MIDNIGHT IN THE PACIFIC

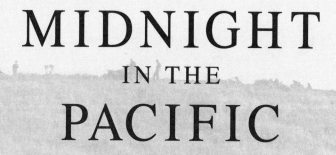

MIDNIGHT
IN THE
PACIFIC

GUADALCANAL
THE WORLD WAR II BATTLE THAT
TURNED THE TIDE OF WAR

JOSEPH WHEELAN

DA CAPO PRESS

Interior design in 10 point Minion Pro by Cynthia Young
Editorial production by Lori Hobkirk at the Book Factory

Frontispiece photo:
Marines advancing to west during final campaign, January 1943. *US Marine Corps*

Cataloging-in-Publication data for this book is available from the Library of Congress.
ISBN: 978-0-306-82459-3 (hardcover)
ISBN: 978-0-306-82460-9 (ebook)

Published by Da Capo Press, an imprint of Perseus Books
a subsidiary of Hachette Book Group, Inc.
www.dacapopress.com

Da Capo Press books are available at special discounts for bulk purchases
in the U.S. by corporations, institutions, and other organizations.
For more information, please contact the Special Markets Department at
Perseus Books, 2300 Chestnut Street, Suite 200, Philadelphia, PA 19103,
or call (800) 810-4145, ext. 5000,
or e-mail special.markets@perseusbooks.com.

LSC-C

10 9 8 7 6 5 4 3 2

It is well that war is so terrible—we should grow too fond of it.

—ROBERT E. LEE AT THE BATTLE OF
FREDERICKSBURG IN DECEMBER 1862

CONTENTS

LIST OF MAPS

MAP 1. Western Pacific Theater, 1942.

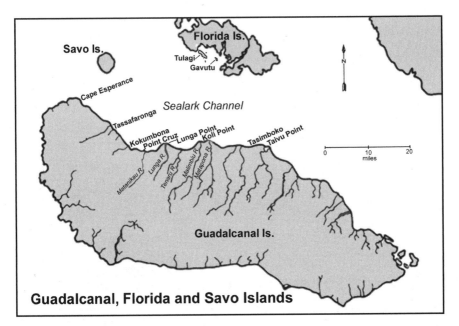

MAP 2. Guadalcanal, Florida, and Savo Islands.

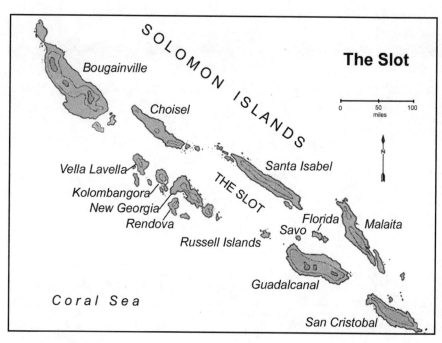

MAP 3. The Slot.

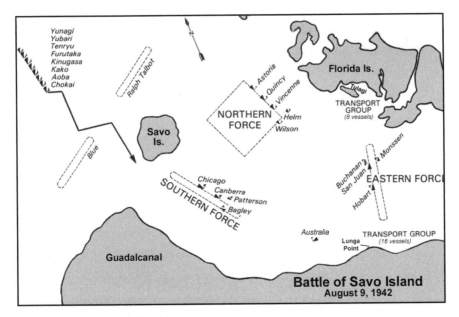

MAP 4. Battle of Savo Island, August 9, 1942.

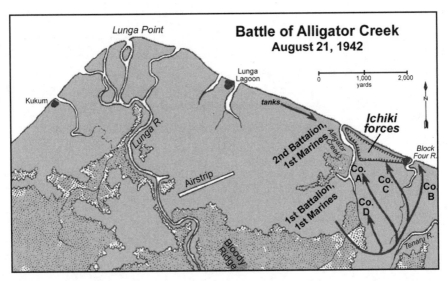

MAP 5. Battle of Alligator Creek, August 21, 1942.

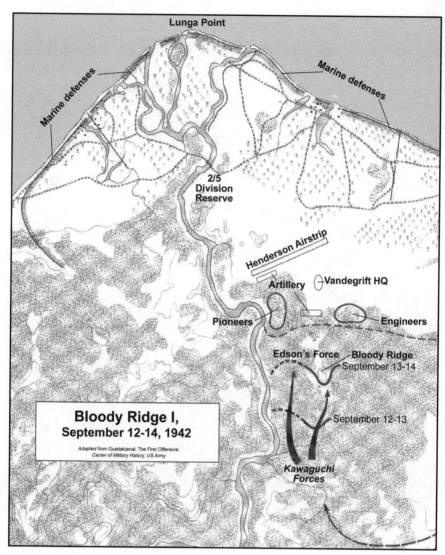

Map 6. Bloody Ridge I, September 12–14, 1942.

MAP 7. Matanikau Offensive II, September 24–27, 1942.

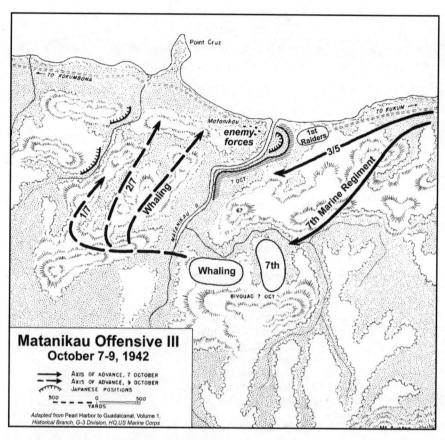

Point Cruz

TO KOKUMBONA

Matanikau

enemy forces

1st Raiders

TO KUKUM

3/5

7th Marine Regiment

1/7

2/7

Whaling

MATANIKAU R.

7 OCT

67

Whaling

7th

BIVOUAC 7 OCT

Matanikau Offensive III
October 7-9, 1942

AXIS OF ADVANCE, 7 OCTOBER
AXIS OF ADVANCE, 9 OCTOBER
JAPANESE POSITIONS

500   0   500
YARDS

*Adapted from Pearl Harbor to Guadalcanal, Volume 1,
Historical Branch, G-3 Division, HQ, US Marine Corps*

MAP 8. Matanikau Offensive III, October 7–9, 1942.

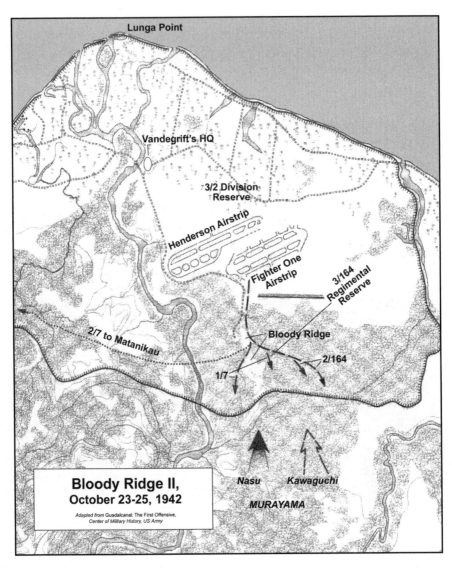

Map 9. Bloody Ridge II, October 23–26, 1942.

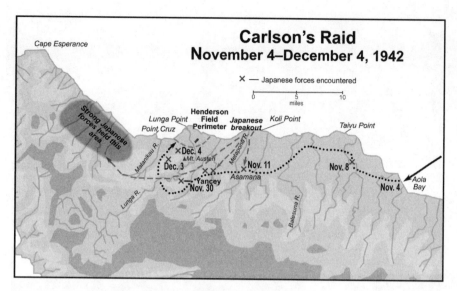

MAP 10. Carlson's Raid, November 4–December 4, 1942.

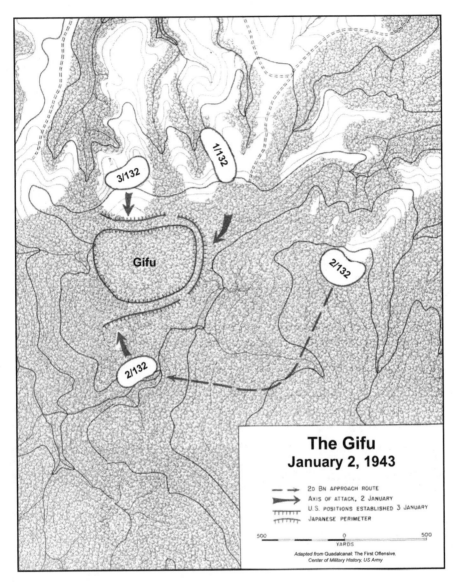

The Gifu
January 2, 1943

2D BN APPROACH ROUTE
AXIS OF ATTACK, 2 JANUARY
U.S. POSITIONS ESTABLISHED 3 JANUARY
JAPANESE PERIMETER

500   0   500
YARDS

Adapted from Guadalcanal: The First Offensive.
Center of Military History, US Army

MAP 11. The Gifu, January 2, 1943.

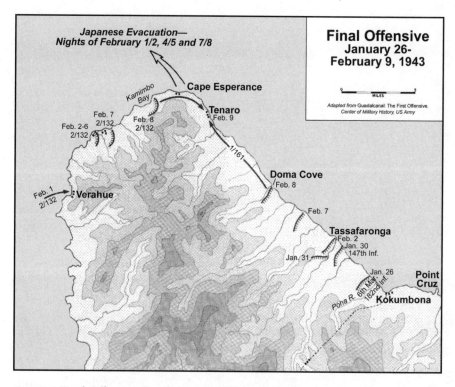

MAP 12. Final Offensive, January 26–February 9, 1943.

Prologue

*If I were king, the worst punishment I could inflict on my en-
emies would be to banish them to the Solomons. (On second
thought, king or no king, I don't think I'd have the heart to do it.)*

—JACK LONDON[1]

MORNING FOG AND THEN A sultry, daylong haze cloaked the powerful US armada's southerly approach to its target on Thursday, August 6, 1942. Six days earlier
the fleet had departed Fiji. Although it had so far eluded detection, the danger
was greater now as it neared the Solomon Islands, patrolled by Japanese naval
aircraft. The eighty-two warships of Operation Watchtower made up one of the
largest naval forces ever assembled. Haze prevented three float planes, sent aloft
at dawn from Japanese-occupied Tulagi Island, from detecting the armada.

By sunset the ships, carrying 19,105 Marines, their food and supplies, and 234
Navy combat aircraft, were 120 miles southwest of Sealark Channel. This would
be the staging area for the next morning's landings on Guadalcanal, Tulagi,
Gavutu, and Florida Islands—the first US land-sea-air offensive of the eight-
month-old Pacific War. Operation Watchtower would also mark the first American amphibious landings since the Spanish-American War, forty-four years
earlier.[2]

During the fleet's approach to the Solomons the young Marines—the enlisted
men's average age was twenty—killed time by speculating about the enemy they
had never met, cleaning their weapons, and sharpening their bayonets. Some
men tried to stay fit with wrestling matches or "good, old-fashioned calisthenics."
They played cards and rolled dice. Whenever possible, they went on deck to escape the hot, fetid ships' holds.

1

The approach from Fiji was often turbulent. Private Marlin "Whitey" Groft of the 1st Raider Battalion counted himself lucky to not be afflicted with seasickness like many of his comrades, who spent long hours topside at the rail, "heaving their guts into the sea."

The men were dirty, but their morale was tremendously high; they were patriotic, Depression-era young men used to hard work and few luxuries. At night they jitterbugged to jukebox music, belted out popular songs, and plucked up their courage with forced bravado.

"They say the Japs have a lot of gold teeth. I'm going to make myself a necklace," said one Marine. Another said, "I'm going to bring back some Jap ears—pickled." Sunday services had been heavily attended. The Marines knelt in prayer in the galley, temporarily transformed into a church, and sang hymns and took communion.[3]

As D-Day neared, white mosquito netting was broken out; using strong Navy coffee, the Marines dyed it dark brown in garbage cans on deck. For reasons unknown, however, the netting would never reach ashore. The Marines were issued three days' worth of "C" rations, their staple food, and "B" rations, which were hardtack crackers.

Rear Admiral Richmond Kelly Turner, a short, balding man who commanded the task force's amphibious group from his flagship, the transport *McCawley*, brooded that night over British military historian Liddell Hart's warning about amphibious operations, inspired by the searing 1915 Gallipoli debacle, in *The Defence of Britain*: "A landing on a foreign coast in the face of hostile troops has always been one of the most difficult operations of war. It has now become much more difficult, indeed almost impossible, because of the vulnerable target which a convoy of transports offer to the defender's air force as it approaches the shore."[4]

Operation Watchtower had been hastily improvised at the behest of Admiral Ernest J. King, the US fleet's crusty commander in chief. Beginning in January King, an old sea dog so tough that he reputedly shaved with a blowtorch, had alone argued for a South Pacific counteroffensive strategy, which countered the prevailing Washington orthodoxy of "Europe First." Mainstream military thinking dictated that a Pacific offensive must wait until early 1943.

King won tepid support for immediate action because of his dire warnings that further Japanese conquests in the South Pacific threatened to sever the sea lanes linking Australia with the West Coast and Hawaii. To protect them, Army and Marine units were sent in the spring to occupy Samoa, the Fiji Islands, New Caledonia, and the New Hebrides. These were remote, malarial, and malodorous subequatorial islands of great physical beauty scattered across the Southern Pacific north of New Zealand and northeast of Australia. An Army bomber group began operating from Efate Airfield. King regarded these new US bases and the airfields under construction in the area as springboards for future offensive operations. Impatient to take the war to the Japanese, King sought a place to begin.

THE SOLOMON ISLANDS ARCHIPELAGO IS the South Pacific's largest island system, with more than nine hundred islands spread over eleven thousand square miles. It was divided into roughly two parts, separated by thirty-mile-wide New Georgia Sound—in American shorthand, the "Slot."

Three hundred miles below the equator and nearly a thousand miles northwest of New Caledonia lay Guadalcanal, part of the British Solomon Islands Protectorate. Guadalcanal's nearly fifteen thousand inhabitants were, for the most part, native Melanesians. Until 1942 it would have been hard to imagine a place of less importance to the world's warring industrial nations.

Volcanic in origin, the remote island was discovered by Spanish explorer Don Alvaro Mendaña in 1568 during an expedition to find King Solomon's fabled gold mines. Despite Mendaña's optimism in naming the island chain the Solomons, they yielded little gold and no gems.

Guadalcanal was named for the Spanish hometown of a ship's officer. Ninety miles long east to west and twenty-five miles wide, it was dominated by riotous jungle. Across its east-west breadth lay a belt of rugged mountains with peaks rising to more than seven thousand feet elevation, punctuated by deep, mist-shrouded gorges.[5]

On the island's northern side the mountains tumbled down to foothills and broken coral ridges covered with four-foot-tall kunai grass. Dense jungle growth clogged the stifling hot valleys and the ravines between them. Along the northern coastline a twenty-mile-long strip of level ground extended six miles inland.

Before the war, European companies, the most prominent of them Lever Brothers, operated coconut plantations on Guadalcanal's coastal plan, harvesting raw copra for processing into coconut oil. On the northeastern coast at Aola, Burns Philp managed a trading station. Marist priests and sisters ran schools in Guadalcanal's scattered small settlements.

Guadalcanal's enchanting views of sea and mountains, its misty mornings and brilliant sunsets, and the Southern Cross etched in the night sky above suggested a tropical paradise, but it was illusory. Guadalcanal's average annual rainfall of more than 100 inches—some areas received 160 inches or more—meant frequent downpours, especially during the monsoon season that lasted from November to May. The rains transformed roads and trails into mires, and the island's streams and rivers into raging torrents.

When it wasn't raining, Guadalcanal was oppressively hot and humid beneath its hundred-foot-high jungle canopy, where the stench of decay permeated the air. Sunshine never reached the ground in some areas, the trees dripped water continually, and it was never dry. There were swamps, enormous saltwater croco-diles, spiders as big as a man's fist, two-foot-long lizards, large land crabs, fire ants, centipedes, giant wasps, tarantulas, leeches, ringworms, and the malaria-carrying Anopheles mosquito; yet poisonous snakes were rare, except for the sea kraits sometimes found on the shores.[6]

UNTIL SPRING 1942 THE US military had no interest in Guadalcanal. Then on May 1, a Japanese air raid impelled Australian officials to evacuate Tulagi, the British Solomon Islands Protectorate's capital, across Sealark Channel from Gua-dalcanal. Two days later, the Japanese Third Special Naval Landing Force—*rikusentai*, or Japanese marines—seized Tulagi and the adjacent islands of Gavutu and Tanambogo. Before long, more than a dozen Japanese seaplanes were teth-ered at new shore facilities on the three islands as well as nearby at the much larger Florida Island. Admirals King and Chester Nimitz, the Navy's Pacific com-mander, began making plans to take back Tulagi.

Then on July 1, US intelligence reported that Japanese construction troops were building an airstrip on Guadalcanal's coastal plain. This was electrifying news, as an enemy airstrip would jeopardize the vulnerable oceanic lifelines con-necting America and Australia. Nimitz and King quickly expanded their invasion plan to include Guadalcanal.

In Wellington, New Zealand, Major General Alexander Vandegrift, the 1st Marine Division's commander, was ordered to attack the Tulagi-Guadalcanal area from the sea on August 1. The news came as a shock to Vandegrift, who was under the impression that his division would not go into action until 1943.

Although the amphibious campaign was officially code-named Operation Watchtower, the Marines nicknamed it Operation Shoe String because of its hur-riedly assembled landing force—two infantry regiments, an artillery regiment, and assorted battalions drawn from across the Pacific—its hasty planning, and its sketchy logistics. Success would depend on surprise and copious luck, most Marine officers believed.[7]

1

August Part I:
Marine Invasion and Naval Disaster

The enemy force is overwhelming. We will defend our positions to the death, praying for eternal victory.

—LAST JAPANESE RADIO TRANSMISSION
FROM TULAGI, AUGUST 7, 1942[1]

The blackest day of the war.

—ADMIRAL ERNEST KING, CHIEF OF US NAVAL OPERATIONS,
DESCRIBING THE NAVY'S DEFEAT AT
THE BATTLE OF SAVO ISLAND

BEFORE SUNSET ON AUGUST 6 the American fleet divided south of Guadalcanal. Rear Admiral Frank Jack Fletcher, Watchtower's tactical commander, positioned his air support group a hundred miles south of Guadalcanal; it consisted of aircraft carriers *Saratoga* (Fletcher's flagship), *Wasp*, and *Enterprise*; the battleship *North Carolina*; and six cruisers. Meanwhile Turner's amphibious force proceeded northwest, skirted Guadalcanal's west coast, and, turning eastward, approached Savo Island in Sealark Channel, where it split again at 2:40 a.m. on August 7 into transport groups Yoke and X-Ray.

Yoke's eight transports sailed north of Savo toward Sealark's northern shore to land nearly five thousand Marines and supplies on Beach Blue on Tulagi as well as on Gavutu, Tanambogo, and Florida Islands. X-Ray's fifteen transports, with fourteen thousand troops and supplies, turned south of Savo and approached Beach Red on Guadalcanal's northern coast.[2]

Before sunset, blue-shirted sailors oiled their winches and tested them by swinging the Higgins boats out from their davits. The Marines checked their packs and resharpened their knives and bayonets. The "hushed, tense activity" did not cease until daylight began to fade, a contrast to the more relaxed atmosphere of previous days. D-Day was now hours away. When nighttime arrived with equatorial suddenness, the command to "darken ship" was issued, and in the silence that followed, the men could hear the wind whistling through the rigging.[3]

At 3:00 a.m. reveille sounded on the transports. After a hasty breakfast in the galley—for many, an apple and two hard-boiled eggs—the Marines made their final preparations prior to climbing down cargo nets to the landing craft. The air was charged with tense anticipation.

Although a handful of officers and noncoms had fought in the distant Great War and the recent Banana Wars, most of the Marines had never fired a shot in anger. Many had learned the "fine points of the art of war," such as throwing and launching grenades, just recently aboard ship. Boot camp had taught them discipline and how to fire and care for their rifles—older bolt-action Springfield '03s with five-round magazines. The Navy refused to purchase the faster-firing semi-automatic M-1 Garands for its Marines, although the Army had them. The hasty deployment and World War I weaponry did not dampen the young Marines' eagerness to meet the enemy.[4]

Just after 6:00 a.m. the roar of swarming Wildcat fighters, Dauntless dive bombers, and bomb-armed Avenger torpedo bombers from the *Saratoga*, *Enterprise*, and *Wasp* drew the eyes of thousands of sailors and Marines to the skies. Making shrieking dives, the combat planes strafed and bombed the unfinished airfield on the lumpy green land mass of Guadalcanal and struck targets across Sealark Channel. Within minutes, flames and black smoke billowed from fifteen wrecked float planes that never got airborne from Tanambogo, Tulagi, and Florida Islands.[5]

"Our ships covered the waters below—dozens of them as far as the eye could see," observed Ensign Harold L. Buell, a dive-bomber pilot flying from the *Enterprise*.

At 6:14 a.m. Admiral Turner's cruisers and destroyers opened fire on Guadalcanal and Tulagi, as Turner and Vandegrift watched from Turner's flagship *Mc-Cawley*, nicknamed the "Wacky Mac." "The concussion of the firing shook the deck of our ship," wrote Richard Tregaskis, a lanky International News Service reporter whom Guadalcanal would make famous, "and stirred our trouser legs with sudden gusts of wind, despite the distance." Flames shot high from a fuel dump hit by the Navy gunners. The air reeked of cordite.

Lieutenant C. Raymond Calhoun, aboard the destroyer *Sterett*, wrote, "It was probably the biggest show of seapower ever assembled in the Pacific at that time, and it was awe-inspiring."

"What a good feeling to know we are doing the dishing out this time," wrote *Sterett* quartermaster Tim Cleere. "Right now it looks as though we are giving them a surprise party."[6]

TWENTY MILES INLAND FROM THE Guadalcanal beaches, amid the high, cold, wet mountain peaks and roaring river gorges, Captain Martin Clemens of the British Solomon Islands Protectorate Defense Force heard the naval gunfire and turned on his radio set. He and his team of natives had abandoned their "coast-watcher" station in Aola, Guadalcanal's administrative center, and withdrawn into the mountains when Japanese troops invaded Tulagi in May.

The Scotsman, a renowned footballer at Cambridge, for three months had shivered through cold nights in Guadalcanal's high mountains while faithfully submitting radio reports to the Royal Australian Navy over his bulky, battery-powered radio-telegraph, which operated only intermittently because of the high humidity. He had reported the arrival of Japanese labor troops and materiel and, since July 6, closely monitored the progress of the airfield project. Since late July there had been a sharp increase in allied bombing attacks on the island, and he was told something big was going to happen. Clearly it was happening today.

Clemens listened on his radio set to air traffic controllers on American carriers talking to their pilots. He could see scores of ships in Sealark Channel, plastering Guadalcanal's north shore from Kukum to Tasimboko.

Clemens had also kept a diary, and in it, on Friday, August 7, he recorded his elation over what he was seeing and hearing: "Wizard!!! Calloo, callay, oh, what a day!!!" As Allied planes roared overhead he "could not resist waving madly and giving the chaps in the air a cheer."[7]

IT WAS SWELTERING ON THE transports despite the early hour. Even before they began climbing down to the Higgins boats, most of the Marines were dripping with sweat. The Marines wore the new sage-green herringbone twill cotton jacket and trousers issued in November 1941 to replace the decades-old issue. On the jacket's four bronze-finished steel buttons appeared in relief the words, "U.S. MARINE CORPS." Stenciled on the jacket pocket was the famous emblem and the letters "USMC."

More conspicuous and nearly as ubiquitous was the new "steel pot" M1 helmet, which covered more of the head than the shallower World War I

"Doughboy" helmet, the M1917. Because not all of the old helmets had been re-placed yet, some Marines still wore the antique headgear.

As the Marines prepared to descend the cargo nets into the landing boats, "Our sailor friends came by, and shook our hands as if we would all be dead before the day was over," wrote Private Sid Phillips.

The *George F. Elliott* rocked in the gentle waves as Private Robert Leckie and his First Marines platoon negotiated the swaying net. "My rifle muzzle knocked my helmet forward over my eyes. Beneath me, the Higgins boats wallowed in the troughs." Weighed down by fifty pounds of gear, the Marines dropped the last three feet from the end of the cargo net into the flat-bottomed boat, known in military parlance as the LCVP (landing craft, vehicle, personnel). It was one of thousands made by Andy Higgins on a roped-off New Orleans street in front of his shop.

Expecting hostile gunfire and casualties on the beaches, the Marines were not talkative as the boats made ready to head for shore, although on Sergeant Jim McEnery's boat the men sang "Roll Out the Barrel" to relieve the tension. The stream of Higgins boats emerging from the transports pleased dive-bomber pilot Buell. "From my grandstand seat in the sky, everything appeared to be proceeding in good order and as planned." From the stern of each boat snapped a three-by-five-foot American flag; the line of flags "seemed to reach to eternity," wrote Phillips.[8]

TASK FORCE YOKE, ITS OBJECTIVE Blue Beach (Tulagi), Florida Island, and the two adjacent flyspecks, Gavutu and Tanambogo, landed its Marines first. At 7:40 a.m. B Company of the Second Marines, 2nd Marine Division, became the first unit to invade Japanese-occupied territory during World War II. Private Russell Miller was the first Marine ashore. The assault troops had to jump over the gun-wales; the newer Higgins models featuring a bow ramp were earmarked for Operation Torch, the North Africa landings scheduled in the fall. Miller and his comrades entered Haleta Village on Florida Island without a hostile shot fired.[9]

After fifteen fighters, fifteen dive bombers, and navy gunfire pummeled Tulagi, now wreathed in clouds of smoke, Colonel Merritt Edson's shock troops, the 1st Raider Battalion, approached the shore at 8:00 a.m. They had covered their M1 helmets with squares of burlap issued the previous night to blur their head-gear's domed shape and dim its reflection. As expected, none of the landing craft reached the beach; the assault's planners had avoided Tulagi's deep-water harbor because it was too obvious. They had chosen a remoter, less likely landing spot, which was guarded by offshore coral formations. Without exception the Raiders' LCVPs became hung up on coral reefs thirty to one hundred yards from shore, and the Raiders had to wade through waist- to armpit-deep water to get to dry land. No one fired on them, and they might have briefly dared to hope that the Navy's preliminary bombing and shelling had wiped out the defenders. If Edson's 828 carefully selected and trained Raiders or the 2nd Battalion, Fifth Marines behind them entertained such a notion, their hopes would soon be dashed.

Tulagi was a hilly, heavily wooded island dominated by a long, 350-foot-high ridge that, as developments would prove, was honeycombed with caves ideal for defense. Bitter fighting would erupt shortly. As the Raiders came ashore near the small island's northwest tip, the Japanese radioed a last message from Tulagi to Rabaul before destroying their radio equipment: "The enemy force is overwhelming. We will defend our positions to the death, praying for eternal victory."[10]

Three miles away at Gavutu the 1st Parachute Battalion landed at noon amid a torrent of machine-gun fire. The parachutists, like the Raiders armed lightly for hit-and-run missions, could have used heavier firepower. As it was, they had only 60mm mortars, light machine-guns, and their '03 Springfield rifles to counter the heavy machine-gun fire raking them from Gavutu's Hill 148 and adjacent Tanambogo, connected to the tiny island by a five-hundred-yard causeway.[11]

AT 9:19 A.M. THE 1ST and 3rd Battalions of the Fifth Marines splashed ashore on Beach Red on the north coast of Guadalcanal, code-named "Cactus." The "Fighting Fifth," famed for its assault at Belleau Wood in 1918, was one of just two Marine regiments—the other being the 6th Regiment—entitled to wear the French Fourragere on the left shoulders of their uniforms.[12]

The Fifth Marines sprinted across the beach, hiked up a low ridge one hundred yards inland, dug foxholes, and braced for enemy machine-gun and mortar fire.

Except for the squawks of alarmed parrots and lories, it was utterly silent.

The Marines began to hope they might be spared a stand-up fight on the beachhead. One had been expected. Intelligence estimates of Japanese strength on Guadalcanal had ranged as high as 5,200, with another 1,850 enemy troops believed to be in the Tulagi area.

The invaders raised their heads and looked around.

"It was a lovely mile-long, gently shelving and sandy beach, ideal for a landing," observed Lieutenant William H. Whyte. "We were puzzled by the stillness. . . . Maybe, we thought, there weren't any Japanese on the island at all."[13]

The Marines began helping themselves to the coconuts knocked to the ground during the naval bombardment, despite a sergeant's shouted warnings that the Japanese might have poisoned them. "We just laughed—and went on husking the nuts, cracking the shells, drinking the cool sweet coconut milk," wrote Private Robert Leckie. "No one bothered to point out the obvious difficulties involved in poisoning Guadalcanal's millions of coconuts."[14]

While the Fifth Marines held the beachhead, the First Marines, arriving in the second wave, passed through and pushed inland toward their initial objective, a prominent hill that overlooked the airfield. The Marines' primitive maps showed the so-called Grassy Knoll to be just a thousand yards away from Beach Red, but it was actually eight miles distant, behind successively higher ridges, and it was impossible to reach in one day. When Colonel Clifton Cates, who commanded the First Marines, informed Vandegrift of the problem, the commanding general agreed to suspend the regiment's mission. Cates's men established a night perimeter a mile inland along the Tenaru River, about two miles east of the airfield.

The Fifth Marines left the beachhead perimeter and marched westward to capture the airfield, five miles distant. In the tall kunai grass some of them became lost, and jittery Marines fired wildly at one other through the grass screen—luckily without casualties. The hours slipped away, and they dug in along the mouth of Alligator Creek a mile from the airstrip. Vandegrift's staff grumbled that for all their experience and training, the Fifth Marines, commanded by Colonel Leroy Hunt, were "sluggish in moving and carrying out their missions."[15]

Although the Marines had encountered no opposition on Guadalcanal, save for sporadic sniper fire, and no casualties except for a man who cut his hand trying to open a coconut, they had been introduced to the hostile natural environment: the sharp-tipped kunai grass, jungle undergrowth that snagged their clothing and slashed their skin, and the oppressive heat and humidity. It was a harbinger of the manifold miseries that lay ahead.

William White of the Eleventh Marines artillery regiment, in top condition when he left the United States, became painfully aware on the first day that two months aboard ship had taken a toll on him and his comrades. "We were sadly out of shape," he lamented. Panting for breath, they found simply moving forward to be "mind-numbing work." "Our clothing, wet with sweat, was like an airtight sack, trapping the heat and making life miserable," he said.[16]

AN EPIC TRAFFIC JAM DEVELOPED at Beach Red as boats unloaded supplies. Every square inch of the narrow, shallow beach soon was jammed with food, clothing, ammunition, and materiel that had been landed haphazardly from Navy lighters. Scores of lighters stacked four deep were waiting to be guided in and unloaded, but there was too little room on the beach and not enough men assigned to unload and move the cargo. "The logistic situation was poor," Colonel Gerald Thomas, the division operations officer, said of the colossal tie-up.

The Navy and Marines disagreed over who was responsible for supplying stevedores. Fearing Japanese counterattacks, Vandegrift would not spare more than the men already detailed from his reserve battalion. The Navy believed its job was to bring the supplies to the beach and no more; it ignored Vandegrift's request to give him more shore workers.

Many of the Marines, told not to help unload supplies but to be ready for Japanese counterattacks, lounged under the palm trees eating coconuts or swam in the lagoon. There was no counterattack.[17]

THE LAST JAPANESE RADIO MESSAGE from Tulagi stunned the Imperial Navy at Rabaul. It knew from the intensified air attacks on Tulagi and Guadalcanal that something was afoot—but nothing of this magnitude. "Enemy forces overwhelming," the message had said. The army high command, preoccupied with the capture of New Guinea, was perplexed. What could possibly be the enemy's interest in Guadalcanal?

At this point the Japanese navy informed the army for the first time that it was building an airfield on Guadalcanal. This surprising lack of communication on a matter as important as a new airfield illustrated the two services' insularity from one another. The army and navy traditionally cooperated only with the greatest reluctance, while jealously guarding their prerogatives. Interservice rivalries would cost the Japanese future victories.[18]

Nonetheless the Japanese reaction to the American landings was instantaneous, although high military officials believed it to be a "landing by a few units for reconnaissance purposes"—no more than two thousand men. Having conquered 20 million square miles—an area five times the size of Nazi Germany's territories—Japanese leaders were supremely confident they could fend off pinpricks such as this.

When Emperor Hirohito announced that he would cut short his vacation and return to the palace to deal with the crisis, the chief of the navy general staff, Admiral Osami Nagano, told him, "It is nothing worthy of your Majesty's attention."

But in Rabaul Rear Admiral Sadayoshi Yamada, in charge of the 25th Air Flotilla, scrubbed that day's planned attack on Milne Bay, New Guinea. Instead, he dispatched to Guadalcanal and Tulagi a strike force of fifty-four planes: twenty-seven Mitsubishi G4M1 medium bombers from the Fourth Air Group—dubbed "Type One Bombers" by the Japanese and "Bettys" by the Americans—with an escort of nine Aichi 99 "Val" dive bombers and eighteen Mitsubishi M6M2 Zero fighters, the best fighter planes in the Pacific.

The Japanese also made sea and ground counterattack plans. Admiral Isoroku Yamamoto began gathering his Combined Fleet from across East Asia for a counterstrike and ordered the waters around Guadalcanal cleared.

The diminutive, fifty-eight-year-old admiral—five-feet-three and 130 pounds—liked to gamble and write poetry. He did not drink, having become a teetotaler after a drunken episode when he was an ensign. Yamamoto had fought in the Russo-Japanese War and had lost two fingers to shrapnel. Later, during two duty tours in the United States, he became fluent in English and cultivated great respect for America's military potential. During his first posting he witnessed some of the early advances in US military air power and returned to Tokyo urging Japan to develop a strong air force. During his second posting Yamamoto took an English class at Harvard and toured the Texas oilfields. In 1939 he became commander in chief of the Combined Fleet.[19]

THE SEVENTEENTH ARMY WAS GIVEN the responsibility of retaking Guadalcanal. The Ichiki Detachment, about two thousand infantrymen whose mission to seize Midway was aborted after the US naval victory, was sent from Guam to the Seventeenth Army for the first ground operation on Guadalcanal. Many Japanese military leaders believed that recapturing Guadalcanal would be as easy as Japan's previous conquests—merely a "mop-up" operation. "With the big success of the southern operations [Southeast Asia], the illusion that the United States and Great Britain were not worth being afraid of began to prevail in the Japanese Army and Navy from the top down," wrote Commander Toshikazu Ohmae, an Eighth Fleet staff officer. "The caution heretofore exercised in operational policies suddenly disappeared."

Lieutenant General Harukichi Hyakutake, who commanded the Seventeenth Army, was less certain of a swift victory than were most of his peers. Before launching his counteroffensive, the general showed a Japanese news reporter Guadalcanal on a map. "This is our new destination—Gadarukanaru. I know you think this might be small-scale warfare. It's true there will be nothing heroic in it, but I'd say it will be extremely serious business."[20]

JAPAN'S TOP ACE, SABURO SAKAI, with fifty-eight victories, had been ready to fly another fighter sweep over New Guinea that day with the crack Tainan Group, veterans of the Philippines and Dutch East Indies campaigns. Two other well-known aces also flew in the group: Hiroyoshi Nishizawa and Toshio Ota. When their mission was canceled and the fighter pilots reported to their command post, they found it in "wild turmoil," wrote Sakai. They received new orders: attack the American invasion force on Guadalcanal's beaches and sink or drive away the troop transports.

Charts were passed around, and when the pilots checked the distance from Rabaul to Guadalcanal, "there were whistles of disbelief," said Sakai. "Five hundred and sixty miles! . . . The distance was unheard of." The Zeros and Vals would have to burn every ounce of fuel they could carry to hit their target and return to Rabaul. The air command advised the pilots to use a dirt airstrip on northern

Bougainville if they ran low on fuel, and it sent a recovery ship and plane off southern Bougainville to collect pilots who were forced to ditch. The improvised strike force was airborne at 8:30 a.m.

Coast watcher Paul Mason heard the drone of the Betty medium bombers when they flew over his southern Bougainville station around 11:30, and he went outdoors to count them; Mason's station was midway on the direct air route between Rabaul and Guadalcanal. To his control station at Port Moresby, Mason radioed, "Twenty-seven bombers headed southeast," evidently not seeing their fighter escort or the Vals. Mason's message was forwarded to Australia, bounced across the Pacific to Pearl Harbor, and then relayed to the invasion fleet, which was reading Mason's report twenty-five minutes after he sent it. The US Navy used its two hours' lead time to prepare for the attack. When the Australian cruiser *Canberra* received the warning the bosun's mate announced, "The ship will be attacked at noon by torpedo bombers. All hands will pipe to dinner at eleven o'clock."[21]

STUBBY-WINGED F4F WILDCATS FROM ADMIRAL Fletcher's carriers *Enterprise* and *Saratoga* rose to meet the Japanese bombers, dive bombers, and fighters. At 1:15 p.m. the first Bettys and Zeros arrived over Savo Island in Sealark Channel, and the Wildcats pounced—as well as they were able to, considering the disparity in pilot experience. Although US Navy pilots had fought at the battles of the Coral Sea and Midway a few months earlier, they lacked the experience of the Tainan Group pilots and had much to learn.

More importantly, the Wildcats they piloted were patently inferior to the Zero. At combat altitude they were slower than the Zeros and only slightly faster than the Betty. The Wildcat had a slower rate of climb and was one-third heavier and less maneuverable than the Zero. But it possessed some advantages, too: the Wildcat had self-sealing gas tanks, making it less liable to burst into flames, and it was armor-plated, enabling it to absorb more punishment than the thin-skinned Japanese fighters. Its firepower—six .50-caliber machine-guns—was superior to the Zero's armament. In designing the Betty and Zero the Japanese had deliberately sacrificed safety for lighter weight and speed. Both warplanes lacked armor protection for crewmen as well as self-sealing fuel tanks that would have made them less combustible. The planes' propensity for catching fire inspired crewmen to nickname them "Flying Cigars" and "Type One Lighters."[22]

THE BETTYS' PAYLOADS SPLASHED HARMLESSLY into the sea, and they turned back. The Wildcats shot down five of them and two Zeros. An hour later, the nine Vals appeared in a second wave over the target area. "Oh boy, we just turned the whole place loose," wrote Roland Smoot, commander of the destroyer *Monssen*.

Five Vals were shot down while diving on the *Mugford*, where they killed twenty-two sailors, but they did minimal damage to the ship; four ditched on the way back to Rabaul. Nine F4Fs were lost from the eighteen engaged, along with a Dauntless dive bomber.

American sailors, when attempting to rescue the downed enemy pilots, were amazed by their determination to die rather than become captives. Ensign Joseph Drachnik of the destroyer *Zane* was on the after-gun mount when one of his 20mm guns shot off the tail of a low-flying Betty and it went into the sea. The pilot crawled onto a wing and stood with his arms defiantly folded. When American officers shouted at him to come aboard, he produced a pistol and began shooting at people on the *Zane's* bridge. The standoff ended when one of the destroyer's 20mm guns suddenly opened fire, cutting the pilot to ribbons and sinking his Betty.[23]

AT TWENTY-FIVE, SABURO SAKAI WAS arguably the most famous fighter pilot in Japan. The descendant of a samurai, he lived by the code of Bushido, especially concentrating on cultivating indifference to pain and an iron will. He was at once chivalrous, cruel, warm, and good-natured. Sakai had been a combat pilot since the beginning of the Sino-Japanese War in 1937. He was one of the first pilots to attack Clark Field in the Philippines in December 1941—and the first to shoot down an American plane over the Philippines.[24]

As he flew his Zero to Guadalcanal on August 7, Sakai was full of confidence: he had defeated every adversary that he had met, and he expected this day to be no different. So he was surprised when a Wildcat piloted by Lieutenant James Southerland rolled away from Sakai's quick burst of machine-gun fire and suddenly shot up toward his belly. Sakai spun, rolled, and tried every evasive maneuver, but the Wildcat matched each one. "Never had I seen an enemy plane move so quickly or so gracefully before," Sakai wrote.

Sakai at last managed to shoot up the Wildcat, but the bloodied Southerland flew on for a time with his canopy open before spiraling down. Southerland bailed out, his chute opened, and he drifted toward the Guadalcanal beach. Sakai turned his attention to a Navy dive bomber, shot it down, and flew into a formation of Grumman Avenger torpedo planes.

An Avenger tail gunner riddled Sakai's canopy, sending shards of glass into his face and head. He passed out. When he regained consciousness, the plane was diving toward the water. Sakai pulled back on the stick, and the plane leveled off. He discovered that he could not move his left arm and leg, and there was a hole in his head and blood on his face. He kept losing consciousness; one time he awakened to find that his plane was flying upside down. Somehow he was able to return to Rabaul and land at the airfield with a nearly empty fuel tank. When he presented himself at the command post and insisted on making a report despite his bleeding wounds, the commander "stared at me incredulously"—just as Sakai blacked out again. He lost sight in his right eye, but returned to active duty in 1944 and survived the war.[25]

TEN AMERICAN LOSSES COMPARED FAVORABLY with sixteen claimed enemy kills on the campaign's first day—especially as these Japanese naval pilots were some of the best flyers in the world. American pilots would face them every day for months.

To be admitted into the elite Japanese aviation program, Sakai had competed with fifteen hundred other applicants. Those selected had to meet nearly impossible physical standards: they had to be able to support themselves on one arm atop an iron pole for ten minutes, swim underwater for at least a minute and a half, and execute somersault high dives. Two-thirds of them washed out; seventy men were in Sakai's graduating class. American pilot training was not as arduous, but US flyers were more adaptable than the Japanese, and they learned quickly. Most importantly, while Japan trained two thousand new pilots per year, the United States graduated twenty-five hundred *per month*.[26]

Admiral Yamada ordered another air strike on August 8, this time hoping to find the American aircraft carriers. Twenty-three Bettys armed with torpedoes left Rabaul with an escort of fifteen Zeros. Unable to locate the carriers, the attack group turned toward Guadalcanal. Bougainville coast watcher Jack Read spotted them and radioed a warning.

The Japanese flight circled to the north this time, eluding the Wildcats waiting for them over Sealark Channel, and attacked the transports from the east. Only a handful of Wildcats met the attackers, shooting down five Bettys and a Zero as the others swooped down on the transports at low altitude, strafing and launching torpedoes. It was up to the ships' gunners to knock them down—and they did, claiming thirteen Bettys.

However, a bomber got a torpedo into the destroyer *Jarvis*, killing fourteen sailors and wounding seven others, and a burning Zero smashed into the transport *George F. Elliott*. The *Elliott* was later scuttled with enough provisions aboard to supply a battalion of Marines, while the *Jarvis* limped away from the battleground for repairs.[27]

THINGS WERE QUIET ON GUADALCANAL, but across Sealark Channel pillars of black smoke billowed from Tulagi, Gavutu, and Tanambogo. Raiders and parachutists battled Japanese troops and laborers fighting from cleverly concealed dugouts, caves, blockhouses, and tunnels "thick with machine guns."

In the first contested American landing of World War II, the 397-man 1st Parachute Battalion landed on Gavutu at noon, August 7. The paratroopers had to wait for the Raiders to first hit Tulagi and then release enough boats to carry the parachutists ashore. More than five hundred Japanese air force personnel, marines, and Korean and Japanese civilian laborers and technicians defended Gavutu and its Siamese twin islet, Tanambogo, outnumbering the attackers and holding the high ground.

Everything about the Gavutu landing was problematic: the thirteen Higgins boats were supposed to deposit the parachutists on the seaplane ramps, but the antiaircraft cruiser *San Juan*, which poured 280 rounds into Gavutu in just four minutes before the landing, turned the ramps into rubble that blocked the landing boats' path. The Higginses veered toward a concrete dock, but some of them got hung up on unmapped coral reefs. The assault troops jumped into chest-deep water and waded one hundred yards to shore under enemy fire. Marines were hit in the boats by bullets that punched through the wooden hulls, in the blood-stained water, and on the dock. Coxswain Henry Marquard, driving a boat in the third wave, thought bees were swarming around his head—they were bullets. Corporal Tony Miksic, shot in the throat, tried to shout "Corpsman!" but no sound came out. Corporal Thomas Lyons leaped from his boat right behind a friend, who was shot dead with blood spurting from his right eye and was knocked into Lyons. Lyons pushed him off, rolled away, and moved on, his training taking over.

Upon reaching the dock, the Marines were swept by rifle and machine-gun fire from caves in Hill 148, Gavutu's dominant feature, and from Tanambogo, five hundred yards away. As men fell wounded around them, parachutist machine-gunners fired at the puffs of smoke coming from the caves. The Marines hugged the ground in their semicircular beachhead as the Japanese depressed their antiaircraft guns to fire on them. The battalion commander, Major Robert Williams, was shot in the chest while attempting to lead B Company in an assault on Hill 148. The attack distracted the Japanese gunners and enabled the rest of the paratroopers to break out of the beachhead after being pinned down for two hours.

Japanese snipers, hidden high up in trees, under buildings, and even in an abandoned truck's engine compartment, picked off the advancing Marines with rifles and machine-guns, timing their shots to coincide with Marine machine-gun fire so that the source of their gunfire was difficult to pinpoint. Camouflaged with palm tree leaves and bark, the snipers could not be seen "unless you were directly under the tree," said Private Robert Howard. Sniper fire, which made a high, flat snap when discharged, sounded like "a supercharged bee" when the bullet passed overhead. The Japanese sharpshooters targeted officers and sergeants who wore conspicuous insignia; the Marines quickly learned to remove rank insignia and abolish saluting and other displays of military courtesy from combat areas.

By 2:30 p.m. the B Company parachutists had reached the top of Hill 148, but the Japanese continued firing from the caves and tunnels beneath the ridge—it would take time to wipe them out. Major Charles Miller, who succeeded the wounded Williams as battalion commander, knew that Gavutu could never be secured until the Marines neutralized Tanambogo's Hill 121, from where the Japanese were raking the Gavutu beachhead with a 20mm gun and heavy machine-guns. Capturing the hill would require extra troops. Brigadier General William Rupertus, the assistant division commander in charge of Tulagi-area operations, had just one uncommitted company to send the paratroopers.[28]

While plans were made to attack Tanambogo, big, blond Captain Harry Torgerson, B Company's inspiring commander, was exuberantly waging a one-man campaign to blast the Japanese from the caves that honeycombed Hill 148. His deadly effective method: shoving planks lashed to fused TNT and gasoline into the caves so the Japanese could not easily throw back the explosives. This also was the procedure adopted by the Raiders' demolitions section, headed by gunner Angus Gauss. Like Gauss, Torgerson had always enjoyed blowing things up, his men said, and the mission he undertook this day was a dream come true.

Outside a particularly large cave, Torgerson prepared an enormous charge, fastening ten blocks of TNT and five gallons of gasoline to a plank. It exploded prematurely as Torgerson was shoving it into the cave. The huge blast blew to pieces a Japanese soldier inside the cave and flattened Torgerson. His trousers were reduced to confetti, but he was not hurt. Picking himself up, he turned to Captain George Stallings, the battalion operations officer, and said excitedly, "Boy, that was pisser, wasn't it?"[29]

At about 6:00 p.m. Captain Edward Crane's B Company of the Second Marines, which had landed on Florida Island but was assigned by General Rupertus to help capture Tanambogo, boarded four Higgins boats. Dauntless dive bombers pounded the islet for ten minutes, and the destroyers *Monssen* and *Buchanan* shelled it. When they were finished not a tree was left standing.

Then the boats went in. The Marines in the first boat landed and deployed along the beach. As the second boat was arriving, a shell from one of the destroyers ignited a nearby Japanese fuel dump. The flames lit up the area like a sports stadium, and Japanese infantrymen aimed a torrent of fire at the splendid targets, hitting Marines and sailors in the boats and ashore. Private Russell Miller, the first Marine ashore on Florida Island, was killed. Crane aborted the operation; all the wounded were re-embarked in the boats. Crane stayed behind with a dozen able survivors. Two returned to Gavutu in a rowboat while Crane and the others walked to Gavutu over the causeway.

Off Tanambogo late the next afternoon, August 8, there appeared another invasion force—two to three times larger than the previous day's. After preliminary attacks by dive bombers and shelling by destroyers, the Second Marines' 3rd Battalion came ashore with two tanks. The tenacious defenders jammed an iron bar into the tread of one of the tanks, and the Japanese swarmed around it and set it on fire with Molotov cocktails, killing most of its crew. Marine infantrymen shot down forty-two of the enemy attackers. That night, with the Marines holding most of the tiny island, the surviving Japanese emerged from their foxholes and dugouts and stormed the Marines' lines. They held. Tanambogo was pronounced secured late August 9.[30]

Five amphibious tractors—in military vernacular, landing vehicles tracked, LVTs—shuttled between Gavutu and Tanambogo on August 9, collecting the wounded and evacuating them to the *President Adams*. This marked the tractor's first appearance during the war; it would become indispensable to later amphibious operations. Armed with two machine-guns, one of the heavily armored tractors helped clear out Japanese-held caves on Gavutu. Late that day, the 1st Parachute Battalion, which had sustained 20 percent casualties, moved to defensive positions on Tulagi and became part of Edson's command. Total Marine casualties on Gavutu and Tanambogo came to 157; Japanese losses totaled more than 500 killed and 20 men taken prisoner—nearly all of them laborers. About 40 swam to Florida Island.[31]

THE TULAGI ASSAULT PLAN HAD appeared simple when Colonel Merritt Edson described it, using the sand table mockup built by British colonial officials Henry Jocelyn and Dick Horton. The 1st Raider Battalion would land where it was not expected, cross the boot-shaped island's one-thousand-yard breadth, turn, and sweep down its two-and-a-half-mile length. It was optimistically estimated that the operation would take no more than six hours. The shipboard cook said when they pushed off, "See you tonight! Chocolate cake tonight!" But simple it was not.[32]

The initial landing met no opposition, as the 350 Japanese marines on the island were watching the southeast, not the northwest, coast. "Everything clicked beautifully," wrote Lieutenant Colonel Samuel Griffith, the battalion's executive officer. As the Raiders pushed southward down the island's long ridge and crossed a golf course, they encountered scattered resistance from log-and-coral outposts, but no enemy concentrations. The Raiders were struck by machine-gun fire and grenades launched by "knee mortars" from the cave-pitted coral ridge when they attempted to advance toward the island's cricket ground, and snipers in trees, rocks, and beneath the former colonial officials' houses targeted them. Incongruously, a Japanese submarine occasionally surfaced in Tulagi's deep-water harbor to lob shells toward the Marines. None of it was serious enough to stop the Raiders. When they stopped for the night, they had captured fully two-thirds of the island. Edson set up his command post in the governor's residence. The main event was still to come.[33]

That night, the Japanese counterattacked—it was a "banzai" attack, shocking in this first manifestation but later a common feature of the Pacific War. The attackers wedged between A and C Companies isolating C Company near the cricket ground, where Captain Ken Bailey, the company commander, killed six Japanese in a bunker before being wounded in the leg. The attackers then turned their full fury on A Company. It became "a savage all-night fight."

The Japanese attacked five times, none of the assaults succeeding. The Marines repelled them with rifle and machine-gun fire, grenades, and, in hand-to-hand fighting, with knives and bayonets. "We were taken by surprise by the viciousness and tenacity of these night attacks," admitted Griffith.

The Japanese fought to the death and committed suicide rather than experience the ignominy of being taken prisoner. "There is a grotesque horror in watching a man activate a grenade and then clutch it to his chest, blowing himself apart before your astonished eyes," wrote Private Marlin "Whitey" Groft.[34]

At daybreak Captain Lew Walt, the A Company commander, was inspecting his lines when he found eighteen-year-old Private First Class Eddie Ahrens, a Browning automatic rifle (BAR) gunner, slumped in his foxhole, covered with blood from head to toe, and barely alive. Beside Ahrens was a dead enemy officer. In front of the foxhole Walt counted the bodies of thirteen Japanese soldiers who had tried to break through Ahrens's position, but had clearly failed.

The captain lifted the teenager, who was still clutching the dead officer's sword, out of the foxhole and carried him to an aid station. A corpsman informed Walt that Ahrens would not survive; he had been shot and bayoneted several times. Walt remembered how Ahrens had refused to quit during the Raiders' strenuous training hikes on Samoa, even when he had collapsed from exhaustion and the extreme heat. At the aid station Ahrens offered Walt the captured sword. "Captain, here's a sword for you. Those guys tried to come over me last night. I guess they didn't know I was a real Marine," he said. He died moments later. Ahrens was posthumously awarded the Navy Cross.[35]

On August 8, Edson pronounced Tulagi secured, although scattered counter-attacks continued, and pockets of Japanese stubbornly held out in caves and bunkers. The last of the strongholds was wiped out with dynamite and grenades on August 10. Historians have found Marine Corps reports to be incomplete, conflicting, and, thus, problematic on the subject of losses on Tulagi, Gavutu, and

Tanambogo. Historian Richard Frank arrived at what is likely the best guess after conducting an exhaustive analysis of company muster rolls for August. His conclusion: Marine losses on Tulagi totaled 45 killed and 76 wounded—121 casualties, 36 fewer than on Gavutu and Tanambogo—while 347 Japanese were killed.

Thirty enemy soldiers and workers hid in Gavutu's caves for weeks. Some slipped away and swam to Florida Island. Others were shot or killed by grenades when they ventured into the open. Mamoru Hara, an eighteen-year-old carpenter, lived for nineteen days on coconuts in a cave among the decomposing bodies of his comrades. He was captured when he emerged in search of fresh coconuts.

The Marines rolled the Japanese corpses into shell craters and threw them into shacks that they then set on fire. "The smell of burning hair and flesh" worsened, if possible, the stench of death and decay that permeated the island.[36]

THE FIRST MARINES SECURED GUADALCANAL'S airfield on August 8 without firing a shot. It was no mean accomplishment to capture Watchtower's primary objective during the operation's second day.

The Marines on Guadalcanal were fortunate to face no resistance during their first wartime amphibious landing. Had a strong enemy force met them at the beachhead the conflation of logistical lapses, spotty supporting fire, and the Marines' abbreviated training and poor physical condition after weeks aboard ships could have jeopardized the entire campaign. Now they would have time to become acclimated to their new environment and to acquire combat skills.

The first nights on the island were memorable for their unknown, unseen terrors. New, strange sounds—the cackles and screeches of macaws and monkeys, the scraping and rustling of large burrowing land crabs—kept the Marines' nerves on edge. Private Robert Leckie was certain that enemy soldiers were whispering in the bushes around him. "I lay open-mouthed and half mad beneath that giant tree," he wrote. Spiders and other crawling insects froze their blood, and the Marines battled swarms of malarial mosquitoes.[37]

As the airfield's surpassing importance slowly became clear, recognition of the Marines' achievement would grow: American forces had executed a tactically difficult amphibious landing in enemy-held territory with air and naval support after just six weeks' preparation.

The Marines were surprised that the airstrip was only a few days away from becoming operational. The airfield was intended to accommodate the Japanese 26th Air Flotilla's twenty-seven fighters and twenty-seven bombers, and from it enemy squadrons could have attacked the New Hebrides Islands and American-Australian convoys. Now the airfield could serve as a platform for a US counteroffensive. The occupation of the enemy airfield, carried out with such ease, was an early turning point in the Pacific War.

A REMARKABLE AMOUNT OF WORK had been done at the airfield in just one month. Japanese Navy Captain Tei Monzen, who was in charge of the project, was so pleased with the progress that he had ordered an extra, celebratory sake ration for the construction workers during the night of August 6, hours before the Marines landed.[38]

The airfield consisted of a thirty-six-hundred-foot runway, with just a small portion still needing grading; a nearly completed airdrome with six hangars and "blast pens"; an air compressor plant for charging torpedoes; a medical clinic; a refrigeration plant; a nearly completed power plant with twin generators; a narrow-gauge railroad; new wooden barracks, never occupied; machine and repair shops; and bridges, encampments, wharves, and an impressive-looking administration building that the Marines promptly nicknamed "the Pagoda" because of its distinctive Asian architecture.

The 11th Construction Corps—about 1,600 Koreans, Ryukyuans, and other laborers under the command of Major Kanae Kadomae—had done the work, while 247 naval troops from the 84th Guard Force provided security. The Japanese had not found time to properly set up two 75mm mountain guns, a triple 25mm cannon mount, two antiaircraft guns, or a pair of radar sets.[39]

In the tent camps between the airstrip and Kukum on the Lunga River it was apparent that the landing had caught the Japanese entirely by surprise, and they "had left by the back door as we came in the front." In one tent were serving dishes set in the middle of the breakfast table, filled with meat stew, rice, and cooked prunes. Around them were bowls and saucers half-filled with food. Chopsticks were scattered on the table and floor. In the tents where they slept the Japanese had left behind shoes, mosquito nets, soap, and other essentials. The reason for their hasty departure became clearer when the Marines saw that shrapnel had torn and flattened some tents and killed two men whose shattered bodies lay nearby.[40]

The invaders' astonishment mounted as they began to inventory the materiel the Japanese abandoned. It ran to four typewritten pages, and included six road rollers; four tractors; three cement mixers; forty-one usable cars and trucks; forty new bicycles; a multitude of tools; 150,000 gallons of gasoline; eighty gallons of lubricating oil; six hundred tons of cement; a large amount of building supplies; a fully equipped, operational radio station; and ten days' food for the Japanese garrison that included canned peaches and pineapple, goulash, and shredded fish, salmon, and crabmeat.

The captured stores included cases of sake and Japanese beer, which the Marines quickly appropriated. "The dirt road paralleling the shoreline became an Oriental thoroughfare, piled high with balloon-like half-gallon bottles of sake and cases of beer." One battalion whipped up a concoction of canned grapefruit juice, "several squeezes" of Pepsodent toothpaste, and, of course, alcohol. The enlisted Marines enjoyed "a rollicking, boisterous life" for about a week until the liquor ran out and officers confiscated the food they had stolen during raids on the stockpile. "What a wonderful week it was!" wrote Leckie.[41]

By day's end August 8, battalions of the First and Fifth Marines formed a battle line along the Lunga River, and the first prisoners were brought in. The Marines, "looking huge by comparison, shooed them along like pigeons." INS correspondent Richard Tregaskis thought they were "a measly lot. None of them was more than five feet tall, and they were puny." Two, bare from the waist down, had been stripped during the Marines' weapons search; a third one wore trousers and a visored cloth cap with an anchor insignia. The naval construction prisoners might have been unimpressive, but the Japanese combat troops that would soon appear would be another matter.[42]

FROM INCEPTION TO EXECUTION OPERATION Watchtower had taken all of forty-five days. Until summoned by Vice Admiral Robert Lee Ghormley to a meeting in Auckland on June 26, Vandegrift had believed that his division would not go into action until early 1943. When they met, Ghormley told the Marine general that he had "some very disconcerting news"—and handed him a top-secret dispatch. It ordered an amphibious operation against Tulagi in just five weeks, on August 1. "I could not believe it," Vandegrift wrote. "Well?" asked Ghormley, tapping the order with his finger. Vandegrift said his division would not be ready to land August 1. Less than a week after the meeting the Navy learned that the Japanese were building an airfield on Guadalcanal. King and Nimitz reluctantly granted a six-day delay until August 7.

It was remarkable that Watchtower got off the ground at all. The two men who divided command of the South Pacific between them both viewed the offensive with grave reservations. Meeting in Melbourne in early July, General Douglas MacArthur and Ghormley agreed that Watchtower should be postponed. MacArthur was commander of the Southwest Pacific Area, which ostensibly included the Solomons, while Ghormley commanded the South Pacific, part of Admiral Nimitz's vast Pacific domain beyond MacArthur's area.

Their overriding concern was lack of air superiority and, secondarily, not enough available shipping to supply the landing force. Japanese airfields were being built on nearby islands, and MacArthur and Ghormley feared the invasion force would run into an aerial buzz saw. The Allies would not be able to gain air superiority from their remote air bases at Efate and Espiritu Santo in the New Hebrides, each more than 550 miles from the landing beaches, much less from the even more distant Tontouta Field on New Caledonia. Air support would depend exclusively on Rear Admiral Frank Jack Fletcher's carrier task force.

MacArthur and Ghormley expressed their reservations in a rare July 8 radio message to the Joint Chiefs of Staff. They were "of the opinion, arrived at independently . . . that the initiation of the operation at this time without a reasonable assurance of adequate air coverage . . . would be attended with the gravest risk. It is recommended that this operation be deferred." Wait until airfields could be built in the Santa Cruz Islands and the New Hebrides, they said, and until they received land-based aircraft.

Admiral King believed the offensive was absolutely worth the risk. He and other Navy officials suspected that MacArthur opposed the campaign because he wanted to lead the first Pacific offensive—an amphibious assault on New Ireland and New Britain with three Army divisions and one Marine division, supported by two carriers. Army Chief of Staff General George C. Marshall suggested that King lead the Marine Corps component. King retorted that the Navy was considering a similar operation—one with the *Army* as the supporting element.

The chiefs compromised: MacArthur ceding operational authority over Guadalcanal and nearby islands to the Navy while being green-lighted to proceed against New Britain, New Guinea, and the rest of the Solomon Islands. The Navy would proceed with Watchtower. This was all arranged before MacArthur's and Ghormley's July 8 message reached the Joint Chiefs. Thus, their objections were brushed aside, and Ghormley was ordered to invade the southern Solomons.[43]

THE NAVY AND MARINES HAD virtually no data on Guadalcanal a month before D-Day. Moreover, only half of the Marine invasion force was in New Zealand— the rest were "spread over hell's half-acre"—when General Vandegrift and his skeletal headquarters staff plunged deeply into the planning phase at the Hotel Cecil in Wellington, New Zealand. They worked from the "black room"—so named to underscore the need for absolute secrecy. The first Allied offensive of World War II necessarily emphasized improvisation instead of the meticulous planning that would characterize future amphibious operations.

The burden of hastily gathering up every scintilla of intelligence about Guadalcanal fell to the division intelligence officer, Lieutenant Colonel Frank S. Goettge. While other D-2 officers went to Auckland and Noumea for information, Goettge flew to Australia to track down former Solomon Islands plantation managers, coast watchers, miners, and traders who had visited Guadalcanal or Tulagi. He interviewed them and located nautical charts. At MacArthur's headquarters in Melbourne, Goettge obtained daily coast-watcher reports and Japanese troop estimates, which ranged from two thousand to several thousand.

Vandegrift proposed landing a reconnaissance team by submarine to scout Guadalcanal, but the cautious Ghormley thought it would be too dangerous. Reports quickly came together on Guadalcanal and Tulagi, yet Vandegrift and his planners lacked good maps.

MacArthur's staff ordered an aerial mapping mission, and by July 20 it had photos of Lunga Point. The photos were sent to New Zealand—and were lost. Unaware of the Army mapping mission, Vandegrift's staff dispatched its own photo reconnaissance flight. Lieutenant Colonel Merrill Twining, the division assistant operations officer, and Major William McKean of Transportation Squadron 26 boarded a B-17 modified for long-range photography flights. They flew over the Tulagi-Guadalcanal area, guided by a *National Geographic* magazine illustration of the Southwest Pacific. Guadalcanal was all of one-half-inch long. "Nothing better was to be had," Twining trenchantly wrote. During much of the flight the navigator read comic books. Three Japanese float planes from Tulagi harbor attacked the B-17, which shot down one of them without sustaining any damage of its own. Twining was pleased that Guadalcanal's north beaches appeared nicely pitched for landing men and supplies, with no evidence of coral reefs to snag incoming boats. Twining and McKean saw no evidence of an airfield, just a flat, burnt area near Lunga Point.

When they landed in Townsville, Australia, to develop their film, they met Lieutenant Commander Eric Feldt of the Royal Australian Navy, who oversaw the Solomons' coast watchers. He shared the latest intelligence from his men and some hand-drawn maps of Lunga Point, Gavutu, and Tulagi that showed the locations of guns and fortifications.[44]

THE 1ST MARINE DIVISION WAS created on February 1, 1941, from the former 1st Brigade. Amoeba-like, prior to Pearl Harbor and immediately afterward, its Fifth Regiment divided to form the Seventh Regiment, provided the nucleus of the 1st Raider Battalion, and contributed manpower, along with the Seventh, to create the First Regiment. The Eleventh Marines provided artillery support for the division. The 1st Marine Division, based at Camp Lejeune, North Carolina, was the East Coast counterpart of the 2nd Marine Division, activated on the same day in San Diego. The 2nd Division consisted of the Second, Sixth, and Eighth Infantry Regiments, and the Tenth Artillery Regiment.[45]

A year earlier the 1st Marine Division practiced amphibious landings in the lower Chesapeake Bay at a place with a portentous name, Solomon's Island, the headquarters of Major General Holland Smith, the Marine Corps' amphibious forces commander in the Atlantic. Smith was studying how to load supplies for amphibious assaults and how best to unload them on beachheads. Proper ship loading and unloading would become important in the Solomons.[46]

In a 1921 treatise that laid the foundations for amphibious warfare doctrine, Lieutenant Colonel Earl "Pete" Ellis had predicted with great accuracy that Japan would attack Hawaii as well as Midway and Wake Islands and said that US victory would hinge upon Marines seizing islands defended by the Japanese. After Ellis died under mysterious circumstances in the Japanese-owned Palau Islands in 1923 while on a secret military intelligence mission, the Marine Corps adopted Ellis's visionary ideas as Operations Plan 712. Between 1934 and 1941 the Fleet Marine Force, with the 1st Brigade operating as its tactical arm, practiced six large-scale amphibious landings and developed a new amphibious warfare doctrine. During these exercises the Marines tested landing craft. They were most impressed with Andrew Higgins's shallow-draft boat and with the amphibious tractor.[47]

IN JULY, THE DIVISION'S SUPPLIES arrived in New Zealand on cargo ships that had been "organizationally loaded" to maximize the use of space; when the ships left the United States no amphibious operations were contemplated until 1943. Between the ships' departure and their arrival in Wellington, Operation Watchtower had been conceived. That meant the ships would have to be unloaded in New Zealand and be repacked for combat so that ammunition, weapons, and supplies were easily accessible. The massive job added up to a big mess on the Wellington waterfront.

Worse, Kiwi dockworkers at Aotea Quay refused to work in the cold winter rain that pelted down ceaselessly day after day. There were no nearby warehouses or shelters where the goods might be kept dry. Marine enlisted men had to do the unloading and reloading, working around the clock, three hundred to a ship. Wellington police ordered the longshoremen off the docks. "We just brushed them [the longshoremen] aside, and there was a lot of hard feeling about it," wrote Lieutenant Colonel Gerald Thomas, the division operations officer. The Marines were kept at the miserable task for days.

The rain damaged the cargo, disintegrated cardboard cartons, and rinsed away labels on canned goods. "In an hour or so you didn't know whether you had a can of corn, peas, or tomatoes." Soon "small mountains of useless, unlabeled cans" loomed over soggy cardboard, cornflakes, and chocolate bars floating amid articles of clothing—"a sea of mush and garbage," wrote Private Sid Phillips. Yet the cargo ships were somehow reloaded with sixty days' supplies, ten units of fire for all weapons—or enough ammunition for ten days of heavy fighting. However, only minimal personal gear made it aboard; bedrolls, trunks, and tents remained in Wellington, along with most of the motor transport. The ships sailed on July 22.[48]

OFF THE FIJI ISLAND OF Koro, Watchtower's eighty-two vessels assembled on July 26 for the first time: Vice Admiral Frank Jack Fletcher's carrier Task Force 61 and Rear Admiral Richmond Kelly Turner's Task Force 62, consisting of the amphibious force and its escort of cruisers and destroyers under British Rear Admiral Victor A. C. Crutchley. Also present was Rear Admiral Leigh Noyes, who led the Air Support Group of all the aircraft in the three-carrier TF-61. The rendezvous marked the important first meeting of all the operation's principals: Vandegrift, Turner, Fletcher, Crutchley, and Rear Admiral John "Slew" McCain, who commanded Ghormley's land-based aircraft (and whose grandson, Arizona senator John McCain, would run for president sixty-six years later). Ghormley had delegated overall command of Watchtower to Fletcher and did not attend the meeting, sending in his stead his chief of staff, Rear Admiral Daniel J. Callaghan.

Fletcher seemed "nervous and tired" when they met in his wardroom aboard his flagship, *Saratoga*, Vandegrift observed. Getting there was a baptism of sorts for McCain, who received a shower of milk when a garbage chute opened just as he began to climb the *Saratoga*'s Jacob's ladder. He arrived on deck "one mad little admiral." These men had never worked together before, and Fletcher's icy, abrupt manner discouraged any potential for amity—Watchtower did not appear to interest him. "He quickly let us know he did not think it [the operation] would succeed," wrote Vandegrift. It was the first of the shocks the Marine general would receive during the meeting.

Fletcher interrupted Turner's presentation to curtly ask him how long it would take him to unload the ships. Five days, replied Turner. Landing all the troops would be completed August 8, but it would take longer to unload the five cargo ships. Fletcher declared that his task force and all of Operation Watchtower's air support would leave in just two days; he was unwilling to expose his carriers any longer.

Fletcher's attitude was somewhat understandable. The carriers were the Navy's greatest strategic asset in the Pacific, and it had lost two of its six Pacific carriers in May and June at the battles of the Coral Sea and Midway. No new carriers were expected until 1943. Thus, all the remaining flattops except the *Hornet* would be cruising eighty miles from Guadalcanal's southern coast, vulnerable to enemy air and submarine attacks. Fletcher suspected that a Japanese carrier was lurking in the Coral Sea and that it might send torpedo bombers against his ships, although air searches had found no sign of one.

Both troops and supplies could not possibly be landed in two days, replied Turner, nicknamed "Terrible Turner" by subordinates because he was "abrasive as a file" and hot-tempered. The lean, beetle-browed admiral and Vandegrift heatedly argued that Fletcher's decision would shift all the risk to Turner's amphibious force by leaving it bereft of air cover.

Fletcher irritably accused Turner of initiating the entire operation. This was largely true: Turner, while heading King's War Plans Division in Washington, had drafted the Guadalcanal invasion plan with other members of King's staff. King was so enthusiastic about Turner's plan and his grand strategy of island hopping through the southern and central Pacific that he had sent him to the Pacific to command Watchtower's amphibious force.

Struggling to quell his boiling "Dutch blood," Vandegrift attempted to explain to Fletcher that this was not a hit-and-run operation and that Fletcher's task force must protect the beachhead until all the supplies were unloaded. Operation Watchtower's object was to obtain a permanent foothold in the southern Solomons. But Fletcher did not appear to be listening to either Turner or Vandegrift; he informed them that he would stay only until the third day. The meeting ended.[49]

THE REHEARSALS FOR WATCHTOWER, STAGED over four days off Koro Island, did little to improve the moods of Vandegrift and Turner. Many landing craft broke down, hidden coral prevented others from bringing Marines to their assigned landing zones, and air support and naval gunfire were wildly inaccurate. Sergeant Ore J. Marion's company of Fifth Marines was landed a mile to the right of its objective the first day and a mile to the left on the second day, when a destroyer continued shelling the beach after the Marines had gone ashore. On the third day Marion's company landed at its assigned place, but as they were reboarding their landing craft to rejoin their transports, their transports left without them because of a report of approaching Japanese ships. They were picked up the next day after spending the night on Koro.

Lieutenant Colonel Griffith, the 1st Raiders' executive officer, described the rehearsal as "just a shocking affair." Vandegrift called it "a bust." It was the only time that Griffith remembered seeing the general despondent. Afterward, Vandegrift "raised all the hell he possibly could" with Turner and Fletcher about the Navy's manifold failures, including slow boat deployment, boat breakdowns, and dangerously erratic fire support. With time Vandegrift tempered his criticism. The rehearsal, he later said, was not so bad "when you think this was the first time that this force, both Navy and Marine, had gotten together" to carry out an amphibious landing.[50]

ALL DAY AUGUST 8 BOATS continued to bring food, ammunition, clothing, and supplies from the five cargo ships to the supply-jammed Guadalcanal beaches. Goods piled up at adjacent landing areas that had been opened up to relieve the logjam. With less than half of the expeditionary force's supplies now ashore, it appeared that Turner had accurately predicted that the process would take five days.

One hundred miles away, Admiral Fletcher, alarmed by the ferocity of the three Japanese air raids on August 7–8, believed that his three carriers were in grave danger. The Japanese air attacks had reduced his operational aircraft by twenty-one planes, and Fletcher's nerves were frayed—he had had little respite since Coral Sea and Midway, the two biggest carrier battles in US history. Moreover, Fletcher believed enemy aircraft carriers would soon be within striking distance of his task force. He was unwilling to expose the Navy's remaining Pacific carriers to the possibility of destruction by enemy torpedo bombers or submarines. It was time to leave.

At 6:07 p.m. Fletcher radioed Turner and Ghormley: "Total fighter strength reduced from 99 to 78. In view of large number of enemy torpedo and bomber planes in area, recommend immediate withdrawal of carriers." He requested that Ghormley send tankers to a rendezvous so that he could refuel. "Fuel running low," he wrote. Without waiting for a reply, Fletcher turned his ships to the southeast at 7:08. At 3:30 a.m. on August 9 Ghormley, hundreds of miles away at Noumea and with no information contradicting Fletcher's assessment, granted Fletcher's request. Ghormley later defended his decision. "When Fletcher, the man on the spot, informed me he had to withdraw for fuel, I approved. He knew his situation in detail; I did not."[51]

Vandegrift knew none of this when he went aboard Turner's flagship *McCawley* late August 8 to meet with Turner and Admiral Crutchley. Turner gave him the bad news. The general was aghast. It was "startling because it was agreed that he would be at least three days in the area when we had our conference" on the *Saratoga*. Shown Fletcher's message citing low fuel as one of his reasons for leaving, Vandegrift was disbelieving. "We all knew his fuel could not have been running low since he refueled in the Fijis"—a tidbit of knowledge that solved nothing. Ships' logs showed that all of Fletcher's ships had several days' fuel remaining at the end of August 8; the carriers had enough to last seventeen days.[52]

Then Turner announced that he too was leaving in the morning because without Fletcher's carrier fighters, his transport force—the only one in the Pacific— was highly vulnerable to enemy dive-bomber and torpedo-bomber attacks. He promised Vandegrift weekly food and supply convoys.

Vandegrift vainly tried to dissuade Turner from leaving: not only were more than half of the Marines' supplies still aboard the cargo ships, but Vandegrift was also not sure that any supplies had been landed at Tulagi because of the heavy fighting. Turner promised to continue unloading all night, giving priority to food, ammunition, and aviation fuel. Tulagi and Guadalcanal would continue to receive supplies until his planned departure at 6:30 a.m. on August 9. When the meeting broke up at midnight Vandegrift boarded a minesweeper that took him to Tulagi for the night.[53]

CRUTCHLEY, TALL, CHARMING, AND NICKNAMED "Old Goat's Whiskers" by his sailors because of his red beard and moustache, had won the Victoria Cross in World War I and commanded the battleship HMS *Warspite* at the Second Battle of Narvik, a British victory off Norway in April 1940. Crutchley was leading the Southern Sector's patrol off Savo Island in Sealark Channel when Turner summoned him at 8:30 p.m. Being twenty miles from the *McCawley*, it was quicker for him to travel there on his cruiser *Australia* than to take a barge. Crutchley placed Captain Howard Bode, the cruiser *Chicago*'s skipper, in charge of the southern group—two cruisers and two destroyers. The group patrolled a north-west-southeast vector blocking the southwestern channel approach. The Northern Force, led by Captain Frederick L. Riefkohl of the cruiser *Vincennes*, patrolled a five-mile "box" north of Bode with three cruisers and two destroyers, blocking the northwest channel entrance between Savo and Florida islands. A force commanded by Rear Admiral Norman Scott covered Sealark's eastern approaches with two light cruisers and two destroyers, while a pair of destroyer pickets was posted west of Savo Island.

Although reports from B-17 pilots and a submarine said that Japanese warships were sailing southeast from Rabaul, Crutchley and Turner did not believe they posed a danger that night. The B-17s from MacArthur's command and the submarine S-38 had spotted the eight vessels on August 7. During the morning of August 8, an Australian Lockheed Hudson reconnaissance bomber had seen Japanese warships off Bougainville's east coast, and the pilot radioed the sighting. A Japanese cruiser picked up the transmission and included it in its action report, contradicting later accounts that the pilot first returned to Australia and had tea before making his report. For whatever reason there was an hours-long delay in relaying the report from Australia to the task force, but Turner and Crutchley received it in plenty of time to take necessary countermeasures.

The sightings excited no alarm, however, because two of the enemy vessels were misidentified as seaplane tenders; it was presumed that the warships were en route to Rekata Bay, 120 miles away, to establish a seaplane base. An attack was not expected until the next morning at the earliest because the Navy believed the Japanese were poor night fighters. That misconception was about to be brutally rectified, along with the errors in ship identification—the enemy force actually consisted of five heavy cruisers, two light cruisers, and a destroyer.

Because a quiet night was anticipated, neither Crutchley nor Bode had bothered to apprise Riefkohl of the temporary change in the Southern Force's command. Everyone in the task force, including Bode, was exhausted after two days and nights of intense activity. Bode turned in, assuming that Crutchley would return around midnight and re-assume command. Crutchley, however, decided to not rejoin the Southern Force after the meeting on the *McCawley* and remained in the Guadalcanal transport area for the rest of the night.

Low clouds blotted out the moon, and lightning flickered through the showers falling around Savo Island.[54]

VICE ADMIRAL GUNICHI MIKAWA, THE soft-spoken commander of the new Eighth Fleet, had ordered four heavy cruisers from Cruiser Division 6 at Kavieng, New Ireland, to rendezvous east of Bougainville with his flagship cruiser *Chokai*, two light cruisers from Cruiser Division 18, and the destroyer *Yunagi*, all sailing from Rabaul. On the morning of August 7 Mikawa described his plan to proceed to Guadalcanal; US cryptanalysts intercepted the transmission, but it was not decoded until August 23. His four ships left Rabaul that afternoon.

Acting on the belief that the American invasion force was small, Mikawa also dispatched a few hundred naval troops on the transport *Meiyo Maru* but recalled it after learning that thousands of Americans had been landed. Before the *Maru* could return to Rabaul, the transport was torpedoed and sunk off Cape St. George by the US submarine *S-38*. All 342 men aboard the ship were lost—the first of many Japanese reinforcements that would die while en route to Guadalcanal.[55]

Mikawa had been at sea continuously since 1939. During the attack on Pearl Harbor he commanded Battleship Division 3, which shielded the carrier attack force whose planes bombed Pearl Harbor. He had urged a second strike on the Americans' repair and refueling facilities, but Admiral Chuichi Nagumo rejected his advice. Mikawa's battleships had helped capture the Bismarck Archipelago and Java. He took command of the Eighth Fleet, whose operational area was New Guinea and the Solomons, upon its establishment, arriving in Rabaul on July 29. In the months since Pearl Harbor Mikawa had more combat experience than any Japanese flag officer.

If all went as planned, Mikawa's strike force would reach the target area during the night of August 8–9. Mikawa ordered every available submarine in his command to the area—at the moment just two could be sent, *I-121* and *I-122*, but by the end of August there would be fifteen lurking around Guadalcanal.

As the Japanese ships neared Guadalcanal Mikawa dispatched scout planes to count the vessels in the landing area and to locate the worrisome American aircraft carriers so he could avoid their search planes. They never found the carriers, but a scout plane reported numerous vessels at Guadalcanal and Tulagi a dozen and a half transports, a half-dozen heavy cruisers, and nearly twenty destroyers, along with two large ships—a battleship (actually Captain Bode's heavy cruiser *Chicago*) and possibly a light carrier.[56]

Amazingly, after the sightings on August 7 and the Hudson's report, Mikawa's strike force had avoided discovery by Admiral McCain's air search network and sailed almost invisibly through the "Slot." Mikawa's arrival west of Savo Island would be a terrible surprise.

Aware that an enemy reconnaissance plane had seen his task force that morning and reported the sighting by radio, Mikawa expected to have to fight his way into Sealark Channel. The cruisers and destroyers that his scout plane had spotted would surely screen the transports anchored off Guadalcanal and Tulagi. To maintain tight control over his strike force Mikawa arranged it in a single, five-mile-long column, with *Chokai* leading.

THE POST–WORLD WAR I WASHINGTON Naval Treaty of 1922 had placed Japan's navy at a five-to-three disadvantage in ship numbers to the United States and Great Britain. Before it abandoned the treaty terms altogether in 1937 and began seriously rearming, Japan focused on torpedo technology and night fighting as ways to level the playing field.

As a result of intensive training in the stormy North Pacific and superior optics, the Japanese Imperial Navy now excelled at night combat. Lacking radar, the navy trained lookouts who had been specially selected for their outstanding night vision. They were drilled in identifying objects four miles away on dark nights through oversized "night binoculars."

Torpedo technology was the other area in which the Japanese gained an advantage inside the naval treaty's parameters. They developed the Type 93 Long Lance, which was superior to any Allied torpedo. The Long Lance could hit targets sixteen miles away or more with a thousand-pound warhead. The torpedoes were hard to spot in the water because they left scarcely any detectable wake; their secret was that they were propelled by pure oxygen rather than compressed air. The standard US torpedo, the Mark XV, had a range that was half the Long Lance's, its depth-setters were faulty, and too often it failed to explode on contact.

The Japanese navy preferred to use torpedoes in ship-to-ship combat, especially at night, because the flash of gunfire betrayed their positions; US Navy doctrine favored guns over torpedoes. So valued were torpedoes that Japanese cruisers—lacking destroyers' built-in torpedo tubes—often carried eight tubes on their decks along with float planes for dropping flares. Japanese destroyer crews could reload their nine tubes in ten minutes—twice as fast as US sailors.

The Japanese navy prized skill in torpedo warfare, and destroyer crews and squadrons often stayed together for years; some sailors spent their entire careers aboard destroyers. By contrast, the US Navy made little effort to keep crews or destroyers together, moving them wherever they were needed. At the beginning of the Pacific War Japan's destroyer avatar, Rear Admiral Raizo Tanaka, declared, "Our torpedo forces were the best night combat forces in the world."[57]

MIKAWA'S PLAN WAS TO SAIL south of Savo Island, torpedo the main Allied anchorage at Guadalcanal, and then proceed to Tulagi to hit the ships there. As the Japanese strike force approached Savo, Mikawa ordered his ships to clear their upper decks of flammables such as aircraft fuel, depth charges, and light oil. It was understood that they were operating under standard night-fighting procedures: no warship opened fire with its guns until the flagship did. Thereafter, each ship was free to choose its own targets. At 11:00 p.m. three heavy cruisers catapulted scout plans to reconnoiter for enemy ships. After reporting by radio what they observed, they were to fly to Shortland Island.[58]

Crutchley's picket line consisted of the destroyers *Blue* and *Ralph Talbot* west of Savo. The *Blue* was posted to the southwest to screen Crutchley's Southern Force, while *Ralph Talbot* was positioned in front of Captain Frederick Riefkohl's Northern Force. Each patrolled a line several miles long, but not synchronously, meaning that large gaps between them—up to twenty-five miles—might occur unexpectedly. Although both destroyers had the new surface SG radar, with a four-to-ten-mile range, their crews were still learning how to use it and did not yet understand how land masses, such as Savo, could block or distort their readings.

Japanese lookouts saw the *Blue* at 12:43 a.m. on Sunday, August 9, and Mikawa had to quickly decide whether to fire on it or to bypass it and hope not to be seen. Mikawa chose to avoid her, and he decreased his ships' speed to minimize their wake. Remarkably, the long line of Japanese warships passed the *Blue* unseen. "Every gun in our force was trained on her," wrote Commander Ohmae, Mikawa's operations officer. The Japanese then watched as a second ship, the *Ralph Talbot*, sailed in the opposite direction without detecting the strike force. "It was a lucky escape," said Ohmae, who stood beside Mikawa on *Chokai*'s bridge during their tense passage into the sound. "Our night lookout training had paid off."[59]

For an hour and a half Mikawa's scout planes thrummed the overcast sky above the eleven Allied vessels patrolling off Savo through clouds, mist, and occasional showers and thunderstorms. Nearly every ship in Crutchley's three forces reported their presence, but no one took alarm—they were assumed to be friendly aircraft.[60]

BEHIND THE *CHOKAI* SAILED THE heavy cruisers *Aoba*, *Kako*, *Kinugasa*, and *Furutaka*; the light cruisers *Tenryu* and *Yubari*; and the destroyer *Yunagi*. They had penetrated Crutchley's destroyer screen and now approached two cruisers, the HMAS *Canberra* and the USS *Chicago*, where Captain Bode was fast asleep. The Allies did not yet know they were there—a testament to Mikawa's nerve and his crews' excellent fire discipline.[61]

At 1:40 a.m. the *Chokai* sighted the *Canberra*. Two minutes later four torpedoes flashed from the *Chokai's* tubes toward the *Canberra's* port bow while its crew prepared to fire its five 8-inch turret guns. Mikawa ordered the lead scout plane to drop flares and waited for his torpedoes to hit.[62]

The soothing pace of events went into hyperdrive. The Southern Force destroyer *Patterson* saw one of Mikawa's ships five thousand yards ahead on a southeast course and at 1:43 blinkered an alert to the *Canberra* and *Chicago*, "Warning, warning, strange ships entering harbor."

Canberra's lookouts reported torpedo tracks in the water, and the helmsman turned her hard to starboard and accelerated. Jolted from a deep sleep by the call to battle stations, Lieutenant j.g. Bruce Loxton, his heart pounding, raced to the bridge. "The night was as black as the inside of a cow" until he reached his battle station and bright green flares lit up the waters south of Savo Island.

Mikawa signaled his strike force, "All ships attack!" As the *Canberra* swung to starboard to avoid the torpedoes, there were flashes of gunfire off the ship's port beam, and she was plastered with 28 five- and eight-inch shells. Fred Tuccito, a sailor aboard *Chicago*, watched the Australian cruiser absorb "hit after hit," wondering, "How could anyone live through such an ordeal?" Some of the Japanese rounds were armor-piercing projectiles that punched gaping holes below the water line and knocked out the electricity and steam power in both boiler rooms. Stoker P. C. Ackerman, his parboiled skin drooping grotesquely, was one of the few sailors that emerged alive from the steam and flames.

Star shells fired by the *Patterson* and *Chicago*, where Captain Bode was now awake and issuing orders, illuminated the area enough to show shadowy ships approaching quickly. Mikawa, however, was not yet finished with the *Canberra*. Lieutenant Commander Mackenzie Jesse Gregory saw a shell explode just below the *Canberra's* bridge, decapitating the gunnery officer, Lieutenant Commander D. M. Hole. He trained his binoculars on the gunfire flashes and saw the Japanese cruisers just a short distance away firing at his ship. "My God! This is bloody awful!" he exclaimed.

Sheets of enemy gunfire knocked out almost all of the *Canberra's* guns and killed most of the gun crews. Fires roared through the ship; her aircraft burned on the catapult like a taper. Lieutenant Commander John Plunkett-Cole, knocked to the deck and momentarily blinded, got up and had his fingers on the torpedo triggers when the ship was hit again. The torpedoes did not fire. Another shell struck, and Plunkett-Cole was on his back, his coveralls smoldering. He exclaimed, "I've been hit in the bum like a bloody sparrow!" Other officers extinguished his smoking clothing.

Sent sprawling over the compass platform on the bridge, C. J. Gunthorp, chief yeoman of signals, got up to find the gunnery officer in a corner, dead; Loxton lying next to him wounded; and Captain Getting mortally wounded in the leg, arms, and head. Other dead crewmen lay in heaps on the bridge, with the wounded shrieking in pain. Commander J. A. Walsh, bleeding from head wounds, took over from Getting and tried to organize firefighting efforts, but there was no water pressure.

The more than two hundred men brought to sick bay with gaping wounds, broken bones, and severe burns overwhelmed *Canberra's* surgeon, Commander C. A. Downward. When the fires spread to the sick bay, the wounded were moved to the forecastle, where they lay for hours in the driving rain, amid the lightning and crashing thunder. Dead in the water, the blazing cruiser listed to starboard. The attack, lasting under three minutes, had been so sudden and overwhelming that the *Canberra* had not fired a shot.[63]

The *Patterson*, pinned by the searchlights of two enemy cruisers, was next up. A spread of torpedoes missed her, but the destroyer trembled violently as a shell crashed into one of its gun shelters, igniting the powder. Two guns were knocked out of action, their crews killed or wounded. The *Patterson* returned fire, and Commander Frank Walker ordered torpedoes into the water, but the crash of his guns drowned out his words. As the swift Japanese strike force passed by, the *Patterson* managed to shoot out the *Yubari's* searchlight and start a fire. The American destroyer transmitted an urgent message, "Warning, warning, three ships inside Savo Island."

A *Chicago* lookout reported torpedoes in the water, streaking toward Captain Bode's ship. Bode ordered a hard turn to port and full speed, but one of the torpedoes tore into the starboard bow and "shook the ship from stem to stern." An enormous plume of water shot like a geyser into the air, dousing the cruiser from the bow to the forward stack. A shell crashed into the starboard leg of the main mast, broadcasting shrapnel across a large area and killing two sailors. The *Chicago* unleashed a salvo from its secondary five-inch battery at one of the blurred shapes passing by, and either it, or one fired almost simultaneously by the *Patterson* struck the *Tenryu*, killing twenty-three men.

Bode's heavily damaged ship sailed west toward ships glimpsed in the distance. When his crew switched on spotlights to illuminate possible targets, there was none; Mikawa's column had pushed on, sailing around Savo counterclockwise into the "box" patrolled by Captain Riefkohl's Northern Force. The *Chicago* continued to sail westward out of the battle area. Bode did not warn Riefkohl that enemy warships would be upon him in just minutes.[64]

THE CAPTAINS OF THE THREE Northern Force cruisers—*Astoria*, *Vincennes*, and *Quincy*, sailing with the destroyers *Helm* and *Wilson*—were asleep in their cabins while Mikawa's eight warships were dismantling the Southern Force. A curtain of storm clouds and mist isolated the Southern and Northern forces from one another. None of the men on watch on the three ships was alarmed by the ghostly flashes in the far distance, or by the vibrations from detonating Japanese torpedoes. These they wrongly attributed to Southern Force antisubmarine action. The distant flares and gunfire flashes finally attracted enough notice for the captains to be awakened and for crews to be summoned to battle stations at 1:48 a.m.[65]

Now the Navy's failure to adequately prepare its fleet for night combat was about to bear poisonous fruit. Other failures would also have fatal consequences: the Northern Force's careless storage topside of high-octane aviation fuel and other flammables as well as some commanders' refusal to use communications and sensor gear, acting on the belief that the enemy could track the signals and target them.[66]

Powerful searchlights clicked on miles away and knifed through the gloom, lighting up the three cruisers at the southeast periphery of their patrol. Utterly misreading the situation, Captain Riefkohl ordered the other Northern Force ships to turn off their lights and signaled, "We are friendly!" Seconds later the Vincennes's radar picked up the blips of unidentified ships just as "a rain of shells" slammed into the Northern Force cruisers. Within minutes all three were burning.

The Kako zeroed in on the Vincennes. Its first two salvos fell short, but then the third raked the cruiser amidships with 8- and 4.7-inch shells, killing officers in the pilot house, including one standing next to Captain Riefkohl. Planes on the hangar deck burst into flames, and electrical power to the guns failed.

The Chokai concentrated on the Astoria, while the Aoba targeted the Quincy.

"Every torpedo and every round of gunfire seemed to be hitting a mark," wrote Commander Toshikazu Ohmae, Mikawa's operations officer.

The tornado of gunfire that roared through the Vincennes killed nearly everyone in the main battery control station, and clogged the bridge and the communications platform with the dead and wounded. "Time seemed to be standing still and everybody was dying," wrote Life magazine correspondent Ralph Morse, who was spending the night aboard the Vincennes after putting in the ship's safe the film he had shot of the Guadalcanal landing—film that he hoped would soon be on its way to his editors stateside. Morse had been on the Hornet for the Doolittle raid and had witnessed the Battle of Midway; now he was once more an eyewitness—this time to a disaster. "The sky was lit up with shelling and fires on ships. . . . Sailors were being hit all around us, and sailors were being killed just next to me."[67]

Two torpedoes crashed into Vincennes's number-two fire room, and raging fires enveloped the antiaircraft stations. Electrical failures sabotaged firefighting.

The forward medical station, its surgeon, and his team were wiped out. Men slipped and slid on the bloody decks and tossed wounded men into the water. With its 9 eight-inch guns, the cruiser took a swipe at a passing enemy ship, the *Kinugasa*, igniting a fire and explosion and sidelining the Japanese cruiser from the fight. But the *Furutaka* plastered the *Vincennes* with more shellfire—the US cruiser sustained fifty-seven hits during the twenty-minute ordeal—and the *Yubari* fired four torpedoes, one of them hitting the number-one fire room and killing everyone there. An assistant engineering officer, Lieutenant Commander Edmund Phillip Di Giannantonio, said the torpedo strike seemed to lift the *Vincennes* out of the water. "She shuddered, shook, throbbed and quivered like a man with a malarial chill, staggered momentarily, and then slowly rolled to port," Di Giannantonio wrote.

Lieutenant Commander Samuel Isquith, a ship's surgeon, and Lieutenant Commander Robert Schwyhart, the ship's chaplain, moved the wounded topside as flaming beams crashed to the deck around them. They placed the men in life jackets and lowered them into the water. Captain Riefkohl, a World War I Navy Cross winner, saw that all was lost, and he stoically performed the dreaded duty of ordering his ship abandoned. Some of the men refused to leave and had to be thrown bodily into the sea.

Warrant Officer Frederick Moody was already in the warm, oily water when the *Vincennes* went down. "Much to our surprise, she settled just as if she wanted to go to sleep." Captain Riefkohl stepped over the railing and walked into the sea as the ship sank, her mast slapping the water nearby. "She turned turtle and went down by the head," with 342 men still aboard. "Oh, Chief, there goes our ship!" Chaplain Schwyhart exclaimed to Chief Petty Officer Bigelow. It disappeared beneath the waves at 2:58 a.m.—neither the first nor the last to go down during this long night. The survivors, in rafts, bobbing in life vests and clinging to debris in the water, watched another ship in their screening column burn on the water nearby.[68]

When the Japanese spotlights found the *Quincy*, which was following the *Vincennes*, the guns of the *Aoba*, *Furutaka*, and *Tenryu* flashed, and dozens of 8- and 4.7-inch shells smashed into the cruiser. The *Aoba* alone fired five salvos at close range. An eyewitness wrote that it was "like red lanterns coming straight at us." The gunfire hit scout planes on deck that were full of aviation fuel, and the *Quincy* became a blazing torch. The *Tenryu* put two torpedoes into her port side, wiping out two fire room crews. A third torpedo, fired by the *Aoba*, struck the stern.

Water flooded the central station, and neither the men below nor their mates on deck could open the hatches because the deck had buckled. "The last I heard were screams of agony and prayers for help" from the doomed men before they fell silent, wrote Quartermaster Second Class Lawrence Morris.

Captain Samuel Moore ordered his wounded ship to charge between the columns of Japanese warships bracketing the *Quincy*. "We're going down between them. Give them hell!" he shouted seconds before a shell smashed into the bridge, killing nearly everyone there.

Wreathed in flames and with guns blazing, the *Quincy* bulled ahead, nearly ramming the *Kinugasa*. Its final shot hit the Japanese flagship, *Choka*; the shell crashed into the chartroom, killing or wounding thirty-six men. It missed Admiral Mikawa by a mere five yards.

Before dying, Moore, sprawled beside the wheel with grievous wounds, had ordered the signalman, the only man standing in the pilot house, to beach the cruiser, but the steering was gone and he was unable to. "No others were moving in the pilot house, which was thick with bodies," wrote Lieutenant Commander John Anderson, the assistant gunnery officer who had sought out Moore for orders, but reached him just as he expired. He "rose up about half way and collapsed dead without having uttered any sound except a moan."

With first aid stations all but wiped out by Japanese gunfire, corpsmen resorted to using boot laces as tourniquets and strips of clothing as dressings. Sailors dragged their burning comrades across the deck, prefatory to tossing them overboard, along with anything that could float. When the order was issued to abandon ship, not everyone went into the warm water. On the gun deck the badly wounded ship's dentist, Lieutenant W. A. Hall, his back to the bulkhead, could be seen pressing the stump of Pharmacist's Mate Paul Scott's leg against his body to staunch the bleeding.

Then a deafening below-decks explosion tore through the ship, and the *Quincy*, her masts burning, capsized and slipped below the waves bow first, her stern rising in the air at 2:38 a.m. Sinking twelve minutes before the *Vincennes*, *Quincy* was the first warship lost in the waters off Guadalcanal. She took with her 370 men—Captain Moore, Lieutenant Hall, and Pharmacist's Mate Scott among them.

Mikawa's operations officer, Commander Ohmae, praised the *Quincy*'s fighting spirit. "She was a brave ship, manned by brave men. . . . She certainly made an impression on our force."[69]

THE JAPANESE HAD NICKNAMED THE *Astoria*, third in line in the Northern Force patrol, "the Coffin Boat of Friendship" because in 1939 she had carried back to Japan the ashes of Japan's former US ambassador, Hiroshi Saito, who had died of cancer in Washington. The *Astoria*'s commander during that historic trip was Richmond Kelly Turner. Her current skipper, Captain William Greenman, had attempted to prepare his crew for night combat, unlike his fellow Northern Force cruiser captains. Greenman had put his crew through a week of night-battle drills before leaving for Guadalcanal. On this night, the *Astoria*'s guns were loaded and manned, and the men had been fed at their battle stations.

Greenman's preparations enabled the *Astoria* to fire the first counter salvo when the *Chokai* opened fire. Then, fearful that he might have fired on one of his own ships, Greenman ordered his gunners to cease fire. Four long minutes passed, with shells splashing around the *Vincennes* in front of Greenman's ship, before he was convinced that enemy ships, not friendly ones, were shooting at them. He ordered his men to resume firing.

During the interlude the *Chokai* found the *Astoria*'s range, and shells began crashing into the gun turrets and amidships, igniting fires on the boat deck and hangar; the planes burned brightly in the night. No longer needing its searchlights, the *Chokai* switched them off and kept shooting. The blizzard of shells, shrapnel, and splinters killed nearly all the *Astoria*'s five-inch gun crews. "Once the enemy started to hit they continued to hit," wrote Lieutenant Commander William Truesdell.

The *Astoria* veered sharply to the right across the *Quincy*'s stern to avoid drifting into her line of fire. In the process the Friendship ship presented an alluring target to Japanese gunners, and she was subjected to a stupefying pounding by four Japanese cruisers. She fired back with her 1.1-inch guns, knocking out two of the *Aoba*'s torpedo tubes and starting fires. But the shellfire silenced *Astoria*'s batteries and killed nearly everyone in the pilot house and the main battery control station, now a gallery of corpses still wearing their headphones. Flames roared in the galley and the hangar, where the extreme heat ignited gasoline cylinders, sending towers of fire high into the air.

With "a deafening roar," steam shot from the number-one stack while ammunition exploded below deck. The superheated steam drove fourteen engine crewmen up to the after mess hall, just as a shell exploded with a blinding flash. Machinist's Mate Second Class Abe Santos, thrown into a metal countertop, had only his pants on when he regained consciousness—his shoes, life jacket, and watch were gone. "I heard guys screaming. One guy was screaming that his arm was blown off." Marine Second Lieutenant Roy Spurlock administered first aid. "The wounds were terrible, beyond anything I had ever seen in my life." Santos, one of just four engine crewmen still alive, scrambled up to the deck, where fires burned "from stem to stern." Santos put on another life jacket, and felt something scraping against his neck. It was a jawbone with teeth still in it.[70]

Water tender Keithel Anthony was led by a lieutenant to help administer first aid to the wounded in the forward mess hall. Anthony had the presence of mind to strap on a gas mask just before an explosion knocked him out. When he regained consciousness, the lights were out, and everyone in the room was dead, including the lieutenant, who had been "blown clear through a wire mesh and his body wrapped around the main steam stack." Suffering from shrapnel wounds to his left arm and left leg, Anthony limped through the carnage. In the machine shop bodies were piled two deep; the men had been overcome by poisonous gas—Anthony's gas mask had saved his life.

The *Astoria* "shook and shuddered" and began to lose speed. She aimed her twelfth and final salvo at the *Kinugasa* but overshot it and instead hit *Chokai*'s number-one turret, killing and wounding fifteen enemy sailors.

An explosion knocked Chaplain Matthew Bouterse to the deck just as he reached the after aid station. He regained consciousness as the aid station began filling with smoke. Two corpsmen led him through the smoke, wreckage, and fire, and they found a ladder to the deck.

Bouterse sat down on the stern in a rain shower. Looking forward at the many fires burning, his eyes fell on a body hanging lifelessly over a rail. It was shrinking as flames below it inched closer. The chaplain was finally pulled away from the horrifying spectacle to attend to a mortally wounded crewman who had asked for him. Bouterse reached the dying man's side before he breathed his last.[71]

IN JUST FORTY MINUTES, MIKAWA'S strike force had crushed the Southern and Northern Forces that guarded the amphibious force's transports. Four allied cruisers were on their way to the ocean bottom. Although it was a masterful demonstration of night combat skills, surprise was the key factor. Commander Ohmae acknowledged this when he wrote, "Had they had even a few minutes' warning of our approach, the results of the action would have been quite different."[72]

Having shattered the transports' screen, the Japanese strike force would have little trouble strangling the infant American offensive in its cradle. Nothing now stood between it and the American transports anchored off Guadalcanal and Tulagi.

When Turner saw flashes of gunfire and flares off Savo, he ordered the transports to stop unloading and to weigh anchor, but they had not yet left. Small craft roared around the area in confusion, their captains expecting an attack on the anchorage at any moment.

However, the bold Japanese admiral who eight months earlier had urged a second attack on Pearl Harbor this time chose to play it safe. He reasoned that it would take two and a half hours to re-form his scattered force and reach the transport anchorages, leaving his ships within easy range of the US carrier planes at daylight. He did not know that Admiral Fletcher's carriers were sailing away. At 2:20 a.m. Mikawa ordered a withdrawal, and his task force sailed back up the Slot without molesting the transports.

His subordinate commanders, elated by the easy victory, were dismayed by Mikawa's decision to retire. "We were all shocked and disconcerted momentarily," wrote Commander Ohmae. The decision also diminished Admiral Yamamoto's joy over the victory. He sent Mikawa a bland congratulatory note: "Appreciate the courageous and hard fighting of every man of your organization." Later, he privately reprimanded Mikawa for failing to attack the transports.[73]

Before Mikawa's strike force reassembled northwest of Savo for the return trip, the picket *Ralph Talbot*, which, with the *Blue*, had missed the fight, tangled with some of Mikawa's ships as they sailed northward into the destroyer's patrol area. Caught in a searchlight, the *Talbot* was fired on by two Japanese cruisers. *Talbot*'s commander, Lieutenant Commander Joseph Callahan, suspected friendly ships were shooting at him by mistake, and he flashed his recognition lights. Momentarily confused by the signal, the Japanese ceased fire—until two cruisers astern went into action, hitting the *Talbot* five times successively and disabling her guns, torpedo controls, and radar, which had been of little use. The *Talbot* got off four torpedoes—they all missed. Listing and in flames, the destroyer drifted into a rain squall that protected her from further punishment.

Mikawa's captains boasted that they had sunk seven cruisers and five destroyers—three times the actual number—while Japanese losses were small: four ships damaged, fifty-eight men killed. Mikawa thought it triumph enough.[74]

ADMIRAL FLETCHER'S COMMANDERS LEARNED VIA "flash report" at 3:00 a.m. about the surface action. Fletcher had turned back toward Guadalcanal two hours earlier because he had not yet received Admiral Ghormley's authorization to withdraw. The report prompted the *Wasp*'s air group commander, Captain Forrest Sherman, to ask the flag officer aboard the *Wasp*, Rear Admiral Leigh Noyes, to continue sailing northwestward with a destroyer screen so that Sherman's air group, trained in night operations, could support Turner's transports. Three times Sherman asked, and each time Noyes refused to forward his request to Fletcher. Ghormley's authorization of Fletcher's withdrawal request arrived at 3:30, and Fletcher again turned southeastward and left the area.[75]

East of Bougainville, the Japanese strike force split up, with Cruiser Division 6's four ships steering for their anchorage at Kavieng, while Mikawa continued on to Rabaul on the *Chokai*, accompanied by the two light cruisers and the destroyer *Yunagi*.

On the morning of August 10, Cruiser Division 6 was seventy miles from Kavieng, sailing in a rectangular formation without an escort. A patrol plane flew overhead. The small US submarine *S-44*, which sighted the four cruisers, was about to exact a small measure of retribution. Lieutenant Commander John R. Moore slipped to within seven hundred yards of them and fired four torpedoes into the

Kako. The cruiser went down in five minutes, taking seventy-one men with her—the first major enemy combat ship sunk by a US submarine in World War II.[76]

FIVE MILES SOUTHEAST OF SAVO before dawn on August 9, the *Canberra*'s survivors struggled to put out the raging fires. Listing more heavily than before, she periodically erupted in concussive explosions. The *Patterson* had sent over hoses and was taking aboard many of the six hundred or so wounded Australian sailors when the destroyer suddenly departed; a hostile ship was reported nearby. "We'll be back!" her crewmen called. The "hostile" was in fact the *Chicago*, with part of her bow gone. In a coda to her error-ridden night, the *Chicago* opened fire on the *Patterson*, mistaking thunderclaps for gunfire, and the *Patterson* fired back. Neither ship was damaged. At daybreak the *Patterson* resumed her evacuation of the *Canberra*, joined by the *Chicago* and the *Blue*.

Admiral Turner said that if the *Canberra* could not retire at 6:30 a.m. with the rest of his screening task force, she would be scuttled. There was no possibility that the *Canberra* could sail anywhere, and at 8:00 a.m. two US destroyers sank her with torpedoes.[77]

The *Bagley*, the only undamaged ship in the Southern Force, came alongside *Astoria* and evacuated 185 stretcher cases as fires raged below decks. Ear-splitting explosions, followed by the crash of collapsing bulkheads, shook the battered cruiser. Nothing could be done to slow the ship's demise; there was no electricity for the pumps and no water for the fire hoses. The crewmen went around collecting the dead and their dog tags. Doctors continued operating on the seriously wounded, filling trash cans with amputated arms, legs, and feet, which were thrown overboard.

When the *Astoria*'s list to port worsened, Captain Greenman reluctantly gave the order to abandon ship, and he went into the water. He shouted, "Turn around, men, and watch your ship go down!" The *Astoria* rolled on her side and sank at 12:15 p.m. on August 9, the fourth Allied cruiser lost during the one-sided battle.[78]

DAYBREAK FOUND THE CHOPPY WATERS of Sealark Channel—soon to be known as Ironbottom Sound after more ships were blasted into its depths—littered with hundreds of exhausted, injured, oil-coated sailors clinging to floating debris and rafts. Sharks circled and sometimes dragged down bleeding survivors to horrific deaths. Abe Santos, the *Astoria* survivor, heard a man in the water near him exclaim that something had bitten him, "then I never saw him again." An *Astoria* shipmate, Charles Gordon, saw a sailor on a destroyer throw a line to a man struggling in the water, but the ship pulled away before he could grab it. Sharks devoured him, "one of the most horrible sights of all the wars I have been in." The waters around Savo teemed with sharks accustomed to feasting on human flesh; area natives followed a long tradition of setting the dead adrift in the sea.

Throughout the morning, sailors pulled more than seven hundred wounded men from the water. They were "mostly incoherent," and many were suffering from severe burns. Lieutenant Commander Isquith, the *Vincennes* surgeon, was rescued around dawn as he began suffering from muscle cramps, a result of treading water for hours next to three lashed-together rafts spilling over with nearly two hundred survivors. A whaleboat towed the rafts and Isquith to a ship, where Isquith put on a pair of loaned pajamas and socks and went to the emergency dressing room. He worked there for the next several hours, treating more than eighty men, before being transferred to a transport, in whose emergency room he continued treating injured sailors.

Wounded men who died after being brought aboard the destroyers were wrapped in canvas that was then weighted and dumped from the fantail after a brief burial service.[79]

ADMIRAL KING DESCRIBED THE NAVY'S stunning defeat at Savo Island as "the blackest day of the war." It was more than that—it was the blackest day in US naval history because, unlike Pearl Harbor, the Japanese attacked Allied warships in a combat zone during a declared war. A shocking 1,077 Allied sailors died in the first major US surface battle since the Spanish-American War. The marginally stronger but numerically inferior Japanese force sank four heavy cruisers—three American, one Australian—and damaged another cruiser and two destroyers. The Japanese did not lose a single ship.

The Imperial Japanese Navy had dealt a heavy blow to the US Pacific fleet, but not a decisive one; it was more of a successful hit-and-run raid than the "decisive battle" the Japanese high command so craved. Afterward Turner's unmolested transports resumed their hasty unloading of the Marines' supplies.

A naval inquiry by Admiral Arthur Hepburn concluded that the fiasco's root cause was "the complete surprise achieved by the enemy." Contributing factors included the Allies' poor readiness despite warnings that the enemy was approaching, communications failures, overconfidence in the radar of the *Blue* and *Ralph Talbot*, and the carrier group's withdrawal, which left the Navy unable to pursue the withdrawing Japanese strike force. US Navy historian Samuel Eliot Morison succinctly summarized the multiple shortcomings as "lack of 'battle-mindedness.'"[80]

Although none of the individual commanders was court-martialed, some of them struggled with feelings of guilt. Captain Bode of the *Chicago*, the Southern Force commander, committed suicide shortly after investigators interviewed him. His lapses weighed on his conscience: his failure to warn the Northern Force or to even issue orders to his own group, the *Chicago*'s departure from the fight, and firing on the *Patterson* by mistake.[81]

For two months, the Navy kept the debacle from the American public. In October press restrictions began to ease after the *New York Times*'s publication of correspondent Hanson Baldwin's articles about the crisis on Guadalcanal. The United States, he wrote, had "nailed the colors to the mast" in the Solomons. News of the Savo Island defeat stunned Americans who had believed everything was going the Navy's way.[82]

The Japanese press went to the other extreme, proclaiming the victory "unrivalled in world history" while claiming that the Japanese navy had sunk twenty-four warships and eleven transports "filled to capacity with Marines." Australia, the reports said, was now isolated and ripe for conquest. English-language broadcasts from Japan, heard by Marines on Guadalcanal, boasted that even though the South Pacific had been swept clean of operational US carriers, there remained "plenty of room at the bottom of the Pacific for more American fleet—Ha! Ha!"[83]

WHILE ALLIED CRUISERS AND DESTROYERS were battling for survival in the black waters off Savo Island, sailors and Marines who were ashore tried to interpret the meaning of the distant gunfire and explosions. "It was a spectacular sight—ships exploding in the rockets' red glare. We had no idea who was winning at first," wrote Lieutenant William H. Whyte, a battalion staff officer with the First Marines. "But we began to get an inkling when the operators of our radio transmitters reported they couldn't get through to our principal ships."

Watching from twenty miles away, the Marines recognized that "the fate of all of us hung on that sea battle," wrote International News Service correspondent Richard Tregaskis. The flashes of gunfire and explosions made them feel "pitifully small . . . in the gigantic whirlpool of war. . . . One had the feeling of being at the mercy of great accumulated forces far more powerful than anything human. We were only pawns in a battle of the gods then, and we knew it."

Admiral Crutchley, whose Southern Force was being knocked to pieces, was also clueless. When the meeting on the *McCawley* with Turner and Vandegrift ended a little after midnight, Crutchley returned to his flagship, *Australia*, and remained in the transport area at Lunga Point. From his ship's bridge Crutchley saw three burning objects off Savo and sent a message to Captain Bode on the *Chicago*: "Report Situation."

Bode replied that the *Chicago* had been hit by a torpedo and was south of Savo, *Canberra* was on fire, and enemy ships remained in the area. Bode's fragmentary report prompted Crutchley to inform Turner that there had been a "surface action" near Savo, but "situation as yet undetermined." Unable to raise the

Vincennes or *Astoria* and alarmed by the flares dropped by Japanese planes in the transport areas off Guadalcanal and Tulagi, Crutchley sent a coded message to seven of his covering force destroyers to rendezvous northwest of Savo Island and engage the enemy if they made contact. But many of the ships were unable to decipher Crutchley's message, and others did not receive it at all. The order was not carried out.

Later, after absorbing the details of the disaster that had befallen his force, Crutchley made no excuses. "The fact must be faced that we had an adequate force placed with the very purpose of repelling surface attack and when the surface attack was made, it destroyed our force."[84]

After meeting with Turner and Crutchley, Vandegrift and his operations officer, Lieutenant Colonel Thomas, boarded a minesweeper for Tulagi to meet with Brigadier General William Rupertus, who was directing operations on Tulagi, Gavutu, and Florida islands. It was after 1:30 in the morning and raining as the *Southard* plowed across Sealark Channel. Star shells, white flashes, and flames lit up the sky around Savo Island. "Jesus, it looked like the 4th of July at Washington Monument," wrote Thomas. "There were shells and star shells going all over the place. . . . We saw a couple of ships blow up—just flashes of fire." Sailors on deck cheered at "the enormous explosions. We all felt elated," Vandegrift wrote. "We were sure our forces were winning."[85]

For Vandegrift and the Marines, all the news was bad: Admiral Fletcher withdrawing his carriers; Admiral Turner leaving later in the day with the remaining warships and transports as well as the supplies that never made it ashore; and the ominous naval battle lighting up the low clouds around Savo Island. By sunset on August 9, the Marines were bereft of naval and air support. The Japanese could shell and bomb them at will.

FROM THE SHORES OF GUADALCANAL, Tulagi, and Gavutu, the Marines looked out over Sealark Channel and saw no ships there, not even Higgins boats. "As the sun set behind the mountains no friendly ships hovered offshore and no friendly planes patrolled the skies. We were on our own," wrote Lieutenant Herbert Merillat, the 1st Marine Division's historian and public relations officer.

The Navy had sailed away with half of the Marines' supplies still on the transports, including all the heavy equipment needed to finish the airfield. Washed up on the beaches of Gavutu were parachutes and boxes of equipment that sailors on the transports had pitched overboard for the 1st Parachute Battalion before leaving. In a box labeled "Major Williams"—Major Robert Williams was the paratroopers' wounded commander—was a case of scotch, a sixteen-gauge shotgun, and shotgun ammunition.

An enumeration of the supplies that did reach Guadalcanal included seventeen days' field rations that, when combined with warehoused Japanese food, might last a month if the Marines received just two meals a day. Also landed were 12 million rounds of .30- and .45-caliber ammunition. The forty-two hundred Marines on Tulagi, Gavutu, and Florida Islands received field rations for four days plus 3 million rounds of .30-caliber and thirty thousand rounds of .45-caliber ammunition.

A Marine enlisted man on Tulagi said hunger quickly became "the single overriding emotion" because so little food had reached the island. Fortunately the Japanese had stored edibles in Tulagi's warehouses, although it was mostly barley.[86]

UNDER THESE PERILOUS CIRCUMSTANCES THE Marines could not have asked for a better leader than fifty-five-year-old Major General Alexander Archer Vandegrift, a calm, mild-mannered Virginian who had spent more than thirty years in the Marine Corps. His grandfather, Carson Vandegrift, a Baptist deacon, was wounded during Pickett's Charge, and young Vandegrift grew up hearing war stories from him and other Confederate veterans in Charlottesville. When his grandfather prayed, Vandegrift said only half-jokingly, it was to "the God of Abraham, Isaac, Jacob, Robert E. Lee, and Stonewall Jackson." When his grandfather first saw him in his Marine Corps dress blues, the old Confederate conceded that he looked military enough, but said he never dreamed he would see his grandson wearing a blue uniform.

Vandegrift attended the University of Virginia before joining the Marines and being commissioned a second lieutenant. He served in Nicaragua and Mexico, was promoted to captain, and was sent to Haiti for several years with the Haitian Constabulary. Between tours in China during the 1920s and 1930s, he helped write the landing operations manual that the Corps used during the Pacific War. He was assistant commandant when he was appointed the 1st Marine Division's commander and promoted to major general.[87]

The morning of the Savo Island battle and the Navy's withdrawal, Vandegrift summoned his top officers to a meeting at his command post. "Singly or in pairs they straggled to my CP, the colonels, lieutenant colonels, and majors on whom so much depended," Vandegrift wrote. "They were a sorry-looking lot with bloodshot eyes and embryonic beards and filthy dungarees." The tired officers slumped to the wet ground around a smoky fire as rain hissed in the flames. They drank coffee from canteen cups and empty, dirty C-Ration tins. On the nearby beach, a procession of small boats landed half-naked survivors of the night's battle, their bodies "black with burns and oil of the sunken ships." Spectrally, the cruiser *Chicago* sailed past, its shot-off bow a forlorn emblem of the one-sided action. "God only knew," thought Vandegrift, "when we could expect aircraft protection, much less surface craft; with the transports gone, the enemy would shift his attacks against us and we could expect surface attacks as well."

Colonel Thomas, the division operations officer, catalogued the priorities of the moment: move the supplies off the beach and disperse and conceal them; dig in; concentrate firepower to repel landings on the beach, the Lunga River, and Alligator Creek; and complete the airfield.

Vandegrift told his subordinate officers to inform their men of their predicament. But, he said, "also pound home that we anticipate no Bataan, no Wake Island. Since 1775 Marines had found themselves in tough spots. They had survived and we would survive."

But the fighting men had already absorbed a more sobering message from the bountiful rumors and scuttlebutt: the Japanese navy had trounced the US Navy, and "we had been abandoned, and were considered expendable."[88]

ON THIS FATEFUL SUNDAY, AUGUST 9, thirty Japanese planes left Rabaul to raid the American transports and beachhead. But they were diverted by a sighting—spurious, it turned out—of a US battleship in the waters southwest of Guadalcanal. The "battleship" was in fact the destroyer *Jarvis*, badly damaged during Saturday's air raid and crawling across the Coral Sea toward Sydney for repairs. The attackers swooped down and sank her with torpedoes, but not before *Jarvis*'s gunners shot down two enemy planes. Because her captain had jettisoned rafts and lifeboats to reduce her draft, none of the destroyer's more than two hundred crewmen survived—adding to the Navy's long "butcher's bill" for the day.[89]

2

August Part II:
Japan Strikes Back:
Tojo Time and Alligator Creek

To defeat the Japanese "we shall have to throw away the rule book of war and go back to the tactics used during the French and Indian Wars."

—MAJOR GENERAL ALEXANDER ARCHER VANDEGRIFT,
AFTER THE BATTLE OF ALLIGATOR CREEK[1]

Most of the men died from the concussion and then were roasted. . . . They were blackened but not burned or withered, and they looked like iron statues of men, their limbs smooth and whole, their heads rounded with no hair.

—LIEUTENANT FREDERICK MEARS, DESCRIBING THE
MACABRE SCENE IN THE *ENTERPRISE* GUN GALLERY
AFTER THE BATTLE OF THE EASTERN SOLOMONS[2]

Cactus can be a sinkhole for enemy air power and can be consolidated, expanded and exploited to the enemy's mortal hurt.

—REAR ADMIRAL JOHN S. "SLEW" MCCAIN,
SOUTH PACIFIC NAVAL AIR COMMANDER[3]

WITH THE NAVY NOW GONE, Vandegrift's Marines had only their own thin resources. They would have to scale back their operational plans to what might be accomplished without air or naval support. Vandegrift and his staff now had two goals: defending the airfield against anticipated counterattacks and making it operational as soon as possible. Vandegrift would not attempt to capture geographical features such as Mount Austen, which overlooked the airfield from the south. The Marines would protect what they had seized; they would win by not losing.

Vandegrift immediately grasped the airfield's tactical and strategic importance. If the Marines could defend the airfield against land, air, and sea attacks and transform it into an unsinkable aircraft carrier, the general and his staff believed Guadalcanal could be held. The presence of American aircraft would mean that the Japanese could not land reinforcements during daylight hours and that air raids would be swiftly counteracted.

In the larger sense, holding Guadalcanal meant preserving the present US-Australian sea lanes; if the island were lost, the longer reach of Japanese air and sea power would necessarily push the lanes eastward. Moreover, victory on Guadalcanal would deal the Japanese their first major defeat of the Pacific War. The outcomes were Manichean in their starkness and import: lose the airfield, lose the island, lose the sea lanes; hold the airfield, and the course of the entire war might be reversed.

As a first step the Marines established an oval-shaped perimeter around the airfield that could be defended by fourteen thousand men. It was a cordon defense consisting of a single line of men, and not the preferred in-depth defensive alignment, for which the perimeter was too small. Vandegrift believed that overwhelming firepower and a mobile reserve could stop any attack. In the meantime he planned to conduct an "active defense" by sending patrols into "Indian territory" to gather intelligence.

East to west the perimeter extended three miles, from Alligator Creek on the east side—on Marine maps incorrectly labeled the Tenaru River, which was in fact two miles farther east—to a series of grass-covered coral ridges, cleaved by jungle-clogged ravines, midway between the Lunga River and, four miles farther west, the Matanikau River.

The First Marines dug in on the west bank of Alligator Creek—a tidal lagoon infested with crocodiles, not alligators—and extended their positions westward along the beach. Vandegrift's greatest fear was that the Japanese would attempt an amphibious landing at Lunga Point near the airfield. Halfway down the beach line the First Marines tied into the lines of the Fifth Marines, whose positions continued westward before curving to the south into the jumble of grassy coral ridges between the Lunga and Matanikau.

The beach defenses were formidable: Marine infantrymen armed with Springfield rifles and light machine-guns and supported by crew-served tripod-mounted machine-guns and 37mm guns. Half-track 75mm guns and amphibious tractors bristling with machine-guns stood ready to move to prepared positions along the water's edge.

Northwest of the airfield the Marines placed their 90mm antiaircraft batteries, while the Eleventh Marines' 105mm and 75mm howitzers were centrally located to deliver supporting fire anywhere on the perimeter that was threatened.[4]

The first patrols left the perimeter on August 9 to find the enemy. Those probing eastward and southward came up empty-handed, but to the west—where the Japanese troops and construction workers had fled August 7—they encountered heavily armed enemy soldiers, who repulsed a Fifth Marines patrol when it attempted to cross the Matanikau, inflicting Guadalcanal's first US combat casualties: an officer killed and several men wounded.[5]

BESIDES BEING THE DAY THAT the Navy left, August 9 inaugurated another unpleasantness: the onset of daily enemy air raids that sent Marines diving into slit trenches and foxholes. A "sing-song whine" signaled the arrival of the Japanese Bettys, followed by the swish of bombs being released, and then explosions. Correspondent Richard Tregaskis quickly learned to prop himself on his elbows in foxholes so that he would not get a concussion when bombs landed nearby. "Some of our people have been so badly shaken by close ones that they have suffered shock and prolonged bleeding from the nose," he wrote.

"Enemy air raids infuriated us all," wrote Vandegrift after ducking into a shelter as six Zeros swooped down on a strafing run. He informed Admiral Ghormley that he hoped to have the airfield operational on August 12 and urged Ghormley to send warplanes as soon as possible.[6]

The full import of the Marines' predicament by now had filtered down through the ranks to the lowliest private. The Navy's departure, coupled with the daily air raids—announced by the clanging of "a dilapidated dinner bell" that sent the Marines running for shelter—was eroding the high morale that had followed the deceptively easy landing. Vanderbilt tried to head off the mounting pessimism by touring the perimeter in his readily identifiable khaki uniform and talking to as many men as possible in the hours before "Tojo time," as the noontime raids came to be known. "I would ask them how they were getting on; what happened during the night, just let them talk about it," he said.[7]

The airfield site, like the northern coastal plain where the Marines landed, was a soil engineer's nightmare, consisting of eighteen inches of black dirt overlying impermeable clay. Rain turned the black dirt into glutinous mud that sat atop the clay until it evaporated or drained to lower ground—which happened to be the airfield, eighteen inches below the surrounding area. Working quickly during the dry season, Japanese construction crews had scraped off most of the black soil to get down to the clay. Now when it rained, the airstrip became a de facto canal. It was dusty when dry, slick and muddy when wet. Rains would hamper air operations until American construction crews could raise the entire runway, lay down perforated steel planking known as Marston matting, and install a drainage system.[8]

The Japanese had begun building the northeast-to-southwest airstrip from both ends, working toward the middle. When the laborers and Japanese soldiers fled during the Marine landings, a nearly two-hundred-foot-long gap remained. Marine engineers estimated that they would need seven thousand cubic yards of earth to fill it and complete a barebones airstrip without taxiways or revetments. The Navy had sailed away with the Marines' construction equipment and digging tools, but the Japanese had thoughtfully left behind plenty of tools to finish the job—shovels, six road rollers, four heavy-duty tractors, a dozen trucks, and a narrow-gauge railroad with two gasoline locomotives and hopper cars that Marine engineers nicknamed the "Toonerville Trolley."

The latter, although somewhat comical in appearance, proved to be indispensable for shuttling large amounts of hand-shoveled fill dirt; without it the runway could not have been speedily completed. The 1st Engineer Battalion went to work on August 9, and three days later, on August 12, it completed twenty-six hundred feet of runway, despite the midday air raids and daily shellings by destroyers and submarines that interrupted or undid work that had been done.

During an impromptu flag-raising ceremony August 10 the airfield was christened Henderson Field in honor of Major Lofton R. "Joe" Henderson, killed during a dive-bombing run on a Japanese carrier at the Battle of Midway. A division air officer, Major Ken Weir, had quickly given the airstrip its iconic name because he did not want it named for "some potbellied old SOB behind a desk in the Pentagon."

On August 12 Navy Lieutenant W. S. Sampson, an aide to Rear Admiral John McCain, set down a PBY-5A Catalina "flying boat" on the airstrip, the first landing at Henderson Field. Another four days labor would finish what would then be a 3,500-feet-long, 150-feet-wide runway. Meanwhile two Marine air squadrons—VMF-223 and VMSB-232, fighters and dive bombers, respectively—and their ground support teams were en route to Henderson Field to introduce a new element into the campaign.[9]

NEAR THE MATANIKAU RIVER ON August 11 the Fifth Marines captured a Japanese naval warrant officer who told intelligence officers that Japanese soldiers were starving in a village west of the river and were eager to surrender. His account appeared to corroborate a report of a white flag seen flying near Point Cruz.

Lieutenant Colonel Frank Goettge, the division intelligence officer, asked Vandegrift for permission to investigate personally, although a larger combat patrol was already planned for that area. It was Goettge who had interviewed Guadalcanal traders, planters, and colonial officials before the landing and helped make a rough map of the north coast. Goettge convinced Vandegrift that he could persuade the hungry enemy soldiers to surrender and possibly end enemy resistance—if he acted quickly. Vandegrift gave his reluctant consent.

After dark on August 12 Goettge's party gathered at the boat dock at Kukum, near the Lunga River's estuary. Goettge planned to make a boat landing west of the Matanikau River with twenty-five men that included most of his D-2 section as well as Captain Wilfred Ringer, the Fifth Marines intelligence officer; Lieutenant Commander Malcolm Pratt, a Fifth Marines surgeon; and a Japanese linguist, Lieutenant Ralph Corry.

Before the operation began, Lieutenant Colonel William Whaling, the Fifth Marines' executive officer, warned Goettge to avoid the area between the Matanikau and Point Cruz, where Whaling's men had encountered strong opposition. Land west of Point Cruz, he urged Goettge.

But just before 10:00 p.m. a Higgins boat put Goettge's men ashore at the very place Whaling had advised him to avoid. The mistake was probably due to a combination of poor visibility and unfamiliar terrain. The men were woefully unprepared for combat, lacking radios, grenades, and automatic weapons, any of which might have made a difference.

The landing was unopposed, and the Higgins boat departed; Goettge intended to push inland to Matanikau Village, where the starving Japanese supposedly were, and return on foot to the airstrip with the prisoners. Goettge set up a perimeter on the beach before he, the Japanese warrant officer, Captain Ringer, and First Sergeant Steven Custer advanced inland toward a two-hundred-foot ridge where they hoped to find the Japanese bivouac.[10]

Suddenly a fusillade of rifle and machine-gun fire from concealed positions on the ridge tore through Goettge's small party. Goettge was killed immediately along with the prisoner, and Sergeant Custer was seriously wounded. Captain Ringer led the survivors back to the beach and sent Sergeant Charles Arndt for help after tracer rounds fired as an SOS signal elicited no response from the Marine lines. Arndt swam out into the channel, found a damaged canoe, and paddled it to Kukum, arriving at 5:00 a.m. on August 13. A second Marine, Corporal Joseph Spaulding, was also sent for help in case Arndt did not make it; Spaulding did not arrive until 7:30 a.m.

At dawn just four patrol members could still fight. Ringer tried to lead them into the jungle, but enemy gunfire cut down three of them. The survivor, Sergeant Lowell Few, plunged into the surf and swam away as Japanese bullets churned the water around him. Looking back at the scene of the patrol's annihilation, he saw flashing samurai swords as Japanese soldiers executed his wounded comrades.

When Arndt reached Kukum and reported the patrol's dire situation, A Company of the Fifth Marines was immediately dispatched by boat. The Marines landed west of Point Cruz, where Goettge was supposed to land but had not. Two platoons of Captain Lyman Spurlock's L Company joined the relief patrol. They worked their way eastward down the beach toward the perimeter, encountering enemy resistance near the mouth of the Matanikau. But they found no trace of Goettge or his men.

ON AUGUST 19 VANDEGRIFT SENT three companies of Fifth Marines on a multiprong mission: to cross the Matanikau sandbar, clean out the Japanese at Matanikau Village, and land at the village of Kokumbona west of Point Cruz to block the enemy's escape.

The operation, which would become known as the First Battle of the Matanikau—there would be four—was a minor success. When Spurlock's L Company reached the outskirts of Matanikau Village, the Japanese launched a daylight banzai attack. Sixty-five of them died, at a cost of four Marines killed and eleven wounded.

Corpsman William Laing was driving a truck back to the perimeter with his friend, Private First Class Larry Westcott, who had been wounded in the lower abdomen and both legs. A grenade thrown by a wounded Japanese soldier exploded nearby, and the blast threw Westcott to the ground and tore open the lower half of his body. When Laing reached his side Westcott asked if he was going to die. "With tears I could not hold back, I grabbed his bloody shirt and lay my head on his chest until life left his body."

B Company, which was supposed to cross the river mouth, was repulsed by intensive enemy fire. I Company, which landed near Kokumbona, had the novel experience of being shelled by two enemy destroyers and a submarine. The I Company Marines drove enemy troops from Kokumbona Village into the hills to the south and then returned by boat to the perimeter.

Another seaborne raid on Kokumbona eight days later, on August 27, proved equally unproductive. Lieutenant Colonel William Maxwell's 1st Battalion, Fifth Marines, was landed west of the village. Its mission was to sweep eastward along the coast toward the perimeter while also blocking the Japanese's retreat into the jungle to the south.

When they landed, Maxwell's men found hot, prepared food at an enemy bivouac, but no Japanese, suggesting a hasty decampment. As they began their eastward sweep the Marines faced a convoluted topography of ridges, cliffs, and gullies that crowded to within just a few hundred yards of the beach. Maxwell sent one company to shadow the main advance from atop ridges to the south, clearing the gullies that emptied onto the beach of any enemy soldiers. But the company could not keep pace with the advance down on the beach, and it had no radio with which to communicate with the battalion. Then, when machine-gun and mortar fire erupted from Japanese entrenched in a gully and at the base of the cliff behind it, progress along the beach stalled. As the day progressed and casualties mounted, Maxwell radioed a request for boats to evacuate his men.

Vandegrift angrily dispatched the Fifth Regiment's commander, Colonel LeRoy Hunt, in a boat to take charge. Hunt relieved Maxwell of command and appointed the next-senior officer in his place. The battalion spent the night on a hill overlooking the beach. When it resumed its push eastward the next morning the Japanese were gone. The division report faulted the operation for being "incredibly slow and its leadership irresolute and faltering." Maxwell was sent home.[11]

DAYS LATER A PATROL FOUND surgeon Pratt's dispatch case and a scrap of uniform bearing Goettge's name. Although official records said that no remains from Goettge's doomed mission were ever found, Lieutenant Colonel Whaling reported seeing shallow graves while leading a patrol over a sandbar at the mouth of the Matanikau—and an arm protruding from the sand. A storm subsequently washed away the sandbar and all traces of the burial sites.[12]

The official report on the Goettge patrol concluded that the white flag seen in Matanikau Village was probably a limply hanging Japanese flag, with the characteristic "meatball" hidden in the folds—and not a signal for parley or surrender. Yet many Marines refused to believe that it was anything other than a white surrender flag, raised to lure Goettge's men to slaughter.

The realization began to sink in that the Pacific War was going to be different from previous US wars—a "take-no-prisoners struggle . . . and fought back in kind," as one Marine described it.[13]

ON AUGUST 15 WORK PARTIES were clearing the last supplies from Guadalcanal's beaches when a tall, sturdily built man with a blond beard and wearing tattered shorts emerged from the jungle near the Marines' eastern perimeter. It was twenty-six-year-old Captain Martin Clemens leading ten armed, bare-chested Melanesians in two columns. They were carrying their rifles at shoulder arms. One of them bore the Union Jack on a short pole. Clemens had been instructed to come down from the mountains to join the Marines at Lunga Point, as had two other coast-watching teams that had taken refuge in the highlands.

The three teams had watched as neat rows of tents went up at Lunga Point in early June and as troops burned off kunai grass on the coastal plain June 20, the day Clemens learned the Japanese had built a wharf. On July 6 the coast watchers radioed a report to their control station on Malaita, which relayed it to Australia, about the arrival of a twelve-ship convoy at the wharf and the unloading of construction equipment, trucks, two small locomotives with hopper cars, an ice plant, and two construction battalions with four hundred naval troops.

Cold, sleep-deprived, and hungry—he had subsisted mainly on yams—Clemens had lost forty-two pounds while in hiding, and he worried about the future. "Things were looking grim. . . . The Japs were all around us, on both land and sea," he wrote. Transports and warships came and went from the northern coast, and Japanese aircraft prowled overhead, often at low altitudes, apparently looking for the coast watchers' hiding spots. Clemens and the other coast watchers—Australian Navy Lieutenant Commander D. S. Macfarlan, responsible for central Guadalcanal, and L. Schroeder and F. Ashton Rhoades, whose territory was the northwestern part of the island—retreated deeper into the mountains, Clemens nearly to the southern coast, and the others to Gold Ridge, a mining camp at four thousand feet elevation.

After observing the Marine landings Clemens, hungry and barefoot, hiked down the hills to Vungana. On August 12 Australian Navy Lieutenant Hugh Mackenzie instructed him and the other two teams to enter the Marine perimeter. Mackenzie had come to the island to operate a coast watchers' radio network, station "KEN," next to the airfield.

CLEMENS AND HIS COMRADES BELONGED to Australian Navy Lieutenant Commander Eric Feldt's Australian Coast Watching Service. From his headquarters in Townsville in northern Australia, Feldt supervised more than one hundred stations in a twenty-five hundred-mile swath of the South Pacific extending from western Papua New Guinea to Vila in the New Hebrides. Twenty-three of them operated in the Solomon Islands. Feldt's coast watchers were planters, traders, colonial officials, soldiers, and naval personnel. They monitored and reported the movement of Japanese troops and ships. The network's code name was "Ferdinand," for the fabled bull that preferred flowers to the arena, a nod to the coast watchers' status as observers, not fighters.

Yet they well knew that the Japanese did not care about the distinction and that they would be executed if captured. Isolated, they faced danger and hardship daily and seldom learned if their reports made a difference. On Bougainville the two coast watchers relied for long periods on supplies that were airdropped in the jungle. Once, one of them pedaled a borrowed bicycle seventy miles over rugged trails to a reported drop site, only to find nothing there.[14]

The Bougainville coast watchers were Guadalcanal's indispensable early-warning system, providing two hours' advance warning of approaching Japanese air raids. The enemy bombers and their fighter escort routinely left Rabaul's air-fields at 8:00 to 9:00 a.m. to begin the 560-mile flight to Guadalcanal.

Jack Read's lookouts often spotted the planes over northern Bougainville, and he would then send the first urgent report. Paul Mason's lookouts monitored Bougainville's southeastern coastline. If the enemy flew over the island or hugged its east coast, both saw the formations—Read first, Mason, thirty minutes later. Unless the Japanese avoided Bougainville altogether, Read, a north Bougainville public servant since 1929, and Mason, a plantation manager, were usually able to alert the Americans that enemy planes were coming.

On four consecutive days Read informed KEN that Japanese planes from Rabaul were on the way: August 29 at 8:25 a.m., reporting eighteen twin-engine bombers and twenty-two fighters; on August 30 at 9:25 a.m., fifteen planes, possibly fighters; August 31 at 8:45 a.m., eighteen twin-engine bombers and twenty-three fighters; and on September 1 at 8:55 a.m., "eighteen bombers, 22 fighters going yours."[15]

WHEN CLEMENS AND HIS MEN reached the First Marines' lines, an outpost guard met them with a loaded rifle. Choking up at the sight of an ally, Clemens was barely able to whisper his name. The guard appeared to know who Clemens was and handed him a cigarette and a piece of chocolate. Before being whisked away in a Jeep, Clemens shook dozens of hands.

Deeply appreciating Clemens's encyclopedic knowledge of Guadalcanal and finding him congenial to his staff, Vandegrift brought the Scotsman into his inner circle. Clemens was detached from Ferdinand to become the Marines' liaison to Guadalcanal's native scouts.

The Melanesian scouts were black, stocky, and muscular, and they possessed great stamina. Their carefully groomed hair stood up four inches or more, and the crown was tinged yellow-red by the lime they habitually applied. Clemens organized them into scout companies that watched and reported native and Japanese activity, recovered downed pilots, and guided Marine patrols. The disastrous Goettge patrol had wiped out Vandegrift's G-2 section, but with the arrival of Clemens and his natives, the Marine general now had a superior intelligence and scouting network.

The Melanesians were skilled in jungle craft and intimately familiar with Guadalcanal's terrain. They could spot cleverly camouflaged positions and were able to distinguish between actual bird calls and Japanese soldiers imitating them to communicate with one another.

Clemens divided the island into five sectors and assigned a chief scout and fifteen to twenty men to each. Later he would organize and manage the native day laborers and the porters who would carry the Americans' supplies on patrols. With Clemens sifting the scouts' reports at Vandegrift's CP and Mackenzie monitoring the coast watchers' Solomons network from his dugout beside the airfield, Vandegrift was now receiving real-time intelligence that enabled him to react quickly to threats.[16]

REPORTS OF JAPANESE SOLDIERS EAST of the perimeter began reaching the Marines on August 13. Natives told a patrol scouting a grassy area for a potential airfield that there were enemy troops farther east. Two days later Clemens and Jacob Vouza, the chief scout for that district, informed Marine intelligence officers that the Japanese reportedly were operating a radio station near Taivu Point, about twenty miles east of the perimeter. That same day Admiral Turner warned Vandegrift that Navy intelligence had intercepted enemy radio traffic indicating that an attack on the perimeter was just days away.

POOR INTELLIGENCE ABOUT THE AMERICAN landings and overconfidence from years of easy victories caused Japanese military leaders to gravely underestimate their enemy. On the basis of an August 10 dispatch by the Japanese military attaché in Moscow and other scattered intelligence, Imperial General Headquarters concluded that several thousand American soldiers had come ashore with orders to reconnoiter the area, destroy the airstrip, and then withdraw. Military leaders resolved to crush the threat but did not believe it would require a disruption of previously laid plans—or much effort at all, for that matter. They viewed their enemy as "very effeminate . . . very cowardly" soldiers who disliked fighting in the rain, or the mist, or at night—"night in particular . . . they cannot conceive to be a proper time for war," said a Japanese battle study.[17]

On August 13 the high command ordered the Seventeenth Army commander, Lieutenant General Harukichi Hyakutake, to seize Port Moresby, New Guinea, and to also send some troops to recapture the Guadalcanal airfield. "Its fighting spirit is not high," the instructions said of the American force on the island. Vice Admiral Matome Ugaki, Admiral Yamamoto's chief of staff, wrote that the mission was "to mop up the enemy remnant, rescue the garrison, and repair the airfield."

At the moment the Seventeenth Army, which on paper was fifty thousand strong, was scattered across the western Pacific, Manchuria, and southeast Asia, from the Philippines to Java, and from the Palaus to Guam, where the closest unassigned unit happened to be—the twenty-three-hundred-man Ichiki Detachment of the 35th Infantry Brigade. Hyakutake believed that it and a small Special Naval Landing Force could recapture Guadalcanal. But if this proved impossible, they should "occupy one corner of Guadalcanal and wait for the arrival of reinforcements," the orders read.[18]

Colonel Kiyonao Ichiki, a former instructor at the Imperial Army's infantry school, was an extremely capable field officer who had commanded battalions in China for several years. His detachment was a "shock unit" whose distinguished history dated to the 1904–1905 siege of Port Arthur during the Russo-Japanese War.[19]

In June 1942 the Ichiki Detachment was poised to assault Midway when the American naval victory caused the landings to be scrubbed. Ichiki and his men were on Guam, waiting to return to Japan when General Hyakutake summoned them to Truk to prepare for the Guadalcanal offensive.

Confident that his elite troops would win an impressive victory with relative ease, Ichiki embarked 917 of his men—a "First Echelon"—on six destroyers at Truk on August 16 to make a speedy landing near Taivu Point. The roughly 1,200-man "Second Echelon" would follow within a week in four slower transports. About 250 men from the 5th Sasebo Special Naval Landing Force were sent to a landing site west of the airfield as a diversion.[20]

"VICTORY FEVER" RAGED IN THE Japanese army following its easy triumphs in China and across Southeast Asia. Japan had never lost a war, having twice repelled the invading Mongols in the thirteenth century—with the assistance of typhoons—and having defeated Russia in 1905. During the twentieth century the army was the driving force behind Japanese expansionism, and it dominated national policy-setting. Modern in weaponry, the army remained feudal in outlook. The army adhered to the samurai warrior code of conduct—Bushido—and revered agriculture as Japan's cultural touchstone; modern industry was regarded as a necessary evil. Feudalism had largely ended in the late nineteenth century with the demise of the two-hundred-year-old Tokugawa Shogunate and the restoration of imperial government under the Emperor Meiji.

The Meiji government was shockingly progressive after the stagnation of the shogunate. It established a representative assembly and eventually a bicameral legislature while encouraging entrepreneurship and rejecting "evil customs of the past." Tenet Five of the Meiji Charter Oath of April 1868 read, "Knowledge shall be sought throughout the world so as to invigorate the foundations of imperial rule." In 1871 emissaries fanned out across Europe and the United States to observe and appropriate foreign methods and technologies. A year later Japan began operating its first railroad.

The new Japanese navy was modeled upon the British Royal Navy and American Admiral Alfred Thayer Mahan's theories, while the army emulated the Prussians and the French. The Meiji diluted the influence of the nearly two million samurai by extending to all males the right to vote and bear arms. Seeing their centuries' old control of Japan slipping away, the samurai rebelled in 1877, and the Meiji government crushed them with modern cannon and rifles.

Yet, even as samurai power faded, Bushido "bamboo spear tactics" endured along with the samurai indifference to death. The Japanese aggressively adopted Western methods and technology but not Western values or philosophy.[21]

In just two decades Japan's military was flexing its muscles in Asia. It defeated China in the First Sino-Japanese War of 1894–1895 and Russia in the Russo-Japanese War of 1904–1905. The Japanese captured Port Arthur and drove the Russian army from Mukden with losses of ninety thousand men while the navy annihilated the Russian fleet at Tsushima Strait, sinking twenty-one Russian warships.[22]

With the creation of the Greater East Asia Cooperation Sphere, Japan began planning to "liberate" the nations of south Asia from Western colonial rule. It promoted Asian solidarity for its member nations—with the Japanese controlling all economic matters. The Sphere's other members supplied oil, rubber, tungsten, and rice for Japan's war industry. Japan granted them limited autonomy. Dissent was ruthlessly suppressed by imprisonment, torture, executions, and massacres.

In 1931 Japan invaded Manchuria. The Japanese believed Manchuria would provide raw materials for Japan's nascent war machine, serve as a market for Japanese products, and eventually become a colony for Japanese emigrants. Near term, Manchuria became a base for Japanese operations in northern China.

In 1937 Japan went to war with China after Chiang Kai-shek and the insurgent communists joined forces to drive the Japanese from Peking and Northern China. The Japanese army piled up victories, much like Napoleon did in Russia in 1812, but China, like Russia 125 years earlier, proved to be quicksand: by 1940 half of Japan's 1.35 million active-duty troops were fighting there, with no end in sight.

In July 1941 Japan signed a mutual defense treaty with Vichy French Indochina and promptly moved troops there, inviting severe international repercussions. The United States, Britain, and the Dutch East Indies froze Japan's assets, stopped oil shipments, and demanded that it withdraw from Indochina and China. Japan suddenly lost access to more than three-quarters of its imported oil. The Japanese opened negotiations with the United States and prepared for war.

As Japan's relations with the West deteriorated, Japanese intellectuals began to systematically eradicate British and US culture in East Asia, hoping to replace it with a new, indigenous culture common to Cooperation Sphere nations. Movie theaters were ordered to stop showing US and British movies; the playing of jazz was forbidden, and even jazz instruments were banned; and baseball was banished. The Ministry of Education ordered schools to remove or destroy American dolls and to put up posters: "Kill the American devils!" exhorted one. Japan tried to ban English but encountered a roadblock: English happened to be East Asia's lingua franca, and it would take years for Japanese to replace it.[23]

BY 1942 JAPAN HAD 2.3 million active-duty troops. Besides striving to increase manpower, the army had aggressively modernized its weapons and equipment during the 1930s, consciously imitating Germany's Wehrmacht, which it deeply admired. Its doctrine emphasized offensive warfare—surprise attacks, even before war was declared, and decisive early victories. Yet the army's samurai traditions remained sacrosanct, especially fanatical devotion to Japan and the emperor, who was revered as a Shinto demigod. The army's other samurai tenets were self-discipline, absolute obedience, and the conviction that death was preferable to surrender. "Those who can die at the right time and leave their spirit forever are fortunate," wrote Vice Admiral Ugaki, Yamamoto's chief of staff.

Grade-school Japanese boys underwent paramilitary training, and when they were teenagers, technical apprenticeships were offered in communications and aviation. Officer candidates attended Ichigaya Military Institute, modeled upon St. Cyr, the French military academy. Enlisted soldiers were recruited and trained in fourteen geographical districts. Wherever they were from, though, the Japanese recruit expected basic training to be harsh. Routinely slapped and punched, the recruits learned to accept physical abuse stoically. Infantry training lasted four months, and competition was fierce among units. Every Japanese soldier carried a copy of Emperor Meiji's Imperial Rescript of 1882, which extolled ancient virtues from the samurai's Code of Bushido.

The Rescript said, "Duty is weightier than a mountain, while death is lighter than a feather." The Field Service Code of January 1941 elaborated, "Meet the expectations of your family and home community by making effort upon effort, always mindful of the honor of your name. If alive, do not suffer the disgrace of becoming a prisoner; in death, do not leave behind a name soiled by misdeeds." The soldiers often burst into song on long marches to keep their morale high. A favorite was the national anthem, "Kimi GaYo," sung while facing toward Japan:

"The emperor's reign will last
For a thousand and then eight thousand generations
Until pebbles become mighty Rocks
Covered with moss."[24]

DURING THEIR INTENSIVE TRAINING, JAPANESE soldiers mastered rudimentary infantry skills, such as bayonet fighting, marksmanship, and night operations. Months of drilling and maneuvers day and night, in every kind of weather, had enabled Japanese soldiers to capture Hong Kong after just a few days' fighting. With thirty thousand troops the Japanese had compelled Lieutenant General Arthur Percival to surrender a British army more than three times larger. The Imperial Japanese Army had swept aside Dutch troops in Java, Timor, and Borneo with relative ease. The myth of the Japanese "superman" was born.

But the seemingly invincible army had an Achilles heel: its anachronistic belief that the spiritual strength of its disciplined infantrymen—and their willingness to attack and fight hand-to-hand—could overcome any adversary, regardless of numbers or firepower. The army's successes in China, Malaya, and the Dutch East Indies (Indonesia) appeared to justify its self-confidence.

ONLY ONCE WAS JAPAN'S STRONG faith in "spiritual power" and cold steel shaken—during the summer of 1939 at Nomonhan, Manchuria. Japan's seizure of Manchuria had brought it into contact with the Soviet Union across a three-thousand-mile border with Mongolia. The Soviets sent mechanized units into Outer Mongolia, and after a series of escalating border clashes, large-scale fighting broke out in 1939 between Soviet and Japanese troops. Two Japanese offensives featuring infantry frontal attacks, weakly supported by artillery and tanks, failed to smash the Soviets.

In August the Soviet commander, General Georgy Zhukov, launched his own offensive after a secret buildup of fifty-seven thousand troops and more than a thousand tanks, armored cars, and artillery. The Japanese did not believe the Soviets could assemble a combined arms force of this size at a railhead hundreds of miles away and transport it to the front lines. But they did.

Taken by surprise, the Japanese troops wilted under the massive Soviet firepower. Using tactics that foreshadowed Zhukov's envelopment three years later of the German Sixth Army at Stalingrad, his army attacked frontally, cracking the enemy defense, while tanks encircled the Japanese 23rd Division, aided by air strikes by more than five hundred Soviet aircraft. Japanese efforts to relieve the besieged division failed, as did the division's attempted breakout: it suffered 75 percent losses before a ceasefire reached in Moscow ended the fighting. Zhukov's brilliant victory attracted the attention of Joseph Stalin, who summoned the general to Moscow and promoted him to field marshal.[25]

The Japanese should have learned from Nomonhan that massive firepower and maneuver could overwhelm bamboo spear tactics; instead, they concluded that they had lost because they had lacked the proper fighting spirit; the solution was to fight with greater determination. Although the army took steps to increase its firepower after Nomonhan, it changed neither its tactics nor its heavy reliance on infantry attacks, night fighting, and the soldiers' "spiritual power."[26]

OVER THE YEARS COLONEL KIYONAO Ichiki had defeated Chinese troops on battlefield after battlefield. He did not expect the Guadalcanal operation to end differently. Ichiki's "victory fever" was abetted by the abysmal intelligence he had received: the American force was estimated to number fewer than eight thousand men and possibly just two thousand. The fact that they were Marines was not known, nor was there any information about the enemy's tactics. Numbers and tactics were unimportant to Ichiki because they were decadent Americans, so their fighting spirit was presumed to be low. Ichiki and his men were confident that "bamboo spear tactics" would rout the Marines as they had Japan's other enemies.[27]

Ichiki's two echelons departed Truk at the same time, but the 1st Echelon, aboard destroyers making twenty-five knots, soon left behind the 2nd Echelon's transports, which were traveling at one-third the speed. On the destroyers the soldiers punctiliously made their morbid battle preparations. They wrote their wills and put them in envelopes with a keepsake, such as a lock of hair or a finger-nail cutting, in case their bodies could not be recovered and returned home. They girded their waists with talismanic "belts of a thousand stitches" given to them by their sisters or girlfriends. The belts supposedly made the soldiers bulletproof— the soldiers knew better, but wore them anyway. Undoubtedly the soldiers also recited, either aloud or to themselves, the words known to Japanese soldiers and sailors everywhere, taken from the ancient poem "Umi Yukaba":

> "Across the sea
> Corpses in the water,
> Across the mountain,
> Corpses heaped upon the field.
> I shall die solely for the Emperor
> I will never look back."

THE FIRST JAPANESE REINFORCEMENTS TO reach Guadalcanal, 113 Special Naval Landing Force troops, came ashore during the night of August 17 at Tassa-faronga on the island's western tip. A little more than twenty-four hours later, at 1:00 a.m. on August 19, six destroyers landed Ichiki's 1st Echelon of 917 men near Taivu Point, east of the Marine perimeter. Three of the destroyers then sailed across Sealark Channel and bombarded the former seaplane base at Tulagi while a fourth destroyer shelled Henderson Field. At Taivu Point only the heavy slap of the waves made by the destroyers suggested to nearby Marine listening posts that there had been a night landing.

Ichiki's men arrived dressed for jungle fighting: heavy shirts, gloves, two pairs of trousers, and cloth-covered helmets that made no sound when they brushed trees and vines. Some wore thin, rubber-soled shoes called *tabis* that were divided into two compartments—one for the big toe and the other for the rest of the foot. Wearing them, soldiers had a better feel for what lay underfoot and might avoid stepping on twigs and making noise. The 1st Echelon arrived with just light arms and two 70mm howitzers; the 2nd Echelon, whose thirteen hundred men were traveling on the slow but roomy transports, was bringing the heavy artillery and antitank weapons.[28]

Impatient and supremely confident that his 1st Echelon could recapture the airfield and defeat the Americans without any help, Ichiki elected to not wait for the 2nd Echelon. His men formed ranks beneath the jungle canopy and began marching westward toward the Marine perimeter twenty-two miles away.[29]

After advancing a few miles toward the Marine lines, the Japanese made their camp. Ichiki sent a thirty-eight-man patrol led by Captain Yokichi Shibuya ahead along the beach to establish communications ahead of the main detachment, which would march that night. Resting during the day and traveling at night, Ichiki's men expected to reach the Marine perimeter during the night of August 20–21.[30]

Vandegrift also sent out a patrol on August 19—eastward to investigate the reports of Japanese troops in that direction and of a supposedly operational radio station thirty-five miles to the east—as well as the listening post reports of a possible enemy landing near Taivu Point. Captain Charles Brush led the sixty-five-man combat patrol from his A Company of the First Marines along the coastal track toward Taivu Point.[31]

That afternoon Brush's men surprised the Japanese patrol, which was "proceeding boldly and carelessly along the beach." Brush launched a frontal attack while sending part of his unit around the enemy left flank. Captain Shibuya was killed immediately. "We are all doomed," Second Lieutenant Shigero Wado thought an instant before he was shot in the right shoulder. Their backs to the sea, the Japanese were nearly wiped out in under an hour; just five of the thirty-eight, Wado one of them, escaped into the jungle. Three of Brush's men were killed, and three were wounded.

While searching the enemy bodies the Marines noted that the Japanese were well equipped, wearing fresh uniforms, and clean-shaven—which meant they were new to the island. Moreover, on their helmets was the five-pointed star of the Imperial Japanese Army and not the anchor and chrysanthemum of the Naval Landing Force. Among the officers' effects the Marines found a code for ship-to-shore communications and detailed maps of the Marine positions.

The maps made Brush uneasy. "They showed our weak spots all too clearly." When Vandegrift and his staff saw the maps, they knew that an attack was imminent and alerted Colonel Pedro del Valle's Eleventh Marines. The artillerymen presighted their guns on likely attack routes along Alligator Creek.[32]

FEW KNEW THE AREA NEAR Taivu Point better than retired Sergeant Major of Constables Jacob Vouza, forty-seven, who was born in a village in the area. In his youth Vouza had earned a reputation as a formidable battler, as befitted his surname, which means "fighter." Vouza served twenty-five years in the Armed Constabulary Force before retiring in 1941. He had spent the last fourteen years of his career on Malaita, the most populous Solomon island and a cesspool of violence. Vouza took an early retirement after being targeted for assassination by a murderous gang whose leader Vouza had had arrested and who later hanged. The death threats persuaded Vouza, his wife, Irene, and their two daughters to leave Malaita and return to Guadalcanal on May 6, settling in a village on the north-central coast. Although he had no formal schooling, Vouza could read and write. The year of his retirement he had converted to Christianity and received the name Jacob during his baptism. Clemens hired Vouza days after his arrival on Guadalcanal, although he wondered whether the middle-aged Melanesian would be of much use after his long absence from Guadalcanal.[33]

Clemens assigned Vouza the dangerous job of scouting the Koli Point area, which was near his village, to determine the size and intentions of the Japanese force there. Unknown to Clemens and Vouza, Ichiki's men had made camp near Koli Point early that morning after a second nighttime march. They were now just five miles east of Alligator Creek.

During the morning of August 20 Vouza and his adopted son, fifteen-year-old Samuel Saki, left their bush village to conduct the reconnaissance. Vouza happened to be carrying an American flag that a Marine officer had given him, but he planned to hide it in a nearby village, realizing that it would be his death warrant if the Japanese caught him with it.[34]

Before reaching that village he spotted a group of soldiers wearing helmets and regular shoes—not the soft-rubber, "cloven-hoofed" *tabis* with the split big toe worn by the Japanese of Vouza's previous acquaintance.

They must be American Marines, Vouza concluded, and he unfurled his flag in a welcoming gesture. It was a terrible mistake—they were Japanese soldiers.

Ichiki's men seized him, tied him to a tree with a large red ant nest at its base, and left him there in the broiling sun while large red ants crawled up his legs and stung him repeatedly. Later, he was brought before Colonel Ichiki, and interrogators demanded to know the location of the American positions. Vouza refused to tell them. Then, an interpreter named Ishimoto, previously a carpenter on a Lever

Brothers plantation on Tulagi and now a Japanese Navy petty officer, identified Vouza as a member of the Armed Constabulary. At a signal, soldiers smashed his face with their rifle butts and an officer slashed his arm with a sword.

Vouza remained silent. "If you do not talk, you die!" an officer shouted. When Vouza remained silent, they forced him to lie down on the ant nest. The ants, he said, "started eating my body." Vouza prayed for God to save him. The Japanese hanged him from a tree by his arms and continued to interrogate him until he lost consciousness. After sunset, his captors cut him down and marched him westward. An officer ordered soldiers to bayonet Vouza to death but not to shoot him, because gunshots would reveal their presence.

Vouza's hands were bound before him, and a soldier stabbed him under his armpit, with the long bayonet penetrating into his throat and splitting his tongue. He was stabbed again, this time in the side, the thrusting blade pushing out of his chest. Attacked a third time, Vouza blocked the thrust with his hands, but the Japanese inflicted several puncture wounds on his chest and abdomen. Vouza slumped to the ground, where he was left to die.[35]

He did not die. With a herculean effort Vouza managed to rise to his feet and stagger into the black jungle, stopping to chew through his wrist bindings to free his hands. Weak from blood loss, Vouza crawled toward the Marine lines, knowing that if he stopped to rest, his life would end.

Private Wilbur Bewley, a sentry at G Company of the First Marines, saw Vouza's silhouette in the dim light and knew by "his large set of kinky hair" that he was a Melanesian. "His bushy hair probably saved his life," wrote Bewley. Marines took Vouza, struggling for breath and his chest caked with blood, to the 2nd Battalion command post of Lieutenant Colonel Edwin Pollock. Pollock questioned Vouza about what he had seen. The sergeant major estimated that 250 to 500 Japanese were poised to attack and described their approach route. The colonel alerted his men to expect an attack by hundreds of Japanese. The onslaught began while Vouza was still at the command post.

A FORTY-FOOT-WIDE SANDSPIT SEPARATED ALLIGATOR Creek's stagnant waters from Sealark Channel, its width varying with the wind and tide. Private Robert Leckie described the creek as "green and evil," lying "like a serpent across the palmy coastal plain. . . . If there are river gods [it] was inhabited by a baleful spirit."

This was the place Ichiki had chosen for his attack, and it was also where the Marines had concentrated most of their firepower. Instead of moving inland and striking farther up Alligator Creek, where the creek bed was dry and the First Marines' defenses were thinner, Ichiki, with minimal reconnaissance, chose to launch a frontal attack—a decision born of haste and hubris.

Anticipating it to be the likely point of attack, Colonel Clifton Cates, the First Marines' commander, had ordered a barrier extending into the surf thrown up across the sandspit. It was erected with barbed wire scrounged from nearby plantation fences because the Marines' barbed wire was still aboard Admiral Turner's ships when they sailed away August 9. Cates later observed, "This wire probably spelled the difference between defeat and a real victory."[36]

At 3:10 a.m. August 21, two hundred men from Ichiki's detachment silently approached the creek and began quietly crossing the forty-five-yard-wide sandbar. They became entangled in the barbed wire, and stealth vanished. They "waved their arms wildly, they shrieked and jabbered"—and they kept coming.

Pollock's battalion opened fire with rifles and 37mm guns loaded with canister from a hundred yards away as the Japanese milled around the wire. Then, as the bottleneck on the sandspit worsened, the Eleventh Marines' 75mm pack howitzers began firing into the penned Japanese soldiers.

Shouting "Prepare to die!" and "Fuck Babe Ruth!" they came in "a dark bobbing mass," "like a bunch of cows coming down to drink." A hurricane of gunfire swept through them "like a broom." Second Lieutenant Goro Ohashi, ordered to lead a platoon across the sandbar, saw streams of tracers "as bright as searchlights" and machine-gun fire "like crimson blossoms" cut down his men.[37]

Rejecting subordinates' pleas to regroup and to try breaching the Marine lines upriver, Ichiki redoubled his efforts to cross the sandbar, training 70mm howitzer, mortar, and machine-gun fire on the Marine positions. The Marines hugged the ground in their shallow holes, "crying, praying, and cursing all at the same time," wrote Private First Class Jim Wilson, and there were increasingly frequent cries of "Corpsman!"

Private Sid Phillips and his comrades set up their 81mm mortar and targeted an abandoned Marine amphibious tractor that the Japanese had turned into a machine-gun position. They hit it dead-on. "A loud cheer went up like a touchdown at a football stadium," Phillips wrote.

Small bands of Japanese troops infiltrated the Marine positions, belying Sergeant Sadanobu Okada's observation that "the enemy's fire was constant. All our attacks were useless." Breaking through the curtain of gunfire, the Japanese threw grenades and attacked with bayonets. Colonel Cates ordered G Company, which had been held in reserve, to counterattack. It cleared the west bank.

Then, a company-size Japanese unit waded beyond the breakers and attempted to come ashore on the Marines' left flank. The enemy soldiers were spotted in the surf, and machine-gun and canister fire shattered the attack at the water's edge.

Albert Schmid was a loader on a three-man machine-gun crew when enemy gunfire killed the gunner. Schmid took over, and the other surviving crew member, Lee Diamond, loaded as they fired, hour after hour, at the attackers across the river. Then Diamond was wounded in the arm, and a grenade blinded Schmid. Schmid continued firing the machine-gun under Diamond's direction for an hour until they were evacuated. Marines counted more than a hundred bodies within the range of Schmid's gun.

Seven enemy soldiers crossed the sandspit and swarmed Private George Turzai's position. He shot five of them, and the two survivors pressed the attack with bayonets. In the darkness one of them accidentally stabbed the other in the back, and Turzai drove his rifle butt into the face of the last one, knocking him into the river.

Private Dean Wilson's automatic rifle jammed, and he grabbed a machete after the Japanese killed his mate, Private Ray Roberts. Enraged, Wilson climbed out of the foxhole and attacked, swinging the machete and killing three enemy soldiers.[38]

Private Robert Leckie and his gunnery comrade had to move their machine-gun about every fifteen minutes—because the Japanese would begin to home in on its muzzle blast. The gunners fired at noises in front of them in the dark. "We never knew if there really was anyone there," Leckie wrote, and they never knew whether they hit anything. "Thus we passed the remainder of the battle; moving and firing, moving and firing."

Privates Harry Horsman and Charles Greer noticed that the 37mm antitank gun to their left had fallen silent and crawled over to investigate. No one was there, and the gun was undamaged. "We gave 'er a go and with good effect," wrote Horsman, knocking holes in the attackers' ranks. When the Japanese set up a machine-gun opposite them, Horsman and Greer fired a high-explosive round over the creek "smack into them."[39]

The roaring firefight continued without letup until daylight. For the rest of the night the Marines mowed down the soldiers that Ichiki continued to send to their deaths.

STILL AT THE BATTALION CP as the fight raged a hundred yards away, Vouza asked that Martin Clemens be notified, and Pollock phoned regimental headquarters to have him sent down. Clemens arrived around dawn and was stunned by Vouza's macabre appearance. "I could hardly bear to look at him." Despite his "gaping throat wound," Vouza managed to gasp out to Clemens what had happened. Expecting to die soon, he dictated "a long last message" for Clemens to give to his wife and children and then collapsed. He was taken to the battalion aid station, where the corpsmen prepped him with ether for surgery and began injecting plasma, serum, albumin, saline, and glucose into his extremities. Fresh blood from native donors replaced the plasma during a long surgery. Doctors were amazed that Vouza was still alive when the operation ended. He would make a rapid recovery and be released from the hospital after twelve days to return to duty.[40]

DAYLIGHT RAISED THE CURTAIN ON a grisly sight: dead Japanese "piled in rows and on top of each other from our gun positions outward." Living Japanese lingered in the coconut grove to the east, and Cates and Vandegrift's operations officer, Colonel Gerald Thomas, sent the division reserve—Lieutenant Colonel Lenard Creswell's 1st Battalion, First Marines—across the dry Alligator Creek streamed a mile and a half to the south. Creswell's men were to envelop the stunned survivors and drive them into the "anvil" of Pollock's battalion on the creek bank.

Most of the Japanese officers were either dead on the sandspit or dispirited by their shocking losses. The leaderless survivors milled around in the coconut grove rather than withdrawing to the east; unaccustomed to defeat, they did not know what to do next. "I no longer heard the sound of our attack," Sergeant Sadanobu Okada wrote in his diary. "I could only hear the roar of the enemies' guns." Okada was one of the very few who escaped eastward and was "very, very sad" to leave behind the bodies of so many friends.

The 2nd Battalion reorganized its positions on the west creek bank while the 1st Battalion brought its hammer down, trudging northward through the kunai grass toward the coconut grove. As the battalion neared the Japanese lines, C Company was ordered to make a bayonet attack. To the Marines' surprise, Japanese soldiers leaped up and countercharged with bayonets. With a crash of wood and steel, the enemies closed in personal combat. "Horrible cries rose as cold steel tore through flesh and entrails," wrote Captain Nikolai Stevenson, the company commander. As Captain Charles Brush's A Company neared the beach, a squad of Japanese jumped up and began running east on the sand. "Line 'em up, and squeeze 'em off," Brush cried. His men killed all of them.

Five light tanks that were supposed to accompany Creswell's men but could not get over the streamed crossed the sandbar into the coconut grove, "pivoting, turning, spitting sheets of yellow flame," and toppling palm trees with Japanese snipers in them, wrote correspondent Richard Tregaskis. "Group after group was flushed out and shot down by the tanks' canister shells." "It was a great sight seeing them [the tanks] running along the beach, weaving through the coconut grove and chasing the fleeing Japs," wrote Colonel Cates.

Japanese soldiers disabled one tank, but when they attempted to kill the crew, other tanks surrounded it and recovered the crewmen. Then they turned and sprayed the enemy infantrymen with machine-gun fire. "The Japs were mowed down like flies," wrote Private First Class Andy Poliny of Brush's company. The tanks ground over the enemy dead, their treads becoming caked with blood and gore, looking like "meat grinders," wrote Leckie.[41]

Hemmed in on three sides, the Japanese tried to break out, but Wildcats from VMF-223, whose arrival at the airstrip the previous day had been greeted with wild excitement, herded them back with strafing runs. The Japanese had just one place left to go. They dashed over the beach into the sea and began swimming. "Their heads bobbed like corks on the horizon," wrote Leckie.

The Marines lay on their bellies on the sand as though they were on the rifle range. "Their heads, small black dots among the waves, were difficult targets to hit," wrote Tregaskis. Wherever the head of a swimming man was seen "a small storm of little waterspouts rose around him as our bullets smacked home." Cates said Pollock's 2nd Battalion "picked them off like ducks in a pond." Many bodies washed ashore over the next few days.[42]

Humiliated by his detachment's annihilation, Colonel Ichiki could see only one honorable ending for him. He burned the 28th Regiment flag—the standard carried thirty-eight years earlier against the Russians at Port Arthur. Then he bowed toward the emperor, prayed to the gods, and shot himself in the head.

The battle had lasted sixteen hours. Just ten Japanese lived to return to Taivu Point, where 80 men from Ichiki's landing force had remained behind. The Ichiki Detachment had lost 813 killed. Fourteen Japanese, 12 of them wounded, became the Marines' prisoners. The First Marines reported 34 dead and 75 wounded. Colonel Cates, who had fought in France during World War I, wrote that he had never seen such a "congestion of dead" as he did that day on the sandspit and in the coconut grove.[43]

THE MARINES NOW LEARNED TO give no quarter. Among the piles of bullet-shredded Japanese corpses lived wounded soldiers still capable of killing and wounding. When they cried for help and corpsmen attempted to give aid, they detonated a grenade or shot the caregiver before being killed. Sometimes they waited for a Marine to pass by—and then stabbed him.

Pharmacist's Mate Second Class Paul Buelow was crawling around the battlefield caring for Marines when he found a dying Japanese soldier. As Buelow placed his medical bag on the ground to examine the enemy soldier's wounds, the Japanese snatched up a bayonet and stabbed Buelow to death. A BAR man who witnessed the ambush killed the Japanese soldier.

Marine Andy Poliny and his comrades saw two Japanese soldiers jump up, carrying a wounded comrade and indicating they wished to surrender. Poliny's sergeant leaped in front of them, crying, "Cut 'em down! Cut 'em down!" As he shouted, the two unwounded enemy soldiers fumbled in their shirts for grenades but were killed before they could detonate them.[44]

Casting aside their customary respect and compassion for a fallen enemy, the Marines made certain the Japanese were dead by shooting them again with rifles and pistols. Tregaskis described the process as "the brutal but necessary re-butcher of the dead. I watched our men standing in a shooting-gallery line, thumping bullets into the piles of Jap carcasses." Lieutenant Herbert Merillat said the Marines justifiably adopted a "kill-em-in-cold-blood" attitude.[45]

Piles of bodies, dismembered and whole, lay everywhere in grotesque attitudes that haunted some Marines for as long as they lived. "I must say I was appalled," wrote Martin Clemens. "There were seven or eight hundred dead strewn in bits over about three acres." Tregaskis saw bodies torn apart by artillery fire, "their remains fried. . . . The tread tracks of one of our tanks ran directly over five squashed bodies, in the center of which was a broken machine gun on a flattened bipod."

A Marine looted the corpses of their gold fillings, keeping his booty in an empty Bull Durham tobacco sack that he wore around his neck. His comrades described his technique: "He would kick their jaws agape, peer into the mouth with all the solicitude of a Park Avenue dentist—careful, always careful not to contaminate himself by touch—and yank out all that glittered." Here too began the Marines' practice of scouring battlefields for souvenirs to barter with sailors and airmen for cash, alcohol, food, and clothing. Samurai swords and Japanese firearms were highly prized, with an Arisaka rifle fetching $35 to $45.

The process of decomposition proceeded swiftly in the tropical heat. Corpses became "puffed up and glossy, like shiny sausages." Leckie was horrified by the swarms of flies, "black, circling funnels that seemed to emerge from every orifice. . . . The beating of their myriad tiny wings made a dreadful low hum."

The stench was so powerful that it disturbed the Marines' sleep and attracted new visitors to the battleground—large saltwater crocodiles. Through binoculars Leckie watched "in debased fascination" as a crocodile feasted on a plump Japanese soldier. But when the crocodile began to tug at the intestines, Leckie remembered that he had swum across the river just an hour earlier, "and my knees went weak and I relinquished the glasses." At night "they kept us awake, crunching," wrote Leckie.

The crocodiles became the Marines' "darlings" because they believed the creatures deterred the Japanese from swimming the creek. The Marines never swam there again either.[46]

The dead were buried August 22. Military police marched Japanese and Korean prisoners to the battleground to perform the gruesome task. The captives responded to the MPs' barked cadence by shouting, "Roosevelt good man, Tojo eats shit!" The POWS piled the reeking corpses onto trucks and dumped them into twenty-five-foot-long pits that were dug with captured Japanese bulldozers and then covered with sand. The burial site was not marked.[47]

In his report to Marine Commandant Thomas Holcomb, Vandegrift expressed his shock at the enemy's seeming disregard for life. "I have never heard or read of this kind of fighting. These people refuse to surrender. The wounded will wait until the men come up to examine them and blow themselves and [the] other fellow to pieces with a hand grenade." A thrice-wounded camouflaged sniper was passed over as dead, but then killed four Marines before he was finally shot dead. "You have to KILL to put them out," emphatically wrote Fifth Marines Captain Lew Walt.

To defeat the Japanese, Vandegrift wrote, "we shall have to throw away the rule book of war and go back to the tactics used during the French and Indian Wars."[48]

WIDELY KNOWN AS THE BATTLE of the Tenaru because of a map error, it was the first full-scale battle between Marine and Japanese infantrymen. Although a clash of battalions, not divisions or armies, it nonetheless revealed a great deal about the combatants' respective characters. In important ways the troops were much alike. Neither side was willing to bend—the seasoned Japanese soldiers embracing their samurai warrior tradition to the bitter end and the young Marines drawing upon their own proud tradition of being the "first to fight" and never giving in. Disciplined and trained to obey and shoot straight, Marines and Japanese alike persevered hardship stoically.

They differed in their leadership—Marine infantry officers adapted tactics to situations, while their Japanese counterparts stuck with a plan, even when it was failing. Because of Captain Brush's reconnaissance patrol, maps and documents taken from dead Japanese officers, and other intelligence, Vandegrift and his subordinates were ready to meet an attack along Alligator Creek.

Lulled by Japan's easy victories in Asia, the Philippines, and Indonesia, Ichiki was unperturbed even when Brush's patrol wiped out his forward communications unit. He never doubted that "bamboo spear tactics"—a frontal attack with bayonets—and "spiritual power" would crush the Americans. After all, it had always worked before. Even as Marine firepower annihilated his men at the sandspit, Ichiki continued the attack over the bodies of his fallen men, until all of them were gone. Tactical inflexibility would become a hallmark of the Japanese army.

FOLLOWING THE SAVO ISLAND DEBACLE and the Navy's abandonment of the Marines, the victory gave Vandegrift and his men a much-needed morale boost. "Yesterday the Jap seemed something almost superhuman, a kind of mechanical juggernaut. But today we had beaten the Jap. The Jap no longer seemed superhuman," the Marine general triumphantly wrote. "Our men had faced the crucial task, stood up to it, and won." Knowing, however, that this would not be the last battle his division would fight on Guadalcanal, on the night of August 21 Vandegrift summoned the 2nd Battalion, Fifth Marines from Tulagi.[49]

The unwelcome news of the defeat reached the Japanese command that same night. "The detachment was annihilated before dawn this morning before they reached the airstrip," said the report from a Japanese coast watcher in eastern Guadalcanal. Vice Admiral Ugaki, the Combined Fleet's chief of staff, wrote in his diary that Ichiki attacked "recklessly, underestimating the enemy." Ugaki was concerned that "the enemy foothold is becoming more consolidated than ours. . . . We can't make light of them."

At Seventeenth Army headquarters in Rabaul the news produced "anxiety" but not discouragement. That was because units of Major General Kiyotake Kawaguchi's 35th Brigade were boarding ships in Truk bound for Guadalcanal and the late Colonel Ichiki's 2nd Echelon was expected to reach Guadalcanal soon.[50]

ALTHOUGH SIGNIFICANT, THE ALLIGATOR CREEK battle did not eclipse the momentous event that had occurred the previous afternoon. At 5:00 p.m. on August 20 the sky over the airfield trembled with the drone of aircraft. The Marines reflexively sprinted for foxholes and dugouts until they saw the white stars on the planes' wings and someone cried, "American!" They were Marine fighters and dive bombers.

Circling the airfield, the pilots and tail gunners threw back their canopies and waved to the men on the ground before landing. "Grim faces brightened as the planes circled the field and came in for landings," wrote Lieutenant Merillat. There briefly reigned that great rarity on Guadalcanal: unmitigated joy. "Our morale soared as the whole complexion of the situation changed . . . from nearly grim despair to delirious confidence," wrote Private Sid Phillips.

"Everybody started cheering and waving their arms and throwing their helmets up in the air," wrote Sergeant Jim McEnery, who got down on his knees and said, "Thank you, Lord." Some Marines wept. Even Vandegrift was choked with emotion and near tears as he went down to the airstrip to greet the flyers. Since Admiral Fletcher's carriers and the battered landing fleet had sailed away, the Marines had been defenseless against the daily Japanese air raids and helpless to prevent the supply drops from the air to Japanese soldiers in the jungle or the nighttime shellings by ships and submarines. But now they had allies.[51]

The two squadrons from Marine Air Group 23, based at the Marine air station on Oahu, had sailed on the Long Island, a converted ocean liner that was the Navy's first escort carrier. They were catapulted from the deck two hundred miles from Guadalcanal because the carrier's four-hundred-foot runway was too short for taxiing takeoffs by fully armed aircraft.

Landing first on the gravel-covered airstrip were nineteen Grumman F4F Wildcats from VMF-223, the Marine fighter squadron led by Major John L. Smith. Twelve of Smith's pilots had been transferred from the more veteran VMF-212 to replace the inexperienced pilots in Smith's squadron while they underwent further training. Landing behind the Wildcats were a dozen Dauntless dive bombers from Marine Lieutenant Colonel Richard Mangrum's VMSB-232.[52]

The F4F Wildcats and the two-man Dauntless SBDs were heavily armed and difficult to shoot down but lacked speed (dive-bomber pilots joked that SBD stood for "slow but deadly"). The Navy was aware of the Wildcats' inferiority to the Japanese Zero in speed, climbing rate, and maneuverability. But until next-generation aircraft rolled off production lines in 1943—the Vought F4U Corsair, the Grumman F6F Hellcat—the Navy had to settle for modifications that added armor, fuel tanks, and folding wings so that more could fit on a carrier's deck, as well as arming the Wildcats with six .50-caliber machine-guns instead of four. The modifications had their drawbacks: the armor and fuel tanks further reduced the Wildcat's speed and climbing rate, and the extra machine-guns used up ammunition faster. Some pilots chose to temporarily deactivate two machine-guns so their ammunition lasted longer.[53]

Within twelve hours of landing at the Guadalcanal airstrip VMF-223's Wildcats were in the air, providing ground support for the First Marines along Alligator Creek and strafing Japanese on the beach. It was the Marines' first ground-support mission since Nicaragua fifteen years earlier. That same day too the squadron leader, Major Smith, an instinctive pilot with twinkling reflexes, claimed the first kill when he shot down a Zero near Savo Island, one of an eventual nineteen shoot-downs by the future Medal of Honor winner.[54]

"Cactus" now being the code name for the Guadalcanal campaign, replacing the amphibious landing phase name "Watchtower," it was only natural that the squadrons became known collectively as the Cactus Air Force. The wooden, Japanese-style building known as the Pagoda served as Cactus's air operations center. When there was an impending air raid the American flag was lowered, a Japanese flag was raised, a bell clanged, and Cactus's pilots scrambled. Later an expropriated Japanese siren warned of imminent attacks.[55]

On August 22, five Army Air Force Airacobras from the 67th Fighter Squadron landed at Henderson Field. Within a week nine more of the Bell P-400s arrived. They had reached the 67th Fighter Squadron in crates, and mechanics had to assemble them. The P-400s were armed with four machine-guns and a 37mm nose cannon. They were ponderous climbers and inferior to Zeros in speed and maneuverability, as they had been to the German fighters when deployed in Europe.

Besides consistently underperforming despite its dedicated pilots' best efforts, the P-400 required high-pressure, bottled oxygen—unavailable on Guadalcanal. Without oxygen the pilots blacked out if they flew above twelve thousand feet, below the altitude at which Japanese fighters and bombers normally operated. Thus, the P-400s were practically useless as interceptors. Vandegrift initially told Admiral Ghormley they were "entirely unsuitable" for Cactus's operations and would not be used except in "extreme emergencies," but they in fact did prove to be excellent ground-support planes with their nose cannon and heavy armament, and they were useful reconnaissance aircraft.

On August 30 two more Marine squadrons landed at Henderson—VMF-224's nineteen Wildcats under Major Robert Galer, and VMSB-231's dozen Dauntless dive bombers led by Major Leo Smith. Their arrival gave Henderson Field sixty-four planes and eight-six pilots, an amazing transformation in just a week and a half, and a testament to Rear Admiral John McCain's determination to commit air resources to Guadalcanal. Daily air sorties, however, swiftly drew down these numbers while also whittling the enemy's ranks of warplanes and experienced pilots.

Downed US airmen were usually recovered because the battleground was above or near Guadalcanal, but Japanese aviators rarely were. The continual attritional air combat had no climactic battle with an ultimate winner and loser. Although almost always outnumbered, the Americans were committed to protecting the airfield and stopping Japanese reinforcements from reaching Guadalcanal. In Galer's words, their mission was to "get the regiment before it got off the ship—hit the ship [and] you get all of it."[56]

It was a peculiar strategic stalemate. Both sides knew that possession of Henderson Field was the key to victory. During the daytime the scrappy Cactus Air Force dominated the seas surrounding Guadalcanal, enabling a thin trickle of supplies and fuel to reach the island while thwarting Japanese attempts to land reinforcements or supplies.

After sundown, control of the seas shifted to the night-fighting Imperial Japanese Navy and its air force, able to land troops and bombard the airfield without interference. The cycle began again at daybreak, when control reverted to the Americans. Only by either destroying Henderson Field or landing enough troops to wrest it from the Marines could the Japanese hope to permanently gain the upper hand. But it lacked the troops to mount a credible attack on Vandergrift's well-armed defenders, and its air raids, sometimes three per day, had not yet shut down the airfield.

From Rabaul it took the Japanese pilots four hours to reach their target and four hours to return. Unless they carried fuel "drop tanks," which extended their range by eight hundred miles, the Zeros escorting the "Betty" medium bombers had just minutes over the airfield before their fuel levels fell below what they needed to return to Rabaul. The Betty pilots, whose range was triple the Zeros', had no such worries. For the long flights the Japanese flight crews packed *koku bentos*—"airborne box lunches."

The Japanese tackled the distance problem by building airfields closer to Guadalcanal, but the projects were slow to reach completion. In the interim they stationed fifty float planes at forward bases—Shortland Harbor, 300 miles from Guadalcanal, and Rekata Bay on San Isabel, 135 miles away. The float planes conducted observation, reconnaissance, and antisubmarine missions, and escorted resupply convoys.

If the Japanese airmen prepared for the raids as though they were heading to lunchpail jobs, the American flight crews were just as matter-of-fact about their preparations for Tojo time, normally occurring between 11:30 a.m. and 2:00 p.m.

When a warning by one of Eric Feldt's coast watchers, usually Paul Mason or Jack Read on Bougainville, reached the Pagoda, the Cactus Air Force went to work. The pilots fired up whatever planes would fly, checking their parachutes, life jackets, and safety belts and making sure their oxygen registered fifteen hundred pounds and their oil was warm and had ninety pounds of pressure before taking off. They climbed to twenty thousand feet—"Angels 20"—to await the enemy.

When the bombers and their escorts appeared, the Wildcats took up positions for an overhead run by turning in the opposite direction of the Betty "V" formation. They then rolled onto their backs and plunged through the screen of Zeros at top speed. Diving right to left to minimize the risk of collisions, they pulled up in climbing left turns for further attacks.[57]

Major Smith issued standing orders to his VMF-223 Wildcat pilots describing how best to approach the Mitsubishi G4M Bettys—nothing but overhead or steep, high-side passes because of the "stinger" in the tail. Besides the dangerous 20mm tail gun, the Betty's top, nose, and ventral turrets were armed with 7.7mm guns. Its Achilles heel—and the Zero's too—was its thin armor plating, and its gasoline tanks, which were not self-sealing and liable to burst into flames when hit by gunfire. Two carrier-based planes, the dive-bombing Aichi D3A "Val" and the Nakajima B5N "Kate" torpedo bomber, would later become ubiquitous in the Guadalcanal campaign.[58]

The Zero, armed with two 20mm and two 7.7mm guns, was faster and more maneuverable than any fighter plane in the Pacific in 1942. The Japanese built it light: its frame was made of a zinc-aluminum alloy, and its armor was practically nonexistent. Its maximum speed was 331 mph, slightly faster than the Wildcat's top speed, but it could climb forty-five hundred feet in a minute, twice the Wildcat's climb rate. The first A6M2 emerged from Mitsubishi's Nagoya plant in 1939 and was hauled by oxcart to a naval station twenty-five miles away. It went into production the following year—hence its nickname of Zero (American pilots also called it the "Zeke"), an allusion to 1940 being the twenty-six hundredth year of recorded Japanese history. Officially designated the Type O Carrier Fighter, it was better known in Japan as the Zero-sen.[59]

Japanese ace Saburo Sakai admired the Zero's "clean, beautiful lines. . . . It was a dream to fly . . . and the most sensitive [plane] I had every flown, and even slight finger pressure brought instant response." The bubble canopy provided good visibility but was also an inviting target. Although the Zero came with a radio, most fighter groups ripped them out, along with their masts and aerials, on the grounds that their fifty-mile range made them ineffective. However, the pilots' real reason was to save thirty pounds of weight, so obsessed were they with squeezing every additional foot per second of velocity from their planes. But without radios the pilots were unable to communicate with the bombers they escorted.[60]

To a Wildcat pilot the Zero's speed and maneuverability made it an extremely dangerous adversary. "He could climb inside of anything, and he had a lot more speed than we did, even carrying more gasoline [in the detachable drop tank]," wrote Lieutenant Commander John Thach, commander of naval fighter squadron VF-3.[61]

Marine Captain Joe Foss, the onetime South Dakota farmer and future ace extraordinaire, later advised his VMF-121 pilots to avoid one-on-one combat with a Zero. If they were alone and encountered a Zero, "you were outnumbered and should go for home. They were not a plane to tangle with unless you had an advantage."[62]

Air combat was intrinsically difficult. Fighter planes traveled at high speeds, twisting and turning in the air; centrifugal force seemed to press a pilot's eyeballs back into his head. Cactus pilots slowly became expert at "deflection shooting"— leading their target so that their bullets and the enemy plane reached the same spot simultaneously. It was much harder than it sounded. Saburo, the Japanese ace, said hitting a target with machine-guns under these conditions was "like trying to thread a needle while running."[63]

LIEUTENANT COMMANDER THACH, LEADER OF the Navy Wildcat squadron VF-3 and a student of air combat, tackled the problem of how to negate the Zero's advantages in order to exploit its light armament and vulnerable fuel tank. During the summer of 1941, while he and his squadron were stationed at Coronado, California, Thach worked alone night after night at his kitchen table, using matchsticks to represent planes. The next day he would test his theories in the air. Thach curbed the throttles of some of his planes so they could play the part of the slower Wildcats, while full-throttle Wildcats represented Zeros.

Thach hit upon the idea of dividing his squadron into two-plane, rather than three-plane, sections and to increase the spacing between leader and wingman to 150 feet to provide more freedom of movement. When one plane was attacked, it "weaved" until the second plane got into position to execute a head-on or side shot at the Zero. His flyers practiced the maneuver until the full-throttle opposition leader was unable to make an attack from any angle without facing one of the throttled-down planes head-on.

Thach exultantly wrote that his Wildcats "at least are getting a shot . . . at least it isn't one-sided. . . . Now we had something to work on, to keep us from being demoralized." Lieutenant Commander Jimmy Flatley, commander of VF-10, christened the maneuver the "Thach Weave." The two-plane section and Thach Weave eventually became the standard operating procedure for Marine and Navy pilots.[64]

Hard data on what made the Zero a superior fighter eluded US military officials through the Battle of the Coral Sea and the Battle of Midway, and a mystique grew up around it. Then, on July 10, 1942, an intact Zero was found crashed in a marshy meadow in the Aleutians, with the pilot's body in the cockpit. Salvaged and loaded onto a ship, the Zero was taken to San Diego, where it was repaired and tested. Pilots discovered other flaws for the Cactus pilots to exploit: the Zero was unable to perform fast rolls, and its engine sometimes cut out during steep dives. Consequently, a Wildcat might shake a pursuing Zero with hard, diving turns. The data generated from the salvaged Zero was incorporated into the design of the Wildcat's successor: the Grumman F6F Hellcat.[65]

Despite the Wildcat's subpar speed and maneuverability, its ability to take punishment was inarguable. One F4F pilot, Lieutenant Lawrence "Cloudy" Faulkner, returned from an air attack on Japanese ships to find a hole in his plane as "big as a dishpan," made by a 20mm round. "They [Wildcats] certainly could take it, and they certainly could dish it out, though sometimes you felt you were in a truck when you wanted a racing car," said Faulkner.[66]

WITH THE ARRIVAL OF THE Cactus Air Force the Marines at last were able to challenge the Japanese for mastery of the skies, and there now ensued an "unending series of encounters" over the airfield. On August 29 eighteen enemy bombers and twenty-two fighters appeared over the airfield. The Marine pilots, who were ready for them after being alerted by the Bougainville coast watchers, shot down two. On August 30 eighteen Zeros attacked the transport *William Ward Burrows*, aground off Tulagi. Eight F4Fs and seven P-400s met them and claimed eight, with four P-400s lost. Rising again to meet a second enemy flight, they shot down eight planes, losing none. On August 31 Smith's forewarned squadron pounced on a forty-one-plane raid and knocked down eleven enemy aircraft.[67]

As the air war heated up, more planes flowed into Henderson—24 on September 4, and 60 eight days later—and even more to the Japanese airstrips at Rabaul, which received 63 on September 1 and 140 on September 12.[68]

Yet as quickly as the US planes reached Henderson, losses from air combat or enemy bombing runs on the airfield reduced their numbers. Of the nineteen Wildcats that had arrived on August 20, just five were flyable ten days later, when two other squadrons arrived.

Admiral McCain, the South Pacific air commander, wrote to Admiral Nimitz on August 31 that Cactus needed two full squadrons of F4Fs or, even better, Army P-38s. These high-altitude twin-fuselage fighters were being flown by MacArthur's Army Air Force over New Guinea—and MacArthur refused to give up any of them. McCain ended his plea by presciently noting, "With substantially the reinforcement requested, Cactus can be a sinkhole for enemy air power and can be consolidated, expanded and exploited to the enemy's mortal hurt." But if not reinforced, the airfield and its defenders "cannot be supplied and hence cannot be held."[69]

On August 26 one-armed Vice Admiral Nishizo Tsukahara, commander of the 11th Air Fleet, asked Admiral Yamamoto's staff for more planes and pilots. His losses were mounting over New Guinea and Guadalcanal. Three days later Imperial Japanese Headquarters agreed to transfer the 21st Air Flotilla to Rabaul from Sumatra and Malaya.[70]

AMERICAN PILOTS, CREWMEN, AND MECHANICS lived in a coconut grove next to Henderson in mud-floored tents or in dugouts. During air raids, they hid in nearby foxholes. They nicknamed their new home "Mosquito Gulch." They worked and slept in their khakis and flight suits, and they wore baseball caps to shield their eyes from the tropical sun—blue caps for pilots, red for crewmen. Gunfire from the Alligator Creek battle roared throughout their first night on the island, causing many of them to wonder what they had stepped into.[71]

At first there was no equipment for fueling the planes or loading them with bombs; it was all done manually. Bomb trucks, carts, and hoists would arrive later. Until then about 140 sailors hand-pumped aviation fuel into the planes from fifty-five-gallon drums and muscled five-hundred- and thousand-pound bombs onto the SBDs.[72]

The primitive airstrip was alternately muddy or dusty, the Wildcats were inferior to the Zeros, and the American pilots were not battle-hardened like their Japanese adversaries. Yet the fact that American warplanes now operated from

Guadalcanal concerned some high-ranking Japanese naval officers, such as Vice Admiral Ugaki, Yamamoto's chief of staff. "We should not let the enemy consolidate its position," he wrote in his diary. "The most urgent thing for us is to destroy these aircraft immediately and render the airstrip unavailable by launching air raids and night bombardments."[73]

TWO WEEKS AFTER THE US Navy sailed away from Guadalcanal, naval activity began to pick up. The night after the Alligator Creek battle Japanese reconnaissance planes spotted three American destroyers escorting a pair of cargo ships loaded with supplies bound for Guadalcanal. Around 3:00 a.m. on August 22 lookouts on the Japanese destroyer *Kawakaze*, which had just landed troops on Guadalcanal and was alerted to the small convoy's presence, saw the destroyer *Blue* sailing ahead of the other ships. What happened next was Savo Island in miniature. The *Kawakaze*'s torpedoes were in the water before the *Blue* even knew there was an enemy ship in the area. One of the fish tore off part of *Blue*'s stern. She limped to Tulagi and was scuttled on August 23, two weeks after having survived the Battle of Savo Island.[74]

Events greater than destroyer ambushes were in progress. The Japanese were poised to launch a combined sea, air, and land effort to recapture Guadalcanal. The operation's ambitious objects were to destroy the US carrier fleet and the Cactus Air Force and to land infantrymen to defeat the US Marines. Three groups were involved: a carrier group, a cruiser group running interference for it, and a transport group. Inexplicably, none cooperated with the others.

Vice Admiral Chuichi Nagumo commanded the formidable carrier force, which consisted of the large carriers *Shokaku* and *Zuikaku*, the light carrier *Ryujo*, battleships *Hiei* and *Kirishima*, five cruisers, and eleven destroyers. Nagumo's three carriers were capable of launching 173 Zeros, dive bombers, and torpedo bombers. More than one hundred miles ahead of Nagumo's large force was Vice Admiral Nobutake Kondo's cruiser group—the Second Fleet, consisting of six cruisers, six destroyers, and a seaplane carrier.

Largely independent of the other two groups were Rear Admiral Raizo Tanaka's three transports carrying Ichiki's 2nd Echelon and a Special Naval Landing Force, convoyed by eight destroyers and the light cruiser *Jintsu*, Tanaka's flagship.

Nagumo's modest contribution to Tanaka's mission would be to detach the light carrier *Ryujo* along with the cruiser *Tone* and two destroyers. They would lure US ships and planes into attacking them while *Ryujo*'s twenty-one planes assaulted Henderson Field. They hoped the distractions would enable Tanaka to safely put ashore the fifteen hundred troops in his transports.[75]

SINCE THE 1920S US NAVAL intelligence officers had monitored the Imperial Japanese Navy's codes and intercepted naval message traffic. Until mid-1942, analysts cleared to read "Ultra" transmissions in Hawaii, Melbourne, and Washington, DC, were snooping on 60 percent of the Imperial Navy's coded radio traffic and deciphering 10 to 15 percent of it. The intercepts aided the US Navy at the Coral Sea and Midway battles.

But then the Japanese changed their code, and they changed it again in July and early August. Soon after the Guadalcanal landings Rabaul radio traffic dropped off sharply, and the intercepted transmissions could not be read at all. Unable to interpret the messages' content, US intelligence officers analyzed transmission frequency, origins, addresses, and patterns for signs of major developments. From intercepted reports by the Truk port director about arrivals and departures of combat vessels, US naval intelligence deduced that a naval buildup was underway.[76]

YAMAMOTO'S THREE GROUPS OF 58 ships and 177 planes sailed toward Guadalcanal on August 23. Their progress was necessarily slowed by radical course changes that were made whenever an American search plane appeared.

A PBY Catalina spotted Tanaka's convoy group and shadowed it, reporting its location to be about 200 miles north of Guadalcanal—west of Admiral Kondo's advance force and Admiral Nagumo's main force. The report prompted Admiral Frank Jack Fletcher, whose carrier fleet was 150 miles southeast of Guadalcanal, to send combat planes from the *Saratoga*. It was Fletcher's first decisive offensive action in two weeks. Commander Harry D. Felt's thirty-one SBDs and six Grumman TBF "Avenger" torpedo bombers hunted for the convoy, which had executed one of its course reversals. General Vandegrift, deeply concerned that Japanese troops would soon land on the island, sent twenty-one Cactus Air Force planes to search for the enemy ships.

Both air groups ran into a squall line and returned empty-handed. With fuel running low, Felt's *Saratoga* pilots landed at Henderson Field. The Navy pilots spent an edgy night in dark, muggy tents, listening to the sounds of wild animals and sporadic gunfire. A Japanese destroyer briefly bombarded the island in the middle of the night, adding to their discomfort. In the morning Felt bequeathed to the Marines twenty-seven 1,000-pound bombs—larger than any bombs on the island—as payment for their hospitality and fuel, and the pilots returned to the *Saratoga*.[77]

In response to a spurious report that Nagumo's carrier group was seen hundreds of miles away, north of Truk, Fletcher decided to send away the *Wasp* to take on oil—refueling having also been his reason for leaving Guadalcanal two weeks earlier. The *Wasp* carrier group, with its sixty warplanes, three cruisers, and seven destroyers, sailed away from the developing battle zone. With that decision, Fletcher reduced his carrier force by one-third, leaving him with two groups, those of the *Enterprise* and *Saratoga,* with their one battleship, four cruisers, eleven destroyers, and 154 aircraft. By sending away the *Wasp,* Fletcher had ceded the possibility of rough numerical parity.[78]

The battle fleets were groping through time, distance, and foul weather toward one another. The Japanese had a general idea of Fletcher's location, but they had been as luckless in locating his carriers on August 23 as he had been in finding theirs.

In fact, the US and Japanese naval forces were more than two hundred miles apart; the battle, when it occurred, would be fought at arm's length—the third carrier battle of the war, after Midway and Coral Sea. Like the previous battles, warplanes would attack ships, and combatant ships would never actually see one another.

NAGUMO DETACHED THE LIGHT CARRIER *Ryujo* as well as its escorts *Tone* and two destroyers to protect Tanaka's transports and draw US carrier planes away from their flattops. Commander Tameichi Hara, skipper of one of the decoy destroyers, the *Amatsukaze,* wrote that the four ships were supposed to "storm" Guadalcanal and distract the US task force. Yamamoto had used the same tactic at Coral Sea when he staked out the light carrier *Shoho* to lure US combat planes from their carriers. The *Shoho* was sunk.[79]

A PBY spotted the *Ryujo* 150 miles northwest of Guadalcanal at 9:35 a.m. on August 24, but Fletcher neither acted on this report nor on a second one a couple of hours later. Only at 1:30 p.m., when the *Saratoga*'s radar picked up bogeys from the *Ryujo* homing in on Guadalcanal, did Fletcher release the *Saratoga*'s air group to attack the enemy light carrier more than two hundred miles away.

Felt's three dozen Wildcats, dive bombers, and torpedo bombers swooped down on the *Ryujo* as its escorts, in a protective cordon around it, filled the air with antiaircraft fire. It did little good. The attack was "carried out like a training exercise" against the nearly defenseless carrier, whose planes were all in the air headed to Guadalcanal. Felt's group missed the target at first—but then Felt laid a thousand-pound bomb on the flight deck. His squadron scored three more hits, and a TBF got a torpedo into *Ryujo.* From over the horizon Admiral Tanaka's attention was drawn to a "gigantic pillar of smoke and flame"—it was the *Ryujo,* burning from bow to stern.[80]

The Cactus Air Force became airborne when the Pagoda picked up *Saratoga*'s radar blip of *Ryujo*'s twenty-one approaching planes. Sixteen Wildcats were waiting at Angels 20 when the Japanese reached Guadalcanal. They spoiled the plan to neutralize Henderson by shooting down three Kate torpedo bombers loaded with conventional bombs along with three of their Zero escorts, while losing three Wildcats.

The Japanese attack group turned back to *Ryujo*, but the carrier's skipper, Captain Tadao Kato, ordered them to land at Buka instead. Lacking the fuel to fly to the airstrip on the northern side of Bougainville, the fourteen planes that survived the flight back to the light carrier splashed down nearby.

By this time, said Commander Hara of the *Amatsukaze*, the *Ryujo* "no longer resembl[ed] a ship . . . [but a] huge stove, full of holes that belched eerie red flames." The *Ryujo*'s escorts picked up seven of the pilots who had ditched as well as about three hundred *Ryujo* crewmen, a third of the carrier's normal complement. At 8:00 p.m. the *Ryujo* sank. Vice Admiral Ugaki acknowledged in his after-action report that the *Ryujo* had stripped away its air defense by sending its planes against Henderson. "This couldn't be helped, and she served as a decoy," he wrote.[81]

MEANWHILE TWO SBD SEARCH PLANES located the Japanese carriers *Shokaku* and *Zuikaku*. Upon learning of the attack on *Ryujo*, at 3:37 p.m. Admiral Nagumo had launched six dozen Val dive bombers, Zeros, and Kate torpedo planes from the two carriers to attack the American carriers. The US pilots radioed their ships with the Japanese carriers' positions and dived on the *Shokaku*. It alertly swerved, and the SBDs' two 500-pound bombs inflicted only minor damage.[82]

When American radar detected the first flight of incoming Japanese planes— twenty-seven Vals and ten Zeros—Fletcher launched the *Enterprise*'s last dive bombers and torpedo bombers to attack the enemy carriers. Then about four dozen F4Fs from the *Saratoga* and *Enterprise* rose to meet the enemy attack group as it bore in on the *Enterprise*. A second wave of twenty-seven Vals and nine Zeros lagged an hour behind the first flight. Indeed, the battle was shaping up to be another Midway: carrier planes attacking one another and their flattops, without the ships ever directly engaging one another.

The first twenty-seven Vals swung around and approached the *Enterprise* from the north; waiting Wildcats met them there. The *Enterprise* flight coordinator lost control of his fighters when the radio circuit was overwhelmed with superfluous transmissions. It became a "pilots' battle."[83]

It lasted fifteen minutes, and six Wildcats were lost. As the Vals dived on the *Enterprise*, their Zero escort fended off most of the Wildcats, but a few got among the Vals, disrupted their dives, and shot them down. The *Enterprise*'s gun crews shot down several others.

But some Vals got through and managed to score three bomb strikes on the *Enterprise*. A bomb that hit the after elevator and plunged through seven floors before exploding in the mess, killing thirty-five men. A second bomb landed nearby and ignited the powder in an ammunition room. The explosion buckled the flight deck and blew out a gallery of two 5-inch guns on the starboard side, killing another thirty-five men.

The third bomb punched a large hole in the deck near the number-two elevator, but no one died. Corpsmen began treating wounded sailors. One of them, Aviation Machinist's Mate Bernard Peterson, suffering from shrapnel wounds, flash burns, and a concussion, staggered to the flight deck, where men lay "with arms and legs missing. A couple of them were pulling themselves over to the side of the ship to commit suicide." Peterson, who was also a qualified gunner, joined a 20mm crew whose gunner had suffered an eye injury. The crew strapped Peterson in, and he was soon firing at diving Vals.[84]

Fires raged throughout the *Enterprise*. Firefighters poured water on burning bedding, foam on burning oil. Asbestos-suited men with air packs entered blazing compartments to rescue crewmen. Medics treated ninety-nine wounded. Four of them died, raising the death toll to seventy-four.

The explosions shorted out the carrier's rudder motor, and the huge ship turned in circles until Chief Machinist William Smith donned a breathing apparatus, entered the furnace-like steering department, and switched on a backup rudder motor. On the flattop's deck, repair parties fanned out with steel plates to cover the holes made by the bombs. Within an hour the battered carrier was making twenty-four knots. It turned into the wind, red-and-white signal flags went up, and it began landing its planes.[85]

Enterprise pilots returned to a ship whose appearance had radically changed during their two-hour absence. Black smoke billowed from fires burning below decks, corpsmen were treating a multitude of wounded shipmates, and repair crews raced from place to place to keep vital functions operating.

Lieutenant Frederick Mears, a TBF pilot from Torpedo Three who managed to land on the damaged carrier (some of his squadron mates were diverted to the *Saratoga*), was appalled and fascinated by what he saw in the gun gallery, which the second bomb had struck. The sailors, some of them still at their stations, had "died from the concussion and then were roasted. . . . They were blackened but not burned or withered, and they looked like iron statues of men, their limbs smooth and whole, their heads rounded with no hair." A gun pointer was in his seat leaning on his sight with one arm. "He looked as though a sculptor had created him. . . . Two or three lying face up were shielding themselves with their arms bent at the elbows and their hands before their face."[86]

With refueling now a priority, Fletcher withdrew to the south with the *Saratoga*, the damaged *Enterprise*, and their escorts as Nagumo headed north with his two carrier groups and Kondo's advance group. The third carrier battle of the Pacific, the Battle of the Eastern Solomons, had ended indecisively, although the fighting would last another day.

Eleven SBDs from VS-5 on the *Enterprise* failed to find *Ryujo*—or any targets for that matter. As night approached, Lieutenant Turner Caldwell decided to lead his dive bombers, known as Flight 300, to Henderson Field instead of trying to find the *Enterprise* in the dark. The Marines gave the naval aviators a warm welcome and shared what they had.

Ensign Harold Buell and his mates, who had not eaten since lunchtime on the *Enterprise*, were introduced to Marine food. "It was barely palatable and came as a shock to carrier pilots who were used to the excellent cuisine served in a carrier wardroom," wrote Buell. To the delight of the Marines, Flight 300 remained for nearly a month—the first carrier planes to operate from Henderson. Meager rations and dysentery would melt thirty pounds from Buell's "already lean frame" by the time he left the island.[87]

REAR ADMIRAL TANAKA'S THREE TRANSPORTS and their destroyer escort continued to plow southward toward Guadalcanal. Despite the Japanese strike force's failure to neutralize Henderson Field, Tanaka intended to land Ichiki's Second Detachment and the naval troops.

After seeing the *Ryujo* in flames, Tanaka requested instructions and was told to withdraw. But the order was then rescinded when the Combined Fleet in Rabaul received a false report that Japanese dive bombers had set fire to two US carriers. Tanaka turned around and resumed sailing toward Guadalcanal.[88]

At daylight on August 25 dive bombers from Lieutenant Colonel Richard Mangrum's VMSB-232 and torpedo bombers from Flight 300 spotted Tanaka's convoy about one hundred miles north of Guadalcanal—and pounced. In the ensuing rain of iron and steel a bomb struck Tanaka's flagship, the *Jintsu*, and set fire to it while momentarily knocking Tanaka unconscious and disabling the light cruiser's communications. A Flight 300 pilot dropped a thousand-pound bomb on the transport *Kinryu Maru*, and the rest of Tanaka's convoy protectively encircled the wounded ships, threw up a curtain of antiaircraft fire, and rescued survivors. With no bombs left, the SBDs returned to Henderson.

A short time later, American B-17s appeared over Tanaka's foundering convoy. The B-17s had a poor record in the Pacific for bombing runs on ships, but this time they squarely hit the destroyer *Matsuki* and sank her. Then Tanaka's destroyers torpedoed and scuttled the *Kinryu Maru*. The convoy's survivors limped back to Shortland Harbor without landing any troops.[89]

"The situation isn't developing to our advantage," wrote Vice Admiral Ugaki. "It is apparent that landing on Guadalcanal by transports is hopeless unless the enemy planes are wiped out." It was a dilemma. To wipe out enemy planes that prevented Japanese troops from landing, more troops had to be landed.[90]

ADMIRAL TANAKA, LONG-FACED AND MUSTACHIOED, had the job of bringing army reinforcements to Guadalcanal by sea. Besides being expert in the use of the "Long Lance" torpedo, he had strong opinions about how to bring in reinforcements, but until the recent transport operation failures, they had not been heeded.

Tanaka believed the troop transports were too slow to complete the three-hundred-mile run from Shortland to Guadalcanal and return before daylight awakened Henderson Field's Wildcats and dive bombers. Destroyers, however, could easily complete the trip before daylight. Although they could not land as many troops as the transports could, they were a faster, surer option, Tanaka believed.

Tanaka's superiors told him to proceed with his nighttime reinforcement and resupply efforts—nicknamed "Rat" operations and later known by the Americans as the "Tokyo Express." On August 31 and September 1 Tanaka's destroyers landed a thousand troops on Guadalcanal.

But then the army forced the navy to revert to using transports and landing barges during the daytime so more men could be landed at one time. Tanaka was recalled to destroyer duty. The change had disastrous consequences for the Japanese. On September 3 Henderson scout planes on dawn patrol up the Slot spotted more than a dozen barges loaded with troops. Sixteen dive bombers took off from Guadalcanal and bombed them in the open sea, sinking several of them.

"I almost felt sorry for the poor Japanese in the barges," wrote Ensign Buell, the Flight 300 pilot. Weighed down by their weapons and gear, many of them drowned when they jumped overboard to avoid the dive bombers' strafing fire. Two days later SBDs sank three more transports, damaged several others, and killed "large numbers" of troops.

The Japanese resumed nighttime destroyer landings. "As we have adopted the new method," wrote Ugaki, "the battle is expected to become a prolonged one." On September 5 three Japanese destroyers put ashore troops east of Henderson Field and then bombarded the airfield. Ugaki said the operation demonstrated the superiority of landing reinforcements from destroyers.[91]

THE ENTERPRISE WAS ON ITS way to Pearl Harbor for repairs that would sideline it for six weeks. As the carrier left the Solomons, a service was held for the seventy-four sailors killed by Japanese bombs. Their remains had been placed in clean mattress covers. Near the number-two elevator on the hangar deck a full ceremony was performed for one of the dead, representative of the seventy-four. As the body was slid off a pantry board into the deep, the ship's band played

"Taps," the Marine guard presented arms, and the assembled crew saluted. The seventy-three other dead sailors, their covered bodies weighted by five-inch shells, were cast from the fantail into the sea.[92]

THE HENDERSON PILOTS GREW ACCUSTOMED to a daily routine of going out on morning and afternoon searches for enemy ships and then withstanding noontime Japanese raids and nightly bombings and shellings. It was "like a broken record . . . day after day with little variance," observed one pilot.[93]

During their breaking-in period Marine and Navy pilots either became fully blooded combat veterans very quickly or became casualties. Cactus Air Force pilots stood a one-in-five chance of being killed or seriously injured, and the preponderance of deaths occurred during their first seventeen days on Guadalcanal. At times Henderson Field itself could be as dangerous as battling the enemy at twenty thousand feet.

Ensign Buell was taxiing for takeoff when the Japanese began shelling the airfield. There was an explosion beneath his SBD. After lifting off to avoid two other taxiing planes, his dive bomber stalled. Buell's plane plowed into a steamroller and broke up, the engine ending up in one place, a five-hundred-pound unexploded bomb in another, and wheels, struts and wings scattered around.

Three Marines roared up in a Jeep. Buell was bleeding from his left eye and so bruised he could barely walk, but he and his gunner had somehow survived. "My God, you've gouged your eye out, sir!" one of the Marines declared. Feeling around his eye with a silk scarf that had been around his neck, Buell discovered a glass sliver from his broken goggles sticking out of his eye. "I pulled the sliver out, blotted the eye, and asked the Marine to shine his light on my face." Through the film of blood Buell could see light, reassurance that his eye would be all right. After treatment Buell returned to duty.[94]

Many young pilots thrived in their dangerous new environment. Second Lieutenant George Hallowell had a mere forty-seven hours flying Wildcats when he landed August 30 at Henderson with VMF-224. The next day squadron leader Major Robert Galer led Hallowell and sixteen other pilots on their first combat air patrol. Two days later Hallowell shot down his first enemy plane, a twin-engine Betty; on September 13 he got another Betty; and the following day Hallowell became an ace when he shot down three float planes.[95]

Captain Loren "Doc" Everton, a Marine Wildcat pilot, got his first kill when he shot down a Betty after it had made a bombing run on Henderson. As he began moving in on his target, "all my hours in the air seemed to do me no good. I had buck fever, and my whole ship was nervous under me." He opened fire from too far away, but then he calmed down and trained his machine-guns on the bomber. "I got up near and saw little pieces of metal flicking off." Its left side erupted in smoke and flame.

"The plane is the thing that dies, not the crew," he wrote—untrue in this particular case because in finishing off the Betty, Everton saw the plane disintegrate and five bodies fly through the air without parachutes. Japanese airmen usually preferred death to the ignominy of capture.[96]

Marine and Navy pilots, however, believed it was their duty to survive and fight again. Captain Marion Carl, who claimed his third, fourth, and fifth kills during the Battle of the Eastern Solomons to become the Pacific War's first Marine ace, was shot down by a Zero two weeks later. He parachuted into Sealark Channel east of Taivu Point and inflated his "Mae West" life vest.

A Melanesian paddled out to Carl in a dugout canoe and took him to a medical practitioner named Eroni, who spoke English and was one of Martin Clemens's scouts. Before they could go anywhere, though, Eroni and Carl had to first repair an eighteen-foot launch that had not run in months. They got it going in two days, and Eroni took Carl to Lunga Point, where Carl gratefully filled Eroni's launch with food to take back with him. When Carl reported to the Pagoda, Brigadier General Roy Geiger, the airfield commander, said, "Marion, I have bad news. Smitty [Major John Smith, VMF-223's commander] has 14 planes now. You still have only 12. What about that?" Carl replied, "Goddammit, general, ground him for five days!"[97]

Lieutenant Richard Amerine, shot down off Cape Esperance in western Guadalcanal on August 30, fought strong currents to reach shore in enemy territory and then spent a harrowing week in the jungle. Two enemy soldiers who were searching for him happened to sit down to rest on the log behind which Amerine was hiding. He rose up and struck one soldier in the head with a rock and strangled the other.

Having shed his trousers and boots during the swim to shore, Amerine put on one victim's trousers and took his pistol, which had three rounds in it. Later he shot a Japanese soldier who was about his size and took his boots. Then he hid as hundreds of Japanese marched past, toting quarters of beef. He used his second bullet while eluding a group of enemy soldiers. Nearing the US lines, he was surprised by a Japanese sentry and shot him with his last bullet.

Martin Clemens interviewed Amerine when he was safely inside the perimeter and had been treated for shock, exhaustion, sores, and weight loss. When Amerine had finished recounting his ordeal, Clemens asked the pilot if he had anything to add. "Oh yes," said Amerine. "What a pity, if I'd only had my net, just think how many beautiful butterflies I could have caught." Clemens learned that Amerine had studied entomology at the University of Kansas.[98]

JAPAN'S COMBINED FLEET WITHDREW AFTER the Battle of the Eastern Solomons and did not return to the Guadalcanal area for six weeks. But Japanese naval and air forces kept the pressure on the Marines. Tokyo Express destroyers and transports landed army troops, and the 11th Air Fleet bombed Henderson Field daily while watching for US convoys bringing reinforcements and supplies to the island. In turn the Cactus Air Force patrolled the Slot looking for enemy convoys.

Moreover, a dozen or more Japanese submarines—I-Boats—lurked in the waters southeast of Guadalcanal. They sometimes surfaced in Ironbottom Sound and lobbed shells into the Marine perimeter, but their primary mission was to sink US carriers, battleships, and cruisers and to stop US reinforcements and supplies from reaching the island. In adopting this strategy, Admiral Yamamoto, so perceptive in understanding air power's crucial role, failed to recognize the importance of the German U-Boats' campaign against American shipping to Great Britain. Rather than assign its subs to decimate the flow of supplies to Australia—and starve America's chief Pacific ally as Germany was trying to do to England—Japan elected to target US warships. But America could build warships faster than they could be sunk.[99]

JUST AFTER DAYBREAK ON AUGUST 31, 260 miles southeast of Guadalcanal in the Coral Sea, Commander Minoru Yokota raised *I-26*'s periscope and, to his great joy, saw an American aircraft carrier, a battleship, and their escort of ten cruisers and destroyers. On the war's first day Yokota's submarine had sunk the SS *Cynthia Olson* off the US West Coast, and since then it had been at sea most of the time.

I-26 edged up to the destroyer screen and fired a full spread of six torpedoes at the carrier, which was Vice Admiral Frank Jack Fletcher's Task Force 61 flagship, *Saratoga*. Spotted by the destroyer *MacDonough*, which instantly changed course to attack the sub, *I-26* went into a steep dive. It was a close call: the sub's superstructure scraped the *MacDonough*'s bottom as two depth charges floated down toward it. However, the destroyer's crewmen had neglected to set the charges, so they did not explode.

But *I-26*'s fish continued to race toward their intended targets. One of them slammed into the *Saratoga* on the starboard side of its island at 7:48 a.m. The strike flooded the engine room and shorted out the two main electrical generators, leaving the carrier dead in the water. Twelve crewmen were injured, including Admiral Fletcher, who was flung into the air by the shock wave and gashed his forehead.

Taken under tow by the cruiser *Minnesota*, the *Saratoga* launched its twenty-one torpedo and dive bombers and nine fighters—VT-8, VS-3, and VF-5—before slowly proceeding to Pearl Harbor for three months in dry dock. The thirty planes were later welcomed into the Cactus Air Force.[100]

FIFTEEN DAYS LATER, THE JAPANESE submarine *I-19*—commanded by Japan's best submarine skipper, Commander Takaichi Kinashi—was operating in the same waters where the *Saratoga* had been torpedoed, now nicknamed "Torpedo Junction." *I-19* was one of several submarines that had been sent to the area to stop reinforcements from reaching Guadalcanal. Indeed, a hundred miles away cruisers and destroyers were convoying the 7th Marine Regiment to the island to bring the 1st Marine Division to full strength.

Through his periscope Kinashi saw twenty-three enemy ships, all within range of his Long Lance torpedoes. The closest was the carrier *Wasp*, the flagship of Rear Admiral Leigh Noyes, who had succeeded Fletcher as Task Force 61's commander. The *Wasp* was the nucleus of one of the two carrier groups operating in the area; the other group revolved around the *Hornet*.

Kinashi watched the *Wasp* turn into the wind and launch eighteen SBDs and eight Wildcats for combat air patrol duty. Many of the forty-five planes that remained on board were being fueled and armed. The *I-19* fired a spread of six fish. As the *Wasp* was turning back to its original course, a lookout shouted, "Torpedoes, starboard side!" The carrier attempted to take evasive action, but it was too late. Two torpedoes, each one carrying a thousand-pound warhead, struck the *Wasp*'s starboard side.

Enormous explosions convulsed the carrier. On the flight and hangar decks planes were thrown into the air, smashing their landing gears when they landed hard, while the planes suspended above the hangar deck broke loose and fell on men and other aircraft. Flames swept through the ship, spreading to ammunition and planes full of fuel and setting off further explosions. The gasoline pumping system was operating at the time, and sheets of oil and aviation fuel spread the flames across the deck. Bombs exploded, water mains broke, and generators were wrenched loose from their moorings. Admiral Noyes, his face singed and his clothing on fire, was hurled to the signal bridge deck. The forward half of the *Wasp* burned furiously.

Meanwhile the other torpedoes fired by *I-19* raced toward the *Hornet*'s five-ship Task Force 17 group six miles away. At 2:51 p.m. one of them took off part of the destroyer *O'Brien*'s bow, and a minute later another torpedo crashed into the *North Carolina*, the first of a new generation of "fast" battleships. The torpedo carved a thirty-two-foot-wide hole, knocked out the number-one turret, and killed six sailors. The battleship withdrew for several weeks' repairs. The *O'Brien* survived the torpedo attack but sank during its voyage to the US mainland for repairs. *I-19* was able to claim the rare feat of hitting three ships with a six-torpedo spread.[101]

At 3:00 p.m., minutes after being torpedoed, the *Wasp* was wracked by massive explosions that turned her into a roaring pillar of fire and smoke. After meeting with his officers, Captain Forrest Sherman concluded that his carrier could not be saved.

At 3:20 Sherman gave the order to abandon ship. The badly wounded were lowered onto rafts and floating mattresses as oil burned on the water around them. A survivor who climbed down near the water before dropping through the burning oil said, "If you had to come up short of the [outer] rings of fire, you always came up flailing your arms to throw the oily flame away from you and get a breath and go down again and go on."

As the *Wasp*'s escorts closed ranks around her to rescue the rest of the twenty-two hundred crewmen, dozens of sharks swarmed to the scent of blood in the water. They voraciously pulled sailors underwater by their hands and feet. Ford Richardson, a sailor on the destroyer *Farenholt*, saw a shark clamp its jaws around a man's midsection and "shake him like a dog shaking a rat." Nightfall finally pulled down the curtain on the scene of horror.

The *Wasp* sank at 9:00 p.m. with 173 men still aboard. Admiral Nimitz criticized Noyes for sailing too slowly through submarine-infested waters, relieved him of command, and assigned him to shore duty. A court of inquiry, however, later exonerated Noyes.[102]

The *Wasp* was the third US carrier taken out of action in a little more than three weeks—the others being the damaged *Enterprise* and *Saratoga*. That left the *Hornet* as the South Pacific's last operational US carrier. Admiral Ghormley ordered Admiral George Murray, the *Hornet*'s skipper and the commander of TF-17, to avoid Torpedo Junction for the time being.[103]

3

September:
"Let George Do It"

We were just holding onto Henderson Field by the skin of our teeth. We didn't have any other foothold on the island. We just had this narrow enclave.

—NEW YORK TIMES CORRESPONDENT HANSON BALDWIN[1]

The word is nobody moves, just die in your holes.

—PLATOON SERGEANT JOE BUNTIN TO HIS MEN BEFORE THE
JAPANESE ATTACK ON BLOODY RIDGE[2]

I can't help entertaining much doubt about the success of the night assault with lightly equipped soldiers. They should be wary of their own conceit.

—VICE ADMIRAL MATOME UGAKI, ON THE EVE OF THE BATTLE
OF BLOODY RIDGE[3]

EVEN BEFORE THE SUBMARINES *I-19* AND *I-26* sent the *Wasp* to the bottom of the Coral Sea and the *Saratoga* to Pearl Harbor for repairs, Admiral Ghormley had outlined a new defensive strategy: he would reserve his South Pacific fleet for major operations. Holding Guadalcanal would be up to the Marines and the Cactus Air Force. The strategy suggested a morally dubious willingness to sacrifice infantrymen and airmen to preserve ships.

"For the present, hostile infiltration tactics and initial shock of a hostile main effort may have to be borne by ground troops and land-based aviation," Ghormley wrote to Admiral Chester Nimitz, the Pacific's commander in chief, on

August 29. While Ghormley's fleet enjoyed "freedom of action," the Cactus Air Force would take "a constant toll of transports and escorting combatant ships, which the Japanese cannot long sustain," he optimistically predicted.[4]

It meant that a month after landing on Guadalcanal the Marines remained largely on their own, save for occasional resupply missions by air or sea. The first friendly ship to dock at Lunga Point was a converted destroyer that landed supplies and an aviation ground crew on August 18. An R4D transport plane from the newly formed VMJ-253 squadron in New Caledonia brought a ton and a half of candy, cigarettes, and ammunition during one of the squadron's first missions.

Allied cargo ships landed supplies during the daytime under the umbrella of the Cactus Air Force. But after sunset the Japanese navy ruled the waters around Guadalcanal, and Allied ships "cleared out like frightened children running home from a graveyard," in the words of naval historian Samuel Eliot Morison. It was a strangely Manichaean tactical situation.[5]

Rear Admiral John McCain, the wiry, chain-smoking Mississippian in charge of the 290 Navy land- and sea-based aircraft in the South Pacific, tried to sustain the Cactus Air Force with new aircraft and pilots and with squadrons orphaned by the loss of their flattops. But the daily grind of combat air patrols, relentless Japanese air raids, and nighttime shellings exacted a steady toll in planes and pilots.

McCain was meeting with Vandegrift on Guadalcanal at the end of August, and they were toasting McCain's visit with a glass of Vandegrift's carefully hoarded bourbon when the air raid siren announced the arrival of Japanese bombers. Later, Japanese cruisers shelled the airstrip. Then, early the next morning, there was another enemy air attack. Down in Vandegrift's dugout McCain said, "By God, Vandegrift, this is your war and you sure are welcome to it. But when I go back tomorrow I am going to try to get you what you need for your air force here."[6]

As promised, McCain told Nimitz, MacArthur, Ghormley, and Admiral King on September 1 that of the nineteen F4F Wildcats that had landed August 20, only five were now flyable. "Pilots in Cactus very tired," he wrote, adding that "40 flyable high altitude fighters" were needed on Guadalcanal; the Army P-400s sent ten days earlier could not fly much above twelve thousand feet, lacking turbochargers and oxygen for the pilots.[7]

In the near term, instead of a large infusion of fighter planes, the Cactus Air Force got Brigadier General Roy Geiger, commander of the First Marine Air Wing, to oversee Guadalcanal's air operations. Geiger's leadership was arguably the near-equivalent of a fighter squadron. Geiger, fifty-seven, had been a Marine officer since graduating from the Parris Island "School of Application" in 1909 in the same class as Vandegrift. Geiger completed flight training in 1917 to become the fifth Marine aviator. He commanded the Marine air squadron that sailed to France in July 1918; it was active in France and Belgium. After the war he served in Haiti, Santo Domingo, and Nicaragua, and he was director of Marine Corps aviation. On Haiti Geiger provided close-air support for Vandegrift's infantrymen. He and Vandegrift were old friends and, like Vandegrift, Geiger was an "Old Breed" Marine to his core—a tough, demanding officer who spared neither himself nor his men.

The Old Breed, wrote Captain John Thomason of the Marines of World War I and the interwar period, "ran curiously to type, with drilled shoulders and a bone-deep sunburn, and a tolerant scorn of nearly everything on earth." They regarded their service in wartime and peace as "an occupation." Another of these characters was Gunnery Sergeant Lou Diamond, a gifted Fifth Marines mortarman with a beer belly, goatee, and a booming voice who was rumored to have hit a Japanese submarine with a mortar round as the submarine cruised along the Guadalcanal shoreline.

The hard-shelled Geiger quickly tired of his men's complaints about the airstrip's abysmal condition. One day after having his fill of gripes, he stalked over to an SBD, started it up, and taxied down the runway, dodging the potholes. Once airborne, he dropped a bomb on a suspected Japanese camp—something no Marine his age had ever done. The complaints stopped. Geiger moved into the Pagoda with his chief of staff, Colonel Louis Woods, a twenty-year aviation officer cast in the same crusty mold as Geiger.[8]

FLYING AT HIGH ALTITUDES ON oxygen, the Cactus pilots suffered piercing gas pains as a result of their twice-daily meals of corned-beef hash, Spam, rice, or beans. There were anodynes that relieved the cramps, but they also had the serious side effect of inducing drowsiness, even unconsciousness, at high altitudes. Geiger tried to supplement his pilots' poor diet with red meat and fruit juices that he obtained for his men's exclusive consumption; whatever had to be done to keep trained, healthy pilots in the air was well worth the effort and cost, Geiger rightly believed.

In the afternoons the pilots on standby "smoked and fidgeted" until combat patrols reported whether enemy ships were sailing down the Slot, and if there were, how many were coming. The pilots then took off to bomb and torpedo the intruders, usually returning after dark.[9]

At night they attempted to sleep in their mud-floored tents next to the airfield—"in the middle of the bullseye," as they described it. It was true: they lived on the front lines, something that pilots rarely, if ever, had done. Besides the naval bombardments, there were harassing nightly air raids by "Washing

Machine Charlie," a rough-running twin-engine plane that dropped small bombs while peripatetically flying over the airfield area, and "Louis the Louse," a single-engine float plane that dropped flares on targets that enemy ships then shelled. These annoyances prevented the pilots—as well as everyone else—from enjoying a night's uninterrupted sleep.[10]

It seemed that there was never any respite at Henderson Field. Day and night the blaring air raid siren sent the pilots sprinting to foxholes and shelters. One night, an earthquake jolted everyone awake. Drenching rain was followed by sauna-like heat that transformed the soupy mud into billowing dirty-gray dust clouds. "You put on clean clothes at nine o'clock and walk down the road and at 9:30 you look like a chimney sweep," remarked INS correspondent Richard Tregaskis.

Tired, stressed, irritable, and weak from chronic diarrhea and malaria, the flyers' hands often shook when they smoked cigarettes, which they did whenever they were not flying. They took to calling themselves the "Nameless Wonders of the Bastard Air Force." "We were a sorry-looking group," wrote Ensign Harold Buell, the dive-bomber pilot from Flight 300, "thin almost to emaciation, in faded, patched, but clean khaki uniforms, bearded with a certain gleam in the eye that would not go away." Flight surgeons examined the pilots and told Geiger's chief of staff, Colonel Woods, that most of them were unfit for duty. "They've got to keep flying," Woods replied. "It's better to do that than to get a Jap bayonet stuck in their ass!" It was noted that the pilots' effectiveness sharply dropped after four to six weeks at Henderson.[11]

THE MARINES' TENACIOUS GRIP ON Guadalcanal had gotten the undivided attention of the Japanese Naval General Staff and the army. At a meeting in Tokyo on August 31 the military leaders conceded that Guadalcanal was no "mop up" operation. The Alligator Creek fiasco, the Cactus Air Force's stubborn resistance, and the Eastern Solomons naval battle had persuaded them that the struggle for the remote island might become the Pacific War's decisive battle. Japanese leaders decided to make recapturing the island their top priority and to delay the New Guinea campaign for the present.

Victory would require the commitment of thousands of soldiers and hundreds of combat aircraft. Imperial General Headquarters assigned responsibility for ground operations to Lieutenant General Harukichi Hyakutake's Seventeenth Army. Relegating New Guinea to secondary status meant temporarily shelving an operation dear to Japanese planners, who saw New Guinea as a bridge to the conquest of Australia and a barrier to Allied attacks on Rabaul.[12]

Major General Kiyotake Kawaguchi's "Kawaguchi Brigade" was given the mission of capturing Guadalcanal's airfield. "Clean up the enemy forces on the island," his orders said. "Seize the airfield, and then as opportunity arises recapture Tulagi and its adjacent islands." This was in line with Admiral Yamamoto's declaration of August 30 that the battle for Guadalcanal must be won on land and that only when Henderson Field was captured could the navy land amphibious troops to secure the island. "There is no other way," wrote his chief of staff, Vice Admiral Ugaki. Whether the Kawaguchi Brigade could prevail was an open question: although Kawaguchi had led his brigade to easy victories in Borneo and Sarawak, he had no other previous combat experience in nearly twenty years' service. But his superiors believed him to be equal to the job of seizing the airfield.

Rear Admiral Tanaka had the challenging job of transporting Kawaguchi's troops over the three hundred miles of water between Shortland Harbor and Guadalcanal—challenging not only because of the enemy but because his superiors at Rabaul and Kawaguchi persisted in interfering with his plans. Tanaka preferred that his destroyer "Rat" operation land the troops over several nights to minimize exposure to US dive bombers. Midnight landings would enable Tanaka's destroyers to be far away from Guadalcanal by daybreak, when Cactus's dawn patrol became airborne.[13]

Kawaguchi wanted Tanaka to transport his men to Guadalcanal on slower but roomier barges—nicknamed "Ant Freight"—arguing that the destroyers lacked space for artillery and food; he said their absence had contributed to the failure of Ichiki's 1st Echelon at Alligator Creek on August 21.

Tanaka opposed Ant operations. The men ended up compromising, with the faster destroyers ferrying most of Kawaguchi's brigade plus the Ichiki 2nd Echelon, the naval landing force, and a battalion of the 2nd Division to Taivu Point. About a thousand other troops—Colonel Okinosuka Oka with Kawaguchi's headquarters and the 2nd Battalion of the 124th Infantry—went by Ant Freight to northwestern Guadalcanal. Kawaguchi, who would land at Taivu Point with his brigade, planned to rendezvous with Oka south of the Marine perimeter and attack it together.[14]

The Japanese had begun postponing landings on bright, moonlit nights, when Cactus pilots, who lacked radar for night fighting on moonless nights, patrolled Guadalcanal's coastline. But during several consecutive nights at the end of August and in early September stormy weather and the waning moon cycle favored Rat operations.

Kawaguchi and his staff came ashore near Taivu Point on September 1. The next morning US planes bombed and strafed the landing area, and an explosion partially deafened the general. After the rest of Kawaguchi's men arrived, he commanded more than three infantry battalions: the 1st and 3rd Battalions of the 124th Infantry Regiment and the 2nd Battalion, 4th Infantry. Also available to Kawaguchi were Ichiki's 2nd Echelon, known as the Kuma "Bear" Battalion;

engineer and artillery units; and two small surviving companies from Ichiki's 1st Echelon.

Believing there were only a few thousand Americans on the island, Kawaguchi was confident that his five-thousand-man brigade and eight howitzers, when united with Oka's one thousand men—actually, just six hundred, because the others had been killed by the Cactus Air Force in heavy seas near Guadalcanal—could accomplish his mission, even without heavy artillery, which was left behind at Shortland. "What we could rely on was only the attack with our bayonets," Kawaguchi later told historian Samuel B. Griffith. Kawaguchi would belatedly acknowledge that he and other Japanese leaders were overconfident and dangerously underestimated the Americans' fighting ability.

Ignorant of the terrain, lacking good maps, and not heeding General Hyakutake's instructions to assess the enemy's strength, Kawaguchi put his pioneers to work clearing a trail through the jungle to the jumping-off point for his attack, tentatively scheduled for September 11. He had no native guides—all were loyal to the Americans and, in fact, were shadowing him and sending reports to Martin Clemens at division intelligence. No Japanese patrols were sent ahead to reconnoiter the jungle.

With no accurate maps and no aerial photos of the terrain south of the airfield, Kawaguchi's pioneers carved out a trail with machetes. His men sometimes were able to travel just a half-mile in two hours, with roots and vines tripping them up. Kawaguchi had succeeded on Borneo and Sarawak without decent maps, reconnaissance patrols, or native guides. He was confident—infected with "victory fever," some of his colleagues might say—that he could defeat the soft Americans just as he had triumphed earlier over Japan's other enemies.

Kawaguchi, however, did have a plan for capturing Henderson Field—and for accepting General Vandegrift's surrender. Three forces would attack simultaneously from different directions, although no one really knew how long it would take for each group to reach its staging area. His main force, the three battalions of the 124th and 4th Regiments, would attack from the south; the Kuma Battalion from the southeast; and Colonel Oka's men from the southwest. Naval gunfire and air strikes would support the assault.

After crushing the Marines, Kawaguchi planned to don his tailored white dress uniform and receive Vandegrift's sword in a surrender ceremony at the mouth of the Lunga River. Afterward his Marine prisoners would be flown to Tokyo and paraded through the streets.[15]

THE JAPANESE SENT MORE SQUADRONS to Rabaul and intensified their daily raids on Henderson Field. Just as maintaining possession of the airfield and keeping it operational was the sine qua non of the Marines' strategy, so was recapturing or neutralizing it the core of the Japanese's strategy. Air battles raged overhead daily during Tojo time and often, too, in the afternoons and at night-time. Bettys and Zeros were shot down every day, and Wildcats and Dauntlesses were either lost or landed with such extensive damage that they wound up in Henderson's thriving "bone yard" at the runway's south end—the ground crews' ad hoc salvage yard.[16]

When inbound Japanese planes appeared, Marines bolted from the Pagoda, one of them sounding the siren while another lowered the "condition yellow" flag, which signified that a raid was expected in forty-five minutes. It was replaced with a Rising Sun "meatball" flag, meaning enemy planes were ten minutes away. Then, "if a person was brave enough, he could see the 'string of pearls' [a bomber formation] coming," said antiaircraft gunner Arthur Farrington. "Their bottoms turned black [as the bomb doors opened] and soon enough one could see the bombs coming down. They sounded like freight cars coming through the air or the 'whoosh' sound a sheet makes when a bed is made up."

Most Marines by this time were in their shelters—safe, they hoped, from shrapnel and bombs. Farrington's dugout was lined with rice sacks and had three thick wooden braces supporting the roof. It did not entirely protect the occupants from flying shrapnel. "We tried to get as much of our bodies as possible under our steel helmets," wrote Farrington. "I used to say, 'Goodbye, toes.'"[17]

While the Kawaguchi Brigade was getting organized near Taivu Point, the Marines received reinforcements of a different sort: the Navy's 6th Naval Construction Battalion—387 men and five officers with two bulldozers, six dump trucks, and a front-end loader. They were the "Seabees," a conflation of the Construction Battalion initials "CB." Their insignia depicted a flying bee wearing a sailor's cap, and carrying a submachine-gun, a wrench, and a hammer. The Seabees on Guadalcanal were experienced construction workers—and over thirty years old on average—who had volunteered to serve as carpenters, electricians, machinists, masons, and truck drivers. The Seabees took over the maintenance of Henderson Field and began building a new airstrip reserved for fighter planes about a mile east of Henderson to relieve congestion there. Fighter One, as it was officially called (pilots nicknamed it the "Cow Pasture" because of its mown kunai grass and no steel Marsten matting) became operational September 9.

The Seabees quickly became proficient in repairing the runways after a Japanese bombing. They waited out the attacks in foxholes, as dump trucks loaded with dirt stood ready nearby, and then swung into action. Commander Joseph P. Blundon, the Seabees' commander, wrote that one hundred Seabees could repair damage from a five-hundred-pound bomb in forty minutes. During one intensive hour they filled thirteen craters while planes circled overhead, waiting to land. The Seabees also built wharfs, roads, bridges, air raid shelters, and electric power facilities—and a still that produced a volatile concoction they called "jungle juice." Entrepreneurial Seabees bartered with the Marines for Japanese swords, flags, and pistols.[18]

NAVY INTELLIGENCE OFFICERS REPORTED A buildup of warships at Truk and Rabaul that they believed portended a new offensive against Guadalcanal. To prepare for an attack, Vandegrift brought to Guadalcanal nearly every unit from Tulagi, Gavutu, and Florida Islands: the 1st Raider and 1st Parachute Battalions and the 2nd Battalion, Fifth Marines; the three battalions added more than fifteen hundred Marines to Vandegrift's fourteen thousand men on Guadalcanal. Rear Admiral Richard Kelly Turner was also sending him the 1st Division's Seventh Marines from Samoa—an additional forty-two hundred combat troops. Two battalions of the Second Marines in the Tulagi area to patrol Florida Island, where they occasionally encountered and destroyed small enemy units. Vandegrift planned to reinforce the Second Marines with the rest of the 2nd Marine Division, now at Noumea.

The Raiders were happy to leave Tulagi, where food had become so scarce that they were eating just two small meals per day while trying to ward off clouds of flies. "The trick was to wave them away and gulp quickly, swallowing our food and as few flies as possible," wrote Private Marlin "Whitey" Groft.

The First and Fifth Marines had been on Guadalcanal a month. They had witnessed the awful aftermath of the Navy's drubbing off Savo Island and watched the cruisers, destroyers, and transports sail away the next day and not return. The Cactus Air Force's arrival had provided a morale boost, but the relentless air attacks and naval bombardments had eroded the Marines' confidence in victory. There was quiet talk of Guadalcanal becoming another Bataan and that "we'd never get off that damned island alive." "We had gotten hold of the notion that we were orphans," wrote Private Robert Leckie of the First Marines. "No one cared, we thought." A sergeant observed that the men in his platoon wrote fewer letters home. "Our necks were out and it was just a question of how far down the Japanese were going to chop," the sergeant said.[19]

Yet the Marines managed to retain their sardonic sense of humor. They said the Navy's guiding principle regarding the Marines was, "Fuck you, George, I'm all right." A saying that became popular during September was, "Let George do it," the Marines being "George." Lieutenant Colonel Merrill Twining, the division assistant operations officer, assigned Captain Donald Dickson of the Fifth Marines, a talented combat artist, to design a "George" medal. On one side of the medal a hand extending from a Navy officer's uniform is shown dropping a hot potato in the shape of Guadalcanal into a Marine's hands. "Faciat Georgius," read the Latin inscription—"Let George Do It." On the other side of the medal a fan whirs behind a cow's rear, suggesting that "the shit just hit the fan."[20]

The Army did not get off lightly either, as apparent in a popular ditty written by an unnamed Marine:

> *"They sent for the army to come to Tulagi*
> *But Douglas MacArthur said 'No!'*
> *He said, There's a reason, it isn't the season,*
> *Besides, there is no U.S.O. "*[21]

Yet the Marines were adapting to Guadalcanal's harsh environment and to their subsistence-level lifestyle. They ate two daily meals, mainly captured Japanese rice and fish. There were exhausting daily patrols outside the perimeter, where the Marines endured extreme heat, torrential rains, and swarms of malarial Anopheles mosquitoes. On patrol they carried only what they absolutely needed and did without everything else, including blankets; they slept in ponchos or shelter halves. Light rations of rice, bacon, raisins, and coffee were considered adequate for four or five days' patrolling.

Armed with the '03 Springfield, each rifleman carried two canteens and forty to sixty rounds of ammunition. Marines on patrol also traveled with light machine-guns—Browning automatic rifles (BARs), mostly—and 60mm instead of the heavier 81mm mortars. The .45-caliber Thompson submachine-gun, the weapon of choice of 1920s gangsters, was a favorite. The Marines liked their stopping power, their deadliness at close range, and their reliability; the Thompson was far superior to the standard-issue .45-caliber Reising submachine-gun, deemed "an absolute dud" that jammed often, was rust-prone, and that the men often simply discarded. The Thompsons were standard issue for the Raiders but for no one else. Marines obtained them by bartering with sailors who stole the submachine-guns from their ships' armories to trade for Japanese officer swords, battle flags, and other souvenirs.[22]

The Marines learned how to move through the jungle without breaking twigs or snagging their clothing on the barbed vines. "We used our ears like bird dogs," wrote Sergeant Ore Marion of the Fifth Marines. Hyper-watchful, they communicated with nods of the head, or a "slight pointing" with a rifle. They were able to distinguish between their own foul odors and the "sweet-sour" smell of the enemy.

They became familiar with the hissing and buzzing sounds made by enemy rifle bullets in the open. In a foxhole the same bullets "snapped wickedly overhead like a whip." The Japanese Arisaka rifle made a higher-pitched, flatter *crack* than the Marines' Springfield, and their machine-gun had a faster firing rate than the Marines'. Knee mortars—Japanese grenade launchers—*twanged* when fired, while heavier mortars made a deeper *thwang*.[23]

Young Marines might have achieved new levels of awareness, but Old Breed Marines—the crusty NCOs who had served in the prewar Corps in China, Haiti, and Nicaragua—deplored their young comrades' lack of water discipline. The 1942 recruit, grumbled Gunnery Sergeant H. L. Beardsley of the Fifth Marines, "can drink more water than six old timers."[24]

The Marines' voice radio sets were—on paper anyway—a valuable tool for maintaining contact with their command posts. But they were unreliable when they got wet, and the dense jungle and deep valleys limited their range and effectiveness. Light radio sets, under the best of circumstances, could transmit and receive at a maximum distance of one to two miles. Even when they were kept dry during the frequent downpours, high humidity steadily corroded circuits and contacts. The best of the sets, used later in the campaign, was the SCR284, with a seven-mile range. Because it weighed 110 pounds, transporting it required several men or a Jeep. A communications medium dating to the Civil War became the preferred one when larger units were in motion: transmission by wire, best when strung overhead, above men and vehicles that could break it.[25]

AFTER BEING FERRIED ACROSS SEALARK Channel to Guadalcanal, the Raiders and parachutists bivouacked near Lunga Point at an abandoned coconut palm plantation. The paratroopers' commander, Major Robert Williams, wounded on Gavutu on August 7, was still recovering. Consequently Colonel Merritt "Red Mike" Edson of the Raiders commanded both the Raiders and parachutists, although Major Charles Miller, Williams' executive officer, nominally remained the parachutists' leader.

The Raiders and parachutists were established to execute hit-and-run raids; however, neither battalion had yet conducted such an operation but had instead operated strictly as amphibious assault troops. Vandegrift brought them to Guadalcanal as a counterweight to the Japanese reinforcements arriving nearly nightly. The general and his staff planned to use the 850 men commanded by Edson for their intended purpose.[26]

In 1940 Marine Commandant Thomas Holcomb foresaw a need for a light infantry unit for reconnaissance and raiding—men who could parachute into enemy territory, hold strategic points until larger forces arrived, and even operate as guerrillas. After watching an Army parachute demonstration in August 1940, Holcomb decided to proceed. Forty men began jump school in October 1940 at the naval air station in Lakehurst, New Jersey, and in May 1941 the 1st Parachute Battalion was born. The paratroopers were a blend of young, athletic men and Old Breed sergeants and corporals with up to ten years' experience. By 1942 Marine jump schools operated at New River, North Carolina, and at San Diego.[27]

Now under Edson's command, the parachutists were in good hands; the forty-five-year-old colonel had been a Marine since 1917. He served in France during World War I, and a few years later he earned his pilot's wings. While fighting the Sandinista guerrillas in Nicaragua during the late 1920s, Edson helped develop counterinsurgency tactics during long patrols deep in the interior and was awarded the Navy Cross. Drawing on this experience, he almost single-handedly wrote the Marine Corps' "Small Wars Manual." In 1937, while with the Fourth Marines in Shanghai, he observed Japanese combat operations firsthand.

Edson also happened to be one of the best marksmen in the United States; he had been a member of five Marine Corps shooting teams, including one that had won the nationals, and he had also been a shooting team coach. Edson was not a flamboyant man, but he often wore a pair of pearl-handled pistols; being the expert marksman that he was, he seldom missed with them. Martin Clemens, who commanded Guadalcanal's native scouts, described Edson as a "tough, shrewd leader."

In May 1941 Edson led the 1st Battalion, Fifth Marines, a "rubber boat outfit" that trained in amphibious landings from Auxiliary Personnel Destroyers. APDs were World War I escort destroyers that had been converted into high-speed transports able to launch Higgins Boats. Each APD could carry 135 men. In August 1941 Edson recommended that the Corps establish a separate fast-strike unit that would land from APDs rather than by parachute. Commandant Holcomb endorsed Edson's proposal.

During the unit's embryonic period the Marine Corps sent to England Edson's future executive officer, Captain Samuel Griffith, and five NCOs to train with and observe the British Royal Marine Commandos. Their report confirmed Holcomb's views on the uses of light infantry units and convinced Edson that his men must be superior marksmen who were in top physical condition. From volunteers and men he recruited on the Quantico, Virginia, rifle range—essentially the cream of the Fifth Marines—Edson formed the 1st Raider Battalion, activated in February 1942. Its senior NCOs were men with ten to fourteen years' experience who had learned guerrilla warfare while fighting in Nicaragua's jungles during the 1930s.

At their Quantico base the Raiders trained hard. Before reveille they ran a mile to the rifle range, where they performed calisthenics and then ran back for breakfast. A full day of training followed. On their daily hikes the Raiders strove for an extraordinary seven miles per hour marching pace—twice normal speed. Once, they hiked with full field packs thirty miles from Quantico to the Manassas Civil War battlefield and returned that night. On one hike company commander Captain Henry Cain dropped dead from heart failure; Edson did not ease up.

They practiced night maneuvers and trained in rubber boats on the Potomac River.

Edson invited retired Colonel Anthony Biddle to instruct the Raiders in bayonet- and knife-fighting. The sixty-five-year-old World War I veteran and hand-to-hand combat legend reportedly crouched empty-handed amid a circle of Raiders armed with bayonets and disarmed them all.

In April 1942 the Raiders were sent to Samoa as part of the American forces guarding the Fijis and New Hebrides. Edson kept them busy with live-fire exercises, close-combat training, rubber boat landings, night reconnaissance patrols, and daily training hikes on Samoa's steep ridges.

A reserved, soft-spoken man with cropped red hair and light blue eyes that were "cold as steel," the wiry Edson's gear at times appeared to be incongruously large on him. Observing how his helmet engulfed his small head, fellow officers called him "Eddie the Mole." He was better-known, however, as "Red Mike," having acquired the nickname in Nicaragua when he grew out his red beard during long patrols, Direct and succinct, Edson was liked and respected by his men for being fair and rewarding good work, but he was not known for his warmth. His executive officer, Griffith, who knew Edson better than nearly anyone, believed he was "in many ways a pretty cold man; I don't know how truly capable he was of loving his fellow man . . . that's just the way he was made."

At the same time that Commandant Holcomb established the 1st Raiders he also created the 2nd Raider Battalion at Camp Elliott near San Diego. Its commander was Colonel Evans Carlson, a minister's son whose egalitarianism—and inspirational slogan, "Gung Ho!," meaning work together—became the battalion's hallmark. During duty tours in China during the 1930s Carlson accompanied Mao Tse-tung and his army on the Long March and into combat against the Japanese. Carlson deeply admired Mao.

Holcomb ordered Edson to send Carlson a company of 1st Raiders to become the nucleus of the 2nd Raiders. After unhappily complying, Edson was outraged to learn that Carlson had rejected half of Edson's officers and most of the enlisted men.

The livid Edson protested Carlson's rejection of his men as "an unjust and prejudicial attitude that has no foundation in fact." The fact that the rejected men were not permitted to return to the 1st Raiders further stoked Edson's anger. Time did not mitigate Edson's dislike of Carlson, and the bad feeling filtered down to his battalion, whose loathing of the Second Raiders was "second only to our feelings for the Japanese," wrote one Raider.[28]

THE RAIDERS AND PARACHUTISTS HAD become thin on Gavutu and Tulagi from their skimpy rice-and-fish meals as well as dysentery and malaria. Poor diet and illness had melted away, on average, more than 20 pounds per man in just four weeks. Private First Class Turner Brown lost 40 pounds. Corpsman Leonard Lintz weighed 165 pounds when he landed on Gavutu; a month later he weighed 115.[29]

The day of their arrival on Guadalcanal, 300 Raiders were sent to Savo Island on the APDs *Little* and *Gregory* to investigate reports that Japanese troops had set up an observation and transmission station there. Finding no evidence of enemy activity, they returned to Guadalcanal. That night, as the two APDs patrolled offshore, a US aircraft mistakenly lit them up with flares, and they were shelled and sunk by three Japanese destroyers that had just landed reinforcements at Taivu Point. Thirty-three sailors died, 70 were wounded, and 238 were rescued. The Raiders mourned the sailors who had "literally cheered us over the side" while landing them at Tulagi. "They were part of us and we hurt for them," wrote Raider Captain John Sweeney.[30]

Because native scouts persisted in reporting an ongoing Japanese buildup near Taivu Point during the first week of September, Vandegrift's staff and Edson decided to execute a hit-and-run operation—the 1st Raiders' first and only such mission.

The Marines spent a miserable night on the APDs, the *McKean* and *Manley*, and a pair of former civilian tuna boats, YP-298 and YP-346—known in Navy vernacular as "Yippies"—waiting for dawn on September 8. "That was a night of utmost suffering and misery," wrote Sergeant T. D. Smith, who spent the seemingly endless hours on a Yippie. With no room to lie down on the deck, the Marines huddled together while sitting up. "With every roll, waves came over the deck. . . . We were awash in cold seawater and vomit. I thought morning would never come." At 5:00 a.m. the ships anchored five hundred yards from the village of Tasimboko near Taivu Point, eighteen miles east of Henderson Field, and began landing the 850 Raiders and parachutists. Hours earlier enemy reinforcements from General Kawaguchi's brigade had landed at the same spot. When they saw the US ships the newly arrived Japanese withdrew into the jungle from their prepared beachfront positions.

Near the beach the Raiders and paratroopers found ample evidence of the Japanese's recent arrival: several hundred neatly stacked field packs full of provisions. In a torrential rainstorm the Marines advanced toward Tasimboko's outskirts. Kawaguchi's rear guard suddenly lashed out at them with rifles, machine-guns, 37mm mountain guns, and 75mm howitzers fired pointblank by an artillery company from the Japanese 2nd Field Artillery Regiment. The artillerists fought alongside disabled soldiers that Kawaguchi had left behind when he led his main force into the jungle. Edson's men, whose heavy armament was limited to 60mm mortars, called in close-air support from Henderson Field. Following colored smoke and panel signals made by the Marines, the dive bombers and

P-400s pinned down the enemy troops. Edson's men were then able to encircle and kill most of them; the rest escaped. Twenty-seven Japanese died, and four guns were captured and destroyed.

Correspondent Richard Tregaskis, who had come along on the mission, struggled to keep up with Edson, "one of the quickest human beings I had ever known." Edson, Tregaskis wrote, "with his humorless grin . . . did not relax. He moved his troops ahead fast, barked at them when they failed to take proper cover." The Japanese disappeared into the jungle, leaving behind an assortment of weapons, including the 75mm guns, and cases of ammunition and supplies stacked ten feet high. There were sacks of rice, cases of canned crab meat and roast beef, sake and beer, a complete radio station, and ten collapsible boats.

The Marines destroyed most of the loot; there was simply too much to carry back with them. After saturating the rice with gasoline, they burned most of supplies and huts in the village, and smashed Japanese rifles, throwing them into the sea with hundreds of antitank mines. But they kept the radio transmitters, six machine-guns, tins of food, sake, and medical supplies. The Marines also took with them the dress whites Kawaguchi had intended to wear when he accepted Vandegrift's surrender. They returned to Lunga Point with the general's uniform nailed to the mast of an APD.

At a cost of two killed and six wounded, the Raiders and parachutists had destroyed Kawaguchi's supply depot, the first of a host of crises his brigade would face. Patrols determined that four thousand or more enemy troops were marching to bivouac areas south and southeast of Henderson Field.

Before Edson's men pulled out, Tregaskis collected all of the enemy papers, notebooks, charts, and maps that he could find. When the strike force returned to Lunga Point, Tregaskis turned them over to the intelligence section at division headquarters. Among them were documents showing that Kawaguchi's objective was the airfield. There was also Kawaguchi's description of the ceremony at which Vandegrift was supposed to surrender his sword. When the general read it, he drily remarked, "It would have been kind of embarrassing, as I forgot to bring my sword with me!"[31]

THE NEXT DAY EDSON, DIVISION operations officer Colonel Gerald Thomas, and their staffs studied their maps and aerial photos of Henderson's southern perimeter, attempting to identify Kawaguchi's probable attack route. "This looks like a good approach," said Edson, pointing to the long, narrow coral ridge immediately south of the airfield. A dirt trail ran along its length; three hills rose from its crown: at its southern tip, Hill 80; six hundred yards to the north, the ridge's tallest feature, Hill 123; and overlooking the airfield, Hill 60. A lagoon lay between the ridge's west flank and the Lunga River.

The topography reminded Edson of tactical situations that he had faced in Nicaragua. The treeless ridgetop was covered with thick kunai grass. Dense rainforest pressed against the ridge from the east, west, and south, which would shield the enemy's movements until the moment of attack. The Japanese called the ridge "Mukade," meaning "centipede," because of the ravines radiating from it like insect legs. The ridge was undefended.

General Vandegrift did not think Kawaguchi would attack the airfield from the south; he believed an attack from the east, across Alligator Creek, or by sea, at Lunga Point, was likelier. On September 9, over the objections of his staff, Vandegrift had moved his command post to a screened shack on a northeastern spur of the ridge to escape the daily airfield bombings. The division's operations staff, with its phones and maps, moved into an adjacent tent.

Edson warned Vandegrift that he had moved to a dangerous spot, but Vandegrift refused to believe that his headquarters was now in the bull's-eye. When Lieutenant Colonel Merrill Twining raised the issue again, Vandegrift barked, "I may not always be right, but I'm always the general."

Making no headway in convincing Vandegrift that this was where the Japanese would attack, Thomas and Edson tried a new tack: if Edson's men moved out of the coconut grove at Kukum to the top of the ridge, they too could escape the falling bombs as well as rest and provide security for Vandegrift's command post. The general agreed to allow Edson's men to bivouac on the ridge and enjoy some R&R. The Raiders and parachutists hiked up the ridge on September 10. Edson told the Marines that it would be quieter there, but they suspected something was in the wind; in their experience the colonel had never sought peace and quiet.[32]

On September 10, Japanese Bettys, escorted by Zeros, bombed Henderson Field once more, and for the first time after a raid Lieutenant Herbert Merillat noticed that he was trembling. "It's annoying to react in this way, but I don't know what can be done about it." During the next day's bombing run some of the Bettys skipped the airfield and, to everyone's surprise, dropped five-hundred-pound bombs and "daisy-cutters" on top of the ridge, killing eleven of Edson's men. Japanese spotters on Mount Austen had radioed Rabaul that day to report that Marines were digging in on the ridge south of the airfield.[33]

Native scouts reported that thousands of Japanese soldiers were continuing to move southwestward, toward the area south of the ridge that Edson's men had just occupied. An Ultra bulletin from the Pacific naval command warned that a Japanese attempt to capture Henderson Field was imminent. "Enemy contemplating early attack Guadalcanal area," the bulletin said.

Vandegrift remained convinced that the attack would come from the sea or east of Alligator Creek, and not from the south. He did not reinforce Edson's small force of just over eight hundred men on the ridge. As the Raiders and paratroopers were fortifying their defensive positions on the ridge, Vandegrift ordered the parachutists to "clean up," because they were "looking like a bunch of Elizabethan pirates." Bushy-bearded, some of them had even begun wearing Japanese loincloths because their trousers had disintegrated. Their lapse in personal hygiene came from necessity; they drank and cooked with their rationed water, leaving none for shaving or cleaning. Bodily filth, which Marines were conditioned to detest, added to the accumulated miseries of hunger, thirst, sleeplessness, fevers, and diarrhea. Considering the manifold crises about to burst upon the Marines, personal appearance was the least of their concerns.[34]

THE NEWS FROM THE NAVY was uniformly discouraging. On September 9 Admiral Nimitz directed Admiral Ghormley to give General Douglas MacArthur "experienced amphibious troops" for his future operations. Ghormley well knew that the Marines on Guadalcanal were his only amphibious troops and could not be spared. But he asked Richmond Kelly Turner, Guadalcanal's amphibious commander, for his opinion. "It was impracticable to withdraw" the Marines, Turner said. The issue was not raised again.[35]

Then, on September 10, Ghormley addressed an alarming top-secret message to Nimitz that said his losses during the past month might prevent him from supporting further operations in the Solomon Islands. Vandegrift was not on the bulletin's distribution list, but his operations chief, Colonel Thomas, picked up a copy when he was in Noumea and shared it with the general and his staff.

On September 11 Turner flew to Guadalcanal to meet with Vandegrift. He "seemed to be under a strain," Vandegrift observed, and he quickly discovered why when Turner handed him Ghormley's grim assessment, which Vandegrift had already seen. Ghormley had also said, Turner told Vandegrift, that the Japanese were going to launch a massive sea, air, and ground attack on Guadalcanal in two to three weeks. Because of shortages of ships, planes, and adequate supplies, Ghormley did not believe he could support the Guadalcanal operation much longer.

This message reflected the "spirit of defeatism" and confusion that New York Times correspondent Hanson Baldwin had sensed during a recent visit to Ghormley's Noumea headquarters. It was also around about this time that Major General Millard Harmon, the senior Army commander under Ghormley, told General George Marshall in Washington that there was "considerable room for doubt" about whether the Marines could hold. Then, very likely because of the prevailing pessimism, General Hap Arnold, the Army Air Force chief, had refused to send a dozen high-altitude P-38 fighters to Guadalcanal, evidently fearing they would be wasted in a lost cause. Prophesied defeat could be self-fulfilling.[36]

Turner handed Vandegrift a second message, handwritten by Ghormley on "social paper." It authorized Vandegrift to make "decisions or arrangements" if dire circumstances so dictated. In other words, it appeared that Ghormley was authorizing Vandegrift to surrender. The general handed the messages to Thomas and told him they would discuss them later.

Turner, who had brought some scotch, now poured drinks. He did not think the situation was as bleak as Ghormley believed it to be, and he told Vandegrift he would bring the Seventh Marines from Samoa to Guadalcanal through the Japanese submarine cordon between the Fijis and the Solomons. Turner, who sometimes thought himself a field general as well as an admiral, wanted to distribute small units of the Seventh Marines all over the island to repel Japanese landings, and he also advocated building a new airfield at Aola, about ten miles east of Taivu Point. Vandegrift strenuously objected to Turner's plan for the Seventh Marines. The regiment, he said, must be kept intact to be used as a strike force. Henderson Field was the prize, he reminded Turner, urging him to land the regiment at Lunga Point.

The general met in the morning with Thomas to discuss Ghormley's messages. "Jerry," Vandegrift said to Thomas, "we're going to defend this airfield until we no longer can. If that happens, we'll take what's left to the hills and fight guerrilla warfare." He told him to swear Lieutenant Colonel Merrill Twining to secrecy and have him draw up contingency plans.

Twining was certain that the division would defy Ghormley's expectations. "The division as a whole had never become totally engaged and in a final showdown remained capable of putting up a finish fight exceeding anything the Japanese had yet encountered."

Vandegrift told his old friend Geiger, Guadalcanal's air commander, what Ghormley had said, adding that he would stay "come hell or high water, Navy or no Navy." If the Marines could no longer hold the perimeter, Vandegrift wanted Geiger to fly out the planes. Geiger replied, "Archer, if we can't use the planes back in the hills we'll fly them out. But whatever happens, I'm staying here with you."[37]

GUADALCANAL HAD BECOME WHAT NAVAL historian Samuel Eliot Morison characterized as a "meeting engagement," much like 1863 Gettysburg—a place of little intrinsic value where both sides had committed themselves to an escalating struggle. The victor would gain a modest strategic advantage: from Guadalcanal the Japanese might interdict the US-Australian sea lanes, while the Americans, if they triumphed, might begin to march through the Solomon Islands to Rabaul. The island lacked any natural resources of use to Japan's or America's war industries, and the battleground was nearly devoid of civilians. In the latter respect it was strangely anachronistic—an eighteenth-century-style battle waged far from cities by modern armies with modern weapons. Guadalcanal's jungles, mountains, and the remote battlefield's difficult logistics had limited the struggle's scope, although not its intensity.[38]

During the run-up to Kawaguchi's attack, Japanese warships shelled the airfield every night. Sometimes twice daily, two dozen bombers escorted by Zeros from the 11th Air Fleet struck Henderson Field. The Cactus Air Force gamely rose to "Angels 20" each day to shoot down a half-dozen or so, but attrition steadily diminished the number of flyable US fighter planes until there were fewer than a dozen. At this critical juncture, as Kawaguchi's men assembled in the dense rainforest south of the airfield, Ghormley's defeatism threatened to jeopardize the operation.

It was the campaign's darkest hour. Hanson Baldwin was surprised to discover upon arriving on Guadalcanal that "we were just holding onto Henderson Field by the skin of our teeth. We didn't have any other foothold on the island. We just had this narrow enclave." Baldwin asked Vandegrift point-blank, "Are you going to hold this beachhead, general; are you going to stay here?" Vandegrift replied without hesitation, "Hell, yes. Why not?"[39]

Admirals Nimitz and Ghormley, meanwhile, tried to reinforce the Cactus Air Force so it could help thwart the expected Japanese offensive, adding sixty planes between September 11 and 13. The Japanese air force at Rabaul, however, increased its air fleet by more than one hundred planes.[40]

AROUND THIS TIME VANDEGRIFT ASKED Nimitz's headquarters to send him one hundred gross of condoms. The request arrived in Hawaii in the middle of the night, and an aide, thinking it might be an important coded message, awakened the admiral. After he had read the message, Nimitz smiled and said, "General Vandegrift is probably going to use them on the rifles of his Marines to keep them out of the rain."[41]

ON SEPTEMBER 12, RAIDER MAJOR Ken Bailey emerged from a transport plane at Henderson Field. Although still recovering from their wounds on Tulagi, Bailey and Lieutenant Astle Ryder had gone AWOL from the naval hospital on New Caledonia and hitched a ride to Guadalcanal. They brought with them mail bags that had accumulated in the rear area over the past six weeks. The Raiders' and parachutists' first mail call of the campaign lifted the men's spirits at a pivotal moment. Besides receiving scores of letters, one Marine, who had not brushed his teeth in more than five weeks, received a toothbrush; within minutes he was offered $50 for it, but he refused to sell.

While his men caught up on news from back home, Edson warmly welcomed the return of the smart, energetic Bailey, his best company commander. Rather than send Bailey back to his former command at C Company, Edson kept him close by as a "roving linebacker," or troubleshooter, for the coming battle.[42]

Edson's men quickly recognized that the ridge was no rest area, although Griffith, the Raiders' executive officer, gamely tried to promote the idea. "Too much bombing and shelling here close to the beach," he told them. "We're moving to a private spot." The Raiders' suspicions were confirmed when Edson told them to round up all the barbed wire they could find. Under a broiling sun they were driven to dig foxholes, open firing lanes, and carve machine-gun positions from the hard coral that underlay the thin topsoil. They dug with folding shovels, bayonets, helmets, and even mess kits—there being few standard shovels or entrenching tools available.[43]

How to defend the ridge with just eight hundred or so lightly armed men posed a tricky tactical problem. Lacking the numbers to create a continuous line and unsure which part of the ridge the Japanese might strike, Edson established a series of mutually supported strongpoints. He believed it would be unwise to concentrate all his men on the ridge crest because the Japanese might simply bypass the ridge and storm the airfield.

His solution was to divide the ridge between the paratroopers to the east and the Raiders to the west and to extend their lines down the ridge into the jungle, even if a concentrated Japanese attack might break them. Double-apron wire was strung along the top of the ridge. In the jungle below, the Marines looped single-strand barbed wire from tree to tree. The Raiders' C Company was positioned farthest from the ridge—to the west between the lagoon and the Lunga River. Edson's advanced command post was on the crest of Hill 123, about five hundred yards behind the ridge's south face. Farther to the north, in a ravine on the ridge's west side, were the battalion headquarters and the communications, medical, and intelligence sections.[44]

Edson inspected his lines and sent out patrols led by native guides to make contact with the Japanese; the patrols reported hearing voices and underbrush being chopped down. Edson and Griffith joined one of the patrols to get a feel for the battleground. Colonel Pedro del Valle, the Eleventh Marines commander, walked the front with his forward artillery observers and Edson. They identified potential enemy assembly areas and attack routes to target. Twelve 105mm guns from del Valle's 5th Battalion would provide artillery support from north of the ridge. The 2nd Battalion, Fifth Marines, which was positioned north of the airstrip, would be Edson's infantry reserve.[45]

Edson's officers established two- and three-man listening posts in the jungle, hundreds of yards in front of the lines, to warn of approaching enemy soldiers.

Sixteen-year-old Private Jim McCarson was sent to one of these so-called Cossack positions. He sat back-to-back with another Raider and tried to control his rising terror. McCarson had lied about his age in order to enlist in the Marines at fifteen, but he might now have repented his haste in getting into the war. "We could hear everything," he said. "Even the crickets sounded like sirens."[46]

Edson's pep talk to his staff officers and battalion commanders emphasized that the ridge had to be held at all costs. If it fell, Henderson Field would be lost, and "it'll be us, not the Japs, roaming the jungles and eating raw coconuts." After the meeting broke up, Edson's words filtered down through the ranks. Platoon Sergeant Joe Buntin told his men manning one of the Cossack positions, "The word is nobody moves, just die in your holes."[47]

THE JAPANESE DEPLOYMENT WAS CHAOTIC. It was an ordeal for Kawaguchi's men simply to reach the staging area south of the ridge; they used marine charts and compasses to navigate in a "zigzag pattern" through the rainforest. Along the twisting jungle trails the exhausted soldiers soon jettisoned most of their artillery, every piece of which had to be carried. However, the Japanese persevered in manhandling a 75mm mountain gun, broken down into its dozen components, and a pair of 37mm antitank guns to the assembly point. There were plentiful 50mm "knee mortars," and four 81mm mortars survived the journey.

Seventeenth Army headquarters warned Kawaguchi that more US Marines were en route in transports to Guadalcanal. Consequently he moved up the date of his attack from September 13 to September 12. The accelerated timetable left Kawaguchi's brigade no time to reconnoiter the Marine positions, and it reached the place from which it would launch the attack after dark on September 12.

The attack order issued that day was an admixture of bravado and fatalism. "Tomorrow after our victorious defeat of the American troops, we will enjoy the treat of President Roosevelt's rations, so eat everything we have to fortify ourselves completely, for we shall win or we shall die, and we'll not need them in retreat."

Not every unit that was supposed to participate in the multiprong assault was present. Colonel Meinosuke Oka's 2nd Battalion, 124th Infantry, was still cutting its way through the jungle, miles from its attack position. Captured Japanese documents indicated that, too late, infantry officers recognized the need for "woodcutters' equipment," compasses, and small whistles to help units maintain contact.

Cactus pilots had bombed Oka's barges in the Slot, inflicting heavy casualties and sending most of Oka's food to the ocean bottom. After landing, Oka reorganized his remaining six hundred men. The battalion was supposed to be taken by barge from Kamimbo Bay, on the western side of the island, to the mouth of the

Matanikau River, but the amphibious mission was scratched because Cactus air attacks had damaged or sunk most of the barges. Instead, Oka's men marched at a snail's pace toward the ridge from Kamimbo, over corduroy ridges and through deep, jungle-choked valleys.

The accumulated lapses in judgment and execution might not have mattered against the inferior armies of China, Borneo, or Sarawak, but they would now. Vice Admiral Ugaki, Admiral Yamamoto's chief of staff, after being briefed that day by confident Seventeenth Army officers on the impending attack, evidently sensed this when he wrote in his diary, "I can't help entertaining much doubt about the success of the night assault with lightly equipped soldiers. They should be wary of their own conceit."[48]

THE OVERTURE TO THE ATTACK commenced a little after 9:00 p.m. when the eight- and five-inch guns of the Japanese cruiser *Sendai* and her three destroyer escorts plastered the ridge and nearby area for over an hour. It was the first of two bombardments that night. Although terrifying to everyone who endured the barrage, the Raiders and parachutists suffered no casualties, mainly because most of the shells failed to explode. A second naval bombardment at midnight targeted the airstrip and the ridge's east side.[49]

Below the ridge Kawaguchi's weary battalions floundered in the inky-black jungle. Only the 1st Battalion, 124th Infantry reached its assembly point at nightfall to carry out its assault on schedule. Oka's battalion, which was supposed to attack from the west, was miles away. Kawaguchi's right wing, the Kuma Battalion, whose mission was to push toward the airfield from the southeast, would also miss the fight. The 124th's 3rd Battalion and the 2nd Battalion, 4th Infantry, blundered around the rainforest for hours. So confusing was the situation in the crypt-like darkness that it was unclear whether either battalion got into the battle at all, aside from probes made against the paratroopers on the ridge's east side.

Kawaguchi and his command group tried to ford the Lunga River, and emerged soaked, muddy, and frustrated. "Due to the devilish jungle, the brigade was scattered all over and was completely beyond control," he said. "In my whole life I have never felt so disappointed and helpless." There would be no coordinated Japanese attack.[50]

Major Yukichi Kokoshu's 1st Battalion did what it was supposed to: it managed to wade the Lunga and then proceed to flank and overrun part of the Raiders' C Company in the rainforest between the river and the lagoon below the ridge.

When enemy troops suddenly flooded C Company's area, the Raiders fell back toward the lagoon and ridge. A bottleneck developed at a log bridge that was the lagoon's main crossing. The Japanese cut off a platoon and with machetes and bayonets hacked some Marines to death.

Others were captured, interrogated, and tortured with knives. Their shrieks of agony unnerved their comrades. "It was horrible and frightening hearing our small group of overrun Raiders screaming as the bastards bayoneted and hacked them with their samurai swords," wrote Private First Class Joseph Rushton. The wounded hid in the jungle when they could.

The Japanese got behind Private Robert Youngdeer's machine-gun section, and as he tried to aid a Marine who had been shot through the legs, a sniper shot Youngdeer under his nose. When he regained consciousness Youngdeer was able to walk and crawl to the ridge. Sergeant Pappy Holdren, who led two wounded Raiders to safety, had fought in World War I at Belleau Wood and the Argonne but said the jungle battle at the lagoon was "the worst situation I've ever been in."

Kawaguchi's uncoordinated attack ended at dawn September 13, when Raiders fought their way down from the ridge to the lagoon and rescued wounded men who had survived the harrowing night.[51]

Edson sent combat patrols into the jungle south of the ridge to establish advanced positions, but they made little headway. He also sent two companies to break up the Japanese salient west of the ridge, near the lagoon. But they had no better luck than the combat patrols. They instead reorganized their lines where the previous night's action had occurred. C Company, which had absorbed the main attack, was pulled back to the ridge, and A Company was sent below the ridge in its place. During the night's fighting one Marine was reported killed and eleven were missing.[52]

That morning, September 13, Edson convened a meeting of his company commanders while he sat on a log eating cold hash from a can. "They were testing, just testing," Edson said. "They'll be back." He told his officers to improve their positions and to give their men a hot meal. "Today, dig, wire up tight, get some rest. We'll need it." With a humorless smile Edson added, "The Nip will be back. I want to surprise him."[53]

The surprise would be a sanguinary one. Edson pulled back his line 400 yards from the ridge's southern extremity to positions 150 yards from Hill 123, the ridge's highest point and his command post. He made his lines more compact along the ridge's east and west sides, moving the western defenses 300 yards to the north. Two platoons of B Company were sent into the jungle as pickets; they were to warn of the enemy's approach and funnel attackers into preregistered artillery "kill zones."

Enemy attackers who reached the ridgetop would now have to cross a hundred yards of open ground to get into the Marine positions. Edson's machine-gunners grimly eyed the exposed area before them in anticipation.[54]

HAVING HEARD NO REPORTS ABOUT the night's attack, the Japanese command in Rabaul sent a pair of scout planes and a Zero escort to Henderson Field in the morning to find out whether Kawaguchi had captured it. Aircraft from the 25th and 26th Air Flotillas were poised to fly in and land for the surrender ceremony if he had.

Even when Wildcats met the Japanese formation over Henderson and shot down four Zeros, the Japanese observers were reluctant to accept Kawaguchi's failure. Just in case he had succeeded, the 11th Air Fleet, when dispatching its usual midday bombing run to Guadalcanal—on this day twenty-seven Bettys and twelve Zeros—diverted the mission to Taivu Point. The air force did not want to bomb Kawaguchi's men if they had captured Henderson, and they believed Marines were still at Taivu Point. The Japanese were wrong on both counts. The Marines were at Henderson, not Taivu Point. The 11th Air Fleet bombed Kawaguchi's rearguard troops at Taivu as they futilely displayed Japanese flags to stop the attack.[55]

DURING THE NAVAL BOMBARDMENTS THE previous night, Admiral Turner, still on the island consulting with Vandegrift, had crouched with him in the general's dugout, uncomfortably close to where the rounds were landing. One shell struck a nearby medical aid station. Vandegrift and Turner examined the blood-stained wreckage the next morning. Shaken by his experience on the island, Turner told Vandegrift before boarding an aircraft leaving that morning, "When I bring the Seventh Regiment in I will land them where you want."[56]

SENT BY VANDEGRIFT TO LOOK over Edson's positions that afternoon, Lieutenant Colonel Merrill Twining was shocked by the condition of Edson's men: "glassy-eyed, mumbling their words and displaying the mechanical high-stepping gait that betrayed utter exhaustion." Yet "their awareness of the gravity of the situation was obviously far greater than our own," he wryly noted. Since the Tasimboko raid the Raiders and paratroopers had slept little. Jungle rot had eaten away their socks, underwear, and footwear (the Army, taking pity on the Marines, sent twenty thousand pairs of shoes from their own stocks). Malnutrition, dengue fever, dysentery, diarrhea, and malaria were rampant in their ranks.

Twining went to see Edson at his command post. The colonel had not slept at all, and he had been busy all that day. "Edson seemed terribly fatigued, but he was in far better shape than anyone else up there," Twining observed. When he returned from his inspection Twining recommended that Vandegrift reinforce Edson with the 2nd Battalion of the Fifth Marines.

But Vandegrift stubbornly persisted in believing that the Japanese main attack would come from the east, not the south. He grudgingly consented only to move two of the Fifth's infantry companies closer to the ridge. Twining later criticized

Vandegrift for "not listening more attentively to Edson's views and estimates of the threat confronting him. . . . Edson felt that we had written him off and that he was very much on his own."[57]

During a late-afternoon inspection of his positions Edson stopped with Captain John Sweeney, the Raider B Company commander, and silently scanned his positions with his field glasses. Before leaving, Edson told Sweeney in his soft, raspy voice, "John, this is it. We are the only ones between the Japs and the airfield. You must hold this position." If the Raiders and parachutists could hold that night, he promised, the Fifth Marines would relieve them in the morning.[58]

AT 9:00 P.M. LOUIS THE Louse chugged overhead and dropped a pale green parachute flare over Henderson Field. It was the signal for seven Japanese destroyers off Lunga Point to begin shelling the airfield. The hour-long bombardment leveled coconut trees where the Cactus pilots and crews were bivouacked, creating squawking pandemonium among the noisy parrots that lived there. "The shells were cutting trees off right overhead," wrote Ensign Harold Buell, the Flight 300 dive-bomber pilot, "and the shrapnel was falling around us like hailstones. The whole thing was a nightmare." The Japanese destroyers sometimes overshot the airfield and hit their own men as they assembled for the main attack.[59]

Colonel Oka, whose sweat-drenched 2nd Battalion, 124th Infantry was hacking its way through the dense jungle to the battlefield, had asked Kawaguchi to delay the night's attack for a day so a battalion that had just landed on the western part of the island, the 3rd Battalion, 4th Infantry, could participate. Aware that he had lost the advantage of surprise by attacking the previous night when he was unready, Kawaguchi refused to delay, although if he had waited, he might have attacked with six battalions rather than five.[60]

Kawaguchi summoned his officers to his staging area, three miles south of the ridge, to go over his battle plan for breaking through the Marine lines and capturing the airfield. Intelligence officers in Rabaul had told him that five thousand Americans defended Henderson. With his and Oka's combined force of more than four thousand soldiers, they would triumph, Kawaguchi predicted. "You must put the enemy to rout and crush them by daybreak. The time has come for you to give your lives for your Emperor." Kawaguchi's troops changed into fresh underwear in order to be clean when they died, and they stacked their packs. Officers made "Xs" with white tape on one another's backs so that their men could see and follow them in the dark.[61]

ON THE RIDGE THE MARINES tensely waited in the coiled silence, devoid of the usual insect noise and bird calls. Then an eerie chanting welled up from the rainforest below. Mantra-like, Japanese soldiers shouted over and over, "US Marine be dead tomorrow!" as they rhythmically slapped their rifle butts and hummed weirdly in harmony. They threw firecrackers to play on the taut nerves of the Raiders and parachutists. The Marines flattened themselves behind their rifles and machine-guns, laid out their hand grenades within arm's reach, and steeled themselves for what was coming.

Private Marlin "Whitey" Groft detected the sweet scent of chrysanthemums on the faint breeze—the Japanese used the extract from the chrysanthemum flower as lice repellant. Then came a wave of terrified small animals "scampering helter-skelter" ahead of the Japanese noisily advancing through the jungle.

The first attack, led by Major Kokoshu's 1st Battalion, 124th Infantry at 6:30 p.m., fell on Edson's right flank—the Raiders' A and B companies and an Engineers company that Edson had placed in the jungle west of the ridge.

Privates First Class Ed Shepard and Russ Whittlesey were in their holes near the lagoon where C Company had been mauled the previous night. Their B Company platoon was one of Edson's "speed bumps"; it would sound the alarm when attacked and funnel the attackers into the prepared artillery-fire zones.

In short order the Japanese overran Sheppard's and Whittlesey's platoon. Most of the Raiders managed to withdraw to the ridge, but Shepard and Whittlesey did not.

Shepard went down with gunshot wounds to both arms and through his right lung, and his rifle sailed into the lagoon. Whittlesey's rifle was blasted from his hands. As he worked frantically to staunch Shepard's bleeding, tearing his own filthy, threadbare shirt into strips for bandages, Shepard ordered him to leave him. "Go to hell, Shep!" snapped Whittlesey as he continued to administer first aid.

He helped Shepard to his feet, and they shuffled toward the ridge; they were behind enemy lines now. Three Japanese soldiers suddenly loomed before them in the inky-black darkness, fitfully lit by explosions and gunfire. Letting Shepard slip to the ground, Whittlesey confronted them with his only remaining weapon, his seven-inch stiletto. Whittlesey's Raider training in hand-to-hand combat took over, and he killed two of the enemy soldiers. The third one bayoneted Whittlesey in the back and ran away. Whittlesey fell to the ground. The wound was serious enough, but when Shepard turned his friend over, he discovered that Whittlesey was bleeding heavily from previous stomach wounds.

"Well, Shep, I guess this is where we came in," said Whittlesey, smiling dreamily. He hummed a few bars from a favorite tune, "I'm Getting Tired So I Can Sleep," closed his eyes, and died. Shepard painfully dragged himself up the ridge to the Marine lines.[62]

AT 10:30 P.M. A RED rocket flare signaled the beginning of the main attack on the center of the ridge. "*Totsugeki!*" cried the infantry officers—"Charge!" Kawaguchi's men surged forward. Mortar rounds whistled, and the air trembled with explosions that shot up geysers of dirt and sent shrapnel whirring. It was followed by a fusillade of crackling, hissing Japanese grenades. The enemy soldiers surged forward, crying "Death to Roosevelt!" and "Banzai!" The Marines arrayed under the brow of the hill lashed back with grenades and machine-guns that buzzed like rattlesnakes.

The fast-moving Japanese assault troops of Major Masao Tamura's 2nd Battalion, 4th Infantry emerged from a dense haze produced by smoke pots they had lit in a gully below the ridge. They raced up the south slope of the ridge, over Hill 80, and into the open area in front of the Raider positions around Hill 123.

In a draw beneath the southeast ridge the attackers dislodged two Parachute Battalion companies. The clouds of smoke gave birth to a rumor that flashed through their ranks—that "totsugeki" was a garbling of "Gas attack!" As the paratroopers fumbled for their gas masks in the smoky darkness, the Japanese, wielding knee mortars and bayonet-tipped Arisaka rifles, piled into them.

Fearing envelopment and remembering the horror stories of Great War gas attacks, the parachutists of B and C Companies sprinted to higher ground as word spread up and down the hill that they had been ordered to withdraw— although they had not. Their A Company comrades on top of the ridge saw them falling back toward them, uncovering their left flank. "There was a great deal of confusion and absolutely no evidence of a centralized command," wrote an A Company parachutist.

Colonel Pedro del Valle's twelve 105mm howitzers heaved and thundered in their positions below the ridge's north rim, and a curtain of metal descended behind the retreating paratroopers, carving gaps in the Japanese ranks and spraying the ridge's approaches with blood and severed limbs.

Officers on top of the ridge labored to stem the stampede. "Get back!" they shouted. "We are not pulling back!" Major Ken Bailey, acting this night as Edson's troubleshooter, waded into the milling parachutists, yelling that the smoke was for concealment and not a gas attack. Brandishing a pistol, Bailey, a commanding, six-foot-three figure, collared and slapped the running paratroopers as metal sliced the air around him. "The only difference between you and the Japs is they've got more guts! Get back!" he shouted. Bailey and other officers stopped the chaotic withdrawal at the ridge's highest point, Hill 123, and reorganized the parachutists for a counterattack.[63]

No sooner had Edson's men repelled the first assault than there came a second one, which they also threw back with grenades, machine-guns, and howitzers. The Japanese kept coming even when wounded many times. "You'd see the tracers go through them half a dozen times—one had to have been hit six or eight times—he'd go down and get back up again," wrote Private Jim McCarson, who saw a dying enemy soldier continue to crawl forward while dragging his intestines behind him. He expired ten feet from the Marine lines.[64]

EDSON CALLED CAPTAIN SWEENEY AT B Company on the radio to ask about his situation. A voice broke in, speaking in stilted English. "My position is excellent, sir!" Sweeney realized that the Japanese must have captured C Company's radio during the previous night's battle. To Edson, Sweeney said, "Cancel that last information, here's my situation," describing it so vaguely that the Japanese he presumed were eavesdropping could glean no worthwhile information. Radio communications were later turned over to Navajo "talkers" who spoke to one another in their native language—one that Japanese code breakers could not decipher. Even if they had cracked it, some Navajo translations would have confounded them—for example, "constant rain" meant "machine-gun fire."[65]

EDSON STALKED THE RIDGE TWENTY yards behind his horseshoe-shaped line around the base of Hill 123, ignoring the bullets that buzzed "like a bunch of hornets" around him, as his three understrength ridgetop companies of paratroopers and Raiders—little more than three hundred men—beat back multiple attacks. Private Groft fired magazine after magazine from his Springfield and threw grenade after grenade at the waves of Japanese coming at the Marines. "More and more just kept materializing out of the darkness, stepping over and on" their wounded and dead comrades.

The Japanese captured two Raiders and tortured them with knives and bayonets until their piercing screams could be heard above the roaring gunfire. The enemy hoped other Marines would come to their aid—and become additional victims. "The whole battalion could hear their screams," said Private Robert Youngdeer, wounded the previous night but returned to duty. The Raiders' discipline held. "The screams filled each one of us with a deep sense of outrage and helplessness, and a yearning for revenge," wrote Groft, whose platoon sergeant was one of those tortured to death.

The Raiders were making their last stand. Tamura's battalion and Major Kokoshu's 1st Battalion, 124th Infantry—without Kokoshu, killed with his sword in his hand at the outset of the attack—repeatedly tried to break through the center of the line. From the division command post at the northern base of the ridge the division operations officer, Colonel Gerald Thomas, could hear "screams and yells all night long," but he also heard a heartening sound: "Edson up there, barking." The Marines' fierce defense of the ridge—afterward known as "Bloody

Ridge" and "Edson's Ridge"—was due largely to one man, Edson. His iron will and fighting spirit inspired the men he had so carefully trained.[66]

Throughout the seemingly endless night del Valle's Eleventh Marines artillery played an equally important role in denying the ridge to Kawaguchi's assault troops—so much so that Japanese survivors described the battle as "artillery hell." The crack 105mm gun crews more than offset the enemy's numerical advantage by laying down the most intensive artillery concentration of the Guadalcanal campaign. The Marine guns broke up attack after attack. Even when del Valle's forward observer team was swept into the jungle and lost during the first attack, the artillerymen were able to sustain a crushing support fire. A Corporal Watson initially took over the team's duties of relaying telephone coordinates to the 105mm batteries, at times aided by Edson, who called in the target coordinates by radio. After one barrage landed just where he had requested it, Edson said, "Perfect. Now march it back and forth."

When Japanese mortar fire cut Corporal Watson's line, he raced to the communications center next to the division command post and phoned in Edson's last instructions to del Valle's gunners: "Drop it five zero and walk it back and forth across the ridge," he said. A few minutes later Edson's runner, Corporal Walter Burak, arrived to say that the range was excellent. "It's right on," he said. "It's knocking the hell out of 'em." Burak returned to the ridge while uncoiling a spool of communication wire that once more linked Edson and the artillerists.

Until communications were re-established with the front line, the artillerists sometimes resorted to firing "by ear"—they could plainly hear the bursting of their own shells and knew the terrain well enough to judge whether they were on target. The crews fired so quickly and continually—the Japanese later described the supporting fire as "automatic artillery—that gunners had to pour water on the barrels to prevent them from swelling. All night long the crews heard the shouted words, "Load! Fire! Load! Fire!" They fired more than two thousand rounds. The roar and flash of the guns transfixed Marines all around the perimeter. Private Robert Leckie, watching the "unbelievable" barrage from Alligator Creek, was "nowhere near either end of it, yet it made my teeth ache."[67]

TWINING LEFT THE DIVISION COMMAND post at 2:00 a.m. on September 14 to check on the situation on top of the ridge. When Twining got there the Marines were under a mortar barrage that was a prelude to a fresh assault. "Edson was up there roaring like a lion getting his men ready," Twining wrote. "Where he found such strength and energy I will never know. Thirteen hours before, I had thought him close to collapse, but he seemed to grow stronger as the night moved on." Edson warned Twining that the Japanese were poised to descend on the division command post "like shit through a goose."[68]

Edson had his hands full with multiple crises. Chief among them was a short-age of grenades and belted ammunition. There was also the problem of the para-chutists' commander, Major Charles Miller, who had remained in his foxhole while his men were leaving their positions below the east side of the ridge. Edson appointed the aggressive Captain Harry Torgerson in Miller's place.

Torgerson's first assignment from Edson was to stop the Japanese from envel-oping the left side of the ridge. Edson ordered him to lead the paratroopers' B and C Companies, which had withdrawn to Hill 123, in a bayonet counterattack to restore their position on A Company's flank. "Do you want to live forever?" Torgerson cried, echoing the words of Sergeant Dan Bailey at Belleau Wood twenty-four years earlier. "Follow me!" They attacked through a hailstorm of Nambu machine-gun fire and, in a brutal hand-to-hand fight, drove the Japanese from the left side of the ridge. During the assault 40 percent of the attacking par-achutists became casualties.

The Japanese attacked again; to Platoon Sergeant George Kelly they resembled an ant swarm. Parachutist Tom Lyons crawled through the eighteen-inch-high kunai grass right up to one of the fast-firing Japanese machine-guns, stood, and threw a grenade. The Japanese gunner stitched Lyons up the middle, knocking him to the ground. Then an enemy soldier stepped on his stomach to see whether he was still alive; when Lyons's eyes flew open, the Japanese bayoneted him in the throat.[69]

Edson and Bailey stood in plain view behind the firing line, talking on field telephones to the company commanders and bringing the howitzer barrage ever closer to where they stood. Private John Ingalls, acting as their bodyguard, lay on the ground, sweeping the oncoming Japanese with his BAR. Sniper bullets plucked at Edson's clothing, pierced Bailey's helmet, and nicked his cheek, splashing his face with blood. Neither man sought cover. "How is he not getting killed?" wondered paratrooper Peter Crocco. At one point Frank Gilbert, a machine-gunner, was standing beside Edson when a sniper's bullet struck near his head. The champion marksman picked up a rifle, aimed, fired, and a sniper fell from a tree, dead.

Richard Tregaskis described Edson as "the bravest, most effective killing ma-chine I met in fifteen years as a war correspondent." He could "wither a man with his China-blue, gimlet eyes . . . as purposeful as a killer's and as unemotional as a shark's." The Marines had the right man at the right place at the decisive moment.

Many Marines did not expect either officer to be alive in the morning and would not have bet on their own chances either. Exhausted, outnumbered, and running out of ammunition, some Raiders began to doubt. "There were so many of them that came over the ridge . . . you could shoot two and there would be six more," observed Private McCarson.[70]

Edson stood on the ridge's highest point and bellowed, "Raiders, parachutists, engineers, artillerymen. I don't give a damn who you are. You're all Marines. Come up on this hill and fight!"[71]

At 2:30 a.m. another red flare arced into the sky. The Japanese plastered the ridge with mortar fire and attacked again. "There was never a moment [until dawn] that there were not Japs in front of us," wrote Captain William McKennan, whose paratrooper company defended the left side of the Hill 123 horseshoe.

The Marines rolled grenades downhill into the assault troops. The machine-gunners peripatetically fired and moved—because the muzzle flashes gave away their positions. They went through belts of .30-caliber ammunition in minutes. "More grenades, more machine-gun belts!" shouted Edson to his operations officer, Captain Jake Irwin. Officers and NCOs from Edson's command post fetched cases of grenades and boxes of belted ammunition and distributed them.

AS THE CRY OF "CORPSMAN!" rang out all night on the ridge, Navy corpsmen risked death to aid the fallen Marines. In William Laing's medical pack were loaded morphine syrettes sealed in tin foil, ready for instant use; quarter grain morphine tablets; two-ounce brandy bottles; and a portable surgical saw that he sometimes used to remove mangled arms and legs that were hanging by threads. Most of the emergency treatment was dispensed at the forward aid station, a tiny tent constructed of ponchos, bits of canvas, and pieces of shattered palm trees. Inside, two corpsmen and a doctor performed emergency surgery on a succession of wounded Marines, while sending the most critically injured men down the ridge by truck to the field hospital.

The doctor's hands "moved as quickly as a card dealer shuffling a deck of cards," wrote Laing, who became a casualty himself while trying to reach a wounded Marine. When he found his patient a Japanese soldier Laing had presumed to be dead stabbed him through the right leg with a bayonet. Laing cried out in pain, and a Marine in a nearby foxhole shattered the enemy soldier's chest with a BAR blast. Laing yanked out the bayonet, doctored himself, and then proceeded to aid the wounded Marine he had intended to treat as well as others as he crawled over corpses under fire.[72]

Private Lewis Johnson, wounded by grenade fragments in the leg, was in the bed of a small truck transporting wounded men to the field hospital when a Japanese machine-gunner shot the driver. The truck coasted to a stop, and the gunner continued firing, killing three wounded Raiders. Johnson painfully dragged himself to the cab, got in, and tried to start the truck. When it would not start, he repeatedly ignited the starter, hiccupping the truck forward three hundred yards and over the hillcrest. Gravity then helped him clutch-start it, and he drove it the

rest of the way to the hospital. Johnson returned to the ridge in the truck and retrieved more wounded men. The hospital treated more than two hundred casualties that night. Eight corpsmen and a doctor were awarded Navy Crosses.[73]

AT 4:30 A.M., AFTER ANOTHER heavy mortar bombardment—dismaying to the
exhausted Marines, who wondered when it would ever end—another wave of attackers tried to drive Edson's men from the ridge. "It is our sincere belief that all
is lost, and our only chance of escape will be to sneak through to the coast for a
naval pickup," lamented one defender.

Edson called Colonel Thomas at division headquarters and said, "I've been hit
hard. I need some men." Lieutenant Colonel William Whaling, a shooting team
comrade of Edson's back in 1921 whose 2nd Battalion, Fifth Marines was in reserve, led a company up the ridge. The reinforcements were fed into Edson's
horseshoe around Hill 123.[74]

As daybreak approached, a Japanese company from Major Tamura's 2nd Bat-
talion, 4th Infantry pushed past Vandegrift's headquarters and overran part of an
Engineers company guarding the new Fighter One airstrip east of Henderson.
Engineers and other Marines counterattacked and drove them back into the jun-
gle. At least one Japanese soldier reached the parked planes—and discovered that
Edson had taken the precaution of assigning a Raider to guard each one.

Ensign Harold Buell was walking to his dive bomber for the dawn patrol when
he saw a Raider sitting in the cockpit, cleaning his automatic rifle. Buell nearly
tripped over the body of a Japanese soldier and then noticed "a large bloody
smear" from the cockpit to the wing flaps. The tall, thin Raider stepped out of the
cockpit and told Buell that he had waited until the enemy soldier climbed onto
the wing and was about to toss a grenade into the cockpit. The young Marine
jammed his BAR into the man's chest and gave him a burst. "Then I pulled him
off the wing so you guys can fly this thing," he said. Buell thanked him.[75]

As Edson had predicted, two Japanese soldiers and an officer swinging a samurai sword rushed General Vandegrift's command post just before dawn. The
enemy officer killed a sentry before Warrant Officer Sheffield Banta shot him
dead. A second soldier was tackled and killed, and the third one ran away.[76]

At daybreak Whaling led the rest of his Fifth Marines battalion to the ridge
and relieved the Raiders and paratroopers. They went to Whaling's bivouac and
had breakfast. "We were pretty badly chewed up; the parachutists took quite a
flogging," said Griffith, the Raiders' executive officer. Bloody Ridge would be the
parachutists' last fight on Guadalcanal.[77]

AT 6:30 A.M. THREE SHARK-TOOTHED Army P-400s from the 67th Fighter
Squadron lifted off from Henderson Field to attack one hundred Japanese troops

reportedly crowded beneath the ridge's southernmost outcropping. Major Ken Bailey and Sergeant Major Jim Childs had drawn a crude map for Army Captain John Thompson, asking him to root out the Japanese with his ground-support planes because the Raiders could not get at them.

Reaching one thousand feet altitude, Thompson and his tiny squadron saw enemy troops massed below them in a clearing. The Army pilots dove to treetop level and, in two passes, slaughtered the surprised soldiers with their .30- and .50-caliber machine-guns and 20mm cannons. Two of Thompson's planes, hit by ground fire, glided back to the airfield and made dead-stick landings. General Roy Geiger rewarded Thompson with a bottle of whiskey, and Vandegrift put him in for a Navy Cross.[78]

IF KAWAGUCHI HAD ATTACKED THE ridge with his five battalions simultaneously, Edson's eight hundred men could not have withstood the onslaught. But only two battalions—possibly twenty-five hundred men—actually participated in the attack. A third one, Lieutenant Colonel Kusakichi Watanabe's 3rd Battalion, 124th Infantry, never went into action. Enraged by Watanabe's failure, Kawaguchi ordered him to commit hara-kiri, but then changed his mind and decided to give him another chance. It turned out that Watanabe had a foot infection and could not walk.

East of the ridge there still remained Kawaguchi's right wing, the Kuma Battalion, consisting of the Ichiki 2nd Echelon, the remnants of the 1st Echelon, and some engineers and artillerymen—together, more than seven hundred men under Major Takeshi Mizuno. During the night, the battalion went into action southeast of the perimeter near the upper Ilu River. Advancing across a plain, Mizuno died leading the initial assault. The fighting continued for several hours. In the morning, six Stuart tanks from the 1st Marine Tank Battalion were sent to dislodge the Japanese. The enemy's four 37mm antitank guns disabled three of the tanks, but the Kuma's attacks failed to reach the airfield.[79]

Late in the afternoon of September 14, after most of the fighting had ended, Kawaguchi's left wing—Colonel Oka's 2nd Battalion, 124th Infantry—finally reached the Matanikau River west of the airfield. During a brief, furious firefight, the 3rd Battalion, Fifth Marines, atop a ridge commanding the coastal road near the Matanikau, drove back Oka's men with 37mm antitank guns, mortars, BARs, rifle grenades, and small arms.[80]

ATOP BLOODY RIDGE, ON ITS slopes, and around its base lay hundreds of Japanese dead, three deep in places. Everywhere were scattered legs, arms, headless torsos, and torso-less heads. Wounded enemy soldiers called for help and detonated grenades when Marines approached to render aid. The few who were captured often shouted "Knife!" and pointed to their bellies, indicating they wished to commit *seppuku*. Raiders said that when the captives realized that no one was going to give them a knife, they appeared relieved and afterward made no attempt to kill themselves, having complied with the letter of the Bushido code.

Throughout the day work parties collected dead Marines' dog tags and loaded their corpses onto trucks bound for the cemetery, where they were unceremoniously dumped on the ground. One of them, paratrooper Tom Lyons, machine-gunned and bayoneted through the neck, was still alive.

When the truck was unloaded at the cemetery, Lyons was on top of the pile. When he began to stir, the terrified driver ran for help. Two corpsmen arrived in a Jeep and took Lyons to the division hospital. He survived.[81]

The Marines discovered that during the night Kawaguchi's men had dragged their 75mm regimental gun to the top of the ridge's southern tip, Hill 80, to fire at the Marines on Hill 123. But the gun never played a role in the battle; its firing pin was too short to detonate the shells. Marines found thirty to forty unfired shells scattered around the gun, each with a small dent in its primer. With a slightly longer firing pin, the gun could have shredded Edson's men with direct fire before del Valle's howitzers silenced it.[82]

One hundred four Marines were reported killed or missing, and 278 were wounded. The 1st Parachutist Battalion, which on August 7 had 397 men, was a shadow of the unit that landed on Gavutu, with just 86 effectives on September 14. It was withdrawn from Guadalcanal four days later. The Raiders reported 234 casualties.

At least 600 Japanese died during the attacks on the ridge, and another 200 were killed in the fighting east of the ridge where the Marines deployed tanks. Kawaguchi reported 505 wounded, but the actual figure was surely closer to 1,000.[83]

INS correspondent Richard Tregaskis toured the desolate battleground on September 14, wary of the snipers still firing from camouflaged treetop perches at the Marines on top of the ridge. "Small fires smoldered in the grass. There were black, burned patches where Jap grenades had burst. Everywhere on the hill were strewn hand-grenade cartons, empty rifle shells, ammunition boxes with ragged, hasty rips in their metal tops," he wrote. On the ridge's southern slope he saw about two hundred dead Japanese soldiers, "torn and shattered by grenades or artillery bursts, some ripped . . . by the strafing planes which we had seen this morning."[84]

AT NO OTHER TIME DURING the battle for Guadalcanal was the outcome as uncertain as during the night of September 13–14 atop Bloody Ridge—when Kawaguchi's assault troops got within a half-mile of Henderson Field and reached the edge of Fighter One. Not only were the Japanese attackers decisively repulsed with heavy losses; the Marines had also proven beyond any doubt that they could beat enemy soldiers once regarded as "supermen." A Japanese survivor paid the Marines a high compliment by acknowledging that they "have *seshin* [spirit] just like we do." Previously, some Marines were unsure whether "we could trust ourselves or not," wrote Sergeant Jim McEnery. "But what happened at the Tenaru and the Ridge gave us a hefty shot of self-confidence."

The 1st Marine Division's final report succinctly stated the reasons for the enemy's failure: a "preconceived scheme of maneuver was rigidly adhered to." It was a hopelessly complex plan, skillfully countered by the Marines tactical defensive changes. Moreover, "the enemy grossly underestimated either our strength, our fighting qualities or both." Two other important factors were Kawaguchi's failure to reconnoiter the Marine positions and his subordinate commanders' inability to improvise ways to exploit opportunities that arose. Inflexibility would be the hallmark of Japanese combat leadership in the months and years ahead. Bloody Ridge would prove to be the critical land battle of the Guadalcanal campaign—and arguably of the Pacific War.[85]

VANDEGRIFT, WHO HAD DOUBTED THAT the Japanese would attack the ridge, admitted that he should not have moved his command post next to what became a major battleground. He moved his CP back to its original location and recommended Edson and Bailey for Congressional Medals of Honor.

By insisting that the Raiders and parachutists repair to the "rest area" atop the ridge, Edson and Vandegrift's operations officer, Colonel Thomas, had prevented the Japanese from capturing the airfield—and winning the campaign. Edson had instantly grasped the ridge's strategic importance and improvised defensive plans—plans that changed with circumstances. He motivated and inspired his men by fearlessly exposing himself to enemy gunfire hour after hour while adjusting his lines and directing artillery fire.

One of his men described Edson's fatalistic attitude toward death as that of a martyr—which was surprisingly close to the truth. In a letter to his wife, Edson wrote, "I am firmly convinced that it is all in the hands of God, anyway, and so one should not worry too much about such things." Some of his men would have disagreed. Although they held Edson in high esteem, they thought he was sometimes too willing to risk their lives. Some of his men gave him the alliterative nickname "Mad Merritt the Morgue Master."[86]

IN A MESSAGE TO HIS superiors in Rabaul, General Kawaguchi reported his mission's failure. "Enemy resistance was unexpectedly strong, so that we suffered a great loss, including battalion commanders. We were forced to withdraw. After regrouping the remaining force on the west side of the [Lunga] river, we are going to plan our move." His battered battalions withdrew southward toward Mount Austen. About eight hundred able-bodied soldiers remained from the two battalions—originally twenty-five hundred men—that had attacked the ridge.

In his journal on September 15 Admiral Yamamoto's chief of staff, Ugaki, wrote that the dense jungle made it impossible for Kawaguchi to coordinate such a complex assault and that too few artillery pieces reached the battlefield. These failings arose from the "conceit" that Ugaki had observed in the Seventeenth Army command. "In short," he wrote of Kawaguchi's offensive, "they made light of the enemy too much. Their operational plans should be more flexible." A Japanese naval officer observed, "The Army had been used to fighting the Chinese."[87]

Grim though it was, Kawaguchi's report was sunnier than the excruciating Japanese retreat over the deep jungle valleys and high ridges, in which hundreds of wounded men were borne on litters in the suffocating tropical heat. By the time they reached Mount Austen their food was gone. They crossed the upper Lunga River, marching west. Becoming weaker by the day, the Japanese buried the few disassembled artillery pieces they had so laboriously borne to the battleground. A Lieutenant Matsumoto wrote, "I cannot help but cry when I see the sight of these men marching with no food for four or five days and carrying the wounded." Without food or medicine, the walking wounded collapsed beside the trail and were abandoned with the litter casualties that lacked men to carry them. The survivors traveled in loose groups, eating tree bark, moss, and betel nuts and drinking from puddles.

Toyoji Hashiba, a squad leader in an artillery battery of the Second Ichiki Echelon, was frustrated by being unable to aid the wounded, or to even share food with them because he had no food himself. At one point Hashiba and his men tossed hand grenades into a river to kill fish for eating. Finding the fish meat too bland, they instead "feasted mainly on the guts which tasted good and bitter." A Sergeant Kashichi described the forlorn retreat in a poem:

> "Flies swarm to the scabs
> No strength to brush them away
> Fall down and cannot move
> How many times I've thought of suicide."

On September 19, Kawaguchi's haggard, barefoot survivors joined their comrades at Kokumbona.[88]

Kawaguchi's defeat prompted Imperial General Headquarters to dispatch Lieutenant Colonel Masanobu Tsuji to Guadalcanal to assess the situation. Tsuji was a rising, influential figure on the Imperial General Staff who had helped plan the campaigns in the Philippines, Burma, Malaya, and the Dutch East Indies. His complaint that the Philippines campaign was not conducted with sufficient harshness resulted in the cashiering of Lieutenant General Masaharu Homma.

After touring Guadalcanal, Tsuji met with Admiral Yamamoto and representatives from the 11th Air Fleet and the Seventeenth Army and told them that the troops were eating weeds and shrubs to stay alive. He asked Yamamoto to send more food convoys. The Guadalcanal troops, Tsuji said, were now "thinner than Gandhi himself." Distraught over the report of the soldiers' suffering, Yamamoto promised more naval protection and even to use his flagship *Yamato* as an escort if needed. Tsuji emphasized that at least another army division must be sent to Guadalcanal and urged Yamamoto to add five high-speed destroyer transports for Tokyo Express runs.[89]

AT DAWN ON SEPTEMBER 18, transports appeared off Lunga Point. Aboard was the long-awaited Seventh Marine Regiment—forty-two hundred combat troops under Colonel John Webb, along with trucks, ammunition, supplies, and heavy construction equipment. While the transports were being unloaded, the destroyers *Monssen* and *MacDonough* shelled Japanese positions west of the perimeter.

The new arrivals were "doubly welcome," wrote Twining—first, they were fresh, well-trained, and well-armed troops, and second, they brought forty-three hundred drums of badly needed aviation fuel, tanks, artillery, engineers, aviation ground crews, communications personnel as well as a thousand tons of rations and post exchange supplies. The food was deeply appreciated because the Marines had run out of captured Japanese rice.

Pharmacist's Mate First Class Louis Ortega said the reinforcements landed with canned peaches, pancake mix, and Spam. They also brought food from New Zealand that initially shocked American palates: lamb tongue, sheep tongue, beef tongue, and calf tongue. Among the supplies were the condoms that Vandegrift had requested—to rain-proof rifle barrels and personal effects. The transports departed with 162 wounded men and the depleted 1st Parachute Battalion, bound for New Caledonia. There, while recuperating from Gavutu and Bloody Ridge, the battalion would build a paratrooper training camp.[90]

In April the Seventh Marines had been sent to Samoa to help protect the critical sea lanes between New Zealand, Hawaii, and the West Coast. Believing that the Seventh would probably be the division's first regiment to face the Japanese in combat, the Marine Corps had filled its ranks with some of the division's most veteran officers and noncoms. The Seventh Marines and a battalion of the Eleventh Marines artillery had sailed from Hampton Roads as the first expeditionary force of the war to leave the United States.

On Samoa, however, the Marines had seen no combat; the powerful gravitational pull of Guadalcanal's "meeting engagement" had shelved Japan's plans to conquer the New Hebrides, Fijis, and Samoa. Now that they were on Guadalcanal, however, the Seventh Marines would see plenty of action.

Admiral Turner had honored his promise to Vandegrift to convoy the regiment to Guadalcanal and to land them at Lunga Point. The Army Air Force had sent B-17 bombing raids against Rabaul to suppress Japanese combat air patrols. This had helped Turner's convoy slip through the Japanese submarine net southeast of Guadalcanal that had sunk the *Wasp* and damaged the *Saratoga* and *North Carolina*.[91]

THE 1ST MARINE DIVISION WAS at full strength for the first time on Guadalcanal. In addition to the division's nine infantry battalions there were the 1st Raider Battalion, five artillery battalions, and the 3rd Battalion, Second Marines from Tulagi. Vandegrift now commanded more than twenty thousand men. He created ten battalion-size defensive sectors.

Bloody Ridge had convinced Vandegrift of the perimeter's vulnerability to attack from the south. He reoriented his defenses so they mainly faced inland rather than seaward. A surprise enemy beach landing, he concluded, was now far less likely because of the presence of the Cactus Air Force. Henceforth, the beaches were closely guarded only at nighttime.[92]

With more than enough troops to defend Henderson's perimeter, Vandegrift wanted to now push westward to the Matanikau River. Vandegrift and his staff planned to establish a horseshoe-shaped position from the Matanikau's mouth to a crossing a mile upriver known as the Nippon, or Log Bridge. Electrically controlled antipersonnel mines would be sown on the river sandbar and booby traps at the bridge.[93]

TWO DECORATED, WELL-KNOWN OLD BREED Marines led the Seventh Marines' 1st and 2nd Battalions: Lieutenant Colonel Lewis B. "Chesty" Puller and Lieutenant Colonel Herman Hanneken.

Forty-nine-year-old Hanneken was five years older than Puller. He had enlisted in the Marine Corps as a private in 1914 and was commissioned five years later when he was sent to Haiti, where American troops were defending US economic interests against a series of peasant revolts. Hanneken tracked down and killed Charlemagne Peralte, a resistance leader, in his hideout and later killed Peralte's successor. These exploits earned him the Medal of Honor. In Nicaragua in 1929 Hanneken burnished his counterinsurgency reputation by capturing rebel chief Augusto Sandino's chief of staff, for which he was awarded the Navy Cross. He also won a second Navy Cross for his Nicaragua service.[94]

Puller had also won two Navy Crosses in Nicaragua after serving five years in Haiti. He was known throughout the Corps as opinionated and colorful, tough but fair. A Virginian who grew up listening to the war stories of aging Confederate veterans, he idolized Stonewall Jackson. Another of his heroes was Julius Caesar; for twenty years he had carried around in his pocket a grimy copy of Caesar's *Gallic Wars*. Younger officers admired Puller's skillful use of terrain and his hand-to-hand fighting prowess. Somewhat of an egalitarian, he believed officers should share their men's hardships; he did, marching along with them with a cold pipe clenched in his teeth. In the mess hall, his enlisted men ate first, followed by the noncoms. Officers ate last, and Puller last of all.[95]

When the barrel-chested Puller came ashore on Guadalcanal, Edson turned to his executive officer and said, "There comes the greatest fighting man in the Marine Corps. We'll have some competition now." After Puller had greeted his old friend Edson, Puller said, "Now show me where they are." A map was handed to him, and Puller, holding it upside-down, frowned at it. "Hell," he said, "I can't make head nor tail of this. . . . Just show me where they are!" The Marines pointed to the hills to the south. "All right," Puller said. "Let's go get them."

His men unloaded landing craft until dusk and bivouacked in a coconut grove near the beach. That night Japanese destroyers shelled the airfield area. Flying shrapnel and falling trees killed three of Puller's men and wounded a dozen others. During the shelling Puller tried to reassure his men. "This won't last forever," he said. "Tomorrow it'll be our turn."[96]

NINE DAYS AFTER THE BLOODY Ridge battle the Marines' embarked on their first major Guadalcanal offensive. It began inauspiciously and nearly ended disastrously. The Seventh Marines' arrival made it possible. Securing the Matanikau River area would prevent all but the largest-caliber Japanese howitzers from shelling the perimeter and give the Marines a platform for future operations to the west. His plan, Vandegrift said, was to use the Matanikau "as a line of resistance . . . bending back to the Ridge, not to the hills . . . and then launch offenses from there." An assortment of Japanese units lurked in the area, among them Colonel Oka's 2nd Battalion, 124th Infantry, which had arrived too late to join in the Bloody Ridge attack.[97]

Because the Seventh Marines' 1st Battalion was fresh and led by the aggressive Puller, Vandegrift selected it to conduct one of the operation's two drives over the Matanikau. Approaching from the Mount Austen area, it would cross the Matanikau at the Log Bridge and push into the area between it and Kokumbona ten miles to the west. The 1st Raider Battalion would make the second thrust, crossing the Matanikau estuary at the sandspit, and then advancing westward along the coastline to establish an operational base at Kokumbona.

But little went according to plan. The first day, September 23, was one of the better ones. On Mount Austen's northern slopes along the upper Lunga River Puller's men clashed with Japanese patrols and outposts and overran an enemy bivouac while the Japanese were at their rice fires. In the ensuing firefight Puller lost seven killed and twenty-five wounded.

Captain Jack Stafford, wounded in the face and neck when his rifle grenade prematurely exploded, was choking on his own blood. Puller unsnapped a large safety pin from his bandoleer and pinned Stafford's tongue to the roof of his mouth, saving his life. He radioed the division with the puzzling words, "Killed Japanese patrol under cloud six thousand yards south of Lunga Point." Division staff officers grasped Puller's meaning, though. On the aerial photograph that served as the division's map, a cloud obscured that particular area.

Puller sent back two companies—one should have sufficed—with his wounded, which included many stretcher cases. The 2nd Battalion, Fifth Marines arrived on September 25 to reinforce Puller's remaining company, C Company.[98]

Puller led his mixed command to the upper Matanikau and then down the narrow jungle path that followed the east bank, intending to cross the river at the Log Bridge, which was a mile from the river mouth. However, intensive Japanese mortar and machine-gun fire from the other side of the bridge made a crossing impossible. Puller radioed for artillery and air support, but they failed to dislodge the enemy troops firing on them from the ridges to the west.

Unable to cross the Log Bridge, Puller's men marched downriver to the Matanikau estuary, where they joined the Raiders, who had earlier tried and failed to cross the sandspit at the river mouth.

Enemy strength west of the river was much stronger than the Marines had anticipated; after Bloody Ridge the Kawaguchi Brigade had drifted into the area, and Colonel Oka's battalion had never left it. Including the fresh troops arriving nightly on the island's northwest coast, more than four thousand enemy lurked beneath the thick jungle canopy west of the Matanikau, invisible to aerial reconnaissance.

Edson was the new commander of the Fifth Marines, replacing Colonel LeRoy Hunt, who had not been aggressive enough to suit Vandegrift and was removed. Edson, Puller, and Lieutenant Colonel Samuel Griffith, the Raiders' former executive officer and now their commander, improvised a plan for September 27: the Raiders would march southward along the east riverbank, cross at the Log Bridge, and flank the Japanese on the western bank while the Fifth Marines' 2nd Battalion attacked across the river mouth. Puller's 1st Battalion would board boats at Lunga Point and go ashore at Point Cruz, a mile west of the river mouth and near where Colonel Goettge's patrol was slaughtered. Puller's men would then march eastward down the coastal road toward the river. Edson was in charge of this hastily conceived operation, with Puller acting as his assistant.[99]

What Griffith later described as a "series of blundering actions" began early on September 27 when the Raiders walked into an ambush. In obedience to Seventeenth Army orders, Japanese troops the previous day had crossed the Log Bridge to the east bank when Puller marched to the Matanikau's mouth. Enemy troops quickly established strong positions, supported by heavy mortars and automatic weapons.[100]

The Japanese barred the Raiders' way up the narrow river path, pinning them with a torrent of mortar and machine-gun fire and hemming them between ridges on their left and the river on the right. Major Ken Bailey, recommended for a Medal of Honor for his conduct on Bloody Ridge, was killed by machine-gun fire while leading the Raider column near the Log Bridge. A sniper shot Griffith in the shoulder as he climbed a steep ridge in an attempt to flank the Japanese. "Good shot," Griffith reportedly remarked as he was dragged to cover. The flanking movement failed.

Miscommunication made matters worse. A garbled radio report from the Raiders gave the mistaken impression that the Raiders had succeeded in crossing the Log Bridge to the west bank and were poised to push northward toward the sea. This misconception set in motion the battle plan's other element. Puller's A and B Companies—which had brought the wounded from Mount Austen to the perimeter—were ordered to proceed with the Point Cruz landing. Major Ortho Rogers, a reservist from Washington, DC, who was Puller's executive officer, commanded the operation in Puller's stead; Puller remained behind to assist Edson.

The three hundred men cast off in boats from Lunga Point without radios or their assigned naval support—the destroyer *Ballard*, which had taken evasive action from an enemy air attack.[101]

The Marines landed in two waves at Point Cruz without opposition and pushed inland about five hundred yards, nearly to the top of a ridge. But then mortar rounds began to explode around them. Major Rogers became one of the first to die when a mortar landed at his feet. "There was so little of him left we rolled the remains in a blanket," wrote Sergeant William Pennington. Within minutes a half-dozen others were killed.[102]

It quickly became clear that the Marines faced a large Japanese force that had deliberately allowed them to penetrate as far as they did in order to envelop and wipe them out. The Japanese pressed the Marines from three sides and attempted to cut them off from the beach. Captain Charles Kelly, who assumed command when Rogers was killed, hastily set up a perimeter on a knoll. The situation could scarcely have been worse. With no radio, the Marines could not summon help.

And then someone had the idea of spelling out "HELP" on the ground with T-shirts in the hope that the message would be seen from the air. The improvised SOS worked: a Marine dive-bomber pilot, Lieutenant Dale Leslie, spotted it and radioed the news to the Fifth Marines on the Matanikau.

Puller urged Edson to renew the assault across the Matanikau sandspit to prevent the Japanese on the west bank from joining the attack on Puller's Marines. But Edson refused. The Japanese across the sandspit were too well established, and the attack would fail, he said. Edson then ordered the withdrawal of the Raiders down the east riverbank.

Puller exploded. "Most of my battalion will be out there alone, cut off without support," he shouted. "You're not going to throw these men away!" He stalked off to the beach and flagged down a landing craft that took him to the *Ballard*, which had concluded its evasive action. The *Ballard* sailed to the Point Cruz beach with several landing craft in its wake to re-embark Puller's men.

With great relief, Captain Regan Fuller watched as the old World War I four-stacker appeared offshore. "She was boiling, with black smoke trailing out behind her," he wrote. When her guns rose to their firing position, Fuller thought it "a lovely sight."

Puller ordered the *Ballard* to shell the coconut grove between the knoll and the beach to clear it of enemy and then to fire along the Marines' flanks as they began withdrawing. By blinker and semaphore, the determined colonel conveyed his instructions to his men; from the knoll Sergeant Robert Raysbrook signaled back.[103]

With its five-inch guns *Ballard* began blasting a path from the knoll to the beach. "We all let out a cheer," a Marine said. "Trees were falling. Japanese were screaming, and we were yelling." With a high-pitched rebel yell, Fuller's men charged down the hill. Platoon Sergeant Andy Malanowski of Baltimore covered the withdrawal with his BAR until he was killed.[104]

Japanese gunfire repelled the first landing boats that approached shore. Puller leaped into one of the boats and led them in while Lieutenant Leslie strafed the enemy with his SBD and flew low to the water, guiding the boats to the evacuation points.

Coast Guardsmen captained the Higgins boats. In the lead boat were Petty Officers First Class Douglas Munroe and Ray Evans. When mortar and machine-gun fire caused another boat crew to balk at continuing toward shore, Munroe, jabbing his finger at the beach, shouted, "We're not leaving 'em there! We're going in!"

Bloodied Marines dashed into the surf supporting wounded comrades as Munroe brought the craft close to shore for loading and Evans covered them with a World War I–era machine-gun. "You came back! Thank God, you came back!"

cried one Marine. Munroe leaped into the other machine-gun turret and turned the boat around for the return trip to Lunga Point.

Seeing that another boat was hung up on a coral reef, Munroe reversed course. With a rope he towed the boat off the reef. As Munroe once more reoriented his boat for the return trip, a Japanese machine-gun bullet struck the base of his skull, and he fell to the deck. Evans drove the Higgins Boat back to Lunga. There he laid Munroe's head in his lap. Munroe opened his eyes and asked, "Did they get off?" Yes, said Evans. Munroe smiled, and died.[105]

Puller remained in a Higgins boat near the beach until all his men were evacuated. The fiasco cost his 1st Battalion eighteen killed and twenty-five wounded. Colonel Gerald Thomas, the division operations officer, credited Puller's "force of will" with having prevented his men's annihilation. Puller's battalion returned to Lunga Point, and all the units involved in the failed Matanikau operation were withdrawn to the division perimeter by midnight September 27.

UNTIL NOW PULLER HAD BEEN the only officer in his battalion with combat experience. He reviewed the recent days' fighting with his officers. "Gentlemen, at least we've all been blooded now. I don't want you to be mooning over our losses and feeling sorry for yourselves or taking all the blame on your shoulder. We've all got to leave this world some day . . . and there are worse things than dying for your country." Puller said that at Mount Austen he "had trouble getting company officers up. I hope you saw that cost us in casualties. . . . I want to see my officers leading." "Stark courage," he said, was an essential quality in an officer.[106]

The Second Battle of the Matanikau was "the only thoroughly unsuccessful campaign of the entire Guadalcanal campaign," wrote Lieutenant Colonel Merrill Twining. "A shambles, really," added Griffith, who was evacuated to New Zealand for medical treatment. He said that Vandegrift was understandably eager to hit the Japanese and gain a psychological edge before their reinforcements arrived. "But everything went wrong."

The operation quickly devolved into piecemeal, jury-rigged actions that were impaired by poor communications and nonexistent intelligence. Instead of facing a few hundred Japanese soldiers, as Vandegrift's staff believed, at least two thousand enemy troops were in the Matanikau area, and thousands more were nearby in Kokumbona.

The division's final report on the Guadalcanal campaign cited the Field Service Regulations' warning against "drifting aimlessly into action" and said the battle was "unpremeditated and was fought without definite purpose other than the natural one of closing with the enemy at once and upon every occasion." The cost of this exercise in futility was 67 killed and 125 wounded. Afterward Edson rarely spoke of the operation, the only failure of his career. When he did, he referred to it as the "abortive Second Matanikau."[107]

THE DAY AFTER THE OPERATION ended, Vandegrift was fuming over a letter from Admiral Turner advising him to continue "clearing out all the nests of enemy troops" and recommending that when the 2nd Raider Battalion arrived it should ferret out remote enemy outposts. The Marine general replied that captured Japanese documents showed that another big enemy push was imminent. The 2nd Raiders, he said, were needed to replace the decimated 1st Raiders.[108]

Vandegrift and his staff decided to do something about the division's erratic patrolling and reconnaissance, which too often resulted in units blundering into firefights against enemy forces of unknown size. Lieutenant Colonel Whaling, who led the 2nd Battalion, Fifth Marines, had volunteered to establish a scout-sniper detachment. Besides being one of the best marksmen in the Marine Corps, Whaling was an accomplished hunter and woodsman, as well as "rugged, fearless, physically like a rock." He selected men who had been avid outdoorsmen in civilian life. One was the middle-aged division postmaster, who was a deer hunter from the South; another was a large, red-bearded Marine known as "Daniel Boone," who became Whaling's acting first sergeant. Daniel Boone set such a fast walking pace that Whaling had to tell him to ease up.

Whaling's 100 to 125 volunteers sharpened their skills during long-range patrols. Then, they crossed the wire in pairs or alone and began bringing back valuable intelligence about Japanese numbers and positions. The scouts were sent back to their regular units to pass along their knowledge. Patrolling dramatically improved; there were fewer successful Japanese ambushes.

After Whaling's volunteers had taught their new skills to their comrades in their old units, they were reconstituted into a semipermanent "Scout-Snipers" unit. Its members initially served as guides and leaders for combat patrols, but as the unit grew in size, the scout-snipers acted as a separate entity during operations.[109]

SHOCKED BY THE DEFEATS AT Bloody Ridge and Alligator Creek, Imperial General Headquarters had suspended its New Guinea operation and had made recapturing Guadalcanal its top priority. The staffs of Admiral Yamamoto and Seventeenth Army commander General Hyakutake met in Truk to discuss the next step. The 2nd (Sendai) Division had already begun assembling in Rabaul for a new Guadalcanal push, but the Japanese leaders decided that this would be more than just another offensive—it would be the decisive one, conducted by twenty-two thousand infantrymen and supported by tanks and heavy artillery.

The buildup would require that at least seventeen thousand fresh troops land at night from destroyers in the coming weeks. "Whatever happens, we must succeed in the coming operation of recapturing Guadalcanal at any cost," Vice Admiral Ugaka wrote in his diary. The offensive was deemed so important that General Hyakutake planned to lead it personally in mid-October.

Known simply as "Plan X," it would be a combined land, sea, and air operation. Besides summoning from Java General Masao Maruyama's 2nd Division—one of the army's highly regarded units, particularly its 29th Regiment—Hyakutake was committing elements of the 38th Division. Led by General Tadayoshi Sano, it was in transit from Sumatra. Its 4th Regiment, under Colonel Nomasu Nakaguma, landed at Kamimbo Bay in late September.

Meanwhile General Kawaguchi's surviving troops and newly arrived reinforcements were to establish strong positions on the Matanikau's east bank, the offensive's starting point. Yamamoto's Combined Fleet and the 11th Air Fleet would bomb and shell the Marine airfield to divert attention from the nighttime landings.

Japanese leaders now recognized the surpassing importance, out of all proportion to its numbers, of the Cactus Air Force; if air and sea attacks destroyed it and wrecked Henderson Field, the chances of Plan X's success would rise exponentially.

Everything possible was done to make this happen. To reduce the 560-mile flying distance from Rabaul to Guadalcanal, which gave Japanese fighter planes scant time over their target, Yamamoto pushed forward the timetable for building a new airfield on southern Bougainville at Buin. That would halve the flying distance to Guadalcanal. The 11th Air Fleet reinforced its air groups in Rabaul so that by October there were eighty-nine fighter and search planes on Rabaul to face the eighty-seven American dive bombers and fighter planes at Henderson.[110]

To support Plan X, Yamamoto pulled in Admiral Kondo's Second Fleet and Admiral Nagumo's Third Fleet. Their three aircraft carriers, large converted carriers *Hiyo* and *Junyo*, battleships, cruisers, and destroyers constituted a powerful naval force.[111]

With little interference from the US Navy, Tokyo Express destroyers were landing up to nine hundred soldiers nightly on Guadalcanal's northwestern coast. Each afternoon the destroyers left Shortland Harbor, reaching the Cactus Air Force's two-hundred-mile patrol limit just before dark. Here they were most vulnerable to air attack, although the fast, maneuverable destroyers were hard to hit. When darkness fell, the convoys continued to Guadalcanal, arriving off the northwest coast around midnight. After landing Hyakutake's men, the Express began the return trip to Shortland, leaving Cactus's patrol range by daybreak.

The destroyers were nimbler than the troop transports, but their limited space meant that few heavy guns or supplies could be landed with the troops. Enemy air attacks, acknowledged Major General Shigesaburo Miyazaki, made transporting troops and supplies to Guadalcanal by sea "extremely difficult." Japanese leaders agreed that the Cactus Air Force had to be wiped out.[112]

4

October: Plan X Showdown

The two lines on the chart were twin fuses, smoldering toward each other. When they met, there would be an explosion.

—ENSIGN C. G. MORRIS, HOURS BEFORE
THE BATTLE OF CAPE ESPERANCE[1]

This is the decisive battle between Japan and the United States in which the rise or fall of the Japanese Empire will be decided. If we do not succeed in the occupation of these islands, no one should expect to return alive to Japan.

—GENERAL HYAKUTAKE'S WORDS BEFORE HIS SOLDIERS
ATTACKED BLOODY RIDGE[2]

We are not in the least downhearted or upset by our difficulties, but obsessed with one idea only, to kill the yellow bastards and we shall do it.

—VICE ADMIRAL WILLIAM "BULL" HALSEY
FOLLOWING THE NAVAL BATTLE OF SANTA CRUZ[3]

VICE ADMIRAL ROBERT GHORMLEY LIVED and worked on his flagship, the *Argonne*, because New Caledonia's Free French government refused to give him lodgings ashore at Noumea. Ghormley rarely left his small shipboard office and, in fact, had neither left the *Argonne* in nearly a month, nor ever gone to Guadalcanal. So Admiral Chester Nimitz and Rear Admiral Richmond Kelly Turner went to Noumea to confer with the South Pacific commander in chief on his flagship. Also attending the strategic summit were General Hap Arnold, the commander of the Army Air Force; Lieutenant General Richard Sutherland, Douglas

MacArthur's chief of staff; and the Southwest Pacific air commander, Lieutenant General George Kenney. MacArthur did not attend.

Arnold remarked on the gridlock in Noumea Harbor, where fifty ships waited to be unloaded. Studying Ghormley's cramped quarters and the tense, weary admiral, gaunt from recent weight loss, Arnold said disapprovingly, "No man—I don't care who he is—can sit continuously in a small office, fighting a war, with all the complicated problems that come up, without suffering mentally, physically, and nervously. . . . A change of scenery is required for anyone doing a wearing job under constant strain." Clearly on edge, Ghormley snapped that no one could tell him how to run his command. "It was obvious to me," Arnold said later, "that the naval officers in this area were under a terrific strain. It was also obvious that they had chips on their shoulders."[4]

After the testy exchange the leaders proceeded to the main question: How to break the stalemate on Guadalcanal, where control of the sea changed hands every twelve hours. By day, US cargo ships landed supplies and food at Lunga Point, and smaller craft skimmed over Ironbottom Sound and shuttled between Guadalcanal and Tulagi unmolested. After sunset, the Tokyo Express fearlessly roved the waters off the island, its destroyers and light cruisers landing troops on the northwest coast and then sailing to Lunga Point to shell the Marine perimeter. By sunrise, the enemy vessels were far up the Slot, usually beyond reach of Cactus's dawn patrol. Indeed, it was a strange situation.

The admirals and generals resolved nothing at the September 28 meeting. MacArthur's staff officers said the general was focused on his New Guinea campaign and could spare few troops or planes for Guadalcanal. The admirals refused to give MacArthur ships, planes, or amphibious troops. General Arnold rebuffed the admirals' request for high-altitude P-38 fighters; they were all needed to support the upcoming invasion of North Africa.

For the time being, Arnold said, the P-40 was good enough, although it in fact was inferior to the Zero in maneuverability and in high-altitude flying. In addition, Arnold said, the South Pacific's airfields could not accommodate more planes. The Navy said new airstrips were under construction.

Although the Army Air Force refused to release P-38s for South Pacific duty, it was establishing the 347th Fighter Group at Tantouta, New Caledonia, with three fighter squadrons. Later, it would add a fourth fighter squadron that included the coveted P-38s.[5]

On September 29, Nimitz flew to Guadalcanal to meet with Vandegrift. The B-17 crew got lost, but the navigator was finally able to get them there by using naval charts. The bomber landed on the muddy airstrip in a rainstorm. Vandegrift took Nimitz around the perimeter to show him the Marine positions, and they talked until 3:00 a.m.

Nimitz told the Marine general that the Navy was writing new regulations and encouraged him to submit proposed changes. Vandegrift immediately offered a suggestion: "Leave out all reference that he who runs his ship aground will face a fate worse than death. Out here too many commanders have been far too leery about risking their ships." Vandegrift's reference to Ghormley was unmistakable, but Nimitz only smiled without commenting.

The admiral later awarded medals during a ceremony outside the division command post. Turning to Vandegrift, Nimitz asked him to step up. To the general's surprise Nimitz read a citation for the Navy Cross and pinned it to Vandegrift's shirt.

When Nimitz boarded the B-17 to return to Noumea, he insisted on riding in the nose. The takeoff did not go smoothly. "We thought [the pilot] was going to run into the trees at the other end of [the runway] and he stopped, with his nose hanging over the edge of the field," Vandegrift reported. Nimitz's aides convinced him to move into the less-exposed fuselage.[6]

Back in Noumea Nimitz had many questions for Ghormley: Why had he not sent the Army's American Division to reinforce the Marines? Why did he not immediately forward fighter planes to Henderson? Why wasn't the Navy doing more to disrupt the Tokyo Express? Ghormley had no answers. Nimitz ordered Ghormley to immediately send to Guadalcanal the American's 164th Infantry Regiment, a National Guard unit from North Dakota.

The Navy's Pacific commander in chief had paid close attention to Vandegrift's running commentary when they toured the perimeter, and he gave Ghormley a to-do list: all-weather runways for Henderson, road improvements, replacing tents with Quonset huts, and upgrading cargo-handling and repair facilities, among other things. He told Ghormley that he should go to Guadalcanal and see things for himself. Nimitz was clearly dissatisfied with Ghormley's leadership two months into the campaign.[7]

Nimitz was not unsympathetic to Ghormley's large responsibilities; Nimitz's own job had taken a toll; he had developed a tremor. At his doctor's suggestion, Nimitz, who had grown up in the Texas hill country hunting and fishing, set up a pistol range outside his office. It helped calm him. Sometimes he steadied his hand by placing a half-dollar on the pistol barrel and firing it without allowing the coin to fall off.[8]

"EQUATORIAL WEATHER" FROM SEPTEMBER 14–27 had given Henderson Field and its stressed pilots a welcome reprieve. Until then the Pagoda had operated in a continual state of urgency, with the hard-nosed airfield operations commanders, General Geiger and Colonel Woods, pushing their pilots and ground crews to their limits and beyond. Wildcats and dive bombers landed and took off with little regard for runway conditions. Arriving planes were refueled and re-armed at "pit-stop speed" and then sent back up. The Japanese raids—sometimes two or three daily—whittled down the number of operational aircraft to a few dozen.

But in late September, storms in the Bismarck Islands had prevented the Japa-nese Bettys and Zeros from mounting raids, while torrential rains and mud grounded the Cactus Air Force. Hoping to gain an advantage during the interreg-num, the adversaries built up their fighter and bomber inventories—the Ameri-cans having lost 66 planes in a month, including 43 Wildcats, half the number received during that period. When good weather returned, Henderson had 87 operational planes, while the Japanese had 180 fighters and bombers at Rabaul.[9]

The raids resumed on September 27 when eighteen Bettys and thirty-eight Zeros flew down the Slot. Eighteen Wildcats met them over Henderson. It was a draw: the Japanese bombers destroyed or damaged ten dive bombers and torpedo bombers parked at the airfield, and Marine and Navy fighter pilots claimed ten kills.

The next day, the Cactus Air Force was alerted well in advance that sixty-seven bombers and fighters were inbound. Thirty-two Wildcats from VMF-223, VMF-224, and VF-5—"Fighting Five," previously assigned to the carrier Saratoga—confronted them above the Slot. The F4F pilots shot down eight Bettys and damaged seventeen others; it was one of the Japanese air force's costlier raids. But they continued without letup. The Japanese were determined to destroy the Cac-tus Air Force.[10]

On September 29 the Japanese unveiled a new tactic: the "fighter sweep." Twenty-seven Zeros and nine Bettys came down the Slot, and more than thirty Wildcats rose to meet them. As soon as the Wildcats appeared, the Bettys turned back; the fighter sweep's objective was to draw the Wildcats into one-on-one combat with the Zeroes and to wear down the Americans by attrition, as the Ger-mans had tried to do during the Battle of Britain. Each side claimed several kills. Rear Admiral Ugaki wrote in his diary that day that he "had to entertain some doubt about our fliers' claim of shooting down so many planes" because Japanese observers on Guadalcanal counted the American planes when they went up and returned, and their numbers did not corroborate the pilots' claims. But the Japa-nese air command was encouraged by the result and sent another fighter sweep on October 2.

Airfield radar detected it just thirty minutes from Henderson, and the Wild-cats barely had time to reach Angels 20 to meet the attack. VMF-223, the first squadron to land at Henderson on August 20, made the first contact with the formation of twenty-seven Zeros. The Japanese aviators shot down the squadron commander, Major John Smith, and pilots Red Kendrick and Bill Lees.

Smith crash-landed in a clearing six miles east of the airfield and walked back. "It was just like a hike," he wrote. "There were a few rivers to ford, of course." The trek took two and a half hours, and along the way Smith came upon the wreckage of an F4F on a hillside, with the dead pilot still at the controls.

Also shot down was Major Robert Galer, commander of VMF-224; he parachuted into Ironbottom Sound and was rescued. Commander Eric Feldt, the coast watchers' leader, extolled the "unabated aggressiveness" of the Henderson pilots, "who fought on day after day, while their friends were killed around them."

When October 2 ended, the Cactus Air Force had fewer than three dozen operational fighters.[11]

ON OCTOBER 3, WHEN THE Zeros came again, twenty-nine Wildcats from VMF-223, VMF-224, and VF-5 were waiting at thirty-three thousand feet, well above the usual Angels 20. They pounced on the twenty-seven Zeros from above. It was a banner day for Cactus: at least nine Zeros tumbled to the ground in smoke and flames, with Captain Marion Carl claiming his sixteenth confirmed kill of the Pacific War.

Although the Cactus pilots almost always met the challenge of interdicting the Japanese raids, attrition necessarily eroded pilots' ties to their planes and squadrons. By early October they often went into action in randomly assigned planes and with wingmen from other squadrons.[12]

Marines and news correspondents sometimes watched the dogfights from Lunga Point, "cheering like a crowd at a football game" whenever a US fighter shot down a Japanese bomber. On radios scrounged from wrecked planes in the bone yard they listened to the "torrent of excited words, most of it unintelligible or garbled by too many people talking at the same time." When an enemy bomber began spinning and plunged into the sea in "a great backfire of ruddy flames and black smoke . . . the watchers on the shore cheered madly, as if our side had made a touchdown."[13]

Japan had begun the Pacific War with a seasoned cadre of pilots, but their numbers were falling and the long decline of Japan's air force had begun. Top fighter ace Sakai, severely wounded on August 7, wrote, "Veteran pilots were killed, leaving us like a comb with missing teeth." Many of the pilot losses were unavoidable, but others were unnecessary; they died rather than use their parachutes, which "seemed to them like flying a white flag," wrote Marine Captain Loren "Doc" Everton, a Wildcat pilot. "About the most honorable thing a Jap can do is die. And I hope they keep right on feeling that way."[14]

AFTER A BOMBING RAID, HENDERSON Field throbbed with activity: there were bomb craters to be filled and fires to be extinguished. The 6th Naval Construction

Battalion—the Seabees, who had completed the Fighter One airstrip east of Henderson on September 9—after a raid went to work filling holes with sand and gravel, laying fresh steel matting, and putting out the smoky fires that burned in the kunai grass. Wrecked aircraft were towed away from the runway. During a twenty-four-hour period in October the Seabees filled fifty-three bomb and shell craters, wrote their skipper, Commander Joseph Blundon.

Sometimes a Japanese shell or bomb failed to explode when it hit the runway, and it had to be removed. "When you see men choke down their fear and dive in after an unexploded bomb so that our planes can land safely, a lump comes in your throat and you know why America wins wars," Blundon wrote. He kept a running total of the Japanese air raids: between September 1 and November 18 there were 146 in which Henderson was hit at least once.[15]

AFTER THE OCTOBER 3 ATTACKS there were no air raids for a week, and new pilots and planes arrived. During the afternoon of October 9 the escort carrier *Copahee* launched twenty F4Fs from VMF-121. They landed at the Guadalcanal airstrip, joining five VMF-121 pilots who had arrived a few weeks earlier. They relieved the gaunt, weary survivors of VMF-223 and VMSB-232, the original Cactus Air Force of August 20, and VMF-224 and VMSB-231, which had arrived ten days later; they had flown combat air patrols and met the daily Japanese air onslaught for weeks on end. VMF-121's arrival marked the end of Marine Air Group 23's tour of duty at Henderson and the beginning of MAG-14's. VMF-223's commander, Major John L. Smith, left Guadalcanal with nineteen confirmed kills.[16]

Newly arrived VMF-121, commanded by Major Leonard "Duke" Davis, would produce the most fighter aces of any Guadalcanal squadron. Its executive officer, a twenty-seven-year-old former South Dakota farmer named Joe Foss, would rack up twenty-six kills in three months on Guadalcanal.[17]

The Japanese were also restocking their airfields. The 26th Air Flotilla sent seventy-two bombers, sixty Zeros, and eight reconnaissance planes to Rabaul to maintain its numerical advantage.[18]

WITH THE TOKYO EXPRESS LANDING fresh troops, artillery, and sometimes tanks on the island each night, General Vandegrift recognized that securing the west bank of the Matanikau River was imperative. If the Japanese controlled the river and its sandbar, their 150mm howitzers could shell Henderson Field at will, and tanks could cross the sandbar to the east bank.

The general and his staff were determined to not repeat the mistakes that had resulted in Second Matanikau's failure ten days earlier and that had jeopardized Puller's battalion. This time, as a result of vigorous patrolling—improved significantly by the influence of Lieutenant Colonel William Whaling's scout-snipers—division intelligence had a better picture of the location of the Japanese strong points.

A dozen men usually went out on the dangerous patrols. Often a Japanese soldier would hide in a covered hole, let the patrol pass, lift the covering, and kill the last man in line. This happened so often, and it was so unnerving, that on many patrols the last man walked backward.

"You have no idea how tiring a patrol is," Lieutenant William Whyte of the First Marines wrote to his father and stepmother after days of "ceaseless patrol activity" in the jungle. The Marines' stamina, Whyte said, was severely tested by the intense heat, the steep coral ridges and deep ravines, and their burdens of food, weapons, and gear.[19]

Division headquarters would coordinate Third Matanikau, and it promised air and artillery support. The operation was similar to its failed predecessor. Vandegrift believed five infantry battalions—or more than four thousand men—would give the Marines numerical superiority. Two battalions of the Seventh Marines, the 3rd Battalion, Second Marines, and Whaling's scout-sniper group would cross the Log Bridge a mile south of the sandspit and turn northward to attack toward the sea along the ridgelines west of the river. Two Fifth Marines battalions would advance toward the Matanikau sandspit to freeze the Japanese on the west bank so the other battalions could get in the enemy's rear. The operation would begin October 7.

LIEUTENANT GENERAL MASAO MARUYAMA HAD recently landed on Guadalcanal with most of his 2nd Division—the Sendai Division—and he was planning to launch what amounted to a mirror image of Vandegrift's offensive. He intended to secure the Matanikau's *east* bank with Major General Yumio Nasu's 4th Regiment, which was replacing Colonel Kawaguchi's decimated brigade. From the Matanikau's east bank, long-range artillery would join aerial bombings and naval shelling in a concentrated effort to shut down Henderson Field. The east bank would be the starting point of the Seventeenth Army's October offensive to capture the airfield.

While Nasu's regiment advanced toward the Matanikau, the remnants of Kawaguchi's brigade, ill, disease ridden, and half-starved from its demoralizing retreat from Bloody Ridge, moved to the rear on the northwest coast. "Rations are gone and our clothing is in rags," wrote one of Kawaguchi's disconsolate survivors. "I wonder how long this will last and pray it will soon be over."[20]

DEATH WAS ALSO ON THE minds of the Marines as they approached the Matanikau from the east. Lieutenant Colonel Julius Frisbee, the Seventh Marines' powerfully built executive officer, attempted to prepare *Time* magazine correspondent John Hersey, the son of Protestant missionaries in China and a Yale graduate, for what he might soon see. Hersey was traveling with a company of the 2nd Battalion, Fifth Marines on a patrol through a valley near the river. Asked by Frisbee whether he had ever seen dead men on a battlefield, Hersey replied that he had not.

"It's possible to think of dead enemy as dead animals," Frisbee said. The "pathetic sight" of dead Marines was different. "They look just like dirty-faced little boys who have gone to bed without being tucked in by their mothers," the colonel said.

Hersey's involvement in Third Matanikau was the basis for *Into the Valley*, one of the first book-length accounts, along with Richard Tregaskis's *Guadalcanal Diary*, of Americans in combat during World War II.

Parakeets and macaws screeched high in the dense rainforest canopy as Hersey and the sweat-drenched Marines picked their way along a stream. Suddenly, Japanese mortar and machine-gun fire erupted from concealed positions. Hersey watched Captain Charles Regaud's heavy machine-gun company teeter on the brink of panic as the word "withdraw" was whispered from man to man. Regaud stood up and bellowed, "Who in Christ's name gave that order?" He lit into them: "You men make me ashamed. . . . Gosh, and they call you Marines." The men hurried back to their positions. Regaud then withdrew them in an orderly fashion while still berating them: "My God, am I ashamed of you guys."[21]

That afternoon, about 150 Japanese troops trapped on the east bank tried unsuccessfully several times to return to the west bank. They made a break that night for the sandbar, but were stopped by I company of the Fifth Marines during a hand-to-hand fracas.

Upriver the Seventh Marines and the Whaling Group bivouacked east of the Log Bridge after overcoming light opposition. They planned to ford the river the next morning.

Unaware that his own offensive was mirroring Vandegrift's, Nasu had sent his 1st and 3rd Battalions to cross the Matanikau and push eastward a mile, near the place where the Marines planned to push westward. Nasu's 2nd Battalion remained south of Point Cruz to support his other units and secure the coastline.

But October 8, the day of attack for both Marines and Japanese, instead brought torrential rains that transformed the hills into mud slicks and the lowlands into bogs that engulfed men, guns, and vehicles. It was a washout.

Colonel Edson, the Fifth Marines' commander, asked Vandegrift to send reinforcements to relieve I Company at the Japanese pocket. Edson's old outfit, the 1st Raiders, which was in reserve for the offensive, arrived early October 8. Fewer than two hundred able-bodied men remained of the original eight hundred who had landed at Tulagi. Major Lew Walt, the former Raider who was now Edson's executive officer, took charge of the Raider remnant. It and two companies of Fifth Marines surrounded the Japanese pocket.

At 6:30 p.m. on October 8 the trapped Japanese once more attempted to break out and reach the sandspit. Behind a smoke screen they attacked en masse, twenty abreast, with automatic weapons blazing, and grenades arcing out of the rear ranks. Bursting from the jungle "in solid waves," they came straight at the Raiders with three Japanese officers swinging two-handed samurai swords. Nine of the first eleven Marines they met died. "It was mayhem first-class, with bayoneting, screaming, shouting," wrote Sergeant Ore Marion of the Fifth Marines. The Raiders fought the Japanese with knives and bayonets. The Marines had just erected a double-apron barbed-wire fence at the sandspit to thwart attacks from the river's west bank. Two heavy machine-guns firing along the fence helped break up the attack.

The fighting ended after forty-five minutes; many of the Japanese soldiers breached the wire and reached the west bank; others were caught in the wire. 'They hit that wire and it really busted them up," said Sergeant Frank Guidone of the Raiders, after seeing dead enemy soldiers hanging on it the next morning. "There were bodies all over, ours and the Japanese, some on top of others, many of them dead, others wounded," wrote Marion. Fifty-nine dead Japanese soldiers were counted. They were recent arrivals on Guadalcanal; in their packs were food, new clothing, and extra shoes.

The already depleted Raiders lost twelve killed and twenty-two wounded; Edson recommended it for a unit citation for what would be its last action on Guadalcanal.

The last Raider killed was Corporal Walter Burak, Edson's runner, aide, and utility man who had won the Navy Cross on Bloody Ridge. Edson had brought Burak with him to the Fifth Marines. The stone-faced 1st Raider Battalion founder reportedly wept when he learned that Burak, who spoke of joining the clergy after the war, was killed by machine-gun fire.[22]

LEARNING THAT ENEMY AIR, LAND, and sea forces were gathering at Rabaul and Shortland Island for a new offensive, Vandegrift scaled back Third Matanikau to a quick envelopment of both sides of the river followed by withdrawal to the perimeter. The abridged version began October 9, when three battalions, along with the Whaling Group, crossed the Matanikau. They turned north toward the sea along three parallel vectors, with Whaling and the 3rd Battalion, Second Marines nearest the river; Hanneken's 2nd Battalion of the Seventh Marines forming the middle prong; and Puller's 1st battalion advancing farthest to the west. For the first time Puller was using native porters—stocky, muscular

Melanesians that Puller hired through Martin Clemens for the price of one twist of tobacco per man, per day.[23]

While Hanneken and Whaling encountered only scattered resistance, Puller's men, ascending a hill overlooking the coastline southwest of Point Cruz, beheld a sight that fighting men usually only dream of. In wooded ravines to the Marines' left and front, they saw a battalion of unsuspecting enemy soldiers—the 2nd Battalion of Nasu's 4th Regiment, his reserve.

The ravines erupted in explosions as Marine mortars and artillery homed in. Unable to counterattack through the shellfire, the Japanese tried to flee the rain of steel by scaling the ravine's opposite slope. It offered no concealment, and Marine machine-gunners slaughtered enemy troops sprinting across the open ground and forced them back down into the ravine—back into the furious mortar and artillery fire. Further attempts to escape also failed. The onslaught ended when the Marines ran out of mortar shells.

In a little over one hour, a 4th Infantry field officer wrote in his diary, 690 men died—practically the entire 2nd Battalion. "Puller did a fine job of pulverizing the Japanese," wrote Lieutenant Colonel Merrill Twining of Vandegrift's staff. During the three-day Matanikau battle the 4th Regiment lost nine hundred killed. Captured documents showed that Third Matanikau preempted the planned Japanese assault by tanks, artillery, and infantry to secure the river's eastern bank—a prelude to the coming all-out offensive.

Among the enemy bodies heaped in the ravines Puller's men found an official order addressed to Japanese soldiers: "From now on, the occupying of Guadalcanal Island is under the observation of the whole world. Do not expect to return, not even one man, if the occupation is not successful. Everyone must remember the honor of the Emperor, fear no enemy, yield to no material matters, show the strong points of steel or of rocks, and advance valiantly and ferociously."

The bodies and packs also yielded boilerplate Japanese atrocity propaganda about the Marines. "The Americans on this island are not ordinary troops, but Marines, a special force recruited from jails and insane asylums for blood lust. There is no honorable death [for their] prisoners, their arms are cut off, they are staked on the airfield, and run over with steam rollers." Japanese prisoners also said they were told that the Marines were men who had killed their mothers or fathers.

That afternoon, most of the Marines withdrew to the Henderson perimeter to meet the consequences of the enemy buildup at Rabaul. The Fifth Marines remained on the Matanikau's eastern bank at the places where the Japanese bridgeheads had been eliminated. Banks of lights were installed, and mines were laid at the sandspit in the belief that the Japanese would try again to force a crossing with tanks, artillery, and infantry.

For the time being Vandegrift's Marines could be satisfied with having re-
deemed their failure at Second Matanikau with a victory two weeks later—one
that cost them 65 killed and 125 wounded.[24]

ON THE NIGHT OF OCTOBER 9 General Hyakutake and his staff came ashore
with more than eleven hundred troops—to learn of Nasu's defeat and loss of nine
hundred men. Rather than expanding their tiny bridgehead on the Matanikau's
eastern bank, the Japanese had withdrawn two miles west of the river.

Hyakutake remained determined to prosecute his plan to recapture Guadalcanal and requested that the 38th Division plus an infantry regiment and an engineer regiment be immediately sent to the island. In a message to the Imperial
General Headquarters the general acknowledged that the situation was "far more
aggravated than had been estimated." In fact, the appearance of Kawaguchi's
starving survivors from the Bloody Ridge and Matanikau battles shocked Hyakutake. With their protruding ribs, loose teeth, grimy and tattered uniforms, and
long hair, they were little more than "walking skeletons."[25]

OCTOBER 9 WAS ALSO THE day that the 1st Battalion, Second Marines, boarded
Higgins boats at Tulagi, crossed Sealark Channel, and landed about thirty miles
east of Henderson Field.

Up to two hundred Japanese survivors of the Alligator Creek and Bloody
Ridge battles were in the area, and Martin Clemens and his scouts had learned
that they were radioing information to their superiors about the Marines from
stations at Gorabusu and Koilotumaria. The Marines were ordered to drive the
Japanese from the area and break up their observation posts.

On August 7 the Second Marines had been the first US troops to set foot on
Japanese-occupied territory during the Pacific War. Encountering scant opposition on Florida Island, the 1st Battalion had been re-embarked on landing craft to
capture Tanambogo. Enemy gunfire had pinned the Marines on the beach and
forced them to abort the mission.

The battalion might have felt that bad luck was still stalking it while crossing
Sealark Channel on October 9: a storm blew up, swamped one of the landing
craft, and eighteen Marines drowned. Shortly after the Marines landed near Aola
Bay, a sniper killed Captain Richard Stafford, the C Company commander.

But the Marines' luck improved. They burst into a Japanese camp at Gorabusu, killed thirty men, and captured an antiaircraft battery, maps, documents,
and one prisoner. After destroying Japanese bases and supplies in the area and
dispersing the surviving enemy soldiers, most of the battalion returned to Tulagi.
Eighty-eight volunteers set out cross-country for Henderson Field, marching

through enemy-held territory and destroying Japanese supplies. Four days later, all eighty-eight reached the Henderson perimeter.[26]

ON OCTOBER 9 TOO, THE *Zeilin* and the *McCawley*—the "Wacky Mac," flagship of Admiral Turner, the South Pacific Amphibious Force commander—sailed from Noumea for Guadalcanal with 2,852 men of the Army American Division's 164th Infantry, nearly one hundred trucks and gun carriers, a dozen 37mm guns, seventy days' rations, sixty days' supplies, ammunition, and 210 men from the 1st Marine Air Wing.

It was the first major US reinforcement since the Seventh Marines' arrival in mid-September, and it marked the Army's introduction to the campaign. Since March the American had defended New Caledonia against a potential Japanese threat that had not materialized.

The American was activated on May 27 under its serendipitous name—a conflation of "America" and "Caledonia," its founding place. It was the only Army division formed on foreign soil and not assigned a number. It had about sixteen thousand men. Its three infantry regiments were former National Guard units: the 132nd Regiment from Illinois; the 164th from North Dakota; and the 182nd from Massachusetts. There were also four artillery battalions, a combat engineer battalion, quartermaster and medical regiments, a signal company, and a mobile combat reconnaissance squadron.

With little else to do over the summer, the American helped the Seabees build an airfield on Espiritu Santo that placed B-17s within six hundred miles of Guadalcanal. Major General Alexander Patch Jr., American's commander, opened an officer candidate school at Noumea to train more junior officers.[27]

Until early October Admirals Nimitz, Ghormley, and Turner had not intended to send American units to reinforce the Marines on Guadalcanal; in fact, no reinforcement of the Marines had been planned. The admirals had wanted to use elements of the American and the 2nd Marine Division to occupy Ndeni in the Santa Cruz Islands. The joint chiefs of staff had included Ndeni in its South Pacific operational plan of early July. Just 330 miles southeast of Henderson, Ndeni was envisioned as a future staging area for medium-range aircraft operating between Espiritu Santo and Guadalcanal and as a base for antisubmarine patrols. At the same time Ndeni's capture would help protect US communications and supply lines to Guadalcanal.

Guadalcanal's emergence as the primary South Pacific battleground had delayed the offensive, but in late September Admiral Turner had drawn up a plan for Ndeni's invasion, which Ghormley was pleased to accept.[28]

Vandegrift, however, believed that the operation would divert resources from Guadalcanal for little gain. Major General Millard Harmon, commander of Army forces in the South Pacific, had slowly come around to Vandegrift's view. On October 6 Harmon weighed in against the operation.

The occupation of Ndeni, Harmon told Admiral Ghormley, "represents a diversion from the main effort and dispersion of force. The situation in Cactus-Ringbolt [Guadalcanal-Tulagi] cannot be regarded as anything but 'continually critical.'" He added, "If we do not succeed in holding Cactus-Ringbolt our effort in the Santa Cruz will be a total waste—and loss. The Solomons has to be our main effort. . . . It is my personal conviction that the Jap is capable of retaking Guadalcanal, and that he will do so in the near future unless it is materially strengthened."

Conversely, there was no danger of the Japanese occupying and developing Ndeni for their own purposes so long as American bombers could fly from Espiritu Santo, Harmon said. He recommended abandoning the Ndeni plan, sending to Guadalcanal an infantry regiment, and intensifying "naval surface action in South Solomon waters." It was imperative too, he wrote, to improve the Guadalcanal runways so they could be used in every kind of weather.

As a result of Harmon's letter, the plan to invade Ndeni was abandoned. Harmon's other recommendations dovetailed with Nimitz's after his visit to Guadalcanal a week earlier, when Nimitz had ordered Ghormley to send Vandegrift the 164th Regiment and to improve Henderson's runways.[29]

ON OCTOBER 11, THE ENEMY reinforcement naval groups collided off Cape Esperance. Rear Admiral Norman Scott commanded Task Force 64, whose two heavy cruisers, two light cruisers, and five destroyers were escorting the 164th from Noumea to Guadalcanal. The troop transports were expected to anchor off Lunga Point the morning of October 13. Ghormley had ordered Scott to "search for and destroy enemy ships and landing craft." Coming from the usually cautious Ghormley, these were fighting orders.

Scott was pleased to be given the opportunity to vindicate the Navy's Savo Island debacle. Cognizant of the Navy's abysmal night-fighting record, Scott had spent the previous three weeks drilling his task force under night-combat conditions and keeping his crews at battle stations from dusk to dawn. Scott was a fifty-three-year-old Navy old-timer from the Annapolis Class of 1911 who, yearning for sea duty after years of staff and office assignments, had finally gotten what he wanted in 1941. Having heard and read the warnings about the Japanese buildup at Rabaul and Shortland, he was expecting—even welcoming—trouble.

About noon on October 11 a B-17 crew spotted Japanese cruisers and destroyers sailing down the Slot. Other reports confirmed the enemy's approach but underestimated its strength. At sunset, Scott's nine ships prepared for action amid the clang of slamming steel doors and bugle calls to battle stations.

The enemy warships belonged to two naval groups that were conducting a routine reinforcement mission to Guadalcanal. Rear Admiral Aritomo Goto commanded one of them—three cruisers and two destroyers that would shell Henderson Field that night. The second group, led by Rear Admiral Takaji Joshima, consisted of two seaplane tenders and six destroyers. Joshima's group planned to anchor off Tassafaronga and land field guns, howitzers, tractors, ammunition, and 728 soldiers.

Admiral Gunichi Mikawa had asked the 11th Air Fleet to help ensure the mission's success by launching a larger-than-usual air attack on Henderson that day. Preceded by a seventeen-plane fighter sweep, twenty-seven bombers and thirty Zeroes had flown to Guadalcanal to paralyze Cactus air operations so that Joshima's convoy could proceed without interference. Indeed, the raid, unfolding during Tojo time, so tied up the Cactus Air Force that it did not interfere with the Japanese ships coming down the Slot, although at a cost of nine Japanese planes.[30]

After reading the ship sightings reports, Scott and his staff pored over their charts hanging from the bulkheads. Calculating time and distances, they set a course that would take TF-64 around Guadalcanal's western coast to a position off Savo Island that night to screen Sealark Channel. Ensign C. G. "Chick" Morris watched *Helena* Captain Gilbert Hoover plot the reports on a chart that showed the location of the opposing forces. "The two lines on the chart were twin fuses," Morris wrote, "smoldering toward each other. When they met, there would be an explosion." "Yes, I think we'll see some action," said Hoover.[31]

As it approached Savo Island at 10:35 p.m., Scott's task force formed a single column. In the lead were destroyers *Farenholt*, *Duncan*, and *Laffey*. Behind them came cruisers *San Francisco*—Scott's flagship—*Boise*, *Salt Lake City*, and *Helena*, with the destroyers *Buchanan* and *McCalla* bringing up the rear. Scott's orders called for the destroyers and their cruiser float planes to light up targets with searchlights and flares, and for the destroyers to quickly release their torpedoes. Building flexibility into the tactical plan, Scott authorized the cruisers to fire without orders from him.

From the northwest the three cruisers of Goto's Bombardment Force approached Scott's group in a column, with the two destroyers flanking the lead cruiser, Goto's flagship *Aoba*. The formation resembled an oversized "T." The *Aoba* and Goto's two other cruisers, the *Kinugasa* and *Furutaka*, had helped demolish the Allied fleet off Savo Island two months earlier. In a complete reversal of the circumstances of August 9, Goto and his commanders did not suspect that American warships were nearby.

When one of the *San Francisco*'s spotter planes caught fire as it was being catapulted, keen-eyed enemy lookouts spotted the flash of light in the inky darkness. But Japanese naval officers, not expecting trouble on this night, dismissed the report and did not act. A US spotter plane reported three vessels off Guadalcanal's northern beaches; they belonged to Joshima's reinforcement group, and not Goto's group. Then, around 11:30 p.m., *Helena's* new SG search radar picked up unidentified ships approaching from the northwest—it was Goto. The contact was relayed to Scott on *San Francisco*.

San Francisco was equipped with the older SC radar. Because Japanese radar receivers could track SC transmissions to the emitting ships, Scott had ordered all SC radar in TF-64 turned off, including the *San Francisco's*. Thus, Scott, the task force commander, was going into action without radar, his cruiser the only one without it as *Salt Lake City* and *Boise*, like *Helena*, had operational SG radar.

Helena's report, though, convinced Scott that this was the main enemy force, and he ordered his task force to reverse course so it might "cross the 'T'" of the Japanese—a centuries' old naval tactic designed to expose an approaching enemy to a fleet's broadsides. Scott ordered his four cruisers and five destroyers to execute a "column left," with the three lead destroyers executing a separate turn ahead of the rest of the column, which would follow the *San Francisco*. The three destroyers would put on speed after making the turn and then fall along the right side the main column. It might have been a classic naval maneuver, but it was not easy to execute, especially in the presence of the enemy.[32]

SCOTT'S FOUR CRUISERS AND TWO trailing destroyers completed their course change at 11:45 p.m. Two of the lead destroyers, the *Farenholt* and *Laffey*, sailed to the right and parallel to the cruisers. However, *Duncan*, the third lead destroyer, had detected enemy ships to the starboard of the turning column and, fearing a strike on the task force's flank, intended to mount a solo attack to preempt it. *Helena's* SG radar reported a target at six miles, and then *Boise's* SG picked up five unidentified ships.[33]

Scott's column was crossing the T of the advancing Japanese column when the American guns began barking. The battle began with a miscommunication: *Helena* Captain G. C. Hoover had radioed, "Interrogatory roger," which he intended to mean, "Request permission to open fire." Scott replied, "Roger," by which he evidently meant, "Message received." But the one-word reply to "interrogatory roger" had a second meaning: "Commence firing!" Hoover so interpreted Scott's reply, and at 11:46 p.m. the light cruiser opened up with her 15 six-inch main battery guns and her five-inch guns, firing ceaselessly in accordance with the new "continuous-fire doctrine" for six-inch batteries, capable of pumping out ninety rounds a minute, "almost like a 6-inch machine gun."

From Scott's flagship Associated Press reporter Tom Yarbrough watched the first salvo flash toward the enemy formation. "The incessant murderous fire that followed threw the Japs into confusion," he wrote. Ninety seconds later, three

Japanese destroyers were burning "and the searchlights were no longer necessary." "She's burning! She's gone!" shouted Commander John Morrow, when a Japanese destroyer rolled over and quickly sank.

The heavy cruiser *Salt Lake City*'s eight-inch guns went into action, their flash and roar mingling with *Boise*'s batteries. *San Francisco* zeroed in on a cruiser three miles away. Fire control radar, which automatically locked ships' guns onto targets, gave the American guns instant lethality.[34]

It was a terrible surprise to Goto and his convoy—as clueless to the Americans' presence as the Allies had been two months earlier at Savo Island. Even as the shells arced toward the Japanese column, Goto had begun sending his recognition signal, thinking Admiral Joshima's reinforcement group was firing on his ships by mistake. When he realized his error, Goto ordered his column to execute a 180-degree starboard turn, which placed his ships at an even greater disadvantage because it neutralized their forward guns.

It was one of Goto's last orders. A shell hit the *Aoba*'s flag bridge, mortally wounding Goto and killing his executive officer and a half-dozen others. Believing he had been wounded by friendly fire, Goto reportedly murmured as he died, "*Bakayaro! Bakayaro!*"—meaning "stupid bastard," either a chastisement of his fellow sailors or himself.

The *Duncan*, mounting its lonely charge on Goto's column, attempted to position itself to launch torpedoes at the *Furutaka*, but the Japanese cruiser swung away and increased speed; *Duncan* plastered it with several salvos.

Unsure of the location of his three lead destroyers, at 11:47 p.m., ten minutes into the battle, Scott abruptly ordered his ships to cease firing so they would not mistakenly fire on the destroyers. But gunners on some of Scott's ships ignored his order and continued firing. The American column sailed northwest in an attempt to parallel Goto's retreating bombardment group.

Scott asked Captain Robert Tobin, the destroyer squadron commander: "Are we shooting at you?" Tobin replied, "I don't know who you are firing at." Unsatisfied with Tobin's oblique reply, Scott ordered Tobin's destroyers to flash their recognition signals. At last reassured, the admiral gave the order to resume firing at 11:51.

San Francisco's lookouts spotted a warship traveling on a parallel course just three-quarters of a mile away, flashing recognition signals in indistinguishable characters. The American cruiser switched on its searchlight, illuminating a Japanese destroyer. It was *Fubuki*. All of Scott's ships drew a bead on her, and within a minute she was dead in the water. A minute later, *Fubuki* exploded and sank.

The American destroyer *Farenholt* was in a highly uncomfortable position— flanked on one side by Scott's cruisers, which were firing at Japanese ships that were on *Farenholt*'s other side. It was probably an American cruiser that tagged *Farenholt*'s rigging, sending shrapnel slicing across the deck, and that then hit the hull just above the waterline, destroying communications. A third shell crashed into the forward fire room.

It was probably also friendly fire that struck *Duncan*, igniting fires and disabling the destroyer's fire control system.

At midnight Admiral Scott ordered a second ceasefire so that he could re-form his column before resuming its pursuit. *Kinugasa* chose this moment to fire on the US cruisers with shells and torpedoes. *Boise* turned on her searchlight to illuminate a target that had appeared on her radar, and the Japanese ships capitalized on the superb firing point. *Boise*'s hull was holed four times, and *Kinugasa* gave the American cruiser a three-minute pasting.

Only when Captain Ernest Small deliberately interposed his *Salt Lake City* between *Kinugasa* and *Boise* was *Boise* able to turn away, with flames leaping from the number-one and number-two turrets, where everyone was now dead. Thunderous explosions rumbled below deck from the magazine, detonated by a below-waterline shell strike. Seawater poured in below deck, providentially extinguished *Boise*'s magazine fire, and prevented other magazines from exploding. As the *Boise* sluggishly turned away, *Kinugasa* and *Salt Lake City* continued exchanging body blows, neither one of them inflicting major damage.[35]

Just before 12:30 a.m. Scott ended his pursuit, turned toward the southwest, and took the roll of his ships as they flashed their recognition signals. He told AP reporter Yarbrough that he had refrained from issuing too many orders, believing they could be confusing in a nighttime battle. "It's largely up to each captain individually. I led them into it and they fought their way out."

Boise and *Farenholt* had limped away from the column, and *Duncan* had gone missing, leaving Scott with three battleworthy cruisers and three destroyers. A few hours later *Boise* rejoined the column, despite its extensive damage and the loss of more than one hundred crewmen. Battered by friendly fire, *Farenholt* sailed fifty miles behind the formation, listing heavily to starboard. The undamaged destroyer *McCalla*, dispatched to locate *Duncan*, found her near Savo Island, where she had been abandoned at 2:00 a.m. Sharks swarmed around the bright aluminum powder cans to which the crewmen clung, ripping to pieces some of the men in the water. *McCalla*'s sailors tried to drive away the sharks with rifle fire. Nearly two hundred *Duncan* survivors were rescued.[36]

AT DAYBREAK THE CACTUS AIR Force flew over the watery battleground, looking for straggling enemy ships. Lieutenant Robert F. "Cowboy" Stout, a Wildcat pilot from Wyoming attached to VMF-212, circled the area to ward off any Japanese aircraft that might attempt to strafe survivors in the water.

"The sea is full of little dots, and every dot is a man swimming, and dying," Stout wrote. "I look at a group of a dozen and try to pull my eyes away from them, but I can't. And then there are eleven, ten, nine, eight. Every dot that's rubbed off the page is a drowned man, and nothing we can do from there in the sky."[37]

The heavily damaged *Aoba* and *Kinugasa* sailed away, while the destroyer *Hatsuyuki* from Joshima's reinforcement group remained with *Furutaka*. At 2:20 a.m. on October 12 *Furutaka*'s crew was ordered to give three cheers for the emperor and to abandon ship. Captain Tsutau Araki refused to leave and went to his cabin to commit suicide. However, his staff had hidden his revolver and samurai sword. Araki went to the bridge to lash himself to the compass and go down with his ship, but the ship sank at 2:48 with 250 men aboard before he could complete the job. He was rescued. Reporting to Admiral Yamamoto in Truk, Araki said he still wanted to die. The admiral and his staff dissuaded him.

Yamamoto had recently protested to the navy minister that the navy's rule that a ship's captain must die with his ship, even after "hard fighting," would rob the navy of some of its best skippers. Going down with one's ship was one of the British navy traditions that Japan had reverently adopted in the late nineteenth century; the Japanese also imported bricks from England to build the Naval Academy at Etajima, a simulacrum of the Britannia Royal Naval College at Dartmouth. If the suicidal tradition continued, Yamamoto wrote, "we shall not be able to get through the war, which cannot be settled soon. There is no reason why we should . . . discourage their [ship captains'] survival, while we are encouraging fliers [another Yamamoto policy] to survive by means of parachute."[38]

While Goto's squadron fought for its life and was prevented from bombarding Henderson Field, Admiral Joshima's reinforcement group had smoothly carried out its mission. Its two seaplane tenders and six destroyers had landed field guns, howitzers, tractors, ammunition, and more than seven hundred troops near Kokumbona without any interference from the Americans. Before daybreak most of Joshima's ships were on their way back to Shortland.

Shirayuki and another Joshima destroyer, *Marakumo*, returned to hunt for survivors from Goto's group, picking up four hundred sailors before being driven off by a US destroyer. By then Cactus dive bombers and fighters were in the air. They sank the *Marakumo*, crowded with *Furutaka* survivors. Later in the day Navy and Marine airmen sank another Joshima destroyer, *Natsugumo*.[39]

At the Battle of Cape Esperance the US Navy claimed its first unmistakable victory of the campaign in an almost mirror image of Savo Island. The Imperial Navy had lost a cruiser and three destroyers. *Duncan*, probably sunk by friendly fire, was Scott's only loss; cruisers *Salt Lake City* and *Boise* and destroyer *Farenholt* were damaged. One hundred sixty-three US sailors perished.

"Providence abandoned us and our losses mounted," read the Japanese official report on the battle. Rear Admiral Raizo Tanaka, in charge of convoying reinforcements and supplies to Guadalcanal, conceded, "It was a crushing defeat for the Japanese Navy. Enemy counteroffensives were becoming increasingly ferocious."[40]

Also during the night of October 11–12, US flyers gave the Japanese a dose of their own medicine. Ten Army planes took off from Port Moresby, flew to Rabaul with no moon to light their way, and dropped seventy bombs on the Japanese residential quarter, killing or injuring 110 men.[41]

THE HIATUS FROM ENEMY AIR raids at Henderson Field was clearly over. Fierce Japanese attacks now targeted the airfield at least twice daily. At 11:30 a.m. on October 13 twenty-four Bettys bombed Henderson and Fighter One, igniting five thousand gallons of aviation fuel and pitting the runways with craters. Three hours later, fifteen bombers hit Henderson again while F4Fs were refueling. Then, at twilight, a pair of 150mm Japanese howitzers began shelling the airfield from more than two miles away—the first time Henderson was hit by enemy artillery. The Eleventh Marines' 105mm howitzers lacked the range to effectively respond. Even worse days lay ahead for the Marines.[42]

Indeed, the "big push" was under way. The Japanese army and navy had repaired their frayed relationship in the interest of defeating the Americans on Guadalcanal. In late September Admiral Tanaka had complained to Yamamoto about the army's piecemeal reinforcement of Guadalcanal. The army, Tanaka said, continued to view Guadalcanal merely as an obstacle to its the primary objective, capturing New Guinea. The navy had also dithered, though. Captain Tameichi Hara, a destroyer commander, conceded that after the American landings the Imperial Navy had let two months go by before preparing to launch a major counter-offense.

Now, however, Japanese task forces were on their way to put ashore thousands of troops and transform Henderson Field into a hellish tableau of smashed planes and burning aviation fuel. By October 13, the Tokyo Express had landed more than ten thousand reinforcements, supplies, and the long-range howitzers collectively nicknamed "Pistol Pete" by the Marines.

With a destroyer escort, six high-speed transports were approaching Guadalcanal with forty-five hundred additional infantrymen, two heavy artillery batteries, an antiaircraft battalion, and a tank company. Their covering force consisted of cruisers and destroyers. A third task force lurked four hundred miles northwest of the island: carriers escorted by battleships, cruisers, and destroyers.[43]

ADMIRAL YAMAMOTO WAS A RISK-TAKER who excelled at games of chance. As a naval attaché in Washington before the war, he was known as a superb poker and bridge player. In electing to attack Pearl Harbor, Yamamoto had gambled and won. However, he had no illusions about what war with the United States meant; he had seen firsthand America's vast resources and its latent industrial capacity. Asked by Prince Konoye whether Japan could defeat the United States, Yamamoto reportedly replied, "I can raise havoc with them for one year, but after that I can give no guarantee." Writing to a friend, he was more pessimistic: "If we should go to war with the United States we must recognize the fact that the armistice will have to be dictated from the White House."

He was careful not to overrate the Pearl Harbor attack's success. "A military man can scarcely pride himself on having smitten a sleeping enemy," he wrote to a friend afterward. In the months following the attack he had grown more cautious.

Now Yamamoto was ready to roll the dice again and break with Japanese naval doctrine that said battleships existed to fight enemy ships, not to support troops on shore. Over the objections of Vice Admiral Takeo Kurita, Yamamoto decided to send the battleships *Kongo* and *Haruna* from northern Bougainville with a fighter escort into Ironbottom Sound to bombard Henderson Field.[44]

THE AMERICAL DIVISION'S 164TH INFANTRY, untested in combat but ably led by Lieutenant Colonel Bryant Moore, landed October 13 at Lunga Point and dug in behind the landing beaches. Private Robert Leckie of the First Marines observed that "their faces were still heavy with flesh, their ribs padded, their eyes innocent. They were older than we, an average twenty-five to our average twenty; yet we treated them like children." With the regiment's arrival, Vandegrift commanded 23,088 troops to the enemy's roughly 20,000.[45]

When transports had finished putting ashore the 164th, along with Jeeps, supplies, ammunition, and some Marine replacements, the 1st Raiders—or what remained of them—boarded the ships for the trip back to New Caledonia. Absent were more than half the men who landed on Tulagi on August 7. Attrition had depleted the Raiders' ranks on Tulagi, at Tasimboko, on Bloody Ridge—where their desperate fighting had by the thinnest margins prevented the enemy from capturing Henderson Field—and in the grinding offensives along the Matanikau.

Some of the Seventh Marines who went to the beach to look over the arriving soldiers and their supplies returned to their battalion dressed in new Army-issue clothing. Colonel Puller wanted to know where they got it. "Colonel, the beach is loaded," he was told. Puller and his first sergeant hopped into a Jeep and drove to the beach. Pistol Pete was lobbing shells at the perimeter, and the new arrivals were crouched in shelters, so Puller and the sergeant were free to help themselves to the Army supplies. When a guard shouted at them from a shelter to leave the supplies alone, Puller retorted, "If you're guarding this stuff, get the hell out here and guard it!" They drove away in their Jeep, which was filled with loot.

Besides being shelled, the National Guardsmen from North Dakota had landed in time to endure the day's two bombing raids. The regiment's first fatality was Corporal Kenneth Foubert, killed by a bomb minutes after setting foot on the island. Later in the day there was another artillery bombardment, followed that night by an unforgettable shelling by enemy battleships. It was a portentously violent welcome.

The Guardsmen's first night on Guadalcanal was a white-knuckle affair—the campaign's most severe naval bombardment. "We had been through 'purple nights' before, but they faded to dainty lavender compared to the events of this and succeeding nights," wrote Lieutenant Herbert Merillat.[46]

AT 1:30 A.M. ON OCTOBER 14 Japanese float biplanes dropped flares outlining Henderson Field for the battleships—red ones denoting the west side, white for the middle, green for the east side. The *Kongo* and *Haruna*, cruising eighteen miles offshore and beyond the range of the Marine five-inch shore batteries, opened fire with their sixteen 14-inch guns as four Japanese spotter planes cruised overhead and gunnery officers with range-finders watched from high in the ships' superstructures. The gunnery crews, firing ten rounds per minute on average, walked their fire back and forth across the airstrip and parking aprons, as "spontaneous cries and shouts of excitement" ran through the Japanese ships. Forty minutes into the bombardment there was a pause as the battleships turned around; the shelling then resumed for another forty minutes. The gunners fired both incendiary and armor-piercing shells, with the latter, normally reserved for sea battles, detonating a moment after impact.[47]

The Americans at Henderson would never forget it. Rather than cowering in a dugout, William White, a field telephone specialist with the Eleventh Marines, went on top of Bloody Ridge with several comrades to watch the show. "Glowing white hot, you could see them rise from the sea, arc across the sky . . . rumbling like a freight train," White wrote. They detonated "with a spectacular flash," the sound of the explosion arriving a moment later.[48]

It was terrifying for those on the receiving end, who first heard a sighing sound, then "a swoosh-swoosh-swoosh . . . rather like a steam locomotive straining to climb a steep hill." Sergeant Kerry Lane, a teenage Marine from North Carolina, wrote that the concussive explosions were "sharp and loud, followed by a swishing sound of hot flying shrapnel, as the metal cut through the trees on the forward side of the ridge." Private Sid Phillips, huddled with his comrades in their bomb shelter, "repeatedly died of terror. . . . Grown men were sobbing and crying like babies." The tremendous explosions "would squeeze our breath out and make us gasp for air."

Merillat lay in a shelter "at the bottom of a quaking heap." The shelter shook "as if it was set in jelly." Captain Joe Foss of VMF-121 dove into a shallow foxhole with his squadron commander, Major Duke Davis. "It seemed as if all the props had been kicked from under the sky and we were crushed beneath," wrote Foss. "Those two hours were simply indescribable. Nothing like them can be imagined." Private Leckie described the sensation of a fourteen-inch shell landing a hundred yards away. "Your stomach is squeezed, as though a monster hand were kneading it into dough; you gasp for breath like the football player who falls heavily and had the wind knocked out of him."

Danny Doyle, a VMF-121 pilot, shared a foxhole with three squadron mates as flames leaped hundreds of feet into the air from a nearby gasoline dump. An ammunition dump exploded. Planes were on fire. In an attempt at levity Doyle turned to a companion and said, "Say, do you think it would reveal our position if I lit a cigarette?"

General Vandegrift and his staff were equally helpless in their dugout. "A man comes close to himself at such times," Vandegrift understatedly wrote. During the brief hiatus in the shelling, Lieutenant Colonel Gerald Thomas, the division operations officer, said to Vandegrift, "I don't know how you feel, but I think I prefer a good [aerial] bombardment or artillery shelling." Vandegrift nodded and began to say, "I think I do . . . " when the thunderous battleship barrage resumed, drowning out the rest of his response. Thomas later said it was "the worst night on Guadalcanal."[49]

Four patrol torpedo boats that had arrived just two days earlier as the advance echelon of MTB Squadron 3 boldly sallied from Tulagi Harbor against the behemoths and their escorts. Around midnight the PT boats, their engines quietly rumbling, set a course for Savo Island to find the capital ships. The speedy little wooden boats fired their torpedoes, but the Japanese, having sighted the Americans, evaded the fish. The PT boats' audacity persuaded Rear Admiral Takeo Kurita to end the bombardment five minutes early. The battleships sailed away after having fired 918 fourteen-inch shells at Henderson Field. Japanese aircraft bombed the airfield the rest of the night.

Daybreak revealed a desolate landscape of fire, smoke, and ruin. It was "a sorry spectacle," remarked Martin Clemens. "We were in a proper mess." Huge craters, large enough to "hide a Jeep," had been gouged in the airfield, and buildings, planes, and fuel burned intensely. Everywhere lay chunks of metal up to a foot long—shrapnel from the battleships' huge shells. From Bloody Ridge, William White and his comrades watched as gas drums exploded one after another and "flames shot up in the air in a noisy, spectacular burst of fire. We could see explosions where our ammunition dumps were located, hear the sound, and feel the earth tremble." They saw personal shelters where nothing remained but "shreds of cloth and shattered equipment." A VMF-212 pilot described his sensations the morning after the bombardment. "You get up in the morning feeling a little gone and spill half the coffee out of your cup, your hand is so unsteady."[50]

Forty-one Marines died, including five members of VMSB-141; its commander, Major G. A. Bell, and four pilots were killed when a shell hit their camp. A shell entombed six men in a dugout; one of them crawled out and tried to dig out the others with his bare hands, aided by other Marines; two were freed; three died. Nearly all the aviation fuel was consumed in raging fires, all the torpedo bombers were knocked out, and just seven of the airfield's thirty-nine dive bombers were flyable. The bombardment dealt more lightly with Fighter One, where twenty-nine of its forty-one Wildcats were still airworthy, as well as four P-400s and two P-39s.[51]

Navy Torpedo 8's Grumman Avengers had been sent to Guadalcanal after *Saratoga* was hit on August 31, but all of its planes were now inoperable. Lacking the means to fight, Navy Lieutenant "Swede" Larsen, Torpedo 8's commanding officer, led his men out of their camp, wrecked during the bombardment, and onto Bloody Ridge with rifles, .30-caliber machine-guns scavenged from their planes, and ammunition and supplies. The torpedo pilots and crewmen joined Major Michael Mahoney's special weapons company of the Seventh Marines south of the airfield. A handful of mechanics remained behind to try to build one useable Avenger from six wrecks; they got it into the air October 22, when it bombed Japanese positions near Henderson.

Lieutenant Frederick Mears wrote that during the morning of October 14 the squadron was ready to break into eight-man groups if the Japanese took the island. "The outlook for Guadalcanal was pretty bleak that day," the pilot wrote. "We began to see a hopeless, losing fight." But in their new home with Major Mahoney's company the pilots absorbed some of the Marines' confidence in eventual victory. "We were no longer in doubt about who was going to hold the field," wrote Mears.[52]

Colonel Thomas was concerned about how the newly arrived 164th Infantry had survived the ordeal. "I was worried that the 164th would go to pieces . . . but it did not affect them," said Thomas. Three soldiers were killed, but the others had gotten into foxholes with the First Marines. A shaken newspaper correspondent wrote that it was "almost beyond belief that we are still here, still alive. . . . We cannot write in this madness, but we keep notes with shaking hands." That morning six of the eight correspondents on Guadalcanal made arrangements to leave.[53]

THERE WAS NO LETUP IN the Japanese attacks as the reinforcement convoy neared Guadalcanal. Two waves of Japanese bombers appeared over Henderson at midday on October 14. Two dozen Bettys dropped their bombs without opposition just before noon. An hour later, a handful of Wildcat pilots, their gas tanks filled with fuel scavenged from wrecked planes, jockeyed their planes around the runway potholes and went up to intercept the second wave—fifteen bombers and ten Zeros—and claimed nine bombers and three Zeros. Captain Foss hid in a cloud when his Wildcat's engine began misfiring, and then by luck a Zero swung right in front of him. "My touch on the trigger was as delicate as a drugstore clerk packing a pint of ice cream. The Jap's wing blew off," and Foss later saw the plane burning on a hillside—his second confirmed kill.[54]

Seabees worked feverishly throughout the day to restore the airfield to normal operations. The naval Construction Battalion was practiced in rapidly repairing bomb craters, but the damage on this morning was of another order of magnitude. The Seabees met the challenge. In one hour Commander Joseph Blundon's men filled thirteen bomb craters while planes circled overhead waiting to land. Even the Seabees' cooks pitched in, passing Marston matting to the repair crews, with the result that no food was prepared for twenty-four hours.[55]

The men of the 164th would never forget their first days on Guadalcanal. "I've seen boats blow up, bombs fall & hit full fuel tanks, planes falling & burning, shells whizzing overhead, men in a panicked stampede," wrote Philip Engstrom. Ed Mulligan said they had no choice but to fight, with the Japanese infantry in front of them and the sea behind them. "North Dakota farmers were mighty poor swimmers and no one could walk on water," he wrote.[56]

THE BOMBARDMENTS, AIR RAIDS, AND Japanese naval buildup inspired a train of ominous headlines in US newspapers: "Japs Believed to Rule Sea in Solomons," "Japanese Fleet Massing North of Guadalcanal as Decisive Battle Rages," "Fate of U.S. Airfield on Island in Doubt." An October 15 Associated Press story warned that "if the battle-hardened Marines and fresh American Army troops recently sent in to reinforce them cannot hold Guadalcanal with air and naval support available to them, then the first American offensive effort will have ended in disaster." An October 16 *New York Times* editorial said the critical battle was at hand. "We know that these American young men will do all that humanly can be done to stand their ground and advance. While we at home work, sleep, amuse ourselves . . . they fight. Guadalcanal. The name will not die out of the memories of this generation. It will endure in honor."[57]

THE TERRIFYING NAVAL BOMBARDMENT, EERILY similar to the thunderous artillery barrages that were hallmarks of World War I, had brutally exploited the airfield's vulnerability to nighttime naval and air attacks. It also revealed that Henderson's air operation might be paralyzed long enough for large numbers of Japanese reinforcements to be landed. Moreover, it darkened Marine and Navy leaders' outlooks. "We were out on a limb," said Colonel Thomas, Vandegrift's operations officer. At the beginning of their third month on Guadalcanal the Marines continued to feel they had been abandoned by the Navy. "We were up there by ourselves."

The sense of being at the last ditch filtered down through the ranks. During the afternoon of October 14 Lieutenant Colonel J. C. "Toby" Munn, aide to General Roy Geiger, the airfield commander, drove over to the Army's 67th Fighter Squadron and gathered pilots and mechanics. "I want you to pass the word along that the situation is desperate," he said.

"We don't know whether we'll be able to hold the field or not," said Munn. "There is a Japanese task force of destroyers, cruisers, and troop transports headed this way. We have enough gasoline left for one mission against them. Load your airplanes with bombs and go out with the dive bombers and hit them. After the gas is gone we'll have to let the ground troops take over. Then your officers and men will attach themselves to some infantry outfit. Good luck and goodbye."[58]

Major Robert Balance exhorted his 1st Marine Pioneer Battalion to prepare to "show their guts" during the climactic battle that everyone knew was coming. "Forget about the dying business; you can't live forever. Think instead about killing, squeezing off those shots, making every round land in one of the little yellow bastards. . . . If die we must, we'll do it with our boots on and our face to the Japs."[59]

Shortly before 2:00 a.m. on October 15 Vice Admiral Gunichi Mikawa, the victor at Savo Island two months earlier, took up a position off Lunga Point with his flagship cruiser *Chokai* and the cruiser *Kinugasa* and bombarded Henderson Field for thirty minutes. On the northwestern side of the island, Japanese destroyers landed more troops, ammunition, and supplies. The cruisers' barrage of more than 750 eight-inch shells added to the destruction wrought by the battleships the night before. Puller's 1st Battalion, Seventh Marines, had just moved from the perimeter to a reserve position beside the airfield, and an intelligence officer described the bombardment as "the most terrifying night of my life."[60]

The next morning, astonished Marines and soldiers saw the masts of Japanese transports and their escorts plainly anchored ten miles west of Lunga Point. They were landing troops and supplies on the beach off Kokumbona under an umbrella of Japanese Zeros. "Through the glasses," wrote Martin Clemens, "I could see them mustering on the beach. There were thousands of them."[61]

There was a mad scramble at the airfield to launch an attack on the amphibious force. Mechanics frantically repaired planes that had been damaged during the night's shelling. P-400 pilots from the Army's 67th Fighter Squadron filled ammunition belts by hand for their planes.

The most pressing need was for aviation fuel for the two dozen planes that were still airworthy. Known supplies had been destroyed during the two nights' bombardment. Told that there was no fuel for his planes, General Geiger snapped, "Then, by God, find some!" Ground crews began draining aviation fuel from disabled planes while the search continued for additional fuel.

A Geiger staff officer remembered that Geiger's chief of staff, Colonel Louis Woods, who was in Noumea, had cached drums of aviation fuel around the airfield. A search yielded more than four hundred drums—each able to keep one F4F airborne for one hour. A note to Geiger from Woods apprising him of the drums happened to be in Geiger's shirt pocket, unread.

The Cactus Air Force was back in business. VMF-121 skipper Duke Davis led five Wildcats into the sky to face the Japanese air screen as ground mechanics continued patching up damaged dive bombers, which were then sent, one at a time, to harry the Japanese landing force. Army P-400s from Henderson and B-17s from Espiritu Santo joined the chaotic air battle.[62]

Geiger halted the piecemeal attacks and marshaled every flyable plane for a coordinated attack on the transports anchored west of the airfield. He gathered twelve: eight fighters, three SBDs, and his personal aircraft, a PBY-5A amphibian whose pilot was Major Jack Cram, Geiger's junior aide.

Cram had been in the habit of using Geiger's "blue goose" for small supply runs between Noumea and Guadalcanal. The previous day Cram had landed the PBY with a torpedo under each wing; they were for Torpedo Squadron 8. Unfortunately none of Torpedo 8's planes was airworthy, and its pilots had joined the Seventh Marines.

No torpedo bombers being available, Cram proposed that Geiger's PBY be used as one—by being jury-rigged with manual-release triggers to drop the fish. In the present emergency neither Geiger nor anyone else objected. Cram planned his torpedo attack with Major Joe Renner, the airfield's operations officer; Cram's crew; and the squadron commanders. Their tactical scheme called for the SBDs to dive on the destroyers and transports from the landward side while Cram ranged farther out and made his run from the sea.

There was a drawback to the plan: Cram had never fired a torpedo. The Torpedo 8 pilots who might have tutored Cram were serving as infantrymen on the perimeter, so Renner briefed Cram during the five-minute Jeep drive to the airfield. Renner was a fighter pilot and knew little about flying torpedo bombers, but his brother piloted one, and Renner passed along what he had told him. "This will be the most screwed-up show in history, but there's no other choice," Renner told Cram. "If it works, miracles are still with us."

After jockeying the PBY into position over Ironbottom Sound, Cram sent it into a steep dive toward the Japanese transports. In amazement he saw that he was traveling 270 mph and that the wings were undulating; flying a PBY above 160 mph was usually discouraged. Cram skimmed over a destroyer and two transports at seventy-five feet as flak peppered his plane and released the torpedoes while approaching a third transport. One of the fish hit its target. Flak sheared off a hatch on the blue goose. Cram banked and headed back to Henderson, with five Zeros after him, strafing him repeatedly. A Zero remained on Cram's tail as he landed on Fighter One, but an alert Wildcat pilot shot it down.

Cram was evaluating the damage to Geiger's plane—starboard engine hit, tail shot up, fuel tanks riddled—when Geiger sent for him.

"Understand you got that plane shot up!" said the leathery Old Breed general.

"Yes, sir."

"How bad?"

"One hundred and seventy-five holes, sir," replied Cram, undoubtedly with a sinking feeling.

Geiger launched into a blistering tirade that included allusions to destruction of government property, even court-martial. When Cram happened to glance at Geiger's aide, Lieutenant Colonel Toby Munn, he saw that Munn was shaking with silent laughter. Munn winked at Cram.

Geiger wound up his diatribe by saying, "Jack, that was a damn fine job," and inviting him to lunch. Later that day, Geiger recommended Cram for the Navy Cross.[63]

GEIGER'S BLUE GOOSE SURVIVED, BUT nine of the eleven other Cactus planes that attacked the transport convoy were lost in the frenzied air battles. The Cactus Air Force remnant, along with Cram and a timely bombing attack by eleven B-17s from Espiritu Santo, sank one transport and forced the Japanese to abandon two others, "beached and burning," while withdrawing the last two. A B-17 bombed one of them and set it on fire near Savo Island. Seven Japanese planes were shot down.

However, forty-five hundred enemy reinforcements and most of their supplies had been put ashore. Yamamoto was keenly aware of the campaign's mounting toll on his resources—and on him personally. "I have resigned myself to spending the whole of my remaining life in the next one hundred days," he wrote to a friend—presciently, as events would show.[64]

WHILE GEIGER WAS ATTEMPTING TO address the aviation fuel emergency, Nimitz was assessing the overall situation on Guadalcanal; unsurprisingly, his evaluation was bleak. "It now appears that we are unable to control the sea in the Guadalcanal area. . . . The situation is not hopeless, but it is certainly critical."

Admiral Ghormley's message that day to Nimitz was even more pessimistic. "It appears to be [an] all-out enemy effort against Cactus, possibly other positions also. My forces totally inadequate [to] meet situation. Urgently request all aviation reinforcement possible." Vandegrift's staff gave Rear Admiral Aubrey Fitch, the new naval aviation commander in the South Pacific, a message that day for Ghormley, not wanting to transmit it by radio.

Tell Ghormley, Vandegrift's staff said to Fitch, "that the Jap has moved in and emplaced artillery of longer range than his [Vandegrift's] which is shelling positions and airfield at will; that enemy surface craft move at will in surrounding waters and shell his positions destructively both day and night and he will be unable indefinitely to hold these positions if this continues." He added that Geiger "can use no more aircraft until avgas situation improves and until destructive enemy fire on airfield from both land and sea is halted."

Fitch passed along the message and acted immediately to address the fuel shortages. Aviation fuel was sent to Guadalcanal on cargo ships, tugs, destroyers, a submarine, and a seaplane tender. Even as he organized this effort, Fitch was uncertain whether it would work. "So long as enemy ships patrol the sea area off Lunga day and night I cannot see how [destroyers and barges] can be brought in with reasonable chance of success."

An airlift of aviation fuel was organized, utilizing all active Army and Navy transport planes in the area. The fuel-carrying C-47s and R4Ds landed at Henderson, unloaded quickly, and then returned to Espiritu Santo for more fuel. The resupply runs lasted a week.

Major Harold Bauer's VMF-212, with twenty Wildcats, was coming from Espiritu Santo; eight SBDs from VS-6 were also en route. Fifteen mechanics led by Gunner Tom Griffis from the Efate air base volunteered to go to Guadalcanal to rejuvenate grounded planes and make them airworthy again. "We were rich in junk," said Griffis. "Planes were scattered around in heaps; there were chunks and fragments and bits of everything." In just one week the mechanics, sleeping on the ground and enduring air raids and shellings, put forty planes back into service.[65]

However, two Navy gasoline resupply missions on October 15 and 16 ended disastrously. Enemy search aircraft spotted the first convoy seventy-five miles from Guadalcanal on October 15: six barges towed by two cargo ships, a tug, a torpedo boat tender, and the destroyers *Meredith* and *Nicholas*. Each barge carried two thousand gallons of fuel and ten tons of bombs.

Certain they had been seen by the Japanese, the American ships turned around, except for the *Meredith* and the fleet tug *Vireo*. But upon receiving a report that two enemy ships were nearby, they too reversed course.

The nervous *Meredith* skipper decided to abandon and sink the *Vireo* because it made such slow time. The *Meredith* had just taken off the *Vireo*'s crew when twenty-seven Japanese planes appeared. In minutes they sank the *Meredith*. A life raft full of *Meredith* survivors managed to reach the *Vireo* before she floated away, but the other life rafts drifted for days—with burned crewmen inside the life rafts and the others hanging onto the rafts' lifelines, where sharks feasted on them. One shark leaped into a raft to tear a chunk of flesh from a wounded man's leg. Just 88 men were rescued. The *Meredith* lost 185 men and the *Vireo* 51.[66]

On October 16 the *McFarland* reached Lunga Point with forty thousand gallons of gasoline, twelve torpedoes, 37mm ammunition, and aircraft flares. As the destroyer-seaplane tender began unloading, 160 ambulatory combat casualties, including battle-fatigue patients, were taken aboard. A submarine periscope was sighted, and the skipper hastened to get underway while still unloading fuel onto a barge.

Fifty minutes later nine enemy dive bombers pounced on the *McFarland* and the gasoline barge, which was cast off just before a tremendous explosion blew it apart. A bomb hit a depth-charge rack on the *McFarland* and destroyed most of the fantail. The panicked patients tried to wrest weapons and life jackets from crewmen struggling with damage control. Amid the pandemonium the engine room crew managed to get the *McFarland* underway at five knots, and it lumbered across Sealark Channel to Tulagi. Twenty-seven men were killed and twenty-eight wounded.[67]

During the night of October 15–16 Japanese cruisers and destroyers returned to bombard Henderson for a third night running, plastering the airfield with more than 1,000 eight- and five-inch shells, adding to Henderson's bone yard of unsalvageable planes. The next morning the Cactus Air Force repeatedly attacked the Japanese landing zones, and carrier planes from the *Hornet*, cruising south of Guadalcanal, carried out seventy-four sorties.[68]

AMID THE BOMBARDMENTS AND AIR raids the Americal's 164th Infantry was still adjusting to its new life in a combat zone. At first the soldiers noticed the small things. For ordnance man Alex Kunivicius it was the parrots that nested in the palm trees in the soldiers' encampment. "They were a nuisance at night with their laughter," he wrote. "They sounded almost human." During air raids "it was as if they were in some large theater, hysterically laughing at some comedian's jokes, all night, without stopping, loud."[69]

"**WHERE IS OUR NAVY? EVERYONE** wants to know," wrote Marine Lieutenant Herbert Merillat, adding, "I still have confidence in them, and feel sure they are doing something to counter this threat. If not, we are lost." "I don't think we have a goddamn Navy," Geiger grumbled to one of his squadron commanders. Even Vandergrift was becoming discouraged, although he never stopped prodding Ghormley to take control of the sea around Guadalcanal and stop the enemy landings and bombardments. He requested more ground forces—a division so that he could go on the offensive.[70]

ON OCTOBER 16, A WEEK after VMF-121 landed at Henderson, VMF-212 arrived from Espiritu Santo with nineteen Wildcats led by Lieutenant Colonel Harold Bauer, enabling the last remaining pilots from VMF-223, VMF-224, and VMSB-232 to depart. Lieutenant Commander LeRoy Simpler's VF-5, the former *Saratoga*-based "Fighting Five," also was sent to the rear after having disproven the naval doctrine that carrier squadrons operated more effectively from aircraft carriers than from land.

Bauer was called "The Coach" by his admiring pilots because he emphasized teamwork—a carryover from his coaching days at the Naval Academy. At Annapolis, too, Bauer had acquired the nickname "Indian Joe" because of his above-average height, dark complexion, and high cheekbones. Bauer had flown to Henderson in September to inspect the airfield in advance of his squadron's deployment. During the inspection visit he had volunteered to go up with VMF-223 and VMF-224. On September 28 he shot down a bomber.

On October 3 he was the last pilot from his squadron to return to Henderson after a dogfight with a slew of Zeros. As he was about to land, Bauer saw a Zero shoot at a pilot who had parachuted from a disabled plane. With just one of his six guns operable, Bauer angrily got on the Zero's tail, shot it down, and then followed the parachuting Marine pilot to where he splashed down in the sea, circling overhead until a destroyer picked him up.

Bauer's engine was spurting flames when he landed, but he was exultant. "The Coach came roaring in like a happy boy," wrote Lieutenant Robert "Pop" Flaherty. Bauer was credited with four confirmed kills that day.[71]

Thirteen days later, as Bauer led his squadron and seven SBDs to Henderson, he saw nine "Val" dive bombers attacking *McFarland* during her ill-fated resupply mission. Nearly out of fuel, Bauer went alone to the *McFarland*'s aid. In a dramatic display of aerial prowess he shot down three Vals, and when he landed, Marines at the airfield cheered.[72]

THE NEWLY ARRIVED PILOTS WERE thrilled to learn combat flying on the job. "I was terribly excited," wrote VMF-212 pilot Jack Conger, who would leave

Guadalcanal with ten and a half confirmed kills. "I hoped it would be my first real chance to draw blood, and that was what I wanted: the blood."

On one of his first missions, to intercept a fifty-six-plane Japanese raid, Conger shot down a Betty. As the enemy bomber plummeted to the sea, Conger's windshield suddenly shattered, glass flew into his left eye, and a piece of metal pierced his left shoe. A Zero had made a "high side" pass at him, stitching the left side of his plane with machine-gun fire and blowing apart his radio. "My whole damn plane was caving in on me. It left me a little woozy." He limped back to Guadalcanal.[73]

Captain Joe Foss and VMF-121 went up with Smith and Carl before they left Henderson and learned about hit-and-run tactics and deflection shooting. Then the replacements had to make their own way. "After a couple of days, we felt like veterans," wrote Foss. The new arrivals were told to strap their oxygen masks on tight; failure to do so invited blackouts and death. "Every time that some new pilots came in we'd always lose a couple of men," wrote Foss.

The rookie Cactus pilots also quickly learned to watch for crossfire when strafing the new enemy destroyers, which would "light up like Christmas trees" when their antiaircraft turrets went into action. "The ship that you're strafing isn't the dangerous one," Foss said. "There's one on each side; they start playing a crossfire into you and they pretty well put it on you."[74]

PRESIDENT FRANKLIN ROOSEVELT AND HIS advisers anxiously monitored the all-out fight on Guadalcanal. Navy Secretary Frank Knox communicated the administration's uneasiness with the situation at a news conference on October 16, when he was asked whether Guadalcanal could be held. "I certainly hope so and expect so," he replied, not sounding very convincing. "I will not make any predictions, but every man will give a good account of himself. What I am trying to say is that there is a good stiff fight going on. Everybody hopes we can hang on."

A series of stories by *New York Times* correspondent Hanson Baldwin, who had spent time on Guadalcanal, began to open Americans' eyes for the first time to the situation's gravity, prompting the Navy to become more forthcoming about its losses. In his first story Baldwin wrote that the United States had "nailed the colors to the mast." The battle, he said, "is a sprawling, intermittent sea, air and land action in which the stakes are high—perhaps eventual victory itself."[75]

At about the same time, Roosevelt shared his thoughts about Guadalcanal with the joint chiefs of staff in a handwritten note. "My anxiety about the S. W. Pac. is to make sure that every feasible weapon gets into that area to hold Guadalcanal, and that having held it in this crisis, that munitions and planes and crews are on the way to take advantage of our success. . . . Our long range plans could be set back for months if we fail to throw our full strength in our immediate and impending conflicts."

The president ordered an immediate canvass of all combat planes inside the United States and requested an inventory of requirements in the South Pacific and on the European front. As a result General Arnold, the Army Air Forces commander, agreed to send 150 planes to the South Pacific, including some of the P-38s that he had been hoarding for Operation Torch, the North African landings planned for November.[76]

Indeed, the Army and Navy agreed that victory on Guadalcanal was crucial to winning the Pacific War, and the intensified Japanese air and naval attacks plainly pointed to something big about to happen. Intelligence reports from Nimitz's command repeatedly warned of a major Japanese offensive. "Predict another attempt [to] recapture Guadalcanal Field impending," said an October 6 bulletin, followed two days later by one that read, "Expect continued enemy reinforcement Guadalcanal by destroyers and small craft almost nightly," and on October 23, "Indications of another Japanese offensive soon. Exact date and place not known but believe will be within two or three days and directed against Guadalcanal."[77]

A day before the last bulletin, Colonel Edson, the Fifth Marines' commander, wrote to his wife, "We are girding our loins for what will probably be the show-down here and may be a deciding factor so far as the length of the war is concerned."[78]

CATHOLIC MISSIONARIES HAD OPERATED SCHOOLS, clinics, and mission churches on Guadalcanal for decades before the Japanese arrived. When the Lever Brothers' employees sailed to Australia, the Catholics elected to stay. Just as they had abused the native Melanesians, the Japanese mistreated the priests and nuns, appropriating their food and furniture and threatening their lives.

On September 3 the Japanese had seized two priests and two nuns from Catholic Station east of Henderson Field after intercepting a message sent to the Marines describing the Japanese dispositions near Taivu Point. Japanese soldiers led Fathers Henry Oude-Engberink of the Netherlands and Arthur Duhamel of the United States—Duhamel had sent the intercepted letter and others to General Vandegrift—and French Sisters Mary Sylvia and Mary Odilia to a hut and slashed their throats. A third sister, in bed with a fever, was spared. One of Clemens's scouts discovered the bodies of the priests and sisters four days later.

Martin Clemens now justifiably feared for the safety of the missionaries remaining at Tangarere Mission on Guadalcanal's southwestern coast. There, Bishop Jean Marie Aubin, coast watcher L. Schroeder, some priests, and eighteen nuns strove to remain beneath the Japanese's notice while struggling with malaria and dysentery.[79]

Clemens was determined to get them out, and a month after the murders of the sisters and priests, the schooner *Ramada* sailed away from Tangarere with Bishop Aubin and twenty-five others. Escorted by an F4F, the schooner rendezvoused with American supply ships that took the missionaries to Buma Mission on Malaita.[80]

On October 9 Clemens and his scouts, after guiding two companies of Second Marines to landings at Taivu Point, reached the village of Gorabusu, where they found a chalice from the Catholic Station that the Japanese had used as an ashtray. A Japanese soldier was found dead in a bed, wrapped in an altar cloth that he had used as a blanket.[81]

ADMIRAL YAMAMOTO HAD ORDERED THE 11th Air Fleet to attack Henderson daily during October without regard for losses. When Kahili Airfield at Buin, about three hundred miles from Guadalcanal, became fully operational on October 20, the Japanese were able to use shorter-range fighter escorts for the bomber runs from Rabaul. Other forward bases were being built on Vella Lavella and Munda in New Georgia, Kolombangara, and Rekata Bay on San Isabel. When completed, the new bases would increase Japanese fighter availability over Guadalcanal by one-third.

On the ground, eyewitnesses sometimes found themselves uncomfortably close to the action. Martin Clemens and his scouts had just landed at Taivu Point to guide the Second Marines on October 9 when, directly above them, a flight of P-400 Airacobras pounced on twenty Bettys. "Bullets and empty cartridge cases fell all around," wrote Clemens. "Then planes started to crash in the sea about us." An Army pilot leaped from his plummeting aircraft just a hundred feet above the water, hitting "so hard that all his clothes came off." The scouts fished him out of the sea, but he died ten minutes later. Another pilot pulled from the water, with one eye dangling from its socket, had a better outcome: a doctor pushed the eye back in and covered it with gauze, and the pilot recovered.[82]

An air raid sent a machine-gunner named Corporal Zachary sprinting for his gun on Bloody Ridge, but the enemy plane was already overhead before Zachary could reach it and dropped an antipersonnel "daisy cutter." William White, a field telephone operator with the Eleventh Marines, and other Marines found Zachary on his back, his lower body twisted and torn. He was conscious but dying. His comrades ribbed him about trying to take on the Japanese plane alone. "The joker banged me a good one," he replied. A doctor added a hospital blanket to the jacket someone had thrown over his shredded midsection, but could do nothing more. Zachary talked for a few minutes, and when he stopped, he was dead. A friend of Zachary's who won often at cards retrieved a wad of several hundred dollars' cash from his own bag and handed it to the sergeant major. Send it to Zachary's family, he said. Tell them Zachary had saved the money.[83]

ON OCTOBER 17 THE NAVY disrupted the daily routine of multiple Japanese air raids with a retributive attack of its own: destroyers *Aaron Ward* and *Lardner* bombarded the Japanese positions west of Kokumbona for three and a half hours with 2,000 five-inch shells. Cactus dive bombers acted as spotters, and B-17s joined in the destruction. The shelling was more effective than anyone might have imagined. Ammunition dumps and enormous food stockpiles disappeared in concussive explosions and billowing black smoke. Among the casualties were twelve hundred large sacks of rice and five hundred boxes of hardtack and canned goods. Captain Toshikazu Ohmae later wrote that the bombardment was "the most fatal reason for further failures" on Guadalcanal.[84]

HAVING GROWN WEARY OF GHORMLEY'S pessimism and his failure to stop the Tokyo Express, Nimitz announced that he was replacing him. The final straw came on October 15 when Ghormley described the developing Japanese offensive to capture the island and conceded to Nimitz that his own forces were "totally inadequate [to] meet the situation." Ghormley's words confirmed for Nimitz the momentous decision with which he had been wrestling for days—whether to relieve the admiral who commanded all South Pacific Allied forces.[85]

Days earlier in Hawaii, Nimitz had told a staff officers meeting, "I don't want to hear, or see, such gloom and defeatism. Remember the enemy is hurt, too, but our job here is to provide them with everything they need on Guadalcanal to fight this battle."

Afterward he detained a few of his officers, including Lieutenant Commander Edwin Layton, the fleet intelligence officer, and asked each of them to advise him about what he should do. Without exception they recommended replacing Ghormley with a more effective leader. Nimitz recoiled from the suggestion; it was tantamount to "mutiny," he said.

But during an impromptu late-night meeting that they requested with Nimitz in his quarters, the officers raised the subject again and pointed out that Vice Admiral William Halsey was now available. The Guadalcanal emergency, they said, justified dispensing with the usual consideration for fellow officers' feelings. Nimitz heard them out and thanked them without further comment.[86]

On October 16, Nimitz told the Navy's commander in chief, Admiral Ernest King, that he was considering relieving Ghormley and replacing him with Halsey. He asked King to comment on the proposal. "Approved," King replied. Halsey's appointment proved to be the great turning point of the naval struggle for Guadalcanal.[87]

UPBEAT, AGGRESSIVE WILLIAM "BULL" HALSEY was the antitheses of the glum Ghormley, who had worked without respite in his quarters aboard the *Argonne* at Noumea because the Free French refused to give him quarters ashore. Ghormley had never visited Guadalcanal. Sent to Washington to await a new assignment, Ghormley underwent a thorough physical examination; it revealed that he had an ulcer and decayed teeth. Nimitz later recalled Ghormley to Pearl Harbor to command the 14th Naval District. In 1945 Ghormley oversaw Navy forces in Germany.[88]

Halsey had been on the "sick list" for months—and had missed Midway—because of what doctors diagnosed as "general dermatitis." The itching was almost unbearable; he was lucky to sleep two hours a night, and he lost twenty pounds. Halsey spent two months in hospitals in Pearl Harbor and Richmond, Virginia, before being pronounced fit for duty.[89]

Halsey's ancestors included sailors—among them the first Long Island whaler to make the perilous journey around Cape Horn. Halsey was a 1904 graduate of the Naval Academy, where he played fullback on the football team. The student newspaper, the *Lucky Bag*, described him as "a real old salt" and "everybody's friend." He sailed around the world with the Great White Fleet on the battleship *Kansas* in 1907–1909.

In 1935, at the age of fifty-two, Halsey enrolled in the Navy's aviator course after he was given command of the aircraft carrier *Saratoga*. Rather than train as a "student observer," he signed up as a "student pilot," the oldest person in Navy history to do so. "With a carrier command ahead of me, I wanted a clear understanding of a pilot's problems and mental processes." He believed that the naval officers of the next war should thoroughly understand aviation.

Aside from those sound reasons, for Halsey there was also the visceral excitement of flying. When he soloed, "it was the thrill of my life." He did not tell his wife Frances that he had switched to the pilot's course until he had logged ten hours in the air alone, knowing she would be "mad as a hornet"; she was—when she read his letter informing her that he was a full-fledged pilot.[90]

Halsey learned of his appointment as the South Pacific's commander when he arrived in Noumea in a PBY patrol bomber with Rear Admiral Raymond Spruance. Before Halsey left the plane, a boat came alongside and he was handed a sealed envelope in which were orders from Nimitz: "You will take command of the South Pacific Area and the South Pacific Forces immediately." Halsey exclaimed, "Jesus Christ and General Jackson! This is the hottest potato they ever handed me!"[91]

One of his first acts was to move his headquarters ashore. When presented with Halsey's request for quarters and office space on the island, the haughty Free French governor, Marie Henri Ferdinand Auguste Montchamp, told Halsey's intelligence officer, Marine Colonel Julian Brown, that he would take the matter "under consideration." When he heard nothing further, Brown returned to Montchamp, who deliberately turned his back on the Marine officer, indicating that he would not respond to Halsey's request.

Enraged by the governor's arrogance, Halsey called for his barge and a Marine guard and went ashore. He stalked to Montchamp's offices, but the governor was not there. Halsey ordered the Marines to surround the building and to raise the Stars and Stripes on its flagpole. He then appropriated the former Japanese consulate and made it his headquarters. Montchamp got the message and grudgingly cooperated. Halsey obtained another building for additional office space, erected Quonset huts, and built facilities for servicemen on R&R. The French made no formal complaint.[92]

Halsey's appointment was one of several actions taken by Nimitz on October 18 regarding Guadalcanal. He ordered a new task force and the Army's 25th Division on Oahu to proceed to the South Pacific. Nimitz also dispatched fifty Army fighters from the Central Pacific, twenty-four submarines, and twenty-four B-17s that would be under Admiral Aubrey Fitch's direction. The carrier *Enterprise*, damaged during the Battle of the Eastern Solomons on August 24 but now repaired, was sent back to the South Pacific.

Fitch had succeeded Rear Admiral John S. McCain as naval air commander in the South Pacific. Vandegrift missed the chain-smoking admiral; they respected one another and enjoyed each other's company. McCain "knew our needs . . . and didn't leave a stone unturned and tried to get us additional air support," Vandegrift wrote. In his farewell message to Vandegrift, McCain wrote, "The planes must find these ships that run in and hit you at night and must strike them before dark."[93]

ON GUADALCANAL THE NEWS OF Halsey's appointment was greeted by loud cheering. It first erupted in the Signal Company bivouac about 9:00 p.m. on October 18 and then spread to units around Vandegrift's command post. "Here were men whooping it up and turning cartwheels in the dark at the best news we had heard since Kelly Turner brought in our Seventh Marines exactly one month before," wrote Lieutenant Colonel Merrill Twining. "The first ray of hope broke through the dark clouds," wrote William White, the field telephone operator from the Eleventh Marines.

Even the usually undemonstrative Vandegrift showed his elation at the news. "The old man was sitting in his tent when I took the message in to him," said a staff officer. "He read it, read it again, and then exploded straight up in the air and let out a war whoop. It's the only time I ever saw him excited." Vandegrift later wrote that he knew Halsey by reputation and "knew of his aggressive nature and that he wouldn't fight a passive naval war and he didn't." He added, "Our drastic, imperiled situation called for the most positive form of aggressive leadership at the top. From what I knew of Bill Halsey, he would supply this like few other naval officers."[94]

A few days later, Halsey met in Noumea with Vandegrift, Admiral Kelly Turner, Marine Commandant Thomas Holcomb, and Army Generals Millard Harmon and Alexander Patch. Vandegrift and Harmon related their "bitter stories"—Vandegrift saying that his men were "practically worn out." Turner "reacted defensively, arguing that the Navy was doing all that it could with its limitations and the enemy arrayed against it."

Halsey asked Vandegrift pointblank, "Can you hold?"

"I can hold, but I've got to have more active support than I've been getting," Vandegrift replied. The Marines especially needed for the Navy to stop the Tokyo Express runs and thwart a troop buildup that could imperil the airfield.

"All right," said Halsey. "Go on back. I promise to get you everything I have."[95]

"I had to begin throwing punches almost immediately," Halsey told Nimitz two weeks after taking command. He ordered Task Forces 16 and 17, led by Rear Admirals Thomas Kinkaid and George Murray and consisting of the carriers *Enterprise* and *Hornet* and up to twenty other ships, to conduct a "sweep" around the north side of the Santa Cruz Islands and to then move southwest toward San Cristobal. He sent Rear Admiral Willis Lee and his smaller Task Force 64 to the area southeast of Guadalcanal.[96]

At his headquarters Halsey imposed a more relaxed sartorial style: his officers were permitted to wear lightweight khakis without neckties rather than the Washington-prescribed new gray uniform. With less success, he tried to erase the ancient interservice rivalries between the Army, Navy, and Marine Corps.[97]

In an ill-advised attempt to improve morale in the South Pacific, Halsey rashly predicted that the Allies would be in Tokyo by the end of 1943. Washington complained that his words could result in a slackening of the war effort.

But his orders were simple and direct. Vandegrift's staff was "delighted. It was a heartwarming change to us," wrote Twining.

Halsey's characteristic aggressiveness was on display at the naval landing area in Tulagi. A handwritten sign in two-feet-high capitals read: "KILL JAPS, KILL JAPS, KILL MORE JAPS!" Halsey's admonition might shock modern sensibilities, but in 1942 it was in step with mainstream sentiment. Besides being routinely disparaged as monkeys, insects, and rodents, the Japanese were vilified in popular songs. One was titled "Mow the Japs Down!" whose lyrics dripped with racial hatred in lines such as, "They're going to be playing taps on the Japs," and "We're gonna have to slap the dirty little Jap." Ernie Pyle wrote that the Japanese were "looked upon as something subhuman and repulsive, the way some people feel about cockroaches or mice."[98]

THE DAY OF HALSEY'S APPOINTMENT also marked the eighth consecutive day of enemy air attacks. The Japanese 150mm field pieces collectively known as "Pistol Pete" also closed Henderson Field. From up to six miles away on the Matanikau River's west bank they were able to hit the airfield with sixty-nine-pound shells without fear of counter-battery fire. Japanese forward observers on Hill 903 west of the airfield watched the shells land and radioed corrections until the artillery fire was on target. The enemy gunners changed their firing positions sometimes daily, making it difficult to find and destroy them.

The barrage forced the Cactus Air Force to shift most of its operations to its Fighter One airstrip a mile east of Henderson for five days. During one attack, when VMF-121 and VMF-212 scrambled Wildcats to meet fifteen incoming Bettys and nine Zeros, the battle raged in the sky above the perimeter.

Lieutenant Lawrence "Cloudy" Faulkner of VMF-212 wrote, "One of them turned back into me from above, and it seemed to me that I could feel the bullets from all six of my guns smashing into him. He exploded; I flew through the smoke and flames and bits of shattered plane." He saw the dead pilot plunge from the sky into the sea.

Lieutenant Robert "Pop" Flaherty's Wildcat malfunctioned and began smoking, but he managed to shoot up a Zero before having to make a water landing. His head banged into the rubber-padded gunsight, knocking him unconscious. When he came to, he was bleeding from cuts over both eyes. He worked himself free from his plane, and natives in two canoes fished him out of Ironbottom Sound.

The Americans shot down seven enemy planes while losing two F4Fs. Captain Joe Foss had two kills, making him an ace after just nine days on the island.[99]

On October 20 a dozen bombers and twenty Zeros raided Henderson. "I was in a sky full of Japs," said Lieutenant Charles Freeman of VMF-212. "They were everywhere, like birds, all taking a peck at me. While I was shooting at one, two more were coming in on my tail." Lieutenant Loren Everton said that at one point "I had one ahead of me, one on each side, and one sliding in from above." Gunfire smashed into his cockpit, spraying his right side with shrapnel. His leg went numb, and he had to lift his leg with his hand to place it on the rudder pedal. Everton somehow managed to land, but his plane "was junk . . . it just went on the [Henderson bone yard] pile."[100]

The raids continued without letup on October 21 and 22, and on October 23 there was a twelve-Zero fighter sweep followed by an attack by sixteen Bettys escorted by seventeen other Zeros.

October 23 was a transformative day for the Cactus pilots. Lieutenant Colonel Harold Bauer, the VMF-212 leader who now commanded all of Cactus's fighter pilots, sent up everything he had: twenty-four F4Fs and four P-39s. "When you see Zeros, dogfight 'em!" he told his surprised pilots, instructions that contradicted the long-standing practice of avoiding dogfights unless necessary. The change was tacit recognition that after two months of intensive air combat, many of Japan's best pilots in the South Pacific were dead, and their replacements lacked their training and experience.

On this day, the pilots clearly remembered, the humidity was perfect for contrails, and the sky was full of them. Lieutenant Jack Conger pursued a dodging Zero and fired a short burst that blew up the enemy plane, hurling the pilot thirty feet into the air. The Japanese airman then plummeted downward, his unopened parachute flapping above him. Conger followed him to the water, where he lay "as though asleep." The Cactus pilots shot down seven planes.[101]

THE CEASELESS ATTACKS ON HENDERSON Field, Yamamoto believed, would enable the navy to land thousands of infantrymen as well as tanks and artillery, and to build up Japanese forces so that in mid-October, General Hyakutake's Seventeenth Army could crush the Marines and capture the airfield.

Most of the more than ten thousand newly landed soldiers belonged to the Sendai (2nd) Division, but they also included two battalions of the 230th Infantry Regiment of the 38th Division. Besides putting reinforcements ashore, the Tokyo Express runs, carried out by ninety-two destroyers, seven cruisers, and four seaplane carriers, also landed eighty artillery pieces from Major General Tadashi Sumiyoshi's 4th Heavy Field Artillery Regiment, forty-six hundred boxes of supplies, and ammunition — 160 tons in all, according to historian Richard Frank.

Counting Kawaguchi's and Ichiki's remnants from the two failed offensives, along with service and support troops, there were now about twenty-two thousand Japanese soldiers on Guadalcanal facing twenty-three thousand Marines and soldiers.

"The victory is already in our hands," Hyakutake messaged headquarters in Rabaul. So confident was he of success that he had chosen the Matanikau River mouth as the place where he would accept the surrender of Vandegrift, who would be required to approach with a white flag and an American flag. Before the Bloody Ridge fiasco General Kawaguchi also had had a surrender plan, as well as the dress uniform he intended to wear for the occasion.[102]

On October 16 the Sendai Division, led by Lieutenant General Masao Maruyama, began advancing with the harrowed Kawaguchi Brigade toward staging points south and west of the American perimeter. Each soldier carried sixty pounds of food, ammunition, and artillery shells. Ten days' rations were expected to sustain the Sendai during its thirty-five-mile trek to Bloody Ridge's approaches. Maruyama believed that his men would be ready to attack on October 22.

In an exhortatory message to his men the general wrote, "This is the decisive battle between Japan and the United States in which the rise or fall of the Japanese Empire will be decided. If we do not succeed in the occupation of these islands, no one should expect to return alive to Japan. . . . Hit the proud enemy with an iron fist so he will not be able to rise again."[103]

The 2nd Division dated to the Imperial Japanese Army of the 1870s. It recruited youths from the Sendai region north of Tokyo, and its headquarters was at Sendai Castle in the Tohoku District—hence, its better-known name. Its recruits were treated more harshly than nearly any soldiers in any army. Beaten and poorly fed to accustom them to privation, the Sendai, before being deployed, marched 122 miles in seventy-two hours with forty-pound packs and 150 rounds of ammunition, running the final miles to their barracks. The division had fought in all of Japan's wars. In 1931 it helped lead the invasion of Manchuria and battled Soviet troops during the 1939 Nomonhan campaign. In March 1942 it had landed at Bantam Bay in Java. Pledging absolute fealty to the emperor, the Sendai's motto was taken from the 1882 Meiji rescript to soldiers and sailors:

"Bear in mind that duty is heavier than a mountain, while death is lighter than a feather."

Although the Sendai division was steeped in tradition and tempered to withstand adversity, some skeptical Japanese officers regarded it as merely average because of its lack of combat experience against well-trained troops. "Though high-spirited, they were not expert fighters," concluded Vice Admiral Ugaki. The division consisted of the 4th, 16th, and 29th Infantry Regiments and artillery and engineer units.[104]

Japanese engineers laboriously hacked out the approach trail—a yard-wide footpath grandly named the "Maruyama Road" in keeping with the general's lofty self-regard. It traversed dense rain forest and rugged, rain-slickened mountains. Construction took fourteen days, longer than expected. Engineers at times had to use ropes to negotiate the steep mountain slopes. Because the jungle canopy concealed the trail from Cactus's reconnaissance planes, Vandegrift and his staff were unsure of the enemy force's size and destination, and their forebodings steadily grew.

Marine intelligence officers asked the redoubtable Jacob Vouza, now recovered from his wounds, to bring them Japanese prisoners to interrogate. The tough, scarred Melanesian with the honorific title of Marine sergeant major was universally respected. He proudly wore Marine dungarees inside the perimeter.

When he was asked to bring in Japanese prisoners, Vouza reportedly replied, "Yes, sir! When do you want them?"

How about tomorrow? replied the intelligence officers.

What time? Vouza asked.

The amused Marines told him 10 a.m.

To the astonishment of Vandegrift's D-2 officers, at precisely 10 a.m. the next day Vouza appeared with two hog-tied prisoners slung between his scouts.[105]

FOURTEEN THOUSAND JAPANESE TROOPS WERE snaking through the hilly jungle west and south of the Matanikau River. Maruyama's nine battalions were tested to their limits in just reaching the jumping-off point on the upper Lunga River near Mount Austen. Worn down by the relentless heat and the rutted, muddy trail over knife-edged ridges, the Japanese began abandoning artillery pieces and discarding shells—and fell behind schedule. Maruyama postponed the attack until October 23.

General Yumio Nasu commanded the Sendai's three-battalion left wing while General Kawaguchi led the right wing's three battalions. The three other battalions would act as their reserve. To divert attention from the primary attack by the Sendai from the south, General Hyakutake planned two assaults along the Matanikau River west of the Marine perimeter. Colonel Nomasu Nakaguma, with roughly two battalions from the diminished 4th Infantry Regiment, was to attack across the river mouth, supported by artillery and tanks commanded by General Sumiyoshi. At the same time three other battalions under Colonel Akinosuke Oka would ford the river a mile upstream near the Log Bridge, and then push north toward the sea, wiping out the two Marine battalions holding the river's east bank.

If those maneuvers succeeded, the Japanese planned to land a battalion of the 228th Regiment east of the perimeter at Koli Point. Its mission would be to capture an airfield believed to be under construction in the area but that in reality did not exist.[106]

Hyakutake had unnecessarily complicated his plan to deceive the Marines, who had only a vague idea of what he was up to. In so doing he had in fact handicapped his own army. What might have been one massive assault on Bloody Ridge had been parsed into four smaller attacks by Maruyama's two wings, Nakaguma's infantry-tank-artillery force, and Oka. They were isolated from one another by distance and unreliable communications.

On October 23, when Maruyama was supposed to attack, he again pushed back the operation by one day—until 5:00 p.m. on October 24. Nasu, commanding the Sendai's left wing southwest of Bloody Ridge, was ready to attack on October 23, but Kawaguchi's right wing was not; Kawaguchi insisted on aiming his attack farther to the east. Weary of the delays and arguments, Maruyama relieved Kawaguchi of his command and appointed Colonel Toshinaro Shoji in his place. Fatigue, rain, and darkness added to the confusion among Maruyama's nine battalions; they had twenty-four hours to put things in order.

Vice Admiral Ugaki fumed over the delay in his diary, "How unreliable they are!" The delay disrupted what was to have been a finely coordinated army-navy operation. Yamamoto had sent the Second and Third Fleets east of Guadalcanal to stop American reinforcements from reaching the island during Maruyama's attack. Ugaki regretted not having sent a naval liaison officer to accompany the Sendai Division.[107]

The postponement order did not reach General Sumiyoshi, who was prostrated by malaria but still directing the planned attack by his tanks, artillery, and Colonel Nakaguma's foot soldiers across the Matanikau sandbar. Unaware that the offensive had been delayed, Sumiyoshi's tank-infantry force attacked on schedule at 6:00 p.m. on October 23.

THE MARINES MIGHT HAVE BEEN unaware of the arduous march by Maruyama's men to their staging area south of Bloody Ridge, but Vandegrift and his staff had presumed that the Matanikau sandspit would be a target of the coming offensive. They had prepared carefully. The 3rd Battalion, First Marines was entrenched on the sandspit's eastern side, and the 3rd Battalion, Seventh Marines had been placed seven hundred yards to the south. Colonel Pedro del Valle's Eleventh Marines had preregistered ten batteries between the river and Point Cruz, a mile to the west. Also in prepared positions were 75mm guns, 37mm antitank guns, and heavy machine-guns. Indeed, the sandspit was probably the best-defended Marine sector. If there was any doubt about Sumiyoshi's intentions, it was dispelled on October 21 when nine tanks lunged toward the sandspit in a preliminary attack. The assault was immediately broken up, with one tank destroyed.

At sunset on October 23 the Marine defenders heard the clanking of a tank approaching from the west. The lead Japanese tank raced toward the sandspit and the Matanikau's east bank, with several medium tanks in its train. At first, some Marines mistook the roar of the tank engines for low-flying enemy planes—until they saw the tanks coming right at them. Gunfire ricocheted off the hull of the lead tank as it burst through the Marines' barbed wire and sped toward their lines.

Private Joseph Champagne reached out of his foxhole with a grenade and dropped it in the tank's tread. The explosion snapped the tread and caused the tank to veer out of control. A 75mm gun on a partially buried halftrack then blew it apart. Within minutes the other Japanese tanks were destroyed by artillery and antitank fire before they could cross the sandspit, and the Marines shot down the tank crews when they tried to flee. "We ripped them with machine guns," wrote Lieutenant William Whyte of the First Marines.[108]

About six hundred of Nakaguma's infantrymen were in assembly areas across the sandspit, poised to cross when the tanks broke through. Forty of the Eleventh Marines' preregistered 105mm guns cut loose, pulverizing the ground where the infantrymen stood, where they intended to attack, and where they tried to retreat.

The Marines could hear the screams of the wounded over the sound of exploding shells. The next morning three Marine Stuart tanks emerged from the jungle and ground over the corpses covering the sandspit and its western approaches. "Soon the ground was covered with gore and intestines," wrote Whyte. Daylight on October 24 revealed a scene similar to the aftermath of Ichiki's Alligator Creek attack, except that in addition to the mounds of bodies—about 650 Japanese lay dead—there were the charred hulls of nine tanks. Remarkably the First Marines reported just two men killed and eleven wounded.[109]

ALTHOUGH THE ATTACK WAS PREMATURE and failed dismally, it accomplished the goal of persuading the Americans that the Matanikau River was where the coming battle would be fought. Even before Sumiyoshi's assault, Major General Roy Geiger, who was acting in Vandegrift's stead while Vandegrift met at Noumea with Halsey and his admirals, had moved Colonel Herman Hanneken's 2nd Battalion, Seventh Marines off Bloody Ridge to a position upriver from the two battalions already occupying the Matanikau's eastern bank.

Like Vandegrift in September, Geiger and the division staff downplayed the threat to Bloody Ridge's southern approaches; they were all but certain that the main attack would come from the west.

This left Colonel Puller's understrength, seven-hundred-man battalion of Seventh Marines to defend a twenty-five-hundred-yard crescent along the ridge's southern brow. He spread out his men to cover both their original sector as well as Hanneken's former area. Puller's line was thin, even with every available man on it. To Puller's left, occupying the southeastern ridgetop, was the Army's 2nd Battalion, 164th Infantry, which had never been in combat.

Unlike the Raiders and parachutists in September, however, Puller's battalion possessed impressive firepower. It had amassed a large number of .30-caliber heavy and light machine-guns and had also scrounged .50-caliber machine-guns from wrecked Wildcats in the Henderson bone yard. In addition, the battalion was armed with six 60mm and four 81mm mortars, and the regiment had sent it a dozen 37mm antitank guns. It was a formidable arsenal compared with the light arms with which the Raiders and paratroopers had defended Bloody Ridge six weeks earlier.

With a cold pipe stem clamped between his teeth, Puller carefully inspected his machine-gun positions on October 24, ensuring that their fields of fire interlocked. Throughout the day, Puller's men deepened their holes and readied their weapons. Barbed wire was wrapped around trees and hung with tin cans filled with stones and grenades with the pins half-pulled. During his inspection of the lines Puller stopped at one well-excavated foxhole, pointed to it with his pipe, and said, "Son, if you dig that hole any deeper, I'll have to charge you with desertion."

In front of their position the Marines had laid down double-aproned barbed wire and mowed down the kunai grass and ground foliage a hundred yards beyond it to create a "kill zone." The soldiers of the 164th called it the "Bowling Alley."

Over Puller's objections, his regimental commander ordered him to send a forty-six-man platoon under Sergeant Ralph Briggs Jr. down into the jungle, three thousand yards from the Marine lines, to alert him of approaching enemy soldiers.[110]

Warning signs of a coming attack on the Marines' southern perimeter began to appear during the day on October 24. A large Japanese force—it was Colonel Oka's men—was spotted on Hill 67, a ridge southeast of the Marine positions along the Matanikau and near Bloody Ridge. Then a Marine saw a Japanese officer on Mount Austen studying the Bloody Ridge positions through field glasses. A scout-sniper returning from the upper Lunga River reported smoke from "many rice fires" rising from the jungle. The reports arrived too late in the day for Geiger and his staff to change their defensive arrangements.[111]

The Sendai Division reached its staging area south of the perimeter during the afternoon of October 24 as torrential rains transformed the trails over which they were to advance to troughs of liquid mud. They had jettisoned most of their heavy weapons during the exhausting, weeklong march through the jungle; consequently they arrived with grenade launchers, mortars, rifles, and machine-guns. They marched the last miles singing their national anthem and bowed toward Japan, pledging their lives to the emperor.[112]

AFTER NIGHTFALL, CLOUDS BLOTTED OUT the moon, and the darkness was complete. It was another layer of difficulty, besides fatigue and hunger—the Japanese had nearly depleted their rations—seemingly designed to interfere with the troops getting to their attack positions. In the confounding darkness, units became intermingled and separated. The attack, scheduled for 7:00 p.m., was delayed.

Colonel Masajiro Furimiya's 29th Infantry Regiment had the job of spearheading the assault. The rain stopped long enough for Maruyama's commanders to position their men for the attack, but there was no time to scout the Marine positions.

At 9:30 p.m. Sergeant Briggs, whose platoon was supposed to sound an early warning of enemy activity, did just that. "Colonel," he told Puller by phone, "there's about 3,000 Japs between you and me." They were all around him, he said, "singing and smoking." Puller told him to withdraw to the east. Remarkably, considering the large numbers of enemy all around, Briggs managed to lead most of his men to a place near the 164th's positions.

At 10:00 p.m. the 29th Infantry launched their attack, crying, "Blood for the Emperor! Marine, you die!" and "Banzai! Banzai! Banzai!" The Marines shouted back, "Blood for Franklin and Eleanor!"[113]

The Japanese hit Captain Regan Fuller's A Company on Puller's left, at the place where his 1st Battalion tied into the 164th Infantry. Within thirty minutes Fuller's men wiped out the attackers with a hurricane of gunfire: two 37mm antitank guns firing canister, four .50-caliber and six .30-caliber machine-guns, eighteen automatic rifles, a 60mm mortar that fired six hundred rounds, and artillery fire. The enemy dead lay in windrows that had to be knocked down to open up firing lanes. Soldiers in a column lay where they fell in formation, each man partially atop the man in front of him, their machine-guns, rifles, mines, and dynamite unused. In stopping the attack Fuller's men had fallen dangerously low in ammunition. "You've got bayonets, haven't you?" Puller said when Fuller apprised him of the situation. Hold at all costs, Puller told Fuller.[114]

THE JAPANESE NEXT STRUCK GUNNERY Sergeant John Basilone's machine-gun section of Puller's C Company to the right of Fuller's A Company. Before the war twenty-five-year-old "Manila John," as he was known, served three years in the Army, mainly in the Philippines, where he was a popular light heavyweight boxer. Basilone left the Army, but disliking civilian life as a truck driver, he enlisted in the Marines in 1940.

Basilone had carefully positioned his two heavy .30-caliber machine-guns—belt-fed, mounted on tripods, and each served by two or three men—and had cleared a field of fire to mow down any enemy troops attempting to climb the ridge. Now, in the darkness, with rain thundering down, the C Company Marines could hear the snip of wire cutters as the Japanese cut pathways through the barbed wire. Basilone told his section to hold their fire until the Japanese were fifty yards away or less.

Then the machine-guns cut loose. "The noise was terrific and I could see Japs jumping as they were smacked by our bullets," Basilone said. "Screaming, yelling, and dying all at the same time." A few of the attackers got into the Marine lines, and Basilone's crew killed them with pistols.

The roaring guns piled up the enemy dead and dying so high that they blocked the gunners' firing lane. During a lull Basilone sent men to push down the bodies. Needing spare gun barrels and ammunition, Basilone ran barefooted and bare-chested to Puller's command post. He returned to the battle line with a half-dozen ammunition belts, each one weighing fourteen pounds, draped over his shoulders and carrying the gun barrels.

In Basilone's absence the machine-gun position on the right had fallen silent. Investigating, he found the two guns jammed and the crew dead or wounded, and he dashed back to his pit to retrieve an operable gun. It weighed 50 pounds with the tripod. With it on his bare back, along with the six ammunition belts—a load of 130 pounds—Basilone led half of his crew to the other gun pit. Along the way they ran into six Japanese soldiers and killed all of them.

Rain continued to fall in torrents. While Basilone cleared the two jammed guns, his crew fired the operable one. When the two guns were working again, Basilone rolled between them through the mud, firing first one, then the other, while his men kept them loaded and the water jackets full.

At one point, when enemy soldiers were crawling toward Basilone's firing position on their bellies beneath the fan of machine-gun bullets, Basilone yanked one of the guns from its tripod, cradled it while flat on the ground, and "mowed down the crawlers." The gun's red-hot barrel scorched his arms.

On the slope below Basilone's position the Japanese made a wall of their comrades' bodies and tried again to knock out the Marine position. Japanese mortar-men zeroed in on Basilone's position, but he moved before the shells began landing.

During another six-hundred-yard trip to the command post for gun barrels and ammunition, Basilone was knocked down by mortar fire, but he got back up and, bleeding, returned with six ammunition belts "banging against my knees," an ammunition box, and full canteens. For his nearly superhuman actions Basilone became the first enlisted Marine to receive the Medal of Honor during World War II.[115]

PULLER STALKED HIS LINES, ENCOURAGING his men. He helped forward artillery observers direct the Eleventh Marines' 105mm howitzers. Lieutenant

Colonel Merrill Twining said Puller's presence "represented the equivalent of two battalions."

His thin line and the relentless attacks—six by 3:30 a.m. on October 25—by Major General Nasu's left wing impelled division headquarters to send elements of Colonel Bob Hall's 3rd Battalion of the 164th into the Marine lines. The Seventh Marines' Navy chaplain, Father Matthew Keough, guided the green Army troops to the lines. The soldiers were distributed by platoon among the Marine units to plug gaps in the line. On the front line, each Guardsman was paired with a Marine.[116]

Other 3rd Battalion soldiers joined their 2nd Battalion comrades on the battle line's southeastern sector, soon nicknamed "Coffin Corner." An Army corporal, William Clark, crawled forward under heavy fire and recovered two light machine-guns whose crews were dead. On New Caledonia Clark had donned a blindfold to teach himself how to disassemble and reassemble a machine-gun in the dark. The skill now proved useful. After dragging the machine-guns to his position, he dismantled them and in the inky darkness assembled a single serviceable gun as men fell around him. With the reconstituted machine-gun, Clark helped repel the Japanese attacks.[117]

At dawn Colonel Furimiya, the 29th Infantry's commander, personally led an assault by his headquarters and colors company. About sixty of Furimiya's men penetrated the Marine line, making a hundred-yard-deep salient. Puller's men crushed it in the morning, although Furimiya and several of his men managed to hide from the Marines. But they were hopelessly cut off from their regiment.[118]

As the Japanese withdrew, Sergeant John Stannard of the 164th Regiment saw the "tips of these bayonets bobbing along above the [high] grass" and called down artillery fire on them, adding to the carnage.[119]

Colonel Shoji, the new commander of Maruyama's right wing, got lost in the jungle and veered too far eastward. His right wing was only peripherally involved in the night's battle.

OVERWHELMING EVIDENCE OF THE AMERICANS' devastating firepower, more than compensating for their smaller numbers, was written in crimson on Bloody Ridge's slopes. Pedro del Valle, commander of the Eleventh Marines artillery, wrote, "The enemy dead along our front were piled high, and in spite of all our efforts to bury them, constituted a definite menace to our health and comfort." Hundreds of Furimiya's men lay dead before, behind, and on the wire, around the foxholes and machine-gun pits of Puller's battalion, and in front of the 164th, now a bloodied combat unit.

Private Bill Walander and other soldiers from the 164th's 3rd Battalion braved sniper fire to search the three hundred charred, dismembered Japanese who lay dead in front of their positions for diaries, maps, and souvenirs. The grass, Walander wrote, was "thick with dried blood."

Army Captain Al Wiest overheard Puller saying of the 164th: "I'll tell you one thing, those farm boys can fight."[120]

Puller asked a prisoner why the Japanese did not change tactics when they failed to break the Marines' lines. The plan had been made, the prisoner replied, and it could not be changed—it was not the Japanese way. Inside their lines Puller's men found 250 dead Japanese from the 16th, 29th, and 230th Regiments. Puller's stubborn defense of his mile-long front on Bloody Ridge earned him a second gold star for his Navy Cross.[121]

AT 2:00 A.M. ON OCTOBER 25 a report reached General Hyakutake on western Guadalcanal and Admiral Yamamoto's headquarters in Rabaul that Maruyama's men had captured Henderson Field. Sent hours earlier, the message declared, "2100 Banzai! The Kawaguchi Detachment captured the airfield and the western force is fighting to the west of the field."

The report was patently false, but before it was debunked, a chain of planned actions predicated on the airfield's capture was set in motion. The 11th Air Fleet's 26th Air Flotilla prepared to fly to Guadalcanal and land at Henderson. Destroyers made ready to embark troops to land at Koli Point, supported by Rear Admiral Tamotsu Takama's Destroyer Squadron Four, which was sailing down the Slot. Yamamoto ordered the Eighth and Second Fleets to approach Guadalcanal.[122]

Early on October 25, a twin-engine Japanese Army reconnaissance plane, escorted by eight Zeros, buzzed the airfield to ascertain whether it was in friendly hands—and was met by a fusillade of rifle and machine-gun fire. The plane crashed in the jungle and exploded. Still unconvinced that the airfield remained in Marine hands, commanders in Rabaul ordered two dozen Zeros to circle the Marine perimeter for two hours and to land if Japanese troops were seen at the field. Henderson Field was initially too muddy from the previous night's heavy rainfall for flight operations, but it finally dried out enough so that Captain Joe Foss and five other VMF-121 pilots could take off and lay the false report to rest.

The Seventeenth Army later offered an explanation: "Control was difficult because of the complicated terrain. Only one enemy position protruding from the south end of the airfield [the hundred-yard salient in Puller's lines] was actually taken, but the airfield itself has not been taken."[123]

AT LAST CONCEDING THAT THE Marines still held the airfield, the Japanese sent eighty-two aircraft to destroy the Cactus Air Force. It was "Condition Red" all day long at Henderson Field on October 25—nicknamed "Dugout Sunday" in acknowledgement of the many hours spent crouched in muddy air shelters. Lieutenant Herbert Merillat described it as "the most intensive aerial fighting of the campaign." It was the apotheosis of the Japanese air force's campaign against Guadalcanal.

The attacks came in seemingly endless succession. Flights of bombers and Zeros were met by Wildcats in frenzied dogfights, with planes plummeting into the sea. General Sumiyoshi's howitzers across the Matanikau River also shelled the airfield sporadically. Vandegrift and his staff did not go into their dugouts, but instead watched the air battles from the command post all day. "There were vapor streaks all over the sky," wrote Colonel Gerald Thomas. "We were too interested to go into the dugouts."[124]

At sea, the Japanese landing vessels and naval support ships continued to sail toward their destinations. Destroyers transporting troops to Koli Point sank the tug *Seminole* and the "Yippie" tuna boat *YP-284* near Lunga Point, to which they were bringing fuel and ammunition. Cactus dive bombers from VS-71, P-39s, and F4Fs from VMF-212 attacked the escorts for the Koli Point landings—the light cruiser *Yura* and five destroyers. They hit *Yura* with two bombs; it was later scuttled. Enemy destroyers then began shelling gun emplacements on the beach, but the Wildcats strafed the warships with their .50-caliber machine-guns, scattering the men on deck. "I concentrated on the center of that destroyer and put about twelve hundred rounds into it," said pilot Frank Drury.

With the help of coastal defense guns, the Wildcats drove off the destroyers, damaging two of them. Zeros, bombers, and dive bombers attacked all afternoon, with the onslaught reaching a crescendo between 2:00 and 3:30 p.m., when it seemed that a new formation appeared over the airfield every few minutes.

"Things got blacker and blacker," wrote Martin Clemens. Between countering the myriad air raids and attacking enemy ships, Cactus fighters and dive bombers were continually in the air, landing only to refuel and reload ammunition.

Lieutenant Jack Conger of VMF-212 fought until he ran out of ammunition, then got on a Zero's tail and chewed it off with his propeller. The Zero broke in half and plummeted toward the sea as its pilot parachuted into the water. Conger's plane stalled and began spiraling downward. Conger bailed out, pulled his ripcord 250 feet above the water, and landed hard.

Marines in a Higgins boat picked him up, and Conger told them to also retrieve the enemy pilot. The Japanese airman, however, refused to get in the boat.

Unwilling to let him die, Conger snagged the pilot's life jacket with a boat hook, and the Marines lifted him out of the water. The pilot whipped out a Mauser automatic pistol, pointed it at Conger's face and pulled the trigger. Nothing happened. Then he pointed it at his own head, but again the pistol did not fire. Conger stopped the Marines from shooting him; instead, they hit him over the head, knocking him out, and got him into the boat. Before turning the enemy pilot over to intelligence officers, the Marines relieved him of his pistol, silk scarf, and other items.[125]

The Cactus Air Force claimed to have shot down seventeen enemy fighters and five bombers, with Captain Foss bagging four Zeros. Two F4Fs were lost, and many others were damaged. At day's end General Geiger had just a dozen flyable Wildcats, eleven SBDs, and six P-39s.[126]

But the numbers didn't matter so much as the fact that the Japanese air force had shot its bolt at Guadalcanal during two intensive weeks of air attacks—a period during which American pilots claimed to have shot down 25 twin-engine bombers and nearly 80 fighter planes. The Eleventh Air Fleet was depleted. Never again would enemy raids equal the onslaught seen between September 27 and October 26, when 228 enemy planes were destroyed while American losses totaled fewer than half that number.[127]

AT HIS COMMAND POST SOUTH of Bloody Ridge, General Maruyama laid plans for a second night attack, believing that this time he could overwhelm the Marine defenders and capture the airfield. His decision to resume the attack was partly inspired by Colonel Furimiya's reckless penetration of Puller's lines. Maruyama could not ignore the fact "that the Commander of the 29th Infantry had carried a Rising Sun banner . . . into the enemy lines."

Meanwhile, Puller steeled his men for another assault. This time, the 1st Battalion would not be alone on the ridge's southern end. Army Lieutenant Colonel Robert Hall's 3rd Battalion, 164th Infantry, took over the eastern portion of the twenty-five-hundred-yard perimeter that Puller's men had alone held the previous night.[128]

Maruyama's "final, death-defying night attack" on Bloody Ridge was placed in the hands of the 16th Infantry Regiment, remnants of the hollowed-out 29th, and a battalion of engineers—all led by Major General Nasu.

At 8:00 p.m. the Japanese stormed up a Jeep road toward the 164th's 3rd Battalion.

They were repulsed, but they continued to attack repeatedly in groups of thirty or more. Hall's men, aided by the Seventh Marines' weapons company, annihilated them, with Nasu and half of the Sendai Division's officers among those killed.[129]

Puller's battalion saw only minor action to the right of Hall's battalion, but four miles to the west Colonel Herman Hanneken's 2nd Battalion, Seventh Marines was pressed to the breaking point on a grassy ridge overlooking a steep valley near the Matanikau River.

COLONEL AKINOSUKE OKA'S THREE BATTALIONS did not reach their staging area on October 24 because of heavy rain; vertical, mud-slickened terrain; and dense jungle. They were ready now, though. Supported by Sumiyoshi's heavy artillery, Oka's more than two thousand men were poised to assault Hanneken's ridgetop defense. Fox Company on the battalion's eastern flank was in the bull's-eye: the Japanese hoped to drive a wedge there between Hanneken and Puller and then push north to the airfield. Providentially, on this spot was Sergeant Mitchell Paige's heavy machine-gun section, which would act the part that Basilone and his gunners had played the previous night.[130]

The son of immigrant Serbs, Paige enlisted in the Marine Corps in 1936 on his eighteenth birthday. In order to make the minimum weight for enlistees, Paige ate dozens of bananas and drank several glasses of water. Now, six years later, he was a twenty-four-year-old "Old Breed" Marine who had served in China, the Philippines, and Cuba.

At 2:00 a.m. Paige's sector erupted in shouting and gunfire. A "seemingly endless wall" of Japanese rose like a wave on the gradual slope ascending to Fox Company's positions. Paige saw "dark shapes crawling on the ground or swirling in clumped knots; struggling men falling on each other with bayonets, swords, and violent oaths."

"Fire machine guns! Fire!" Paige shouted.

One of his gunners was bayoneted and lifted in the air; Paige shot the attackers. A Japanese officer swung a two-handed samurai sword at Corporal Raymond Gaston as he lay on the ground. He blocked the murderous blows with his rifle until it splintered. As the officer again raised his sword to deliver the killing blow, Gaston "caught his man under the chin with his boondocker, a violent blow that broke the Japanese's neck."[131]

The Marines beat back the first attack, but it was followed at 3:00 a.m. by a second one that knifed through Fox Company's line and gave the attackers possession of a ridge spur. After the assault troops had passed through the line, Paige sprayed a full belt into their backs as they were about to attack the company command post behind his position. Paige continued to fire bursts until steam rose from his machine-gun's barrel.

"In front of me was a large pile of dead bodies," he wrote. "I ran around the ridge from gun to gun trying to keep them firing, but at each emplacement I found only dead bodies. I knew then I must be all alone."[132]

Paige commandeered a machine-gun from adjacent G Company and, also borrowing its crew and several riflemen, formed a skirmish line. They launched a bayonet attack, beating the enemy soldiers in a race to an abandoned machine-gun, which Paige began firing—the only gun in action at that forward position. It drew enemy fire from many quarters, wounding three volunteers who were keeping Paige supplied with ammunition.

With three captured machine-guns, the Japanese occupying the ridge spur enfiladed the rest of the 2nd Battalion's positions. Major Odell Conoley, the battalion executive officer, organized a scratch force to retake the spur: communications men, runners, cooks, mess boys, and stretcher bearers—no more than two dozen men. Supported by Paige and his machine-gun, Conoley's Marines recaptured the position and the machine-guns.

Then Paige organized his riflemen for a frontal attack, shouting orders in Japanese for them to stand up and hurry. To his surprise about thirty Japanese soldiers concealed in the tall kunai grass in front of the Marines stood up. Paige fired a long burst into them, "and they just peeled off like grass under a mowing machine."

He wrenched the .30-caliber gun from its tripod, laid the red-hot water jacket across his left arm, ignoring the burning pain, and slung belts of ammunition over his shoulder—150 pounds in all, "but the way I felt I could have carried three more without noticing it." "Let's go!" he shouted to his riflemen. "Whooping like a bunch of wild Indians," they charged downhill, firing from the hip, cutting down everyone in their path until they reached the jungle's edge.[133]

Shortly after dawn the Japanese withdrew, leaving 298 of their dead on the ridge spur and scattered throughout the ravine below.[134]

WHEN HE LEARNED ABOUT PAIGE'S actions the next morning, Puller, wanting to shake Paige's hand, paid him a visit. Hanneken was putting him in for a medal, Puller told Paige, adding that he was recommending Basilone for one too. The gunners knew one another—they had met at New River, North Carolina, where they swapped stories about their prewar Philippines service. For his heroics on Bloody Ridge Paige was awarded the Medal of Honor and received a battlefield commission.[135]

The 164th Infantry had earned the Marines' respect. In a change from their habitual deprecation of Army infantrymen as "doggies," the Marines addressed the men of the 164th as "soldiers." Colonel Clifton Cates, the First Marines' commander, wrote to Lieutenant Colonel Bryant Moore, the 164th's commander, "The officers and men of the First Marines salute you for a most wonderful piece of work. . . . We are honored to serve with a unit such as yours."[136]

HUNDREDS OF BLOOD TRAILS DISAPPEARED into the dense jungle below the ridge, where the Sendai Division was preparing to withdraw along the "Maruyama Road." In low spirits, Maruyama's division gathered up its wounded and began the dreadful march to friendly territory west of the Matanikau River.

The Right Wing under Colonel Shoji had failed again to join the battle; for unexplained reasons, the three battalions remained on the defensive all night. As Maruyama's battered division limped off to the west, Shoji's nearly intact battalions began marching eastward to the Koli Point area.

The corpses of more than twenty-two hundred Japanese soldiers were strewn across Bloody Ridge's slopes, in the ravines below, and in the jungle. The painstaking troop buildup, the relentless air raids, and the marshaling of fleets for the big "October push" had been squandered in a series of piecemeal ground attacks. Not only were the assaults poorly coordinated and executed, but their objectives were the same as Kawaguchi's in September—adding up to a colossal failure of leadership and imagination.

"Had all three [Japanese forces] struck us at once, we would have been in great difficulty," wrote Lieutenant Colonel Merrill Twining. Because they did not, some of the Japanese army's finest units were annihilated—the 29th and 16th Infantry Regiments and the Kawaguchi detachment, according to the Marines' final report on Guadalcanal. The American victory was achieved at a relatively low cost: eighty-six Marines and nineteen soldiers from the 164th Infantry killed. The 164th supervised the burial in pits, using bulldozers and dynamite, of nearly eleven hundred recovered enemy bodies.

REAR ADMIRAL RAIZO TANAKA, THE destroyer squadron commander, later said that the failure to land "a completely equipped army force" on Guadalcanal was due to the Cactus Air Force, "which was supposed to have been eliminated, but was not." Lieutenant Colonel Masanobu Tsuji, the Imperial General Headquarters officer sent to assess the situation after Kawaguchi's defeat in September, accepted blame for the debacle, saying he "underestimated the enemy's fighting power" and deserved "a sentence of ten thousand deaths." He asked to remain on Guadalcanal with the Seventeenth Army. His superiors instead summoned him to Tokyo to make a report.[137]

While conceding the October push's failure, Major General Shuichi Miyazaki, the Seventeenth Army's chief of staff, said he was not giving up. "We think we are forced to make a new offensive with more strength on a much larger scale."[138]

Maruyama's return march to the upper Matanikau and beyond was a ghastly ordeal for the beaten army. Each day, wounded men dropped along the side of the trail, never to rise again. Stretcher cases were abandoned when their bearers grew too weak from hunger to continue carrying them. With each passing day, the once-proud Sendai Division bore more of a resemblance to a procession of fasting pilgrims with walking sticks than it did to a combat unit.

Lieutenant Keijiro Minegishi wrote in his diary, "We haven't eaten for three days and even walking is difficult. On the uphill my body swayed around unable to walk. . . . I must take a rest every two meters. It is quite disheartening to have only one tiny teaspoon of salt per day and a palmful of rice porridge."

Squad leader Toyoji Hashiba wrote that he would have killed himself but for his fear that "many men might follow my actions and slaughter themselves." As it was, "a good many" men elected to commit suicide by blowing themselves up with hand grenades. When Hashiba and his companions finally arrived at a beach east of Cape Esperance, they had become so weak from hunger and thirst that they were able to travel just two hundred meters a day.[139]

A Sendai soldier who made the first night's attack against Puller's battalion on October 24–25 understatedly observed in his diary that "our attacking didn't work out too well" and recorded the deaths of two comrades. A few days later during the retreat, he wrote, "It seems like most of our company was stamped out. . . . The enemy planes are still flying and seem to be looking for us. We must admit that we are defeated. We are praying for the dead."[140]

Admiral Ugaki irritably catalogued the Seventeenth Army's shortcomings in his diary: shoddy reconnaissance of terrain and enemy positions, army leaders' inability to properly direct and coordinate the attacks, removal of Kawaguchi from command of the Right Wing immediately before the battle, and Colonel Oka's failure to obey orders and, instead, advancing "at his own discretion." General Maruyama, wrote Ugaki, was suffering from "chronic neuralgia," and his staff, which should have taken on more responsibility, was "incompetent." "The navy was skeptical about the future after seeing three failures by the Army," he wrote.[141]

ONE SOLDIER WHO DID NOT join the retreat was Colonel Furimiya, the 29th Regiment's commander. During the first night's attack, Furimiya and a handful of his men became trapped behind the Marine lines. Except for Furimiya and a captain, the rest were killed by Marines the next day. After trying and failing to escape several times, the colonel tore up the regimental flag, ground it into the mud, and wrote a farewell letter to General Maruyama, instructing his captain to deliver it after his death. "I am sorry I have lost many troops uselessly and for this result which has come unexpectedly. We must not overlook firepower," he wrote ruefully. "I am going to return my borrowed life today with short interest." Furimiya stood, bowed in the direction of the emperor, and ordered the captain to shoot him in the head. The Marines found the letter beside his body.[142]

SAILING TOWARD GUADALCANAL WAS THE largest Japanese fleet yet seen in the South Pacific: four aircraft carriers, five battleships, and fifty-eight other warships. This was the naval component of Yamamoto's "Plan X" for capturing Guadalcanal. The "October push's" other elements had failed; the air and land attacks had neither suppressed the Cactus Air Force nor defeated the Marines on the ground.

The gambler in Yamamoto, however, believed that victory on Guadalcanal was still possible—if the Combined Fleet could destroy Admiral Thomas Kinkaid's and Willis Lee's task forces. They included thirty-three warships, among them two battleships, *Washington* and *South Dakota*, and two carriers, *Hornet* and *Enterprise*. Halsey had summoned the "Big E" to the South Pacific from Pearl Harbor even though she was still undergoing repairs.

The Combined Fleet held a daunting edge in warships as well as 212 planes to the Americans' 172—if the naval groups of Admirals Chuichi Nagumo, Nobutake Kondo, and Hiroaki Abe were able to launch a concerted attack. Yamamoto's warships had full tanks for this operation, despite fuel shortages in Japan and in the navy. Nagumo's timidity was a concern; sightings of American scout planes had already caused him to twice turn back from Guadalcanal despite Yamamoto's exhortation to "not hesitate or waver."[143]

Nagumo commanded the Striking Force, or Third Fleet, with the preponderance of the naval force's carrier planes on three flattops—*Shokaku*, *Zuikaku*, and *Zuiho*. West of Nagumo was Kondo's Vanguard Force, with one carrier, the *Junyo*. Kondo was to coordinate with the Seventeenth Army on Guadalcanal while Nagumo warded off US carrier attacks from the east.

The Japanese sailed south on October 25 toward the Santa Cruz Islands, while Kinkaid's smaller Task Force 61 sailed north. That day Japanese search planes spotted Lee's Task Force 64 near Guadalcanal, where it was assigned to protect the beachhead. The Japanese suspected that Lee's warships were bait, while US carrier groups lurked nearby, waiting to pounce.[144]

Before dawn on October 26, the enemy fleets were two hundred miles apart and groping for one another in the gray light, neither one certain of the other's position. The Japanese launched their search planes first—float planes, shortly after 4 a.m.—followed by Kate dive bombers thirty minutes later. The weather favored offensive air operations: broken cumulus clouds, pregnant with rain, occupied half the sky, providing hiding places for attack planes.

Just before 5:00 a.m. the *Enterprise* launched a combat air patrol of sixteen SBDs, each one carrying a five-hundred-pound bomb. Working in pairs, the pilots were under orders to search a two-hundred-mile quadrant to the west and north.[145]

BOTH NAVIES' BATTLE PLANS MIGHT be described as a distillation of Confederate General Nathan Bedford Forrest's famous maxim: "Get there first with the most men." In this sense, a carrier battle was not so different from a cavalry fight, its immediate object being to cripple the enemy's flight decks before its own were struck.

Yamamoto's commanders got their search planes into the air first on October 26, accurately communicated the position of the US warships first, and struck first with dive bombers and torpedo bombers. Admiral Kinkaid's fleet would not make up the lost time.

Frustratingly for the Americans, the advantage could easily have been theirs. Nighttime-flying PBY Catalinas from Espiritu Santo attempted to provide Kinkaid with intelligence on the location of Nagumo's carriers at 3:00 a.m. But a communications glitch delayed the sighting report's relay by two hours.

Two PBYs had found Nagumo's carriers at about 2:00 a.m. and even dropped five-hundred-pound bombs near *Zuikaku*, panicking the skittish Nagumo into ordering all the carrier planes in *Zuikaku*'s, *Zuiho*'s, and *Shokaku*'s hangars disarmed and degassed. He temporarily reversed course to the north.

At 3:00 a.m. one of the PBYs radioed the carriers' position, but the report did not reach Kinkaid until 5:00—after he had already dispatched the paired SBDs from *Enterprise*. Thirty minutes into the search patrol, about eighty-five miles from *Enterprise*, one of the SBD search teams spotted a lone Kate torpedo bomber flying in the other direction; neither acknowledged the other's presence, nor did they when they encountered one another during their respective return flights.[146]

Nagumo was just as eager to locate the American carriers. At 6:30 a.m. Japanese float planes that had been on patrol since 4:00 a.m. spotted the *Hornet*—the carrier that had launched the Doolittle Raid in April—and radioed her position to Nagumo. Flight crews swarmed the decks of the *Shokaku*, *Zuikaku*, and *Zuiho*, readying their planes for an attack. At 7:10 a.m. the first of sixty-five Kates, Vals, and Zeros rose from the carriers and flew toward the American carrier group two hundred miles away.[147]

Enterprise's search patrol SBDs located the Japanese battleship and carrier groups between 6:17 and 6:50 a.m. and radioed their positions to Kinkaid. When the reports reached Admiral Halsey in Noumea, his terse message to a fleet accustomed to Admiral Ghormley's caution was electrifying: "Attack. Repeat. Attack."[148]

Above Nagumo's carrier group, Zeros intercepted two SBDs that had reported the enemy ships' location and disrupted their bombing runs. The American pilots shot down two Zeros before turning back. Two other SBDs that located *Zuiho* fifty minutes later were luckier. During their diving runs on the light carrier, Lieutenant Stockton Strong and his wingman, Ensign Chuck Irvine, planted two 500-pound bombs on the carrier's stern, taking it out of the fight. But *Zuiho*'s planes had already left to attack the American carrier group.[149]

At 7:30 a.m., twenty minutes after the Japanese carrier planes were airborne, twenty-nine planes left *Hornet* to strike Nagumo's carriers, and around 8:00 the *Enterprise* dispatched nineteen planes from Air Group Ten—whose other aircraft had comprised the earlier search patrol. *Hornet* launched a second strike group of twenty-five planes at 8:15. There were now seventy-three American planes in the air.

A second wave of Japanese planes left Nagumo's carrier group at about the same time as *Hornet*'s second group; more than 130 Japanese planes were on their way to attack Kinkaid's ships.

ODDLY, *ENTERPRISE* AND *HORNET* PILOTS were operating independently of one another, while sometimes flying literally side by side. Not keyed into one another's communications networks, they would fight separate battles, limiting their effectiveness.

Air Group Ten's nineteen planes went into action earlier than anticipated, about midway to their target, and the encounter was costly. Some of the fighter pilots had not yet charged their .50-calibers; some torpedo bombers had not turned on their radio transmitters. Nine Zeros from *Zuiho* flashed out of the sun, sending two TBFs tumbling into the sea, and badly damaged two others, which then turned back and splashed down near the task force. The Zeros also shot down three Wildcats from Lieutenant Commander John Leppla's four-plane division, including Leppla's; he did not survive.

Lieutenant Commander Jimmy Flatley, who led the other four-Wildcat division, deplored the group's lack of preparedness, writing in his report, "Eternal vigilance or eternal rest." The air group notified *Enterprise* that enemy planes could be expected in thirty minutes.[150]

At about 9:00 a.m. the first wave entered Kinkaid's combat air patrol zone. A local squall concealed *Enterprise* and, because Nagumo believed there was only one American carrier in the area, his pilots expected to see only *Hornet*. Minutes later they did. The nearly new, 824-feet-long carrier, commissioned almost exactly one year earlier, was the seventh US ship bearing the name. Sailors on her escort ships would fondly remember her generous dispensation of hundreds of gallons of ice cream every time a destroyer came alongside.[151]

A proper air defense might have mitigated the storm about to burst upon *Hornet*, but errors in judgment and commission imperiled the flattop. *Enterprise*'s fighter director, who was responsible for positioning the thirty-eight planes defending both carrier groups, was new to the job. Halsey had appropriated his predecessor, a veteran of Midway, for his staff. The severe enemy threat calamitously magnified the new director's mistakes.

He had placed the task force's air patrol too close to the carriers—within ten miles—and at an altitude three to four thousand feet below where the enemy usually flew. That left too little time for the Wildcats to break up attacks, and gave the Japanese dive bombers the advantage of diving with the F4Fs below them. In another error due to the flight director's inexperience, the Japanese approach vector was relayed to the pilots in relation to the ships' heading—useless information unless the pilots could see the ships.[152]

Black smudges in the distant sky announced the enemy's approach through the outer ring of antiaircraft fire. And then, just as the Japanese dive bombers appeared, a *Hornet* gun officer rendered half of the ship's five-inch antiaircraft battery useless by mistakenly sending the five guns into "stops," freezing them with the barrels pointed horizontally.[153]

Associated Press correspondent Charles McMurtry was on *Hornet*'s signal bridge, above the flight deck, awaiting the expected attack, when two waves of Japanese Vals appeared. "Suddenly the air seemed filled with planes and smoke bursts of our five-inch shells and tracer bullets of our antiaircraft guns, as every one of the ships in our task force let go," he wrote. Fifteen dive bombers penetrated the curtain of fire thrown up by the escort screen of cruisers and destroyers.

Hornet's guns claimed the lead dive bomber a few hundred feet inside the screen, but then a burning Val piloted by the squadron leader, Lieutenant Commander "Mamo" Seki, slammed into *Hornet*'s stack during a wild suicide dive. The plane's wing sheared off on the signal bridge a few feet from where McMurtry stood, and the wreckage crashed onto the flight deck. Two of the plane's bombs exploded. "The whole ship seemed to shudder under [the] bombs," McMurtry wrote. Inside the wrecked bomber's cockpit, which came to rest under the forward elevator, sailors later found a chart of the Panama Canal, suggesting that it might be a future enemy target.[154]

Then, seven Kate torpedo bombers converged on *Hornet* from three directions, flying "so low over the water it was difficult to pick up the blue-gray silhouettes against the clouds and ocean." The bombers had to "jump over the masts of the destroyers in the screen," according to a *Hornet* officer. Spotting the foaming wakes of two torpedoes slicing through the water toward her, Captain Stephen Jurika, the operations officer, shouted, "Torpedoes on the starboard side approaching ship!" Nothing could be done. When the fish struck, it felt as though "the ship was a rat being shaken by a bull terrier, just literally shaken."[155]

Three more bombs hit the flight deck. One of them, with a delayed fuse, exploded four decks below. A disabled Kate then plowed into a forward gun gallery and exploded near the forward elevator shaft.

Within ten minutes *Hornet* was dead in the water, "six fires burning, no power, no lights, no water, no radio, very limited intraship communication, some guns knocked out, some casualties," wrote McMurtry. Jurika said the ship was in no danger of sinking; however, it was unable to move because it had no power. As everyone turned to trying to extinguish the fires and save the ship, a sailor shouted, "We will save her and come back and wipe out those Japs. We'll save her, we'll be back."[156]

WHILE *HORNET* WAS BEING REDUCED to a burning, drifting hulk, a dozen or so dive bombers from her scattered first strike group were nearing Nagumo's carrier group. At 9:25 a.m. the Wildcat escort engaged Nagumo's combat air patrol, and the SBDs continued flying unescorted. Five minutes later, they sighted *Shokaku* and *Zuiho*, the latter spewing smoke from the search patrol strike two hours earlier.

Lieutenant Jimmy Vose and eleven dive bombers swooped down on *Shokaku* amid a cloud of Zeros, hitting the carrier with six 1,000-pound bombs that smashed into the flight deck, forward and amidships, and near the after elevator. The explosions left gaping holes in the flight deck, shredded the upper hangar, and "twisted" *Shokaku*'s antiaircraft guns. As the dive bombers peeled away from the carrier, tail gunners saw flames leaping skyward through the pall of smoke.[157]

Six torpedo bombers from *Hornet*'s first strike group could not find the Japanese carriers, but they did locate Admiral Abe's battleships, cruisers, and destroyers. They attacked the cruiser *Tone* but scored no hits. *Enterprise*'s much-reduced attack group also failed to locate the carriers. Its four torpedo bombers made a run on the cruiser *Suzuyi* in Abe's group, but without success.

Hornet's second strike group of dive bombers and TBFs also attacked Abe's force, targeting the heavy cruiser *Chikuma*. Dive bombers hit the bridge twice, killing nearly everyone there. Captain Keizo Komura was wounded but lived. The SBDs' bombs also knocked out a torpedo tube mount and disabled an engine. Nearly two hundred Japanese sailors died, but the ship, battered and smoking, remained afloat and was escorted to Truk for repairs.[158]

MINUTES AFTER *HORNET* WAS DISABLED, intercepted radio transmissions revealed to the Japanese the presence of a second US carrier, *Enterprise*. This was unexpected; *Enterprise*, insofar as the Japanese knew, had been sent to Pearl

Harbor for repairs after the Battle of the Eastern Solomons two months earlier and had not returned. But Halsey, days after being named commander of the South Pacific, had ordered her to the South Pacific, even as repairs on her continued.

At 10:17 a.m. part of the second Japanese wave, looking for the second carrier, found her. Vals from *Shokaku* went into their balletic dives to bomb *Enterprise*—and entered a maelstrom of antiaircraft fire that shot nearly all of them to pieces.

While undergoing repairs at Pearl Harbor *Enterprise* was equipped with state-of-the-art antiaircraft guns, 40mm BoFors mounted as twins and quads. The Bo-Fors fired faster, at a rate of 100 to 120 rounds per minute, and were effective at intermediate range and up to 12,500 feet elevation. The Swedish-designed guns were adapted to US specifications to replace the older 1.1-inch guns.[159]

The combat air patrol, positioned too low and too close to *Enterprise*'s screen, was nearly as ineffective as it had been in defending *Hornet*. But the roaring BoFors and radar-directed five-inch gunfire from the antiaircraft cruiser *San Juan* and *Enterprise*'s other screening ships shredded the attacking Val squadron. "As each plane came down, a veritable cone of tracer shells enveloped it," a pilot said. Some dive bombers, however, slipped through the curtain of gunfire.

"I think that son of a bitch is going to get us!" Commander John Crommelin exclaimed as a Val took aim at *Enterprise*. It dropped a five-hundred-pound bomb on the flight deck's forward overhang; the bomb traveled downward and punched through the port side, exploding outside the ship. A second bomb hit the forward elevator but did not detonate until it reached the third deck, where the blast killed forty men. A third bomb was a near-hit that sent shock waves through the ship.[160]

Kate torpedo bombers from *Zuikaku* then appeared, low to the water. The *Enterprise* captain's "superb maneuvering" made all their torpedoes miss. Lieutenant Stanley "Swede" Vejtasa of VF-10 and his wingman, Lieutenant Dave Harris, were ten thousand feet above the Kates and swooped down on them. Vejtasa destroyed six.

A Kate smashed into the forecastle of *Smith*, a destroyer in *Enterprise* formation, setting the entire forward half of the ship ablaze. From the control room Lieutenant Commander Hunter Wood phoned steering instructions to Chief Quartermaster F. Riduka in the steering engine room, and together they expertly guided *Smith* through the formation, hanging in the wake of the battleship *South Dakota*, which helped douse the fires.[161]

A freak occurrence doomed *Porter*, another *Enterprise* escort. A stricken US torpedo bomber ditched near the destroyer, and the impact jarred loose an unfired torpedo from beneath the plane's wing. The fish veered erratically through the water—toward *Porter*, which was preparing to retrieve the torpedo bomber's crew. Fighter planes spotted the careering torpedo and tried to detonate it with machine-gun fire before it reached the destroyer. They failed; the torpedo struck *Porter* amidships, sending a column of water a hundred feet into the air and killing fifteen men. The destroyer *Shaw* took aboard *Porter*'s crewmen and scuttled her with gunfire.[162]

JUNYO WAS ADMIRAL KONDO'S ONE-CARRIER division; a recent accidental fire had damaged his other flattop, *Hiyo*, which was sent away for repairs. *Junyo* had launched eighteen Vals and twelve Zeros at 9:00 a.m., and a little after 11:00 they appeared above the American fleet. The immobile *Hornet* presented an easy mark, and the airmen were looking around for additional targets when a radio message from *Junyo* alerted them to the presence of the second US carrier. The pilots spotted *Enterprise* almost immediately. The "Big E" had just begun taking aircraft aboard when the Vals poured out of the clouds.[163]

A near-hit jammed an elevator and flooded some compartments. The main radar was knocked out. Lieutenant Brad Williams, *Enterprise*'s radar officer, climbed the radar aerial as bullets and shrapnel whizzed around him, and he lashed himself to the antenna so his hands were free to make repairs. He was successful. The radar was activated—with Williams still attached to it—and it made a dozen revolutions before the lieutenant's cries attracted attention. Someone stopped the radar long enough for Williams to climb down.[164]

A *Junyo* dive bomber scored a hit on the forward turret of the battleship *South Dakota*, which had helped shield *Enterprise* from worse punishment; her gunners, firing the new 40mm BoFors, were credited with twenty-six shootdowns. The enemy bomb wounded *South Dakota*'s captain and four dozen men. Another Val dropped an armor-piercing bomb on the antiaircraft cruiser *San Juan*, damaging her steering control so that she swerved erratically through the formation.[165]

Despite the large hole in her flight deck, *Enterprise* managed to take aboard sixty of her own aircraft and forty-eight of *Hornet*'s in the cramped landing area. Planes crowded the flight deck because the forward elevator was out of commission and one of the two deck elevators was jammed.[166]

HORNET DRIFTED WITHOUT POWER AS her crews fought valiantly to control the numerous fires. At 11:23 a.m. the cruiser *Northampton* took her under tow—until the line broke and a thicker cable was substituted. At 1:30 p.m. the towing operation resumed. But more enemy warplanes were on the way; at 1:15 *Junyo* had launched a second attack, this one targeting the helpless *Hornet*.

While *Junyo*'s fifteen Kates and Zeros were flying to the battle zone more than two hundred miles away, Admiral Kinkaid ordered *Enterprise* and her escorts to withdraw southward. He was unwilling to risk the last operational US carrier in the South Pacific to provide air cover for *Hornet*. *Hornet* would have to be towed to a safe port before Japanese torpedo bombers got her. *Northampton* tried, but it could make just three knots while tethered to the huge carrier.

The destroyers *Russell* and *Hughes* peeled away from the consorts surrounding *Hornet* and began quickly transferring wounded sailors and aviation personnel from the carrier until they could take no more. "We knew a major Japanese task force was bearing down on us," wrote Edwin Hooper, a *Hornet* officer. Hooper began swimming away from the carrier toward the destroyer escorts, blowing a whistle and yelling, "Follow me!" to other able-bodied men in the water. While Hooper was in the water, reports reached *Hornet* at 3:15 p.m. of *Junyo*'s approaching second wave. *Northampton* cast off just before the bombs and torpedoes began coming down. To the swimming sailors, the explosions in the water "felt like you had been hit by a blockbuster."[167]

Amazingly, with no air support and only manually operated antiaircraft batteries, *Hornet*'s gunners managed to bring down two Kates and a pair of Zeros. But then there was a flash, followed by a "dull rumbling noise," wrote Commander Edward Creehan, the ship's engineer officer. A torpedo had struck the carrier. "The deck on the port side seemed to crack open and a geyser of fuel oil which quickly reached a depth of two feet swept all personnel at Repair 5 off their feet and flung them headlong down the sloping decks of the compartment to the starboard side."

Her after engine took on seawater, and *Hornet*'s list increased to 14 degrees. Captain Charles Mason gave the order to abandon ship. As life rafts were being launched, more Kates struck, followed by a half-dozen Vals, which scored near-hits that violently shook the carrier.[168]

After the lifeboats were launched, the destroyers *Mustin* and *Anderson* took up stations a thousand yards from *Hornet* and plastered her with five-inch shells, hoping to set her afire and scuttle her. But the crew had done its job too well. "We had turned off all the hoses, all the cocks, to the gasoline systems," wrote Captain Jurika, the operations officer. "They were firing incendiary shells . . . everything, at the waterline." When that did not sink her, they launched 14 torpedoes into her. At 8:40 p.m., when her escorts departed, she was "a blazing wreck, still afloat, in spite of I don't know how many torpedo hits." *Hornet* refused to go down.[169]

It was left to Japanese destroyers to finish off the burning hulk early the next morning. Four torpedoes did the job at 1:35 a.m. on October 27—ironically,

Navy Day—when for the first time a US warship that was still afloat was abandoned and sunk by an advancing enemy.[170]

Kinkaid's decision to leave *Hornet* without air protection embittered flyers.
Being a nonaviator, Kinkaid might not have appreciated the pilots' attachment to
their carrier, or the importance of upholding naval tradition by not leaving her to
the enemy. Although his rationale—preserving *Enterprise*—was sound, it was
probably no coincidence that Kinkaid was the last nonaviator to command a US
carrier in battle during the Pacific War.

As Kinkaid turned south, the battered Japanese carrier force sailed north toward Truk, low on fuel. The Battle of the Santa Cruz Islands, the Pacific War's
fourth carrier battle, was over. US and Japanese aircraft carriers and their squadrons would not duel again until 1944 in the Philippines Sea.

AMERICAN MATERIEL LOSSES EXCEEDED THE Japanese's. On the sea bottom
lay one of Halsey's only two operational aircraft carriers in the South Pacific,
while the other was limping to Noumea for repairs. *Porter* was gone, and *South
Dakota* and *San Juan* would need repairs before returning to action. All of Yamamoto's ships remained afloat when the fighting ended, although the carriers
Shokaku and *Zuiho*, a cruiser, and four destroyers had been heavily damaged.
Shokaku and *Zuiho* would be out of commission for months.

But the comparative naval losses were not the most important consequence of
the Battle of Santa Cruz. Even though it was clearly a tactical victory for Yamamoto and marked the acme of the Japanese carrier fleet, it was not a Japanese
strategic victory.

Captain Tameichi Hara, who better than most understood the Pacific War's
unfavorable calculus for the Japanese, said the victory was not decisive enough.
"The head and tail of the Japanese opponent were versatile and flexible—contrary
to Midway—and they struck back effectively with what force they had." Moreover, America's enormous industrial capacity meant that its losses could be
quickly made up, unlike Japan's. "We must win every battle overwhelmingly,"
Hara wrote. "This last one, unfortunately, was not an overwhelming victory."[171]

Even Hara's sober words did not tell the whole story. The Japanese air fleet,
which had suffered a rapid attrition of experienced pilots since August, had lost
heavily at Santa Cruz: sixty-nine planes shot down, twenty-three others damaged and unable to return to their ships, and 148 Japanese pilots and crewmen
dead. The fast-firing BoFors guns and the grouping of *Enterprise*'s escorts inaugurated a new age of antiaircraft defense that would be fully realized in the carrier battles of 1944. US carriers would then no longer operate inside
independent escort screens but in groups, surrounded by rings of battleships,
cruisers, and destroyers.

The impact of the Americans' cruelly efficient antiaircraft defenses was reflected in Lieutenant Commander Masatake Okumiya's description of *Junyo*'s planes limping home from their missions. "There were only a few planes in the air in comparison with the numbers launched several hours before," he wrote. "The planes lurched and staggered onto the deck, every single fighter and bomber holed. Some planes were literally flying sieves." The weary pilots who emerged from their cockpits described flying through skies "choked with antiaircraft shell bursts and tracers."

A young squadron leader, Lieutenant J. G. Shunko Kato, was "so shaken that at times he could not speak coherently" about his first combat mission, Okumiya wrote. "Young and lacking experience in circumstances where his friends died all around him, he had suffered a nasty shock." Yet Kato climbed back into his plane and led six Vals on another sortie. The Japanese might replace planes and ships, although not nearly as rapidly as America's defense factories, but the loss of veteran pilots was irreversible.[172]

Admiral Fitch's squadrons had lost eighty-one planes but just twenty-four air crewmen, a tribute to the American flyers' determination to survive and the strenuous efforts made by rescuers. The recovery of downed airmen helped sustain a cadre of able, experienced flyers. The Americans were winning the battle of pilot attrition.

Nimitz made no attempt to mitigate the defeat, citing the loss of two ships, planes, and sailors and airmen—in all, 262 dead. "Despite the loss of about three carrier air groups and damage to a number of ships, the enemy retired with all his ships," he pointedly noted.[173]

Japanese broadcasts exaggerated the "brilliant war results" achieved by the "invincible navy" at the Battle of Santa Cruz: four US aircraft carriers sunk, along with a battleship, a cruiser, a destroyer, and another large ship.

The government claimed that since the war began, 609 US warships and transports had been sunk, and 3,702 Allied planes destroyed. Naturally the emperor expressed his satisfaction with the results, while regretting the loss of "many capable fliers."[174]

"The nation was drunk on false victories," wrote fighter ace Saburo Sakai, appalled by the propaganda-fueled sense of unreality that he witnessed in Yokohama when he arrived to recover from his wounds. On street corners, crowds listened to blaring radio reports trumpeting great victories. "Every time the announcer mentioned another major defeat over the enemy loud cheers and cries resounded through the streets."[175]

The Japanese government's extravagant claims blinded its people to the fact that the Pacific War was at a watershed, just as the Axis powers were approaching their limits on other side of the world. While Halsey's and Yamamoto's fleets struggled, German armies were fighting at Stalingrad and El Alamein, and an American task force was on its way to North Africa to launch Operation Torch.

THE ASSOCIATED PRESS REPORTED NOVEMBER 1 in a story published in US newspapers nationwide that Japan's October push had failed. "The most powerful mobilization of sea, land and air forces Japan ever placed in action was insufficient to achieve its objectives. . . . Officers who are directing operations feel today that Guadalcanal can and will be held against the enemy."[176]

The Japanese were not ready to give up on Guadalcanal, though. They were planning an even larger combined forces campaign in November. Guadalcanal now surpassed tactical and strategic considerations—it had become a symbol and a point of national pride for both Japan and the United States.

In a letter to Nimitz on the last day of October, Halsey catalogued his needs— for more planes, ships, and escort vessels to "keep the pot boiling" in anticipation of the next battles for the island. "We are not in the least downhearted or upset by our difficulties," the feisty admiral added, "but obsessed with one idea only, to kill the yellow bastards and we shall do it."

In the margin of Halsey's letter Nimitz scrawled, "This is the spirit desired."[177]

5

November:
Halsey's Navy Triumphs

For Christ's sake, Jack, what are we going to do? Throw potatoes at them?

—*HELENA* PLOTTING ROOM OFFICER AS US SHIPS
SQUEEZED BETWEEN ENEMY WARSHIP COLUMNS
DURING THE NAVAL BATTLE OF GUADALCANAL[1]

The sound of their motors was as triumphant as the march from Aida, and we cheered and jigged and waved our arms at them passing overhead, urging them on. The enemy was running! The siege was broken!

—MARINE PRIVATE ROBERT LECKIE THE MORNING
AFTER THE NAVAL BATTLE OF GUADALCANAL[2]

The enemy's replacement rate is three times ours; the gap between our strengths is increasing every day; and to be honest things are looking black for us now.

—ADMIRAL ISOROKU YAMAMOTO, LATE NOVEMBER 1942[3]

THE 1ST MARINE DIVISION WAS riddled by malaria, dysentery, scrub typhus, dengue fever, and assorted other vile tropical afflictions that included ringworm, skin ulcers, and jungle rot—or trench foot—from continually wet feet. Jungle rot bore holes in the skin; ringworm scarred it. Dysentery was responsible for diarrhea so severe that men sliced open the seats of their trousers to obtain relief quicker, sometimes twenty or more times daily. "A solid bowel movement was a cause for rejoicing," wrote one sufferer. Dysentery grounded Army pilot Doug Canning and some of his 67th Fighter Squadron mates; they were sent to New Caledonia to recover. Gastroenteritis hospitalized INS correspondent Richard Tregaskis with diarrhea, nausea, and a high fever.

Guadalcanal's scourge, however, was malaria, spread by the ubiquitous Anopheles mosquito, which proliferated in the mangrove swamps in such large numbers that Marines wore socks on their hands and wrists when they slept and sometimes covered their faces with black head nets while on night watch. Despite these and other countermeasures, their eyes were often puffy and their lips swollen from insect bites. There was a chronic shortage of mosquito netting, and as the 1st Marine Division's final report acknowledged, "This factor was largely responsible for the high incidence of malaria."

Malaria tormented them with symptoms oscillating between intensive sweating and bone-rattling chills; when the symptoms debilitated them, they went to the medical tent for a day or two, after which they were usually able to return to the lines. A malaria sufferer described what it was like: "Even while I was shaking with cold, my nose was hot . . . my eyeballs must have been on rubber bands hitched to sore places in the back of my brain, for every time I moved my eyes I could feel the stretch clear to the back of my skull, and my skin felt raw and dry even while cold and wet." The symptoms sometimes recurred for years.[4]

During October and November US malaria cases on Guadalcanal spiked to around 5,000. In November the rate was 1,781 cases per thousand men per year for all military service branches on Guadalcanal. In other words, nearly everyone had malaria at one time or another, or multiple times; its severity varied. Lieutenant Colonel Merrill Twining, the division assistant operations officer, estimated that it affected at least 90 percent of the original landing force.[5]

Still, many so-called effectives were in fact wasting away. Tregaskis wrote that during one air raid he jumped into a slit trench and found it "crammed with sick people. The feverish, emaciated wrecks . . . were a pitiful sight."[6]

The Japanese combated malaria with quinine, a derivative of the cinchona tree bark; Japan happened to occupy Java, the single place where cinchona was plentiful. Lacking access to quinine, the Allies relied on atabrine, a synthetic drug originally developed in Germany. When taken regularly it suppressed malaria's worst effects, although it did not eradicate the disease. Winthrop Company obtained a license in 1931 to make atabrine, initially with German chemicals. Winthrop and other companies had then embarked on a crash program to make millions of tablets with their own ingredients.[7]

Atabrine stained the skin yellow—sometimes strikingly so. Once, a sergeant reportedly told a young Marine that he would not send him on point during a patrol because he was "yellower than a Jap" and feared his fellow Marines might shoot him by mistake. Many Marines mistakenly believed that the yellow tinge was permanent and that atabrine caused impotence. For those reasons, many avoided taking the prescribed one tablet, twice daily, three days per week unless compelled to—and few units required their corpsmen to routinely dispense the pills. "Line officers did not see that their men took their tablets," a 1st Marine Division medical officer sighed. It was too bad, because atabrine sharply reduced the odds of getting full-blown malaria to just one in ten. But many young Marines chose to spurn the atabrine regimen, and they suffered the consequences.[8]

The omnipresence of atabrine inspired a song set to the popular tune "Tangerine":

> *"Atabrine for malaria,*
> *That's the pill that keeps the chill away.*
> *Try to grin; don't let it scare you,*
> *If you start to change color that's OK. You can see what*
> *It's done for me,*
> *Look! My face is gray; my hands are turning green,*
> *But we have to get the Japs on the run*
> *And when it's all said and done,*
> *We owe it all to Atabrine, we don't mean quinine,*
> *We owe it all to Atabrine."*[9]

On average the Marines lost thirty-five pounds each while on the island because of the cumulative effects of malaria, dysentery, and dengue fever. Fatigue, weakness, and heat exhaustion were common plaints. Cuts became infected. "Day by day I watched my Marines deteriorate in the flesh," lamented General Vandegrift.[10]

Three months in the sweltering tropics, where rain fell in torrents daily and nothing ever dried completely, also "melted away" the Marines' underwear and socks and rusted their shirt buttons, which then fell off. The Marines resorted to using communication wire to close their shirts.[11]

When the Navy sailed away with half of their supplies, the Marines initially subsisted on captured rice or oatmeal, eaten twice daily, sometimes with prunes. In mid-September they received their first shipment of food—New Zealand lamb, sheep, and beef tongue; Spam; and C- and K-rations. For weeks they consumed no fruit or vegetables.

Their habitual élan ebbed with their body weight. "Our strength was being slowly sapped," wrote Private Robert Leckie, "and a sort of physical depression afflicted many of us." Their world shrank to their squads. Unless they were sent on patrol, veterans sometimes did not leave their foxholes even to eat. Stress and sleeplessness made it worse, and some men developed the fixed "thousand-yard stare" from sunken, red-rimmed eyes—a sign that they had battle fatigue, or had "gone Asiatic," and might have to soon be shipped out. Skin around their eyes became drawn tight, and "the constant stare of pupils ... seemed darker, rounder, more absolute."[12]

The Marine leadership was not immune to the effects of stress after three months of combat operations. At division headquarters officers grew "nettlesome and irritable" and "became largely a group of introverts, short-tempered and unable to coordinate our activities as effectively as before," Lieutenant Colonel Twining reported.[13]

The enlisted men found an anodyne in sardonic humor, as in the Marines' adaptation of the British song, "Bless 'Em All."

> *"For we're saying goodbye to them all*
> *As back to our foxholes we crawl*
> *There'll be no promotion*
> *This side of the ocean*
> *So cheer up, my lads,*
> *Fuck 'em all!"*[14]

Besides disease and poor rations, the Marines now had to endure the November rains, described by Twining as "singularly unpleasant." Mold grew on clothing and gear, and rats, "big and fat," swarmed the encampments. Flies fed on Japanese corpses, which emitted a continuous "cloying, sickening odor" in the jungle outside the bivouacs. The fat flies buzzed constantly around the Marines, especially at mealtime, when they tried to brush them off their food with one hand while eating with the other. Insects invaded the men's tents; Tech Sergeant Horace McGothlin discovered that catching a small lizard and sequestering it in his tent was an effective countermeasure.

The rains sometimes sprang ghastly surprises. During one nighttime deluge "a terrible stench" nearly overpowered one New Zealand pilot. When the water ebbed he saw wedged in the bushes outside his tent half of a corpse; it had washed down from the hillside.[15]

BUOYED BY THE DIVISION'S ANNIHILATION of General Masao Maruyama's Sendai Division on the slopes of Bloody Ridge and its emphatic repulse of the Japanese "October push," at 6:30 a.m. on November 1 Vandegrift's Marines went on the offensive. With the Eighth Marines aboard transports en route to Guadalcanal and the 2nd Marine Raiders Battalion and the America's 182nd Infantry soon arriving, Vandegrift was willing to now commit a larger force than he had during the three previous Matanikau operations. He intended to drive the enemy from the area between the Matanikau River and Kokumbona, which lay twelve miles west of Henderson Field.

If the offensive succeeded, the Marines could establish an advanced patrol base at Kokumbona. "We want to give them a sense of futility," said Lieutenant Colonel Gerald Thomas, the division chief of staff. An ancillary goal was the destruction of the 150mm Pistol Petes that had shelled Henderson Field for weeks, or at least forcing their relocation beyond bombardment range of the airfield.[16]

It was going to be the first combined arms operation on Guadalcanal since the amphibious landing on August 7. As cruisers shelled the Point Cruz area, P-39s and dive bombers, directed to targets by forward air observers with signal panels, would attack Japanese infantry and artillery positions. B-17s from Espiritu Santo would strike Kokumbona.

Colonel Merritt "Red Mike" Edson, the former Raiders commander, knew the terrain all too well from the Second and Third Matanikau offensives. This time two battalions of Edson's Fifth Marines would lead the assault over the Matanikau and westward, aided by the 3rd Battalion, Seventh Marines; Lieutenant Colonel William Whaling's scout snipers; and the Second Marines' 1st and 2nd Battalions, recently arrived from Tulagi. In reserve was the 164th Infantry Regiment. The Eleventh Marines and 3rd Defense Battalion would provide artillery support.[17]

On Halloween night, October 31, the First Marines' 3rd Battalion took up positions on a hill west of the Matanikau to shield engineers building three bridges over the river that night. At daybreak, as air strikes, artillery shellfire, and naval gunfire pounded the Japanese, the Fifth Marines crossed the river on the bridges, made of planking and fuel drums. The Whaling Group and the Seventh Marines battalion forded the Matanikau farther upstream to guard the Fifth Marines' left flank. Behind them came the Second Marines.[18]

The Fifth Marines' 2nd Battalion negotiated the coral ridges inland against little opposition. However, the 1st Battalion, advancing near the beach, ran into Japanese dug into jungle ravines at the base of Point Cruz. The battalion found itself in a close-range infantryman's brawl, at times hand-to-hand. Casualties mounted rapidly. Private William Seiverling Jr. and his platoon attacked enemy positions in a gully, where he killed a sniper. Then, Seiverling single-handedly covered the platoon's withdrawal, killing several Japanese before losing his own life. Corporal Terrence Reynolds Jr., firing a BAR from the hip, was killed as he threw back a Japanese counterattack.[19]

On November 2 the 5th Regiment's 3rd Battalion under Lieutenant Colonel Lew Walt flanked the Japanese and, with bayonet and grenade charges, drove them from the ravines to an area of beachside cliffs honeycombed with caves. Mortars and artillery failed to dislodge them. The surrounded enemy soldiers tried to break out with a bayonet attack early November 3, but they were repulsed. Later in the day the Fifth Marines crushed the pocket, silencing the grumbling from division headquarters that its advance was taking too long. The Marines killed more than three hundred Japanese and captured a large number of heavy weapons, including a dozen 37mm guns, which explained the enemy's stubborn resistance.[20]

To stop the Marine drive Hyakutake emptied his Seventeenth Army headquarters of service troops, engineers, and even wounded men and sent them to the front. An antitank battery and labor troops were moved to Point Cruz. Hyakutake requested reinforcements, and the 38th Division's 228th Infantry Regiment, already poised to sail to Guadalcanal, hurriedly embarked from Shortland Harbor on seventeen destroyers, landing on Guadalcanal at Kamimbo during the night of November 3.[21]

Colonel John Arthur's Second Marines and the 1st Battalion, 164th Infantry took over for the Fifth and Seventh Marines and continued advancing on November 4. The Second Marines had scant combat experience and had never operated in Guadalcanal's dense jungle undergrowth. Their introduction to both became forever etched in their memories. "We had to hack our way through with bayonets and machetes," wrote squad leader Jim Sorenson. "Thorny vines clutched at our dungarees and tore them like barbs on a wire fence. . . . The heat was stifling, even breathing was difficult . . . our clothes were soaked through from sweat." Reaching a ridgetop, his squad ran into a hurricane of machine-gun, grenade, and mortar fire that cut down many of them.[22]

They were two and a half miles from Kokumbona when the offensive was suspended—because hundreds of Japanese troops had been seen east of the Henderson perimeter. Vandegrift pulled back his men to defensive positions.[23]

UNEASY ABOUT THE GUADALCANAL CAMPAIGN, Roosevelt administration officials hedged their forecasts and parsed their words. During a news conference on November 6 FDR enigmatically said the operations were not large-scale but conceded that Guadalcanal's importance might be greater than their size suggested. Afterward, Navy Secretary Frank Knox told the perplexed press that Roosevelt meant that Guadalcanal might not be critical to the Pacific War's outcome. "Even if we lost the Solomons," Knox said, sounding like a man trying hard to convince himself, "it wouldn't be decisive. If the Japs take them, it still wouldn't be decisive."[24]

WHILE THE 228TH INFANTRY WAS landing at Kamimbo, about a thousand other Japanese reinforcements from a sister unit, the 230th Infantry, came ashore on the same night, November 2–3, east of Koli Point. Koli was also the destination of Colonel Toshinaro Shoji's three unbloodied Sendai Battalions. Shoji's men had acted as Maruyama's right flank at Bloody Ridge on October 24–26, but they had fought little. Afterward Shoji's twenty-five hundred men began marching toward the northeast coast.[25]

US naval intelligence intercepted a radio message informing Shoji of the planned Tokyo Express reinforcements. The information was passed along to Vandegrift, who sent Colonel Hanneken's 2nd Battalion, Seventh Marines to the area to waylay the Japanese when they came ashore. After a draining, twelve-hour march, the Marines bivouacked east of the Metapona River, about three miles from Koli Point and a dozen miles from the perimeter.

Around midnight Hanneken's men watched in tense silence as an enemy cruiser, three destroyers, and a transport glided past them. Signals were flashed to the ships from the beach a mile to the east, and troops and supplies were landed under the ships' guns in the rain.

Hanneken's men did not interfere. "It was a horrible thought knowing how much firepower they could bring to bear on us," wrote Sergeant Mitchell Paige, one of the heroes of the second Bloody Ridge battle. "I was praying that no one would accidentally trip a trigger.... No one even dared to whisper as they continued to unload troops and supplies." After putting about a thousand men ashore, the ships glided away at 2:00 a.m. The reinforcements included two battalions from the 230th Infantry, three artillery and antiaircraft batteries, a company of engineers, and a unit that specialized in seizing airports and had captured the one in Hong Kong.[26]

Hanneken attempted to notify division headquarters about the landings, but his wet radios did not work. He prepared to attack in the morning. Just after daylight the Marines advanced to the east and, to their surprise, encountered Japanese soldiers marching in formation toward them on the beach, oblivious to their presence. "We could hardly believe it," Paige wrote, "for this was truly a machine gunner's dream, perfect grazing fire at troops in formation."[27]

But a premature Marine rifle shot scattered the Japanese like birds, and the enemy replied with heavy mortars and howitzers. Hanneken's battalion was then hit from the rear by flanking Japanese troops. Still unable to contact division headquarters and with his casualties mounting, Hanneken conducted a fighting withdrawal from the Metapona to the west. Several hours later, the battalion reached the Nalimbiu River, closer to the perimeter, and dug in.

The 2nd Battalion's radio began working again, and Hanneken asked division headquarters for reinforcements and air support. It was then when Vandegrift suspended the 4th Matanikau offensive.

The air support arrived quickly, but the Cactus Air Force planes bombed and strafed Hanneken's positions, not the enemy's, adding to his casualties. It took three urgent messages to stop the friendly fire attacks.

That afternoon, November 3, Colonel Puller's 1st Battalion was withdrawn from Bloody Ridge and loaded into boats at Lunga Point. It landed late that night at a small beachhead established by Hanneken's men near the Nalimbiu estuary.[28]

THREE DAYS PASSED WITH LITTLE fighting while the combatants moved into their respective positions. The Japanese crossed the Metapona to Tetere to the east, and Shoji received orders to march to the upper Lunga River. Leaving behind five hundred men at Gavaga Creek near Tetere to occupy the Americans, Shoji prepared to lead his three thousand other troops inland, to the south.[29]

Vandegrift had swiftly put together a strong combined force to attack Shoji: The American operation had mushroomed to four infantry battalions, a pair of tank companies, the Cactus Air Force, and naval warships—all of which would pound the Japanese after driving them into a pocket. With his troops now operating both west and east of Henderson Field, Vandegrift was compelled to form a new organizational structure. A brigadier general would command each of the two sectors: William Rupertus, arriving November 3 from Tulagi, was placed in charge of operations east of Henderson, while Edmund Sebree, the Americal Division's assistant commander, oversaw operations to the west.[30]

After conferring with his battalion commanders, Hanneken and Puller, Rupertus realized there were more Japanese in the area than he had initially believed. He delayed taking offensive action until after the arrival of two 164th Infantry battalions that were marching overland to the area.[31]

Early November 7, Hanneken and Puller advanced eastward, while the 164th's 2nd and 3rd Battalions under Colonel Bryant Moore pushed north toward the beach. The Marines encountered few Japanese—they had all gone east with Shoji. The next day Hanneken's and Puller's battalions crossed the Metapona and hemmed the Japanese from the east and west across a large swatch of dense jungle bisected by Gavaga Creek. Between them lay an unknown number of Japanese soldiers in strong positions.[32]

The two Americal battalions approached the area to seal the southern side of the pocket, and the 3rd Battalion got ahead of the 2nd. In an attempt to catch up, the 2nd made a night march. But 3rd Battalion machine-gunners mistook their comrades for enemy soldiers, killing two of them and wounding a dozen others. Then, Vandegrift abruptly withdrew the 3rd Battalion so that he could resume the Fourth Matanikau operation. Sebree objected—both battalions were needed to seal the south side of the Gavaga Creek pocket.

Thus, the climactic tactical move was left to the three companies of the 2nd Battalion, 164th Infantry. Upon knitting together the inland flanks of the Seventh Marines' 1st and 2nd Battalions, the battalion would then pounce with the Marines on the trapped enemy.

But the friendly-fire casualties had made the Army battalion cautious, and it moved slowly through the swamps. Now fully aware of the Americans' intentions, the Japanese resisted fiercely. Between November 9 and 11 the 164th's 2nd Battalion fought in hip-deep water, discolored by mud and blood, trying futilely to close the gap between the Marine battalions. Rupertus contracted dengue fever, and Sebree took over as commander.

During the nights of November 9–10 and 10–11, Shoji slipped around the Americal battalion and into the jungle to the south with most of his men. Left behind were more than 450 dead Japanese soldiers, either killed in action or by suicide.[33]

Although Shoji had gotten away with about 3,000 men and was now on a long southwesterly march to the upper Lunga River near Mount Austen, the Americans had staunched the growing threat to Henderson Field from the east. They had lost 40 killed and 120 wounded—among the latter, Puller, wounded for the first time in his twenty-three-year career.[34]

PULLER'S BATTALION HAD LEFT ITS bivouac near the mouth of the Metapona River at first light on November 8 to resume its march toward Gavaga Creek in pursuit of the Japanese. After skirmishing with the enemy rear guard throughout the morning, at 2:00 p.m. artillery and machine-gun fire swept Puller's men. A 77mm shell blew Puller off his feet and riddled his legs and lower body with shrapnel. Struggling to his feet to help a man repair a field telephone wire, Puller was shot by a sniper through his upper arm and fell to the ground.

Lowered into a foxhole with the repaired field telephone, Puller helped call in artillery fire and planned the next day's attack. That night, however, he discovered that he was unable to walk and informed his regiment that he could no longer lead his men; Major John Weber, his executive officer, took over.

Puller proved to be a difficult patient, strenuously objecting when a corpsman tried to attach an evacuation tag to his uniform. "Take that and tag a bottle with it. I can go under my own power," he barked. Puller limped to the beach and crawled aboard a landing craft that took him to the division field hospital.[35]

LIEUTENANT COLONEL EVANS CARLSON'S 2ND Marine Raider Battalion had landed November 4 at Aola Bay, about twenty miles east of Gavaga Creek, to provide security for construction of an airfield that was opposed by Vandegrift, Roy Geiger, and Slew McCain. Their opinions had been ignored; the airfield was Admiral Richmond Kelly Turner's idea, and it had Halsey's support. Not only was the site thirty-five miles from the perimeter, but Marine engineers had concluded that the ground was too marshy to support aircraft landings and takeoffs. In due time they would be proven right, and the project would be abandoned.

In the meantime, a five-hundred-man Seabee battalion had landed at Aola with the 2nd Raiders, as well as a battalion of the Army's 147th Infantry, some Americal Division artillery, and Marine artillerists armed with coastal and antiaircraft guns.[36]

Two days after the 2nd Raiders arrived, Vandegrift persuaded Turner to release them to help the Seventh Marines mousetrap Shoji's men.[37]

LIKE NO ONE ELSE, EVANS Carlson had tested the limits of the prewar Marine Corps' surprising tolerance of iconoclasts. A Connecticut Congregational minister's son, Carlson was in the Army during World War I. In 1922 he entered the Marine Corps and was selected for officer training. Carlson earned a Navy Cross a decade later in Nicaragua while fighting insurgents. In 1935, while assigned to President Franklin Roosevelt's security detail in Warm Springs, Georgia, Carlson and the president became friends. In Roosevelt, Carlson gained a powerful ally.

Roosevelt liked the raw-boned captain's boundless energy, autodidactic curiosity, and their conversations. At Warm Springs, Carlson and his wife, Etelle, dined with the president and first lady. Carlson moved on to a new assignment but remained in contact with the president.

In 1937 Carlson received orders to go to China to observe the early phases of the Sino-Japanese War. Roosevelt, who habitually short-circuited the chain of command, asked Carlson to send letters directly to him with detailed descriptions of what he saw there. Carlson traveled with Mao Tse-tung's Red Army—coincidentally at the same time that Marine Captain Samuel B. Griffith was accompanying the Japanese army—and also spent time with Chiang Kai-shek and his Nationalist forces. Sworn enemies before the Sino-Japanese War, Chiang and Mao were now reluctant allies against the Japanese.[38]

Carlson's experiences with the Red Army changed his worldview. He traveled on foot a thousand miles in fifty-one days with Mao, Chou En-lai, and their Eighth Route Army, once marching fifty-eight miles in thirty-two hours while subsisting on handfuls of rice. The Marine major admired the army's egalitarianism, guerrilla tactics, and spirit of "Gung Ho"—a motto that Carlson later adopted. Officers and enlisted men wore the same uniforms, ate the same food, and shared the same hardships. Officers explained their objectives and tactics to their men, a rarity in most armies, and convened "education" sessions regularly to cultivate proper spirit. Carlson wanted to lead this way and to utilize Mao's hit-and-run guerrilla tactics in combat.

In Shanghai, Carlson fell in with a group of left-leaning writers who met frequently to discuss politics, philosophy, and promoting tolerance in the world. Among them was Edgar Snow, who was then writing his best-seller *Red Star Over China*, which described Snow's travels with the Chinese Red Army in 1936. Their intensive conversations advanced Carlson's communist education.

In his letters to Roosevelt and then publicly Carlson praised Mao's army and criticized the US policy of continuing to supply Japan with steel, oil, and other material while officially proclaiming neutrality. He strongly advocated an embargo against Japan. When his opinions began appearing in newspapers, the Navy threatened disciplinary action unless he desisted; instead, Carlson resigned, wrote two books about the Chinese communists, and went on a nationwide speaking and writing tour.

When war with Japan appeared imminent in 1941, Carlson applied for his old commission as major and was granted it—as a reservist. His return dismayed many Marine officers, one of them Merritt Edson, who deplored Carlson's infatuation with Chinese communism.[39]

IN LATE 1941 THE FORTY-FIVE-YEAR-OLD Carlson and the president's son, Marine reservist Captain James Roosevelt, began lobbying the Marine commandant to create a unit that would be a unique amalgam of the British Royal Marine commandos and the Chinese Communists. Edson's "rubber boat" battalion was already experimenting with many of these ideas, had been for months, and seemingly had the inside track. But pressure from the Roosevelts persuaded the Navy and Marine Corps to authorize not one but two commando-style raiding units: Edson's 1st Raider Battalion at Quantico and Carlson's 2nd Raiders near San Diego.[40]

To Edson's consternation, the nucleus of the 2nd Raiders Battalion came from Edson's battalion—in all, seven officers and 190 enlisted men. Carlson selected the rest from volunteer applicants from throughout the Marine Corps.

Carlson addressed the assembled applicants beforehand, and they never forgot the impression that he made on them. "He was typically Nordic, raw-boned, angular-faced, with a generous mouth. He was not exactly grim, but austere, and he commanded immediate respect," wrote Brian Quirk.

Carlson and Roosevelt, who had become the 2nd Raiders' executive officer, interviewed the volunteers in darkened rooms amid exploding firecrackers and thrown knives twanging into a wall. They were asked whether they could unflinchingly cut an enemy soldier's throat or choke him to death, and whether they could go without food or sleep for days and walk fifty miles in a day.

Carlson rejected half of Edson's officers and three-fourths of the enlisted men and sent the rejects to other units as replacements. Edson never forgave Carlson.[41]

The battalions reflected their commanders' divergent beliefs and personalities. The culture of Edson's 1st Raiders jibed with Marine Corps orthodoxy, albeit more demanding physically. Carlson's battalion trained as hard physically as Edson's men and, like them, emphasized small-unit tactics. It was in a third area, "ethical indoctrination," that Carlson's battalion significantly differed from Edson's.[42]

At their training camp at Jacques Farm north of San Diego, Carlson made "Gung Ho!" the Second Raiders' battle cry, and convened "gung ho" meetings regularly. Each session began with the singing of the "Star-Spangled Banner," "God Bless America," and the "Marines' Hymn." Carlson lectured on the origins of the Pacific War, from Manchuria to China to Pearl Harbor, and expounded on the values that they were defending. He then invited his men to air their grievances. Carlson's officers wore no badges of rank. Carlson wanted to abolish all social distinctions between officers and men.[43]

Although some of Carlson's methods and beliefs raised eyebrows, his fellow officers respected his leadership and fighting ability, even if he was a "pinko." Colonel David Shoup, a future Marine commandant, once reportedly joked in defense of his friend Carlson, "He may have been Red, but he wasn't yellow."

BEFORE DAYBREAK ON AUGUST 17, 1942, Carlson's men carried out the first major US raid of the war. Two hundred twenty Raiders emerged from submarines off Japanese-held Butaritari Island, Makin Atoll, climbed into rubber boats, and headed for shore. Their ostensible mission was to destroy an enemy seaplane base and weather station, but the raid's planners also hoped that it would divert Japanese attention away from Guadalcanal.

Everything that could go wrong did. A storm nearly swamped their boats, and the Raiders had to bail with their helmets. Two rafts loaded with medical supplies and ammunition were swept away. Soaked to the bone, the Marines landed at 5:20 a.m. in the wrong place amid crashing, fifteen-foot breakers.[44]

An accidental burst from a light machine-gun alerted the more than one hundred Japanese troops on the island. The Raiders wiped out the first truckload that arrived, but more followed. Snipers harried the Marines, and a dozen enemy planes appeared, but then bombed and strafed their own men. Two seaplanes landed Japanese reinforcements; the Raiders shot them up. All day, the Raiders clashed sharply with the Japanese defenders.

The Raiders were supposed to return to the submarines by evening, but their attempts were baffled by powerful waves that upended or drove their boats back to the island. Just eighty men were able to fight through the surf and reach the subs; the others, exhausted and drenched, lay on the beach.[45]

Around midnight, Carlson, despondent over his failure to get off the island, stunned his men by announcing that he had decided to surrender. Japanese reinforcements and aircraft would arrive after daylight, he reasoned, and he saw no other option. But surrender meant that the president's son, James Roosevelt, would also become a captive—an enormous propaganda coup for the Japanese.

Carlson's note to the Japanese garrison commander said he wished to surrender his men "according to the rules of military law." The Japanese courier never delivered the note—a Raider mistakenly shot him in the dark.

Evidently in a better frame of mind the next day, Carlson sent patrols to inform everyone of a new evacuation plan to be executed that night. A Marine blinked a Morse code message by flashlight to the submarines, arranging a rendezvous near a lagoon on the other side of the island. In the meantime eighteen dead Raiders were buried in a mass grave; Carlson, the minister's son, said a prayer over each man. At 11:00 p.m. the Marines reached the submarines.[46]

Only when the Raiders reached Pearl Harbor, where the Navy feted them as heroes—Carlson claimed the Raiders killed between 100 and 150 enemy soldiers—did Carlson realize that 12 of his men were unaccounted for. Their fate remained a mystery until the end of the war, when Louis Zamperini, an Army Air Corps bombardier captured by the Japanese, reported that while he was held on Kwajalein, he saw scratched into a cell wall nine names beneath the words, "NINE MARINES MAROONED ON MAKIN ISLAND, AUGUST 18, 1942." A native told Zamperini that they were beheaded.[47]

ON NOVEMBER 6, CARLSON'S RAIDERS began the fifteen-mile trek from Aola Bay to the area from which Shoji's 3,000 men had already slipped away. C and E Companies, which had arrived at Aola Bay on November 4 from Espiritu Santo, began the march with about 250 men. A few days later three other Raider companies joined them. The Raiders were ordered to pursue and destroy Shoji's troops.

Carlson had recently reorganized each of his squads into three 3-man fire teams, each of them armed with an M-1 carbine, a BAR, and a Thompson submachine-gun. No comparable Japanese unit could withstand such a volume of firepower. Carlson's innovation soon became the Marine Corps standard.

Each Raider carried four days' rations, whose ingredients were influenced by Carlson's close observation of Mao's army: rice, bacon, tea, raisins, salt, and sugar, augmented daily by a "Type D" chocolate bar. Air drops of food were planned every four days.[48]

On November 12 Carlson's Raiders were traveling south along the Metapona River toward the village of Asamana when they caught up with part of Shoji's rear guard and remnants of the 230th Regiment. Shoji's men were bathing in the river, laughing and splashing. The Raiders silently lined the riverbank and began shooting the defenseless enemy soldiers. "It was like shooting birds," said Private First Class Jesse Vanlandingham. When the screams, exploding grenades, and thump of bullets ended, about 120 naked bodies floated in the crimson water.

Other Japanese units in the area counterattacked. During the intensive firefights Carlson called in an air strike, identifying the target with T-shirts arranged in the shape of an arrow. Carlson claimed his men killed 160 enemy soldiers.[49]

Fifty scouts led by Sergeant Major Jacob Vouza and one hundred native porters joined the Raiders. The scouts were excellent trackers who claimed to be able to smell the Japanese. They guided Carlson's men and ranged ahead, following the trail of Shoji's battalions. The porters carried the Raiders' extra ammunition and supplies, enabling them to cover ground quicker. "Vouza's logistical ability was always excellent," wrote Lieutenant Cleland Early.[50]

Operating as the hit-and-run guerrilla troops they were trained to be, the Raiders repeatedly fell upon the Japanese flanks and rear and then melted back into the jungle. Their fluid tactics kept Shoji's men off balance. Often marching parallel to the Japanese left or right flank, Carlson would send a patrol to harass the enemy rear, and when the Japanese turned to fight, would rip into their flank with his formidable firepower. The Raiders moved every day, never staying more than one night in a place. Carlson set the example for his men. "He was everywhere and seemed never to be tired!" said Private Ashley Fisher. Carlson's men struck the Japanese a dozen times and cleared the area between the Metapona and Tenaru Rivers.[51]

At one point a Raider captured by the Japanese was found dead beside the trail, his face slashed by knives and his testicles stuffed into his mouth. In retaliation, Carlson ordered the immediate execution of two Japanese prisoners. Thereafter, the Raiders killed every enemy soldier that they encountered—they took no prisoners. The Japanese were "too treacherous," said Carlson. "They killed most of our medical corpsmen who tried to help them so we take no chances."[52]

On November 17, Vandegrift summoned Carlson to division headquarters. The Marine general ordered the 2nd Raiders to continue their march southwest and to find the Japanese trails that connected Mount Austen and Kokumbona to the west. They were to also ferret out and destroy the Pistol Pete howitzers on Mount Austen that had intermittently shelled the airfield for months.[53]

During the next weeks, Carlson's men crossed some of Guadalcanal's most formidable terrain: coral ridges; stifling-hot, vertical jungle valleys; and soaring precipices. The meager ration of rice, bacon, tea, and raisins seemed only to whet the young Marines' roaring appetites. Food replaced sex as their principal topic of discussion. The men griped to Carlson, "Goddamn rice, colonel! We're hungry!" Twice they killed and butchered wild steers, but most of them could not digest the rich meat after subsisting for weeks on their Spartan diet.[54]

On November 28, they located one of Pistol Pete's firing positions on a coral ridge between the Lunga and Tenaru Rivers, but the field piece was not there. They climbed the eastern slopes of Mount Austen, the mass of rock and jungle looming above Henderson Field that had tantalized the Marines since they landed on the island. Using ropes to scale the cliffs, they entered areas where no other Marine had ever ventured. On November 30, at a large abandoned Japanese bivouac, they found a 75mm gun—one of the Pistol Petes—and a 37mm antitank weapon.

That same day, in what Carlson described in his report as "the most spectacular of any of our engagements," a seven-man Raider squad led by Corporal John Yancey discovered a Japanese bivouac occupied by up to one hundred enemy troops. There were no sentinels, a surprisingly common Japanese failing. In a torrential rainstorm Yancey and his men charged through the bivouac with automatic weapons blazing. Running up and down the slope shouting, "Hi, Raider!" so they would not shoot one another, they slaughtered seventy-five enemy soldiers in their shelters, as they attempted to flee and as they tried to reach their weapons, which were neatly stacked in the middle of the camp—and useless to them.[55]

Captain Oscar Peatross's B Company encountered ten Japanese in ragged uniforms sitting around a fire. Left behind by the main body of survivors from General Hyakutake's ruinous October offensive, "they were a pitiful sight: emaciated beyond words, pale and sickly looking; one had a crutch, and another had a crude homemade splint," Peatross wrote. The Raiders killed all of them.

The rest of Shoji's men pushed on to the upper Matanikau and beyond. No more than one thousand of the three thousand enemy soldiers that had fled Gavaga Creek managed to rejoin the Seventeenth Army.[56]

On December 2, Vandegrift ordered Carlson to end the "Long Patrol" and to bring his men into the perimeter. Convening a group meeting, Carlson announced the news to the Raiders, who stood and sang the "Marines' Hymn" and "Onward, Christian Soldiers." Carlson split his men into two columns, with one following the Tenaru River to the perimeter, and the other tracing the Matanikau's northward course. On December 4, the thin, ragged, bearded Raiders entered the perimeter. "Oh my God. The walking dead!" exclaimed one Marine. Others cheered them all the way in.

During their four-week mission, Carlson's men had driven the Japanese from eastern Guadalcanal and Mount Austen to the western part of the island. In the jungles and on the highlands they had repeatedly defeated the Japanese by utilizing guerrilla tactics, their automatic weapons, and Carlson's "Gung Ho!" philosophy. During their 150-mile march, the 2nd Raiders killed at least 488 Japanese soldiers.

The Raiders lost seventeen killed and eighteen wounded. Two hundred and twenty-five others were evacuated after becoming ill with malaria, ringworm, dysentery, or other debilitating ailments.[57]

IN NOVEMBER, HALSEY AND YAMAMOTO both decided to go all-in on Guadalcanal. No longer a "meeting engagement" on a remote, forgettable island, it had become the Pacific War's decisive battle, symbolizing America's and Japan's commitments to victory. Guadalcanal was now on the minds and lips of ordinary Americans and Japanese.

The October push had revealed deep, possibly congenital flaws in Japanese thinking: unnecessarily complex planning, poor reconnaissance and coordination, and a fatal inflexibility.

The slaughter of the Sendai Division on Bloody Ridge and the Japanese navy and air force's failure to destroy the Cactus Air Force and neutralize Henderson Field inspired no serious self-examination, and few changes.

Encouraged by the tactical naval-air victory at the Battle of Santa Cruz, Japanese strategists were now planning a third combined army-navy offensive. The November push was to be the biggest yet—the Tokyo Express landing tens of thousands of infantry reinforcements, the massing of powerful naval forces, and daily raids by the 11th Air Fleet.

The failures of the September and October pushes did not challenge Japan's underlying faith in spiritual power's inherent superiority to firepower and economic power. General Suzuki Teiichi, president of Japan's Planning Board, wrote, "The key to final victory lies not in the material fighting strength of the nation, but in the spirit which infuses strength in all directions. . . . Material wealth does not decide the outcome of a war."

Between November 2 and 10, Admiral Tanaka's Tokyo Express destroyers delivered several thousand troops and tons of supplies to Guadalcanal during more than sixty-five nighttime destroyer and cruiser shuttles. The stealthy landings at Taivu Point east of the Marine perimeter and at Kamimbo and Tassafaronga to the west had increased Japanese manpower to more than twenty-five thousand troops.

Yet this was only the prologue to an even more ambitious troop buildup. Captain Toshikazu Ohmae, sent by Yamamoto to Guadalcanal after the failure of the October offensive, had urged using overwhelming naval power to neutralize Guadalcanal's airfield so that large numbers of troops could be landed at once.

The November plan called for land-based 11th Air Force bombers to pound Henderson daily during the first phase. Then, battleships and cruisers would bombard Henderson Field and Fighter One on two consecutive nights, silencing the Cactus Air Force so that the transports could land the troops.

November 13 was provisionally designated "Z-Day"—when up to thirteen thousand men would be landed. Most of them would belong to the 38th Division, but there would also be special naval landing force troops. If the operation succeeded, General Hyakutake's Seventeenth Army would easily surpass thirty thousand troops, equipped with plentiful long-range artillery for bombarding Henderson and Fighter One.

Additional troops, including the 51st Division from China, would arrive during subsequent weeks in the lead-up to the campaign's "decisive battle" in December. Fought by ground forces, it would be supported by a massive naval bombardment of Henderson Field. Japanese military orthodoxy dating to the Russo-Japanese War asserted that decisive battles determined wars' outcomes, and leaders were certain that the Pacific War would be no exception.[58]

Monitoring of the Japanese army's encrypted four-digit call signs strongly suggested to US naval intelligence that something was in the wind. There was a significant spike in radio traffic involving the Solomon Islands—"excellent indications" of a looming attack. Intelligence analysts estimated that there were seventeen thousand Japanese soldiers on Guadalcanal and that another nineteen thousand were in transit.

On November 10, south Bougainville coast watcher Paul Mason reported the largest enemy fleet that he had ever seen: at least sixty-one ships, plus up to a dozen transport ships carrying possibly fifteen thousand troops. Nimitz wrote to Halsey, "While this looks like a big punch, I am confident that you with your forces will take their measure."[59]

MASON'S AND JACK READ'S TIMELY warnings about Japanese air raids had long rankled military officials in Rabaul. In early November, a hundred-man detachment along with tracking dogs was landed on Bougainville at Buin to hunt down the men.

The Japanese never really had a chance of finding them. Mason and Read knew the mountainous, heavily wooded island's vast trail system intimately, and the Japanese did not. Mason and Read went into deep hiding in the mountains, shielded by the loyal natives.

Scouts spotted the tracking dogs and notified Mason; he called in an air strike, and a Catalina PBY's bomb killed all the dogs. The natives sent the pursuers on wild goose chases, while the scouts busily created false trails for them to follow. Unable to find either Read or Mason, the Japanese suspended their manhunt.[60]

BESIDES BEING REINFORCED BY SEABEES, the 2nd Raiders, and a battalion of the independent 147th Infantry Regiment east of Henderson in early November, the Americans on Guadalcanal also added thirty planes to the Cactus Air Force. They included Wildcats, torpedo and dive bombers, and eight of the coveted Army P-38s—bringing the number of operational aircraft to seventy-seven. Moreover, two Army B-26 squadrons at Espiritu Santo lay within flying distance of Guadalcanal. Almost daily, additional reinforcements, ammunition, food, and supplies were now arriving by ship.[61]

Halsey had promised Vandegrift that he would send every warship that he had to Guadalcanal to disrupt the Tokyo Express. They included the *Enterprise*, even as repairs of her recent bomb damage continued during her trip to the area;, and two of the new, fast battleships, *Washington* and *South Dakota*. On November 10, Halsey was reading summaries of Yamamoto's attack orders that Navy intelligence had decrypted. They described the enemy's intentions, but with an important omission: the plan for battleships to shell Henderson Field and destroy the Cactus Air Force.[62]

PRESIDENT ROOSEVELT HAD ORDERED THE joint chiefs of staff to make Guadalcanal its top priority. "My anxiety about the Southwest Pacific is to make sure that every possible weapon gets into that area to hold Guadalcanal," he said.

Publicity, however, was the weapon Roosevelt began to personally wield from Washington. With the president's approval—and possibly at his suggestion—*Time* magazine put Vandegrift on its cover in early November. When the Marine general learned that he had become a celebrity, he was pleased—not by the attention that it brought to him, but "because it seemed to bring the real meaning of the campaign home to the American public." With public attention focused on Guadalcanal, Vandegrift believed the US government could no longer prosecute the campaign "on our only too familiar shoestring."[63]

TWO CONVOYS WERE ON THEIR way to Guadalcanal with more than five thousand reinforcements. Four transports left Noumea on November 8 under Admiral Richmond Turner's command with two battalions and the headquarters of the Americal Division's 182nd Infantry, the 101st Medical Regiment, a Marine replacement battalion, and more artillery. Their escorts, led by Rear Admiral Daniel Callaghan, included cruisers *San Francisco* and *Portland*, light cruisers *Helena* and *Juneau*, and ten destroyers.

The next day, a second naval force under Rear Admiral Norman Scott left Espiritu Santo with three transports bearing assorted air and ground replacements, food, ammunition, and the 1st Marine Aviation Engineer Battalion. The transports' escorts were the antiaircraft cruiser *Atlanta* and four destroyers.

Japanese scout planes snooping the waters southeast of Guadalcanal spotted the two convoys as they approached Lunga Point. Scott's group got there first, on November 11, the twenty-fourth anniversary of the end of another war, which was far from the minds of the troops who hurriedly disembarked amid a Japanese dive-bombing attack. The nine Val dive bombers, escorted by a dozen Zeros, were met by Cactus's Wildcats. All of the Vals were shot down either by the Wildcats or the convoy's antiaircraft gunners. Two hours later, a raid by twenty-seven Bettys and five Zeros suspended the unloading again. Only one vessel was damaged, the transport *Zeilin*, after her passengers had gone ashore.

Turner's transport group expected trouble when it arrived the next day, on November 12. Callaghan's and Scott's escort ships fanned out to ward off enemy submarines and to counter air raids while the transports were unloaded. Work stopped when a Bougainville coast watcher warned that Japanese warplanes were on their way. At 2:00 p.m. sixteen Bettys armed with torpedoes and escorted by thirty Zeros swooped down on Turner's ships. The canny admiral deftly positioned them so that the torpedoes ran through the water parallel to the ships, all of them missing their targets.

His gunners went to work along with twenty-two Wildcats and Army P-400s flying protection overhead, including six VMF-121 Wildcats led by ace Captain Joe Foss. Fighter planes and antiaircraft guns shot down eleven bombers plus some Zeros, with Foss bringing his total kills to twenty-three since October 9. Four US planes were lost.

"On our third salvo we made our first kill," wrote C. Raymond Calhoun, the destroyer *Sterett*'s gun director. "The plane hit the water with a crash, skidded, tumbled, came to a stop, and burned like all the fires of hell." The *Sterett*'s gunners knocked down a second plane, then saw a burning bomber crash into *San Francisco* and explode in "a huge ball of flames," killing fifteen crewmen and wounding twenty-nine.

The violent reception notwithstanding, Scott and Turner managed to put ashore the troops, weapons, and supplies entrusted to them.[64]

AIR RECONNAISSANCE REPORTED A LARGE number of Japanese battleships, cruisers, and destroyers advancing from the north and northwest toward Guadalcanal. Turner had been Guadalcanal's amphibious force commander since landing day and knew intuitively what to expect next—a bombardment to suppress the Cactus Air Force so that enemy reinforcements could land. Coast watcher Paul Mason had seen them November 10, packed in a dozen transports.

Scott's and Callaghan's overmatched cruisers and destroyers would alone have to meet the coming attack. Even though Halsey had put all his chips on the table, the *Enterprise* and her escorts, and Rear Admiral Willis Lee's two battleships and their escorts were nearly two days' sail away.

During the afternoon of November 12, Turner buttoned down the landing area. He sent away the six transports—the damaged *Zeilin* had already left—with an escort of three destroyers and two minesweepers. They made for Espiritu Santo.

Turner chose Callaghan, who lacked combat experience but had fifteen days' seniority over Scott, to command the thirteen warships that would face the Japanese fleet. Turner's selection of Callaghan, until October 30 a staff officer and previously Admiral Ghormley's chief of staff, followed Navy protocol, but Scott would have been a smarter choice. An experienced combat officer, he was the Navy's only surface force commander to have won a battle: at Cape Esperance, a nighttime battle—like this one was shaping up to be.[65]

Vice Admiral Hiroaki Abe led the Raiding Group sent by Admiral Kondo, the Advanced Force commander, to bombard Henderson Field, Fighter One, and the Cactus Air Force that night. It was almost a month to the day after the battleships *Kongo* and *Haruna* had memorably plastered the airfield with more than nine hundred shells. The battleships *Hiei* and *Kirishima* this time would shell the island; their gun turrets were stacked with antipersonnel high-explosive rounds. The light cruiser *Nagara* and fourteen destroyers—three of them manning a picket line to the west—were the two dreadnoughts' escorts.

If the bombardment silenced Cactus, Admiral Mikawa, leading a squadron of cruisers and destroyers, would join Admiral Tanaka and his twelve destroyers in convoying 13,500 reinforcements in eleven transports to Tassafaronga and Cape Esperance.

Callaghan entered Ironbottom Sound with his thirteen warships. Besides having one ship fewer than Abe, he was at a decisive disadvantage in the metal that his squadron could throw per broadside, the ages-old yardstick of naval power. In this respect Abe's ships held a three-to-one edge.

Callaghan had arranged his ships in a single column, like an eighteenth-century admiral going into battle: four destroyers in the vanguard; two heavy cruisers and three light cruisers in the middle; and four destroyers bringing up the rear, spaced 500 to 750 yards apart. This was the configuration that Scott had used at Cape Esperance when he had crossed Rear Admiral Aritomo Goto's "T."

The formation might have accomplished its aim if Abe's squadron had also approached in a single column, but it did not—its three or four loose formations made Callaghan's precisely spaced ships look like ducks in a shooting gallery.

NOT ONLY WAS SAN FRANCISCO the hometown of Admiral Callaghan, the cruiser of that name had been his first wartime command. Thus, for purely sentimental reasons, Callaghan had selected it as his flagship. Unfortunately, it lacked the new SG radar set, which provided a 360-degree display of surface waters for more than ten miles. The technology was a stride in early target identification, especially useful against an enemy that relied on lookouts. Four of Callaghan's other warships had SG—the light cruisers *Helena* and *Juneau* and the destroyers *O'Bannon* and *Fletcher*. As the enemy fleets raced toward a headlong encounter, Callaghan, in the middle of his column, was relying on SG plots radioed to him by *O'Bannon* and *Helena*.[66]

It was 1:24 a.m. on November 13—"Friday the Bloody Thirteenth," as many would remember it. "We had thirteen ships, November the 13th, and the last ship was the *Fletcher*, and she was the 445, which added up to thirteen! I've always felt, as a result of that battle, that thirteen was my lucky number," wrote John Chew, *Helena*'s air defense officer. The simple fact that he survived validated Chew's superstition.

Helena's SG radar picked up three Japanese groups fifteen miles ahead. By the time its report reached *San Francisco* by TBS (talk between ships) radio at 1:30 a.m., six minutes had elapsed, and the combatants were four miles closer to one another. At 1:42 the lead destroyer, *Cushing*, made a hard left and reported that it was moving into position to fire torpedoes at three or four targets ahead. *Cushing*'s captain requested Callaghan's permission to do so.

The *Cushing*'s abrupt course change nearly caused a collision, and Callaghan made matters worse by dictating course corrections that reached some ships but not others. As the American warships tried to avoid running into one another, Japanese vessels appeared on both sides of the formerly neatly aligned column, now in disarray.

At the instant *Cushing* was requesting permission to fire fish, Abe's Raiding Group sighted the Americans—eighteen minutes after *Helena*'s initial report. The meeting was evidently unexpected: crews on Abe's two battleships frantically swapped out the incendiary shells they had readied for bombarding Henderson Field for armor-piercing shells for surface combat. The switch took another eight minutes.

The milling American ships had not yet opened fire, although Callaghan at 1:45 a.m. ordered them to stand by to do so. Adding to the confusion was the gabble of voices clogging the Americans' voice communications circuits.[67]

The leading Japanese ships that now hemmed Callaghan's column on both sides. Abe's warships opened fire at 1:48, fully twenty-four minutes after the *Helena*'s initial radar sighting.

When *Hiei*'s and *Akatsuki*'s spotlights bathed the *Atlanta*'s bridge in white light, the cruiser began firing at the searchlights. Her guns' powerful recoil rocked the ship, spilling books from shelves, tipping chairs, and scattering papers everywhere. It was too late. Four enemy ships now had *Atlanta* in their cross-hairs, and shells battered the cruiser from two sides. She fought back with salvos from her five-inch guns. Then a torpedo fired by the *Akatsuki* struck *Atlanta* amidships; the explosion lifted the cruiser out of the water and killed nearly everyone in the forward engine room.

THE TWO COLUMNS OF JAPANESE warships enclosing Callaghan's ships were so close in places that American torpedoes did not have time to arm before they struck the enemy ships. *Helena*'s frustrated plotting room officer burst out to John Chew, the air defense officer, "For Christ's sake, Jack, what are we going to do? Throw potatoes at them?"

"Odd ships fire to starboard, even to port!" Callaghan barked, in an attempt to impose order on the bizarre tactical situation. Some of the ships' guns were pointed the wrong way, including Callaghan's flagship, an even-numbered ship whose guns were aimed starboard. The American column plunged forward, its guns hammering at the swarming Japanese ships.[68]

Inside the Guadalcanal perimeter, air raid sirens wailed, horns blew in the tank park, and a bell clanged in warning of an impending naval attack on the air-field. A Japanese observation plane flew over Henderson and dropped green flares. Everyone braced for a naval bombardment. Instead, there came a ceaseless rumble of guns and gun flashes from near Savo Island, informing them that the Navy had intercepted the Japanese bombardment force.

"The star shells rose, terrible and red. Giant tracers flashed across the night in orange arches," wrote Marine Private Robert Leckie, who watched the fireworks from Bloody Ridge. "Sometimes we would duck, thinking they were coming at us, though they were miles away." Distant explosions made the ground quake underfoot, "as though the great whale had been harpooned, as though the iron had smacked into the wet flesh. Some great ship had exploded." When a ship was hit and erupted in a fireball, the watching Marines were silent, fearful it had been one of theirs. The explosion's concussion "would flap our clothes."[69]

Indeed, the explosions swiftly followed one another. *Atlanta*'s demise fol-lowed the torpedo strike and an explosion that knocked out power, setting her adrift. She calamitously wandered into *San Francisco*'s line of fire and absorbed 19 eight-inch rounds intended for a Japanese destroyer that had just moved out of range. The salvos buckled decks, smashed bulkheads, and strewed bodies and body parts everywhere. One of the shells killed Admiral Scott and three staff officers. The *Atlanta* burned from stem to stern.[70]

Admiral Callaghan, horrified by his ship's inadvertent decimation of the *At-lanta*, shouted, "Cease firing! Our ships!" intending the order for just his ship. But his open TBS mic broadcast it to the entire squadron. Consequently, at 1:54

a.m. some ships stopped firing while others did not. Realizing his error, Callaghan exhorted the squadron's gunners to concentrate on the battleships, as one of them, *Hiei*, loomed out of the night near *San Francisco*. "We want the big ones, boys; we want the big ones!"[71]

Callaghan got more than he bargained for when *Hiei* took the measure of his flagship and fired five or six salvos into her, inflicting fifteen major-caliber strikes, many from fourteen-inch bombardment shells; *Hiei* had not finished changing over to armor-piercing ammunition when she went into combat. Four 14-inch rounds crashed into *San Francisco*'s bridges, with devastating effect, littering the navigation bridge deck with "bodies, helmeted and life-jacketed, limbs and gear. . . . The siren was moaning and water was raining down through holes in the deck above" from the ruptured gun-cooling systems, wrote Lieutenant Commander Bruce McCandless. Killed on the flag bridge were Admiral Callaghan and four lieutenant commanders on his staff. *San Francisco*'s commander, Captain Cassin Young, awarded the Medal of Honor for his actions at Pearl Harbor, was mortally wounded.

Hiei, the light cruiser *Nagara*, and *Hiei*'s sister battleship, *Kirishima*, then continued battering *San Francisco* with murderous fire that knocked out steering, silenced most of her guns, and ignited numerous fires. The sick bay was evacuated when three feet of water surged into it.

Lieutenant Commander Herbert Schonlan, the damage control officer, succeeded to command upon the deaths of every superior officer. He concentrated on suppressing the twenty-two fires raging on the ship. That left Lieutenant Commander McCandless, the officer of the deck, to conn the burning flagship, hit forty-five times, away from the main action as crewmen stuffed mattresses into shell holes near the water line. Eighty-three men lay dead.[72]

During the chaotic back-alley brawl in the dark, the combatants fired at whatever target happened to be in front of them. Within a quarter of an hour, several ships on both sides were burning or sinking. Ablaze and pummeled by shellfire, *Cushing* drifted without power or means of self-defense—her guns knocked out, her torpedo mount jammed, dead sailors everywhere—as the cruiser *Nagara* circled and continued to pump shells into her. *Cushing*'s crew was ordered to abandon ship.[73]

Laffey, facing the looming *Hiei*, gamely riddled the battleship's bridge until it collapsed. A dazed Admiral Abe survived. *Hiei* found itself in the exasperating position of not being able to fire its fourteen-inch guns at the much smaller *Laffey* because the guns could not be depressed far enough. *Laffey* fired two torpedoes, but at such close range that they did not have time to arm. However, the destroyer's concentrated fire damaged the battleship's communications system as it moved down the line.

Laffey's modest triumph was brief; a torpedo fired by one of the three enemy destroyers trailing *Hiei* and *Kirishima* plowed into her after hull, wrecking her propulsion and steering. The Japanese destroyers then shelled her as she drifted. A magazine exploded, and she sank. *O'Bannon* swerved to avoid the sinking ship's bow and threw life jackets to sailors in the water as she passed.[74]

Sterett and *O'Bannon* raked *Hiei*'s superstructure with their five-inch guns, and the battleship was soon "beautifully illuminated by her own fires." Their shellfire blew away chunks of *Hiei*'s superstructure like "a knife cutting through a block of butter," wrote an American sailor. *Hiei* depressed her fourteen-inch guns as far as they would go and fired, but the rounds passed ten feet above *O'Bannon*. Japanese sailors could be seen diving overboard with their clothes on fire. Two torpedoes, possibly fired by *Monssen*, hit the battleship at the waterline, and there was a huge explosion.

Aaron Ward led the rearguard destroyers as the column hurtled onward. "Every American ship took the bit and raced at Admiral Abe's forces," wrote executive officer Julian Becton. It "did somewhat resemble the charge immortalized by Tennyson" ("The Charge of the Light Brigade"). *Aaron Ward* fired "every gun that would bear, launching torpedoes port and starboard." After an exchange with *Yudachi*, the Japanese destroyer was left dead in the water. As *Aaron Ward* continued through the enemy formation, three 14-inch rounds crashed into her, along with two 8-inch shells and five smaller-caliber strikes.[75]

"Our formation had ceased to function as a force," said the Navy's combat narrative of the melee. "Each ship had become an independent entity faced with the problem of not firing on friendly vessels."[76]

A Japanese destroyer appeared off *Sterett*'s starboard bow; *Sterett* trained her five-inch guns on her and fired a pair of torpedoes. The enemy ship exploded with "a tremendous roar . . . her stern came completely out of the water." A fireball shot skyward, and the destroyer burned and then rapidly went down. "Oh, you poor son of a bitch," a *Sterett* sailor shouted. Then it was *Sterett*'s turn to absorb punishment—from *Nagara* and other ships. Multiple strikes left her number-three gun "a shambles," damaged her torpedo and ammunition-handling rooms, and knocked out her steering. Captain Jesse Coward switched steering to the engines and pulled the burning destroyer out of the battle while a damage assessment was made.

Ensign Perry Hall, who went below to check on damage, reported that "bits of burning bedding smoldered on the bunks, burnt bodies were scattered about the deck, the stench of burning flesh and powder made breathing difficult. . . . Bodies, mattresses, and other debris sloshed back and forth with the movement of the ship," as seawater poured through a shell hole just above the water line.

Willie "Red" Hammack, who was helping treat the injured, found the wardroom full of wounded men—on stretchers, on the deck, or sitting and waiting until the doctor, Lieutenant Harry Nyce, could get to them. "Some were full of shrapnel holes, some were gut-shot, and some were badly burned. . . . There wasn't a whimper from a single man in that wardroom," wrote the amazed Hammack, who aided Nyce in performing multiple amputations.[77]

Captain Tameichi Hara, one of Japan's leading torpedo experts, commanded the destroyer *Amatsukaze*, which had joined the *Hiei* in smashing up the *San Francisco*. Now she zeroed in on a destroyer near the end of Callaghan's column, *Barton*, and fired eight torpedoes. Two smacked into the destroyer, and "pillars of fire" streaked hundreds of feet into the air. *Barton* broke in two and sank, "so quickly that I rubbed my eyes in disbelief," Hara wrote. "There was a roaring ovation from the crew" of the *Amatsukaze*.

Compounding the *Barton* tragedy, *O'Bannon* ran over her survivors in the water, and *Barton*'s depth charges detonated, killing more crewmen. Three minutes later Hara's crew fired four more torpedoes at the light cruiser *Juneau*, holing her.[78]

In this rumble in the nighttime by twenty-seven warships, no one was safe for long, and the *Amatsukaze* was no exception. Blindsided by a cascade of six-inch-gun salvos from *Helena*, the *Amatsukaze* lost her steering, hydraulics, guns, and radio, and she began burning. Absorbing thirty-seven hits and suffering forty-three crewmen deaths, she steamed in circles, her rudder jammed.[79]

Star shells burst over *Monssen*, second-to-last of the four trailing destroyers. Her torpedo men had just fired five fish at a large vessel two miles away, reporting two strikes, and then her gunners swept the decks of an enemy destroyer. *Monssen*'s captain, Lieutenant Commander Charles McCombs, believed the star shells were American, and he blinked a recognition signal at the ship that fired them.

Two searchlights instantly stabbed through the darkness and smoke, pinning *Monssen* in a sunburst of light. Too late McCombs realized that the star shells were unfriendly ones. His men opened fire on the nearest spotlight, and it went out. "Then all hell broke loose. We started getting hit with heavy caliber shells on both sides," wrote McCombs. Ten rounds hit amidships, ten around the bridge, and another killed everyone in the number-one gun turret. More shells crashed into the engine room and the captain's and chief's quarters. In minutes, every gun was disabled, and *Monssen* was burning furiously, dead in the water. McCombs gave the order to abandon ship.[80]

After *Portland* lit up *Akatsuki* with shellfire and fire from other US ships sent the Japanese destroyer plunging to the ocean bottom, a torpedo blew away a large part of *Portland*'s starboard afterdeck. Everyone in the steering room died. With her rudder jammed to the right and two propellers sheared off, *Portland* circled to starboard, firing 4 six-gun salvos at the *Hiei* that ignited new fires.[81]

The slugfest, lasting thirty-four minutes, was one of the most intensive sea battles ever fought. When it ended, the Japanese had won a decisive tactical victory. Twelve of the thirteen US ships had been sunk or damaged, and 1,439 sailors, officers, and Marines were dead or dying. Yet Admiral Abe's Raiding Force had not gotten off lightly. Five destroyers had been lost or damaged, and *Hiei*, hit eighty-five times by shellfire, was slowly limping northward away from Guadalcanal.

The circumstances persuaded Abe to cancel the bombardment of Henderson Field planned for early that morning and to withdraw his ships in the train of the *Hiei*. Informed of the changed plan, Yamamoto at 3:44 a.m. postponed by one day the troop landings scheduled for November 13–14, until the night of November 14–15. Admiral Mikawa's Eighth Fleet of cruisers and destroyers, along with Admiral Tanaka and his transports and destroyer escorts put in at Shortland Harbor to wait.

The delay, however, did not mean Yamamoto was scaling back the November push—far from it. Callaghan's squadron had baffled Abe's plan to shell Henderson and neutralize the Cactus Air Force, but Vice Admiral Nobutake Kondo, commander of the Advanced Force, planned to send Mikawa and his cruiser-destroyer force to Ironbottom Bay that night to carry out Abe's unfulfilled bombardment mission. And on the following night, when the 13,500 soldiers were sailing to Guadalcanal in eleven transports, Kondo intended to hit Henderson with his Bombardment Force to safeguard the landings against Cactus Air Force attacks.

DAYBREAK RAISED THE CURTAIN ON an appalling scene of broken ships, broken men, fire, and smoke. Oil-coated survivors clung to floating debris, bobbing among the torsos of dead comrades. Near at hand, *Atlanta*, adrift near Lunga Point, was no longer burning, but she was clearly doomed. Nearly two hundred men had died on her, and bodies and severed limbs littered the decks when boats came alongside to take off the wounded. Pillars of smoke rose from the destroyers *Cushing* and *Monssen* and the Japanese destroyer *Yudachi*. Aaron *Ward* lay dead in the water east of Savo Island.

Higgins boats manned by sailors and Marines plied the oily waters, pulling aboard survivors from *Barton* and from *Monssen*—before she exploded and sank at 9:00 a.m. By day's end, more than eleven hundred casualties flooded Guadalcanal's medical facilities, where the first order of business was to remove the black oil and sludge caked on the survivors. Luckily for the wounded, the Army's 101st Medical Regiment had landed the day before.

The casualties included ships as well as men—not far from the landing beaches the stricken *Portland* cruised in a clockwise orbit, her rudder stuck. Despite her extensive damage, she managed to rake *Yudachi* with several salvos and sink her. A towering smoke plume on the northern side of Savo Island marked the slow, troubled passage of the crippled *Hiei* as it steamed in circles.[82]

The tug *Bobolink* from Tulagi was about to take *Aaron Ward* under tow when *Hiei* began firing two-gun salvos at her, straddling the stricken destroyer but not hitting her. The battleship stopped its lackluster shelling when Cactus Air Force planes began homing in on it.

The first search patrols were in the air at dawn. It did not take them long to spot the *Hiei*, "forward turrets smoking . . . after turrets dangling," ten miles north of Savo Island, accompanied by three destroyers. It was a rare opportunity for the Cactus Air Force, which had never before had the chance to destroy a Japanese battleship. The pilots made the most of it.[83]

At 6:15 a.m. a dive bombers from VMSB-142, which had arrived at Henderson the day before, hit *Hiei* with a thousand-pounder. An hour later torpedo bombers from another newly arrived Marine squadron put a torpedo into the battleship on its first mission. The bombers returned at 10:10 and struck *Hiei* with a second torpedo.

Enterprise had left Noumea for Guadalcanal on the 11th with Kinkaid's Task Force 16, and at daybreak November 13, was 280 miles south of the island. Believing—falsely, it turned out—that enemy carriers were 150 miles west of Guadalcanal, Kinkaid decided to clear the *Enterprise* for a possible carrier battle by sending extra planes to Guadalcanal. Eight bombers from Torpedo Squadron Ten, the so-called Buzzard Brigade, lifted off the flattop, accompanied by six Wildcats from VF-10. At 10:00 a.m. the planes spotted *Hiei*, and the torpedo bombers scored three hits.

Lieutenant Albert "Scoffer" Coffin's exultant torpedo squadron then landed at Henderson Field, a mere thirty minutes away from the doomed battleship. Brigadier General Louis Woods, who had succeeded Roy Geiger as Cactus's commander, was surprised and delighted by the Buzzard Brigade's appearance. "Boys, I don't know where you came from, but you look like angels dropping out of heaven to us."

Dive bombers hammered *Hiei* throughout the day, and Wildcats tangled with twenty-three Zeros sent from the carrier *Junyo* to protect the battleship, shooting down eight of them. Fourteen Army Air Force B-17s from Espiritu Santo even took a crack at *Hiei*. High-altitude bombing of ships was rarely successful, but on this Friday the Thirteenth a bomber pilot got lucky; one of the fifty-six five-hundred-pound bombs, dropped by the B-17s from fourteen thousand feet, hit its target.

At 3:30 p.m. Admiral Abe ordered *Hiei* abandoned and scuttled, but Yamamoto countermanded the order. Use the battleship as a decoy, he said, to divert the enemy's attention from the task force sailing from Shortland to bombard Guadalcanal that night. Orders notwithstanding, survivors were taken off the thirty-year-old battleship by 6:00 p.m., and it sank hours later. The first Japanese battleship sunk during the war took 450 men to the bottom with her.[84]

CAPTAIN GILBERT HOOVER, COMMANDER OF the lightly damaged *Helena*, took charge of Callaghan's mangled task force and left the area early November 13 for Espiritu Santo. With him were the smoldering cruisers *San Francisco* and *Juneau*, and destroyers *Fletcher* and *Sterett* acting as escorts. The *O'Bannon*, whose sonar gear was damaged by the *Laffey*'s exploding depth charges, sailed ahead to apprise Halsey of the night's battle; the task force was under radio silence, and Hoover did not want to give away its location. Moving at thirteen knots because the damaged *San Francisco* and *Juneau* could muster no greater speed, the sad little convoy entered Torpedo Junction, the area south of San Cristobal Island near where the *Wasp* had been sunk on September 15.[85]

MINORU YOKOTA HAD CREDIBLY COMMANDED the *I-26* since it was commissioned exactly a year earlier. It sank a US supply ship headed for Hawaii the day of the Pearl Harbor attack and, later, took down a cargo steamer off the Canadian coast. On August 31 *I-26* torpedoed *Saratoga*, sending her away for four months of repairs.

On the morning of November 13, *I-26* was cruising southeast of Guadalcanal when her lookouts sighted three enemy cruisers and two destroyers. She fired a full spread of torpedoes. They missed the *San Francisco*, but fifteen hundred yards to *San Francisco*'s starboard lay the light antiaircraft cruiser *Juneau*, chugging along on one screw, down twelve feet by the bow. Just before 11:00 a.m. an *I-26* torpedo struck *Juneau*'s port side, near where she had been hit the previous night.

The torpedo detonated *Juneau*'s forward magazine, and "she leaped from the sea in a blinding burst of light," wrote Lieutenant C. G. Morris. From *Helena*'s bridge Morris saw a five-inch gun turret soar into the air above the *Helena*'s stack. The *Juneau* "blew up with all the fury of an erupting volcano," wrote Lieutenant Commander McCandless, who witnessed the explosion from the bridge of the *San Francisco*. "There was a terrific thunderclap and a plume of white water that was blotted out by a huge brown hemisphere a thousand yards across, from within which came the sounds of more explosions."

When the dark cloud lifted, "we could see nothing of this fine 6,000-ton cruiser or the 700 men she carried," wrote McCandless. A large chunk of plating smashed into the side of *San Francisco*'s bridge, a few feet from where he was standing, and another piece of debris broke an enlisted man's legs.

"The *Juneau* had vanished as though she had been a mirage," wrote Morris in amazement. An oily patch of sea marked her grave. Shocked *Helena* crewmen walked the decks as though in a trance.[86]

Captain Hoover, whose friend Captain Lyman Swensen was the *Juneau*'s skipper, did not stop to search for survivors. He was unwilling to risk other ships being torpedoed. He pressed ahead, signaling to a B-17 overhead that had been drawn to the area by the massive explosion: "*Juneau* torpedoed and disappeared lat. 10° 32' S, long. 161° 2' E at 1109. Survivors in water. Report Comsopac." The Flying Fortress pilot dutifully relayed the report to Henderson Field, but the message inexplicably went no further.

About one hundred survivors, their faces blackened by oil, clung to rafts and debris from their ship. Some were badly wounded. "Shoot me! Shoot me!" a sailor whose leg had been blown off pleaded with Allen Heyn, who had suffered painful shrapnel wounds. He towed the man to a raft, which was filling with shocked survivors.

Among them was George Sullivan, one of five brothers from Waterloo, Iowa, that were on *Juneau*. They had requested to be assigned to the same ship. Sullivan was looking for his four brothers, calling out their names as he swam around, "Frank! Al! Matt! Red!" He wiped oil from his mates' faces so he could identify them. Sullivan found his brother Albert hanging onto a rope attached to Heyn's raft. But Al soon died along with other survivors who began succumbing to wounds, lack of food and drinkable water, vivid hallucinations, the broiling sun, hopelessness—and relentless shark attacks.

George Sullivan fell victim to the sun, his hallucinations, and, finally, to the sharks that circled the crewmen, pulling them underwater one by one. He announced one night that he was going to swim to San Cristobal Island, which was more than fifty miles away, for buttermilk and a meal. His mates tried to dissuade him. But George jumped from the raft into the water and swam out twenty-five yards. There three sharks overtook him and tore him to pieces.

Admiral Halsey learned about the *Juneau* disaster the next day, November 14, when Hoover's ships reached Espiritu Santo. Rescue aircraft and a destroyer were dispatched—to the wrong location. Ten days would pass before the last of just ten survivors was found. Six hundred eight-seven crewmen perished.[87]

Following the Sullivans' deaths, the Navy revised its personnel assignment policy to prevent brothers from serving together on the same ship. President Roosevelt wrote the Sullivans' parents, Tom and Allita, "The entire nation shares in your sorrow. I offer you the gratitude of our country." The parents were invited to Washington to meet First Lady Eleanor Roosevelt. In 1943 the Navy christened one of its new destroyers *The Sullivans*.[88]

Halsey convened a committee of three high-ranking naval officers, including Admiral Turner, to question Hoover about his decision to not rescue *Juneau* survivors. When they had finished their investigation they recommended that Hoover be removed from command. "Reluctantly, I concurred," wrote Halsey, despite Hoover's otherwise stellar war record and three Navy Crosses. Hoover was reassigned to naval headquarters at Pearl Harbor. Later, after closely reviewing the case, Halsey concluded that he had been "guilty of an injustice"—and that Hoover should not have been relieved.[89]

ON THE AFTERNOON OF NOVEMBER 13, just hours after the *Juneau* was blown to pieces, the *Sterett*'s crew stood in ranks on the destroyer's fantail. Twenty-eight bodies lay under canvas shrouds in a neat row on the deck, blood puddling under them. A detail of bluejackets stood at attention with rifles at "order arms." Captain Jesse Coward read the service for burial at sea from the Book of Common Prayer and spoke with pride of the dead crewmen. The color detail raised its rifles and fired three volleys. The victims' names were called out, and the dead were lifted onto a wooden slide and committed to the deep.[90]

The sacrifice near Savo Island early November 13 of Callaghan's task force—and of Callaghan, Scott, and more than fourteen hundred other fighting men—had spared Henderson Field and the Cactus Air Force what would have been another terrible bombardment by Japanese battleships. Although Abe had triumphed, the bloody surface action was just the opening movement of a symphony of death on the water.

HALSEY'S BATTLESHIP GROUP, WITH *WASHINGTON* and *South Dakota* as its nucleus and led by Rear Admiral Willis Lee, would not arrive off Guadalcanal until 8:00 a.m. on November 14—giving Mikawa's cruisers carte blanche to bombard the Cactus airfields overnight. Fears of enemy submarine attacks had slowed the progress of the two battleships and the *Enterprise*, with its six dozen planes, and the group remained at a safe distance south of Guadalcanal.

But Halsey intended to risk it all, overriding his subordinates' concerns that sending battleships into the confines of Ironbottom Sound would limit their maneuverability and needlessly expose them to the enemy destroyers' Long Lance torpedoes. Halsey ordered Lee to proceed with his battlewagons ahead of the *Enterprise*. The square-jawed admiral intended to honor his promise to General Vandegrift to give him everything he had.

Confident of success, Mikawa departed Shortland Harbor early November 13 with four heavy cruisers, two light cruisers, and a half-dozen destroyers to bombard Henderson. Waiting at Shortland to begin sailing later that day to Guadalcanal were eleven transports and Admiral Tanaka's eleven-destroyer escort.

At about 1:00 a.m. on November 14 Mikawa's Outer Sea Force of cruisers and destroyers reached Savo Island, where he detached Rear Admiral Shoji Nishimura's Bombardment Unit. It consisted of the heavy cruisers *Maya* and *Suzuya*, the light cruiser *Tenryu*, and four destroyers. They reached shelling range of the airfield at 1:30 a.m., when Washing Machine Charlie, whose engine's uneven growl was all too familiar to the Americans, dropped illumination flares.

Maya and *Suzuya*, each carrying about 500 eight-inch, high-capacity shells, commenced firing, targeting Henderson and Fighter One. Pilots and ground crewmen crouched in their muddy shelters with hundreds of sailors who had lost their ships the previous night, escaping watery graves only to now face new terrors. The shells screamed down on the perimeter for thirty-seven minutes as the Marines and sailors cursed and prayed. "You just sit in your foxhole and tremble," wrote Lieutenant Archie "Hap" Simpson, an SBD pilot. Out of ammunition and harried by a pair of PT boats led by Lieutenant Hugh Robinson, Nishimura's Bombardment Unit rejoined Mikawa and began sailing back up the Slot.

For all their sound and fury, the 989 eight-inch shells fired by Nishimura's cruisers inflicted surprisingly little damage—and missed Henderson Field altogether. On Fighter One, three planes were destroyed and fifteen others were damaged. Nishimura had failed to neutralize the Cactus Air Force and had instead whetted the pilots' appetite for revenge when daylight returned.[91]

THE MOOD IN WASHINGTON GREW more somber when the news arrived of Callaghan's surface battle, and his death as well as Scott's. It darkened further with the report that Japanese cruisers had bombarded Henderson. And then came word that Japanese transport ships were filled with fresh troops sailing down the Slot, and that there was no US surface force to stop the massive reinforcement. It was whispered that Guadalcanal might have to be evacuated.

Navy Undersecretary James Forrestal later told historian Samuel Eliot Morison that the tension in Washington over Guadalcanal during November equaled the apprehension felt the night before the 1944 Normandy landings.[92]

The best anodyne for Washington's anxiety would be a decisive victory.

AT 6:30 A.M. ON NOVEMBER 14, a dawn search patrol from Henderson Field spotted Admiral Mikawa's bombardment force 140 miles west of Guadalcanal, evidently on its way to a rendezvous with Tanaka's transports and destroyers. A strike force of eleven planes was quickly launched from the airfield—a mix of fighters, dive bombers, and torpedo bombers from Cactus and Torpedo Ten. High above the Slot the pilots saw spread below them Mikawa's Eighth Fleet: four Japanese heavy cruisers, four light cruisers, and six destroyers. After days of air raids, nighttime bombardments, and other hard usage, such juicy targets and the prospect of revenge were an elixir for the weary Cactus pilots. Major Joe Sailer's group singled out the *Maya*, while the torpedo bombers concentrated on *Kinugasa*, which had fought at Savo Island on August 9. The attackers scored hits on both cruisers.[93]

Enterprise, about 200 miles south of Guadalcanal, launched its search patrol at 6:08 a.m.—ten SBDs, each one armed with a five-hundred-pound bomb. One of them reported seeing unidentified planes 140 miles to the north, flying toward the *Enterprise*. Admiral Kinkaid scrambled an attack group of Wildcats and SBDs led by Lieutenant Commander James "Bucky" Lee, commander of VS-10, with orders simply to fly toward Guadalcanal and attack whatever Japanese forces they encountered. Then, two of *Enterprise*'s search planes spotted Mikawa's fleet.[94]

Two other search pilots, Ensigns R. A. Hoogerwerf and P. M. Halloran, had also located Mikawa's fleet and pounced on the cruisers. Flying too low, Halloran's SBD struck the *Maya*'s main mast and crashed into the cruiser, igniting shells and fires, and killing Halloran and thirty-seven Japanese sailors.

Mikawa's ships were attracting American planes like sugar drawing ants. Bucky Lee's group dove at the cruisers, rupturing *Kinugasa*'s fuel tanks and dooming her; at 11:40 a.m. she capsized and sank. The heavy cruisers *Chokai* and *Maya*, light cruiser *Isuzu*, and destroyer *Michisihio* all sustained damage, but sailed on with the rest of Mikawa's fleet to their planned rendezvous with Admiral Tanaka's Reinforcement Force.

The Cactus and *Enterprise* pilots were so preoccupied by their attacks on the Eighth Fleet that two hours passed before they were drawn to the richer target of Tanaka's eleven transports and eleven destroyers, now sailing southeast toward Guadalcanal.[95]

The slow-moving transports had cast off the previous afternoon, expecting to reach Cape Esperance during the night of November 14. At 9:49 a.m. Lieutenant j.g. Martin Dean Carmody and his wingman, Lieutenant j.g. W. E. Johnson of the *Enterprise* spotted them 150 miles northwest of Henderson, between New Georgia and the northwest tip of Santa Isabel. They dived on a large transport, but missed. Attacked by seven Zeros, Carmody and Johnson became separated, and Johnson was shot down; he and his tail gunner were never seen again. But the location of Tanaka's transport group was now known. Plowing southeastward at eleven knots, the transports were sitting ducks.[96]

EVERY PLANE THAT COULD "CARRY a bomb or fire a gun" was readied at Cactus and on the *Enterprise* to attack the transports. Major Sailer left Henderson at 10:40 a.m. for his second sortie of the day with eighteen dive bombers, seven torpedo bombers, and six F4Fs. Thirty minutes later, the group was over the transports, and the bombing and strafing began, as Zeros from the 11th Air Fleet and float planes vainly tried to deflect the American warplanes. SBD pilots Ensign L. Robinson and Lieutenant (Junior Grade) R. D. Gibson of VB-10 each released a thousand-pound bomb at two thousand feet over a transport, and both hit amidships. As the dive bombers pulled up, their rear gunners sprayed the decks with sheets of machine-gun fire.[97]

When the bombers had expended their ordnance, they returned to Cactus to be rearmed and refueled, and they immediately took off again. Major Harold Buell, an *Enterprise* dive-bomber pilot, described "a superhuman effort from the ground support personnel [that] kept a steady stream of SBDs and TBFs shuttling back and forth from the field to the convoy targets."

The transport decks ran red. "We would get down real low on our dive, and we could actually see them [the troops]. They must have packed them on those ships," wrote Second Lieutenant Archie "Hap" Simpson. On the transport decks, soldiers ran around firing their rifles at the diving planes, wrote Marine dive-bomber pilot John McEniry. Some pilots vomited in their cockpits when they saw at close hand the slaughter they inflicted when they machine-gunned soldiers in the transports and in the water.

"It was a terrible picture of destruction," said Lieutenant Commander Jimmy Flatley, commander of VF-10, nicknamed the "Grim Reapers." "We could see the Jap soldiers on the open decks, as tightly packed as a football crowd in a stadium." Many of them belonged to the 229th and 230th Regiments of the 38th Division; a sister regiment, the 228th, had landed near Kokumbona a week earlier and fought the Americans during the abbreviated Matanikau offensive.[98]

Every American warplane within striking distance was dispatched. The *Enterprise* launched a second attack group at 2:12 p.m.; fifteen B-17s from Espiritu Santo joined the turkey shoot and scored a direct hit on a transport. Ten B-26s were loaded with torpedoes and thousand-pound bombs and, with four P-38s as escorts, set out from Espiritu Santo to bomb the transports and afterward to land at Henderson. Bad weather forced the P-38s to turn back, and the B-26s landed at Henderson without dropping their bombs.[99]

Admiral Tanaka would never forget this day of "carrier bombers roaring toward targets as though to plunge full into the water, releasing bombs and pulling out barely in time . . . each hit raising clouds of smoke and fire as transports burst into flame and [took] the sickening list that spelled their doom . . . the tragic scene of men jumping overboard from burning, sinking ships."[100]

By late afternoon, five major air attacks had sunk six of the crowded transports. A seventh turned back to Shortland because of damage. Just four pressed on. Tanaka's destroyers plucked thousands of soldiers from the Slot's waters, but the bombs and strafing runs had killed hundreds of others.

LIEUTENANT GIBSON'S SBD WAS SHOT up, but he managed to return to Henderson Field. Ensign Robinson found himself sandwiched between Zeros—one on his tail and another making a head-on run. Robinson pulled away slightly, and then a 20mm round struck his engine. It stalled and burst into flames. By side-slipping, Robinson was able to extinguish the engine fire and another blaze in the rear cockpit. He tipped his plane into a steep dive, with the Zero still pursuing him, and his engine restarted. Still diving, Robinson rolled to the right, with bullets clattering like hail against his plane, then turned left, and then right again, with his thousand-pound bomb still in place, enhancing his diving speed. He pulled out of the dive at 2,500 feet while racing at 320 knots, but the Zero remained behind him. He executed a "Split S"—an aerial U-turn—but that did not shake the Zero either. Robinson then flew low among coconut trees on one of the Russell Islands and climbed over the hills as the Zero continued firing at him. He dove at a 30-degree angle to gain speed, then rocketed upward toward a cloud bank. The Zero's pilot then decided that he had had enough, waggled his plane's wings in a salute to Robinson's skillful aerobatics, and broke off their duel. When Robinson returned to Henderson Field he counted sixty-eight holes in his plane.[101]

Enemy warplanes and antiaircraft fire claimed five Navy and Marine planes; the Japanese lost twice that number.[102]

THE DAY'S LAST US CASUALTY might have been Lieutenant Colonel Harold Bauer, the aggressive skipper of VMF-212 known as "Coach." He had remained behind on Guadalcanal to wrap up the affairs of his squadron. After a month on Cactus, VMF-212 had been relieved and was going to California with ninety-two kills to its credit.

But Bauer could never resist taking a crack at the Japanese. Around 4:00 p.m. on November 14, he went up with his friend Joe Foss and his fighter squadron, VMF-121, on one of its last missions of the day. During a strafing run on one of the surviving Japanese transports, Bauer, Foss, and Second Lieutenant Boots Furlow were attacked by two Zeros. Bauer shot down one of them and turned back for Henderson Field, while Foss and Furlow dealt with the other Zero. When Foss and Furlow were flying back to Guadalcanal, they saw an oil slick in the water and Bauer swimming in his life jacket. Foss tried to drop his life raft to Bauer, but it got hung up in his plane and did not fall.

Exactly a week earlier, it had been Foss treading water after being shot down near Malaita. He had fended off circling sharks by breaking chlorine capsules in the water. At nightfall, a man in a canoe with a lantern pulled Foss into his boat, an instant before a flying fish attracted by the light smashed the lantern. The Australian boatman and a priest paddled Foss to shore, and he was later rescued.

With that memory fresh in his mind, Foss was reluctant to leave Bauer even though he was low on fuel, but Coach gestured to him to return to Cactus. Reaching the airfield, Foss and Joe Renner, the airfield operations officer, hopped into a PBY reconnaissance plane and flew to where Bauer was last seen, but by then darkness had fallen, although the flickering of burning Japanese transports in the distance partially illuminated the area. Bauer was never seen again. He was one of five Cactus pilots—Foss would be another—later awarded the Medal of Honor. Bauer was officially credited with downing eleven enemy planes.[103]

WHILE RELAYS OF BOMBERS PUMMELED Tanaka's transports throughout the afternoon of November 14, Japanese reconnaissance planes were aloft, looking for enemy ships that might interfere with the troop landings. They spotted the six ships of Admiral Lee's Task Force 64—Lee's first flag command—sailing north toward Guadalcanal. Admiral Kondo, sailing south with fourteen ships, warned Tanaka, still on his way to Guadalcanal with his four intact transports and nine destroyers. When he reached Ironbottom Sound, Tanaka waited north of Savo Island until Kondo's ten-warship Advanced Force and Rear Admiral Shintaro Hashimoto's Sweeping Unit of four vessels dealt with Lee. Tanaka would then dash to the island with his diminished reinforcements and supplies.

The Japanese snoopers erroneously reported that Lee's task force consisted of two heavy cruisers and four destroyers. The cruisers were in fact the battleships *Washington* and *South Dakota.*

REAR ADMIRAL WILLIS LEE, FIFTY-FOUR, was the best gunnery officer in the fleet—a rarity for an admiral. It was just one of the traits that set him apart from the run of high-ranking naval officers. His wire-rim spectacles and mild, scholarly appearance had earned him the nickname "Doc," a nod to his resemblance to the bespectacled *Snow White* dwarf. Lee was known for chain-smoking Philip Morris cigarettes while filling the backs of envelopes with calculations on gunnery algorithms and wave theory; indeed, gunnery was Lee's vocation and avocation. He presided over a group of officers with postgraduate instruction in ordnance that met informally on occasion and called itself the "Gun Club." *Washington*'s gunnery officer, Edwin Hooper, said the "highly scientifically oriented" Lee had once concluded that the Navy's "temperature and density corrections for the 16-inch powder" were in error—and he had proved it to the Bureau of Ordnance.

The great-great-grandson of the third US attorney general, Charles Lee, and possibly a distant relation of Robert E. Lee's, Admiral Lee was both scholar and warrior. Besides being what another generation might describe as geekish, he was a crack shot. In 1920 he was a member of the US Olympic rifle team that won five gold medals as well as silver and bronze medals at Antwerp. During the Vera Cruz expedition in 1914, Lee, a member of the landing force, killed three snipers with a rifle while he sat in the open to draw their fire. His peers nicknamed him "Ching Chong China Lee" because he had so enjoyed his early-career posting to China.[104]

Lee trained his men to adapt quickly to unexpected circumstances by introducing surprising variables to his gunnery practices. Sometimes he assigned relief crews to fire the turret guns, or he changed up the targeting. Although demanding, Lee was well-liked; he typically called out a cheery "Good morning!" to his officers and enlisted men, and liked to tell and listen to a good joke.

More relevant to the present circumstances, Lee had closely studied radar systems and understood how they worked—better than most of the men who operated them. His flagship, *Washington*, like *South Dakota*, was equipped with the state-of-the-art SG surface radar. Unlike admirals Callaghan and Scott, Lee appreciated the SG's advanced features and intended to use them to their best advantage when he went into combat.[105]

Even greater advantages than Lee's mastery of SG radar were his cool-headed leadership and his good fortune in commanding two of the new generation of fast battleships—the dry-docked *North Carolina* was another of that class—capable of cruising at twenty-eight knots and crewed by eighteen hundred sailors. Each was armed with nine 16-inch guns; *Washington* also had 20 five-inch guns, and *South Dakota* 16 five-inchers. Each battleship's broadside carried twice the metal of the *Kirishima*.

KONDO'S ADVANCED FORCE GLIDED SOUTH through calm waters on this clear, moonlit night. The admiral was confident that his fourteen warships would have little trouble brushing aside the six American ships misidentified as cruisers and destroyers. Then, after his battleship and cruisers had bombarded the airfield and destroyed the Cactus Air Force, nothing would stop Tanaka's transports from landing reinforcements. With luck, General Hyakutake could then overwhelm the enemy's ground forces and claim the great prize, Henderson Field.

Lee's ships formed a column, with destroyers *Walke*, *Benham*, *Preston*, and *Gwin* sailing ahead and screening *Washington* and *South Dakota*. Task Force 64 was created expressly for this emergency. The four destroyers were selected from four different divisions strictly on the basis of how much fuel was in their tanks; none of them had ever sailed together. Lee did not issue a formal operational order because there had been no time to draft one; instead, orders were blinkered or semaphored as developments warranted. Lee did not know the whereabouts of Kondo's force, only that it was traveling south toward Guadalcanal.[106]

Lee did know Tanaka's location, and he set TF-64's course to intercept the enemy destroyers and transports; his ships would reach the Savo Island area at midevening. As their ships passed Guadalcanal's coastline, Lee's sailors could see Tanaka's transports burning in the distance.

Seeking information on Kondo's whereabouts, Lee raised Henderson Field, but Cactus's radio room had no new information. Then, his radio room picked up a transmission from some American PT boats: "There go two big ones, but I don't know whose they are." Concerned that his task force was about to draw friendly fire, Lee radioed Henderson: "Refer your big boss about Ching Lee; Chinese, catchee? Call off your boys!" Vandegrift was a personal friend of Lee's and was familiar with his nickname. So too were the PT boat commanders; they assured Lee that they were not after him.[107]

Under a setting quarter-moon Lee skirted Savo Island's western shore while bearing to the north, and then completely circumnavigated the fateful island until his task force was pointed west. The sea was glassy; starlight reflected on the water.

Kondo had divided his fourteen ships into three groups. Hashimoto's light cruiser *Sendai* and three destroyers comprised the Sweeping Unit east of Savo Island; west of Savo, Rear Admiral Susumu Kimura led a screen consisting of the light cruiser *Nagara* and four destroyers. Behind Kimura came Kondo's big guns, the Bombardment Unit that would carry out Abe's thwarted mission of two nights earlier: battleship *Kirishima*, cruisers *Takao* and *Atago*—the latter was Kondo's flagship—and two destroyers.

While sailing west between Savo and Guadalcanal, *Washington*'s SG radar picked up Hashimoto's four ships east of Savo, ten miles away. The contact disappeared as Savo's land mass interposed, but radar contacts to the west multiplied as Lee's ships neared Kondo's two principal groups.

In a public address announcement to his crewmen, *Washington* Captain Glenn Davis warned that they were going into action soon. "We might be ambushed. A disaster of some sort may come upon us," he said. "But whatever it is we are going into, I hope to bring all of you back alive. Good luck to all of us."

At 11:16 p.m. Lee told his captains to fire when ready. A minute later *Washington*'s sixteen-inch main battery homed in on the leading Japanese ship, ten miles to the west, and her five-inch guns targeted other vessels that were closer. *South Dakota* opened fire a minute later.[108]

Kimura's destroyers and cruiser unleashed a blizzard of gunfire and torpedoes that shattered Lee's four destroyers. A rain of shellfire wrecked *Preston*, and "the whole after part of the ship soon became a mass of flaming wreckage." She listed to starboard, rolled onto her side, and sank at 11:37. Some eyewitnesses later said the destroyer was struck by friendly fire—from *Washington*. A torpedo and an enemy cruiser salvo smashed *Walke*, blowing apart the forecastle and superstructure deck as far aft as the bridge. She, too, sank, and her depth charges exploded, killing and injuring crewmen in the water. Nearly two hundred men died in the two sinkings. *Gwin* and *Benham* were heavily damaged, but remained afloat. Lee's destroyers had not fired a single torpedo, but they had screened the battleships from the enemy destroyers.[109]

With her five-inch secondary battery, *Washington* plastered Kimura's lead destroyer, *Ayanami*, leaving her in flames and dead in the water. Lee ordered *Gwin* and *Benham* to retire, clearing the area for action by the two battlewagons—just as *South Dakota*'s circuit breakers tripped and she suffered a critical six-minute electrical failure that disabled her radar screen.

Washington launched two life rafts while steaming by the wreckage of *Walke*. Through binoculars, *Washington*'s Hank Seely saw dozens of men clinging to floating wreckage amid burning oil. "The screams and smell of burning flesh, the sight of those burning men, almost scraping alongside the ship, is never to be forgotten." As the battleship glided past, men in the water shouted encouragement: "Get after 'em, *Washington!*"[110]

Kondo ordered the *Kirishima* and the heavy cruisers *Atago* and *Takao*, which he had held back northwest of Savo, to proceed to Lunga Point to bombard the airfield, dismissing reports that the two enemy "cruisers" were in fact battleships.

Around midnight, eleven miles west of Savo, the Bombardment Unit neared *South Dakota* as she regained power. The battleship fired at a cruiser eight miles away, and her salvo set ablaze her own scout planes; the next salvo blew two of them overboard and put out most of the fires. As *South Dakota* veered around TF-64's wrecked destroyers, their flames silhouetted her for Kondo's ships.

Searchlights from the lead Japanese ship lit up *South Dakota* like a Christmas display. The battleship fired at the lights and put them out, but other enemy warships now trained their spotlights on the battleship, and *South Dakota* was riddled by 14-, 8-, 6-, and 5.5-inch shellfire from five ships. The onslaught knocked out her radar, directors, and fire control instruments; started fires; and ruptured five fuel oil compartments. Commander Paul Backus, a *South Dakota* gunnery officer, said an 8-inch salvo turned the bridge into a shambles and wrecked the chartroom behind it. Backus's roommate, assistant navigator Dwight Moody, was standing at the chart table when a shell crashed into the room, cutting in two a young sailor behind Moody, but sparing Moody. The concentrated attack on the battleship—twenty-six strikes in four minutes—killed thirty men, wounded sixty others, and rendered *South Dakota* impotent.[111]

Washington passed unnoticed behind the burning destroyers during *South Dakota*'s shellacking and sought targets for a retaliatory shelling. Hooper, *Washington*'s gunnery officer, noticed that one of the enemy ships was "considerably larger" than the other, and "I shifted the main battery onto this target." It was *Kirishima*, five miles distant.[112]

It was a rare opportunity for Lee's gunners to square off against an enemy battleship. They did not waste it. Three 16-inch salvos smashed into *Kirishima*, and it spewed black smoke, steam, and flames. *Washington* then pumped sixteen- and five-inch shells into the Japanese battleship until its guns fell silent at 12:07 a.m. and it turned away. In seven minutes *Kirishima* was hit nine times by *Washington*'s sixteen-inch guns, each projectile weighing twenty-seven hundred pounds—and up to forty times by her five-inch batteries. Lee proudly said *Washington*'s main battery performed as though it were participating in "a well-rehearsed target practice."[113]

At 12:32 Kondo withdrew his Bombardment Unit without firing a gun at Henderson Field. Japanese destroyers pursued *Washington*, which deliberately led them away from the damaged American ships. *Kirishima*, listing to starboard and burning uncontrollably, limped off to the southwest, attempting to reach Kamimbo on western Guadalcanal. However, she was unable to make any headway and could not be steered. "There seemed to be no prospect of using the engine as ninety percent of the engine room crew was killed," wrote Vice Admiral Ugaki, Yamamoto's chief of staff.

Around 3:00 a.m. Captain Sanji Iwabuchi lowered *Kirishima*'s ensign as her surviving crewmen chorused "banzais." He transferred the emperor's portrait to the *Asagumo* and ordered *Kirishima*'s valves opened.

A short time later *Kirishima* rolled over and sank, the second battleship lost by the Imperial Japanese Navy in two days. The Japanese reported 249 sailors killed during the sea battle—more than 200 of them *Kirishima* crewmen—but the losses were probably much higher; US dead numbered 242.[114]

Crews battled fires on the still-seaworthy *South Dakota*. Unable to contact *Washington* because of damage to his ship's communications systems, Captain T. L. Gatch withdrew *South Dakota* from the battle zone. Later Halsey ordered Lee and what remained of his task force to return to Noumea. *South Dakota* was sent to the United States for repairs.

Walke and *Preston* had gone down off Savo Island, but the torpedoed *Benham* remained afloat, although her bow had been blown off. While under escort by the *Gwin* to Noumea, the *Benham*'s situation worsened. Her crew was taken off, and she was abandoned during the afternoon of November 15. *Gwin* scuttled her by firing a shell into her magazine.[115]

HALSEY RELISHED THE IMPROBABLE NAVAL victory, which he believed prevented Guadalcanal from becoming another Bataan. Rejecting the warnings of cautious subordinates and defying Navy doctrine, Halsey had risked his two battleships in the confines of Ironbottom Sound. Lee's triumph had validated his wager.

"The use we made of them [the battleships] defied all conventions, narrow waters, submarine menace, and destroyers at night," Halsey said. It was "a decisive American victory by any standard." Had the Imperial Japanese Navy won the battle, "our troops on Guadalcanal would have been trapped as were our troops on Bataan." Vandegrift, Halsey said, "would have been our 'Skinny' Wainwright, and the infamous Death March would have been repeated."[116]

Vandegrift was deeply grateful for the Navy's timely intervention. "We thank Lee for his sturdy effort of last night," he wrote to Halsey. "We thank Kinkaid for his intervention of yesterday . . . but our greatest homage goes to Scott, Callahan and their men," who stopped Admiral Abe's attack on November 13. "To them the men of Cactus lift their battered helmets in deepest admiration."[117]

Halsey paid homage to his two dead admirals when he was promoted from vice admiral to four-star rank on November 26. He directed Vice Admiral William Calhoun to send his three-star pins to the widows of Admirals Scott and Callaghan. "Tell them it was their husbands' bravery that got me my new ones."[118]

REINFORCEMENT FORCE COMMANDER TANAKA NOW fulfilled his obligation. He had tenaciously shepherded the four remaining transport ships with their troops and supplies to the beaches of western Guadalcanal. He now deliberately ran them aground, fifteen miles west of Henderson Field at Doma Cove and Tassafaronga.

It was Petty Officer Tsuji's fourth campaign, and he had never seen ships being beached, much less been aboard one. On the deck of the *Yamura Maru*, he began to pray "as if the hour of our death were arranged," he wrote in his diary. The last transport was run aground at dawn, watched by hundreds of American sailors from the sunken destroyers *Walke* and *Preston* as they clung to floating debris in Ironbottom Sound. Its mission completed, Tanaka's destroyers departed for Shortland Harbor.[119]

Hours earlier, Marines on the island had watched the drama in Ironbottom Sound, attempting to interpret the ribbons of tracers, the kinetic white flash of guns, arcing shells, and the explosions and fires like a soothsayer reading tea leaves—while praying for the Navy to win. At daybreak, the sound of planes warming up at Henderson and Fighter One gave them their answer.

"The sound of their motors was as triumphant as the march from Aida, and we cheered and jigged and waved our arms at them passing overhead, urging them on," wrote Private Robert Leckie.

General Woods, the Cactus Air Force's commander, asked Vandegrift whether his pilots should concentrate on Tanaka's destroyer escorts or on the transports. The transports, replied Vandegrift. Artillery, air, and destroyer commanders had reached the same conclusion.

Just before 6:00 a.m. the first Marine and Navy dive bombers appeared above the transports as they were still being unloaded, and began dropping five-hundred- and thousand-pound bombs on them and on the supplies stacked on the beaches. Marine 155mm artillery joined in the destruction.

Wildcat squadrons climbed to Angels 20 to fend off twenty Vals and Zeros that materialized over Savo Island in a hopeless attempt to shield the transports. Just two escort planes survived the Cactus fighters' onslaught.[120]

The Cactus dive bombers and torpedo bombers homed in on the beached transports. Major Joseph Sailer flew with pilots from VMSB-132 and VMSB-142 as they scored five bomb strikes on the transports and strafed them with .50-caliber machine-guns. *New York Times* correspondent Foster Hailey was a passenger in a torpedo bomber that passed between two burning transports. "It was like looking down into the crater of a volcano," he wrote. "The decks had been burned away, leaving only the hulls."[121]

From amid the crash of falling bombs and artillery shells there arose a new sound: the boom-whoosh of naval gunfire. The destroyer *Meade*, captained by Lieutenant Commander Raymond Lamb, had sallied from Tulagi Harbor and was bombarding three transports beached at Doma Cove and Tassafaronga. With her 40mm machine-guns, she blasted the shoreline. Then *Meade*, along with a motley of small boats, rescued more than two hundred sailors from *Walke* and *Preston* who had been in the water more than twelve hours.[122]

All day the F4Fs, dive bombers, torpedo bombers, and P-39s from the 67th Pursuit Squadron, along with some newly arrived B-26s, came and went from the Henderson airfields, and "we never tired of saluting them," wrote Leckie. He and his comrades felt enormous relief after months of worry and tension. "The enemy was running! The siege was broken!"[123]

Two *Walke* survivors, Seaman Dale Land and Machinist's Mate Harold Taylor, reached shore under their own power, landing barefooted behind Japanese lines. For two weeks, they survived on stolen Japanese food and coconuts. They got their hands on a Japanese rifle and bandoleer and began shooting enemy soldiers wherever they found them. On December 5, Taylor, walking ahead of Lamb, opened fire on a group of Japanese sitting around a fire, killing three or four of them. The survivors killed Taylor. Land got away and eventually reached the American lines.[124]

THE WATERS AROUND THE BLAZING transports—*Kinugasa Maru, Hirokawa Maru, Yamura Maru,* and *Sangetsu Maru*—were crimson-stained, and body parts tumbled in the surf. Some pilots became ill at the gruesome sight as they flew low over the ships. In the afternoon, an SBD pilot bombed a large ammunition dump, and the sound of the gigantic explosion was heard throughout the perimeter.

On the *Yamura Maru*, Petty Officer Tsuji had prayed to Kannon, the Buddhist Goddess of Mercy, while his captain drove the transport aground and bombs fell around his ship. The transport was hit, and chunks of metal and mangled bodies whizzed through the air. Tsuji, his shipmates, and the soldiers they were ferrying scrambled down the cargo nets and ran into the jungle. Later that day, they hiked to a construction camp and slept among the headstones in the Pioneer Forces Cemetery—the place where Tsuji and many of his comrades would die weeks later of hunger.[125]

Just 2,000 of the 13,500 reinforcements that embarked for Guadalcanal reached the island, and many of them were wounded and without weapons. Landed with them were fifteen hundred bags of rice and 260 cases of ammunition, although dive bombers destroyed much of the ammunition that day. "This amount of staple foodstuff could not support our forces there more than several days," wrote Vice Admiral Ugaki when he learned of the resupply effort's failure.[126]

TENSION HAD SPIKED ON GUADALCANAL when the news spread that a mighty Japanese fleet was on its way to destroy Henderson Field and the Cactus Air Force, and to land thousands of reinforcements. "Our fate depended on the outcome," wrote Martin Clemens. During the morning of November 15, when the naval battle's result was still unknown, "pandemonium" prevailed at division headquarters when the phone lines went out and contact was lost with many units.

But when reports of Admiral Lee's victory reached the Marines, the tension was replaced by jubilation. "This was the biggest battle of them all," Clemens declared. When told that Tanaka's transports had been destroyed, Admiral Halsey exclaimed, "We've got the bastards licked!"[127]

The epic naval-air battle of November 12–15, whose ferocity has few modern-day counterparts, cost the Imperial Japanese Navy two battleships, a cruiser, three destroyers, ten transports, and the lives of thousands of sailors and soldiers. Japan could not readily recoup the losses. Its leaders reconsidered their all-in plan to recapture Guadalcanal.

The sinking of two light cruisers and seven destroyers had fewer consequences for the United States, whose production was expanding weekly. However, the deaths of seventeen hundred servicemen were sobering—just seven hundred fewer than the total killed in the Pearl Harbor attack.

WHILE THE COMBINED FLEET DISPLAYED its usual tactical proficiency during the two surface actions, its reluctance to concentrate its superior forces as Halsey had done was a strategic failure. Halsey risked the *Washington* and *South Dakota* in Ironbottom Sound's confines and placed the *Enterprise* within supporting distance. He also reinforced the Cactus Air Force with Air Group Ten's seventy-seven aircraft.

Yamamoto, however, flinched from the opportunity to destroy the enemy fleet in a decisive battle and gain complete control of the seas around Guadalcanal. Had he risked his two other battleships or the carriers *Zuikaku* and *Zuiho* and their aircraft, the outcome might have been dramatically different.

Committing the battleships *Kongo* and *Haruna*, the cruiser *Tone*, and more destroyers to the night battle of November 14–15 might have tipped the scale to Admiral Kondo's advantage, enabling him to bombard the Guadalcanal airfields. But they were not risked. With only the auxiliary carrier *Junyo* in supporting range, Tanaka's force lacked adequate air protection.

Finally, the navy permitted Mikawa's cruiser force to retire while insisting that the four transports and the destroyer escorts that had survived the American air onslaught continue to Guadalcanal. The presence of Mikawa's cruisers would have ensured that more supplies and troops got ashore than the few that did, but exposing the cruisers in American-controlled waters was deemed too risky.

When US Navy and Marine pilots sank the battleship *Hiei*, it stunned Japan's top admirals, who were already frustrated and displeased by Admiral Hiroaki Abe's failure to neutralize Henderson Field on November 13. Abe and *Hiei*'s commander, Captain Masao Nishida, were summoned to a military court of inquiry in Tokyo. Neither of them offered a defense, and they were retired with pensions and barred from public office. Because of his connections in the Imperial Navy hierarchy, Admiral Nobutake Kondo avoided the disapprobation that ended Abe's and Nishida's careers.[128]

IN MELBOURNE, FLAGS WERE FLOWN from the city hall in celebration, and a London newspaper hailed the US victory in "the greatest sea battle of the war."

The Roosevelt administration's reaction was more subdued, although Navy Secretary Frank Knox did declare at a news conference on November 16, "We have at the moment naval supremacy around Guadalcanal." His announcement came with a caveat: while the US Navy was spread across the globe, the Japanese navy still had the advantage of "operating in comparatively narrow waters." Yet Knox also recognized that "the process of attrition operates more against them than against us. Remember that we build faster with our greater resources than they do."

A Tokyo radio broadcast claimed that the US fleet had been "annihilated" and that the Navy's "miserable defeat is kept in the dark." But Japanese naval commanders knew the truth. At a meeting following the battle, Vice Admiral Ugaki said Japan's troops on Guadalcanal now faced "an acute shortage of foodstuff and ammunition." While assuring fellow officers that the Navy would improve the supply situation by establishing forward air bases and neutralizing enemy air strength, Ugaki warned that American "fighting spirit is high, too," and that victory was not guaranteed. In his journal Ugaki went further, acknowledging "the fervent fighting spirit of the American forces."[129]

THE TIDE OF FATE AND fortune had turned on Guadalcanal. The November 12–15 Naval Battles of Guadalcanal were the emphatic culmination of Halsey's decision to commit all of his resources to holding the island. Yamamoto was now reluctant to send capital ships to bombard the airfield or to meet the US Navy in battle. The Japanese had lost its appetite for wagering everything on a decisive naval battle for Guadalcanal.

Although mastery of the sea and air around Guadalcanal had slipped through their fingers, the Japanese had not completely given up. Perhaps twenty thousand Seventeenth Army troops remained alive on the island, supplied by nightly Tokyo Express runs. Yet the likelihood of a Japanese victory was waning as Allied strength waxed. Moreover, a new enemy had arisen to haunt the Seventeenth Army: starvation.[130]

Coming eighty-seven days after the Marine landings in August, Guadalcanal's turning point coincided with cheering news elsewhere for the Allies. At El Alamein the British Eighth Army defeated General Erwin Rommel's Afrika Corps. On November 8 British-American forces had landed in French North Africa and were advancing eastward. And in Russia, the Red Army was poised to counterattack and encircle the German Army at Stalingrad.

AFTER THE CLIMACTIC NAVAL VICTORY, the Japanese reinforcement convoy's destruction, and Carlson's Long Patrol that had rid eastern Guadalcanal of Japanese troops, Vandegrift ordered a new Matanikau River offensive. With six battalions from three regiments, he planned to clear the Japanese from the coral ridges and jungle between the Matanikau River and the Poha River near Kokumbona.

Ground down by three months of combat, the 1st Marine Division remained inside the perimeter, and fresher troops led by Brigadier General Edmund Sebree conducted the offensive. His force consisted of two recently arrived battalions of the Americal Division's 182nd Infantry Regiment of the Massachusetts National Guard, the Americal's 164th Regiment, and the Eighth Marines.

Sebree inexplicably chose his two least experienced units, the 1st and 2nd Battalions of the 182nd, to spearhead the attack to the west—perhaps reasoning that because they were freshest, they would perform best. On November 18, the 2nd Battalion crossed the Matanikau River and turned southwest. Lieutenant Colonel

Bernard Twombley's men reached their objective a mile away, Hill 66, after struggling in the heat and humidity. Lieutenant Colonel Francis MacGowan's 1st Battalion crossed the river on November 19 and marched due west, occupying ridges east of Point Cruz.

A nearly mile-wide gap lay between the two battalions, and during the night of November 19–20, Colonel Yoshitsugu Sakai's 16th Regiment erupted from that area's knobs, ravines, and coral ridges and crashed into MacGowan's left flank. The green Army battalion began giving way. Sebree and MacGowan somehow stopped what nearly became a stampede.

The 1st and 3rd Battalions of the veteran 164th Infantry were recalled from a rest area and pushed into the gap. "There were some pretty pissed off North Dakota farmers up there, as mad at the Massachusetts boys [the 182nd's two battalions] as at the Japs," wrote John Hagan.

The 164th's battalions threw the enemy off a grassy knoll but were pinned by machine-gun, mortar, and artillery fire, as was MacGowan's battalion near the coast. The 1st and 2nd Battalions, Eighth Marines, relieved the 164th and attempted to advance through the jumbled terrain, but they made no headway. The well-entrenched Japanese used every terrain feature to their advantage. A sense of futility gripped the battalions.

Colonel Gerald Thomas, Vandegrift's chief of staff, went to the front for a firsthand look. Observing the 182nd, he "didn't like what I saw at all." No one was attacking, and no officers appeared to be in the vicinity. Thomas told Major General Alexander "Sandy" Patch, the Americal's commander, about the situation. "He [Patch] was very downcast, and he said, 'I realize that that regiment that I have up there's not doing well." Thomas suggested that Patch pull back for "a complete reorganization."

Vandegrift was "furious" over the lack of progress. Patch told the Marine general that he wanted to wait until his 132nd Regiment reached Guadalcanal before resuming the attack. On November 23, Vandegrift suspended the offensive. It had cost the lives of 134 soldiers and Marines, with little to show for it. Combat Marines deplored the 182nd's conduct at Point Cruz and its abandonment of mortars and rifles. "Army lines break once in a while!" wrote Private First Class Arthur Farrington.

The Americans held a line from just west of Point Cruz to Hill 66, a mile and a half to the south. Neither combatant appeared eager to renew the battle until they were reinforced. In the meantime, both sides patrolled aggressively, while continually improving their entrenchments. Occupying a ridge near Hill 66, the 164th lost men almost daily to snipers and shell bursts. The steady attritional losses resembled World War I trench warfare, inspiring the nickname "Matanikau meat grinder."[131]

The bitter stalemate west of the Matanikau would last until mid-January.

LIEUTENANT GENERAL HITOSHI IMAMURA AND the staff of his new Eighth Area Army, which commanded the Seventeenth and Eighteenth Armies, were planning major operations to recapture Guadalcanal in late January, and to secure areas of New Guinea. "We must by the most furious, swift and positive action deal the enemy annihilating blows to foil his plans completely," he wrote. "It is necessary to rouse the officer and men to a fighting rage."[132]

But Admiral Yamamoto, who tended to look at the larger picture, had become pessimistic. At a meeting at Truk on November 21 with his old friend Imamura, Yamamoto said, "The enemy's replacement rate is three times ours; the gap between our strengths is increasing every day; and to be honest things are looking black for us now."

In fact, before November ended, discrete discussions about withdrawal from Guadalcanal were occurring throughout the Imperial Navy, the rationale being that it would be wiser to secure New Guinea, thereby protecting Rabaul. On November 26, Yamamoto's chief of staff, Vice Admiral Ugaki, wrote in his diary, "A great change, the strategic policy for abandoning Guadalcanal and securing Eastern New Guinea, won't be easy because of the army's stubbornness. . . . I requested the senior staff officers to determine the limit of terms beyond which the recapture of Guadalcanal would be impossible. . . . I think we must ask the high command to send the chief of the Operations Bureau to discuss the matter with us."[133]

ON GUADALCANAL THE TENACIOUS SEVENTEENTH Army soldiers dug deeper into their reverse slope positions. Of the nearly thirty thousand Japanese troops who had reached the island since August, just thirteen thousand were fit for duty on November 20—about one-third the present US fighting force. Combat wounds, illness, and starvation had claimed the lives of ten thousand Japanese troops, and thousands of others were alive but largely incapacitated.

Incapable of major offensive action with such diminished numbers, the Japanese went on the defensive, vowing to make the Americans pay for every yard. Ill, malnourished, and wounded soldiers manned the ingeniously constructed redoubts, resolving to fight to the death if necessary. Their zealous fatalism might have been praiseworthy had they not been the Americans' mortal enemies.

A Seventeenth Army report described how its debilitated units were deployed: "The force at the front line position was divided so that those who could not walk due to illness or injury took charge of the defence of positions; those able to walk by utilizing a stick took charge of transportation and cooking in the rear area, and those who were comparatively healthy disturbed the enemy from the rear."[134]

The Marines were very much aware of their enemy's steady deterioration. Lieutenant Herbert Merillat said that recovered Japanese diaries chronicled the soldiers' deepening despair. One diarist's entry was a *cri de coeur*: "Where are our friendly aircraft? Where is the might of the Imperial Navy? Have they forgotten we are on the island?" Recalling the Marines' own sense of abandonment in August and September, Merillat sardonically added, "Familiar words."[135]

While conditions worsened dramatically in the Seventeenth Army, they were improving just as rapidly inside the American lines. The Eighth Marines had landed on November 4–5. Two weeks later the first mail in weeks arrived. On Thanksgiving Day, November 27, everyone received a large serving of turkey, potatoes, cranberry sauce, and pumpkin and apple pie.

At the end of November, nearly two hundred planes crowded Guadalcanal's three airstrips; they included B-17s, B-26s, P-38s, and even New Zealand Hudson A-29 bombers. With Tojo time no longer a daily occurrence, the Cactus Air Force was freed to provide close air support for ground troops and to interdict Tokyo Express runs farther up the Slot. Air transport squadrons flew in food, supplies, ammunition, weapons, and gasoline, and they flew out the sick and wounded.[136]

Supplies arrived regularly and in profusion compared with the lean days of August and September, but the Japanese navy had not completely ceded the waters around Guadalcanal to the Americans. On November 28, the cargo ship *Alchiba*, escorted by five destroyers, was unloading aviation fuel, bombs, and ammunition at Lunga Point when a Japanese midget submarine launched by *I-16* fired a torpedo past the destroyer screen. It struck the *Alchiba*, which began burning furiously. The ship's captain, Commander James Freeman, showed exemplary presence of mind in immediately weighing anchor so that if *Alchiba* sank, she would not block the Lunga anchorage. Freeman deliberately ran her aground two miles away. The *Alchiba* burned there for four days but, amazingly, survived to sail again. Freeman was awarded the Navy Cross.[137]

Halsey reorganized the South Pacific Force, assigning the repaired *Saratoga* and *Enterprise*, whose forward elevator was still inoperable, to anchor two carrier groups. The *Washington* was mated with her repaired sister, *North Carolina*, to lead a battleship task force that would also include the *Indiana*. The *Maryland* and *Colorado*, which were en route to the South Pacific, would be the core of a second battleship group. Rear Admiral Thomas Kinkaid, who had commanded *Enterprise*'s Task Force 16 during the climactic November 12–15 battles, was appointed to lead the new heavy cruiser Task Force 67.[138]

THE NOVEMBER 29 BULLETIN FROM Admiral Nimitz's headquarters warned that the enemy planned to reinforce Guadalcanal and Buna. Buna, on New Guinea's eastern tip, was where thirty thousand US and Australian troops were fighting Japanese troops in jungles as miserable as Guadalcanal's. The prize was strategic positioning: for the Japanese, a stepping stone to Australia; for the Allies, a window on Rabaul.[139]

The next day's bulletin, based on decrypted Japanese messages, read, "Believe attempts to transport supplies to Guadalcanal by destroyers possibly also Marus [transport ships] now under way. Enemy submarines also heading for Guadalcanal."[140]

As the Japanese convoy approached Guadalcanal, Kinkaid was detached from the heavy cruiser TF-67 to take over a new command in the North Pacific. Rather than delay Kinkaid's transfer until after the enemy threat was addressed, Halsey appointed Rear Admiral Carleton Wright to succeed Kincaid. Although he was a competent thirty-year veteran, Wright lacked surface combat experience, and he was replacing one of the ablest naval officers in the Pacific. Wright readily adopted Kinkaid's operation plan for TF-67—personally commanding three heavy cruisers, assigning a heavy and light cruiser to Rear Admiral Mahlon Tisdale, and giving Commander William Cole command of the four destroyers.

Callaghan's defeat on November 13 had led to new tactical protocol that required destroyers to fire torpedoes as soon as they acquired targets, which had long been the Japanese practice. The new rules also stipulated that task force commanders must direct operations from ships equipped with modern surface radar. Wright obeyed the second guideline; his flagship *Minneapolis* had SG radar. In fact, each of his three groups had at least one ship with surface radar and another with SC medium-range radar. But destroyer captains still needed Wright's permission to fire torpedoes.[141]

Halsey ordered Wright to take TF-67 from Espiritu Santo to Tassafaronga and stop the Japanese resupply run. On paper, Wright's five cruisers and four destroyers were a capable-enough naval force. But Wright was going into his first surface combat against a Japanese master: "Tenacious Tanaka"—Rear Admiral Raizo Tanaka, the wily, veteran commander of Destroyer Squadron 2, Tokyo Express avatar, and expert in night combat.

Tanaka was arguably the most knowledgeable man in the Imperial Japanese Navy on the subject of heavy torpedoes—particularly the Type 93 Long Lances carried by his destroyers and wielded with such lethality by their well-drilled crews. Each torpedo packed an unusually large, thousand-pound warhead that, because it was propelled with pure oxygen, could travel faster and farther than any American torpedo while leaving an almost invisible wake.[142]

Because his flagship, the cruiser *Jintsu*, was being repaired, Tanaka moved his flag to the destroyer *Naganami*. Tanaka's Tokyo Express had made the run many times, but Tanaka certainly could not forget that Tassafaronga was where, just fifteen days earlier, US warplanes eviscerated the four transport ships that he had escorted.

Warned that American destroyers and transports were in the area, Tanaka avoided the Slot when he left Buin, and sailed east via Bougainville Strait, then turned south for Indispensable Strait. An American search plane overflew the Japanese squadron around 10:00 a.m. on November 30, and Tanaka braced for a bombing attack by the Cactus Air Force. Yet, for some reason, Wright did not receive a sighting report; either the pilot did not see Tanaka's ships, or the report was lost.

Tanaka's destroyers were to put ashore supplies and some reinforcements but were not to pick a fight—only engaging if compelled to. It was a straight resupply run. Tanaka's crewmen would push overboard half-filled barrels of food and medical supplies to float in the water just off the beach, while sending soldiers to shore in small launches. Then, the destroyers would turn around and sail as speedily as possible back to Shortland Harbor.

The new resupply method followed two weeks of attempts to provision the Seventeenth Army via submarines, airdrops, and small ships moving along a chain of bases. Each scheme had proved inadequate, so now high-speed destroyer runs to drop supplies in barrels were planned every few days, augmented by submarine resupply missions. On this night, the decks of six of Tanaka's destroyers were cluttered with eleven hundred barrels, roped together in pods of two hundred, to be thrown overboard and retrieved by soldiers from the beach.

Since the failure of the November offensive a fortnight earlier, the condition of the Japanese troops on Guadalcanal had become dire. Soldiers had consumed all of their food staples and were reduced to "eating wild plants and animals. Everyone was on the verge of starvation, sick lists increased, and even the healthy were exhausted," Tanaka later wrote. Nonetheless, Tanaka's veteran destroyer captains implicitly understood that if enemy ships attacked them, destroying the enemy took precedence over resupplying the troops.[143]

During their approach to Guadalcanal, the admiral ordered his destroyer commanders to not fire their guns if they encountered the enemy—it would give the enemy an aiming point. Instead, he said, they were to discharge their torpedoes at American gun flashes. The six destroyers crowded with supply drums carried just one torpedo for each tube. Tanaka's flagship *Naganami* and the *Takanami*, which was acting as a picket a mile distant, were unencumbered by supplies and carried the normal complement of Long Lances.[144]

TF-67's five cruisers—*Minneapolis*, *New Orleans*, and *Pensacola* under Wright and *Northampton* and light cruiser *Honolulu* under Tisdale—sailed astern of the four destroyers. *Dayton*, *Fletcher*, *Maury*, and *Perkins* were expected to make the first radar contacts and then, when authorized to do so, launch radar-controlled torpedo attacks. The cruisers would then join in with radar-controlled shellfire. Although the plan appeared sound, it glossed over the fact that Wright's force would likely face a well-drilled, seasoned enemy destroyer squadron whose specialty was night combat. Moreover, Wright neglected to implement an important part of Kinkaid's tactical plan—picketing one or two destroyers five miles ahead of the task force to warn of approaching warships.[145]

Wright sent away the cruisers' float planes—most of them went to Tulagi—to avoid the possibility that they would become obstructions or fire hazards during night combat. He was certain that when they were needed, the float planes could be quickly summoned from Tulagi to drop flares.

Just before the task force entered the channel between Guadalcanal and Florida Island, Wright's ships nearly collided with three US transports and five destroyers that had just landed reinforcements and supplies and were now returning to Espiritu Santo. Halsey ordered two of the destroyers, the *Lamson* and *Lardner*, to join Wright's task force. Because it was too late to brief the commanders about the operation, Wright sent them to the rear of his column, behind his cruisers, without orders. The task force proceeded to Ironbottom Sound. The water was black and smooth as obsidian under cloudy skies.[146]

At 11:06 p.m. *Minneapolis*'s SG radar picked up two vessels fifteen miles away, off Cape Esperance. As Wright's task force closed the distance, the two blips grew to several. At 11:16, now four miles from the Japanese, Commander William Cole sought Wright's permission for his destroyers to fire torpedoes. Wright hesitated, believing the distance, seven thousand yards, was too great for the Mark XV torpedo.

Four or five minutes passed before Wright granted Cole authority to fire. Wright, a Navy "big gun" admiral who did not fully appreciate torpedo warfare, was evidently preoccupied with deciding when to open fire with his batteries.

The delay was fatal. By the time Cole received permission to fire, the enemy destroyers were moving away from Cole's destroyers.

When their twenty-four fish finally entered the water, yellow flames were spurting from *Minneapolis*'s eight-inch guns, which fired four salvos at a ship lit by star shells. *New Orleans* joined in, and reported scoring hits on a destroyer that appeared to burst into flames.

Cole's torpedoes were now in a stern chase, meaning they would have to travel even farther than when he first requested permission to fire. No hits were confirmed: they either missed their targets or, as often happened with the Mark XV, the torpedoes passed beneath the enemy ships because of faulty depth settings, or the magnetic and contact exploders failed to work. Cole's destroyers zigzagged to the north, away from the battleground, while firing their guns at distant targets, "without observed result."[147]

The Japanese lookouts spotted the American ships an instant before the *Minneapolis* opened fire, and Tanaka barked the orders: "Stop unloading! Take battle stations!" His veteran destroyer crews, who had fought and trained together for years, instantly went into their well-rehearsed battle routines. "Close and attack!" Tanaka ordered—the signal to his three divisions to mount a mass torpedo attack.[148]

Its detached position from the rest of Tanaka's squadron and its relative proximity to Wright's task force made the *Takanami* appear bright and clear on American radar—and a perfect target for Wright's five cruisers, whose radar automatically trained their guns on it. The entire line fired on *Takanami*. As the hits multiplied, the Japanese destroyer replied with counterbattery fire, which made her an even better target.

The cruiser captains initially believed that they had sunk several enemy ships, when they were all evidently firing on the same one, *Takanami*. "For a brief moment victory seemed to be ours."

At this juncture, flares dropped by the float planes in Tulagi would have clarified the situation for Wright's gunners. But glassy surface conditions in Tulagi Harbor deprived the planes of the lift needed to become airborne, although they tried for an hour and a half. When they finally did get into the air, they arrived too late to influence the battle's outcome.

A MILE BEHIND *TAKANAMI*, TANAKA'S seven other destroyers lurked like ghost ships near the Guadalcanal coastline. Tanaka's destroyers swung around to a course parallel to Wright's ships, accelerated to forty knots, and moved into firing positions. Four of them managed to first push some of their drums of supplies into the water. The American cruisers' gun flashes gave Japanese torpedo men targets to aim for, and they lashed back with spreads of their twenty-four-inch Long Lance torpedoes—up to fifty of them.[149]

At 11:27 p.m. Wright's task force was violently disabused of any notions of a quick and easy victory. The first two torpedoes struck Wright's flagship, *Minneapolis*, exploding in the bow compartments and a forward engine room and sending a tower of flames and water skyward. The water crashed down onto the deck and put out most of the fires, but a section of the bow dragged in the water, and *Minneapolis* listed to port.

A minute later, a torpedo smashed into *New Orleans*, next in line, as she swerved to avoid *Minneapolis*. It ignited *New Orleans*'s powder magazine and tore off her bow. The *New Orleans*'s decapitated bow glided aftward along the port side, tearing and denting her hull just above the waterline. The bow sank, a steel mausoleum full of dead sailors, with its guns pointed skyward, as a column of fire reached twice as high as *New Orleans*'s foremast.

Then the *Pensacola*, veering to the windward side of the burning ships, was silhouetted by their flames and, at 11:39 p.m., was struck by a torpedo that blew up a fuel tank. Fires raced through the cruiser, transforming the mainmast into a blazing torch and roasting everyone in Control Aft.[150]

The *Honolulu*—nicknamed the "Blue Goose" and regarded as a lucky ship—upheld her reputation when she swerved to the lee side of the burning ships and escaped the torpedoes still coursing through the black water. Weaving, she moved northwestward, firing her guns. His flagship a shambles, Wright transferred command of the task force to Admiral Tisdale on the *Honolulu*.

At 11:48 p.m. two torpedoes slammed almost simultaneously into the fifth cruiser, *Northampton*; many crewmen felt just a single explosion. The blast ripped the port side and detonated five-inch ammunition. Oil spewed onto the afterdeck and caught fire. Catastrophic flooding caused an immediate list. *Northampton* lurched to a halt, dead in the water.[151]

Tanaka ordered his squadron to break off contact and withdraw. A short time later, *Oyashi* and *Kuroshio* were dispatched to rescue crewmen from the *Takanami*, but they aborted the operation when US ships drew too near. Just 33 of *Takanami*'s crew of 244 reached Guadalcanal alive.[152]

Flames engulfed four of Wright's five cruisers. *Northampton*'s prognosis was poor; she was listing 20 degrees to port. But *New Orleans* appeared to be in worse shape, with 120 feet of her bow gone, everyone dead who had been inside it, and both forward turrets seared by a flash fire. A surge of seawater tamped down the major fires, but concussive explosions of aircraft bombs in the magazine jolted the cruiser.

Chaplain Howell M. Forgy was on the bridge when the torpedoes went into her. He was slammed into the steel bridge shield. A wave then washed over the bridge, leaving a foot of water on the deck and soaking the chaplain. "I opened my eyes to find we were in a cave of fire. . . . I could see the fire reaching more than hundreds of feet above the mast. . . . The great wall of flame all around me actually dried my sopping uniform in seconds," he wrote. Forgy began "trying to pray a sort of message to tell God I was ready" to die.[153]

Lieutenant Commander Hubert Hayter, Ensign Andrew Foreman, and Lieutenant Richard Haines refused to leave *New Orleans*'s central damage control station even when toxic gas began seeping in. Given permission to evacuate, Hayter ordered everyone to put on a gas mask and sent the sailors up the narrow escape hatch to the deck. Knowing that he was too big to fit through the small hole, Hayter gave his gas mask to a sailor who lacked one. Aided by Hayter, Foreman, and Haines, most of the enlisted men escaped. When their turn came to leave, the officers were unable to climb the ladder, and they died of asphyxiation at their station, among the 182 *New Orleans* crewmen killed.[154]

Admiral Tisdale ordered the destroyers *Fletcher* and *Drayton* to rescue *Northampton* crewmen. They plucked sailors off life rafts, pulled them from the sea, and dragged cork-buoyed nets through the water to gather as many others as possible. "All these men were in filthy, oily water," wrote Joseph C. Wylie Jr., a *Fletcher* officer. They were taken below decks and brought up in relays to be hosed down and issued clean, dry clothing. "The cooks turned to," wrote Wylie. "The galley was just running for the next 48 hours." Although 58 *Northampton* crewmen perished, 773 survived.

At 2:40 a.m. on December 1, Captain Willard Kitts ordered *Northampton* abandoned. Twenty minutes later, *Northampton* rolled over and sank stern first.[155]

Fires raging on her, *Minneapolis* wobbled into port in Tulagi, aided by the tug *Bobolink* and PT boats. Also managing to reach Tulagi were *New Orleans*, aided by the destroyer *Maury* and making just two knots, and *Pensacola*.[156]

TANAKA HAD AGAIN DEMONSTRATED WHY he was regarded as one of the Imperial Japanese Navy's best combat officers. He had put on no less than a graduate seminar in night surface warfare. A Japanese analysis of the battle said the American cruisers, ready for surface battle, were aware of Tanaka's destroyers before the Japanese even knew enemy ships were present. But by hesitating at the crucial moment, Admiral Wright squandered his advantages in numbers, firepower, and technology. The Japanese critique blamed it on American incompetence: "His fire was inaccurate, shells [im]properly set for deflection were especially numerous, and it is conjectured that either his marksmanship is not remarkable or else the illumination from his star shells was not sufficiently effective." With binocular-equipped lookouts instead of radar, Tanaka had won almost effortlessly, at a cost of just one destroyer.

For the US Navy, it was another Savo Island debacle. In thirty minutes of combat the *Northampton* was sent to the depths of Ironbottom Sound, and three sister cruisers were so crippled that they did not return to service for nearly a year. As the historian Samuel Eliot Morison wrote, the cruisers had been "picked off like mechanical ducks in a carnival shooting gallery." The names of nearly four hundred officers and seamen who died were added to the long roster of American sailors who perished during the Guadalcanal campaign.[157]

Wright did not brood over his losses—because he claimed victory, while acknowledging that the dark night and his task force's distance from the enemy ships made reports of Japanese losses problematic. However, based on his commanders' claims, Wright asserted that his warships had sunk two light cruisers and seven destroyers—more Japanese ships than were present. For their roles in the hypothetical victory, Wright recommended that all of his cruiser captains receive Navy Crosses. They received their medals, as did Wright and Tisdale.

Besides inflating the Japanese losses, Wright's action report lavished praise on his cruisers' gunnery, which was in fact barely adequate and responsible for sinking just one destroyer. "The gunnery performance of our cruisers was excellent," he wrote.

Wright disparaged Commander Cole's decision to fire torpedoes from seven thousand yards—"it is improbable that they were very effective"—while approving of the destroyer commanders who did *not* fire their torpedoes. Yet, had Wright immediately granted Cole permission to fire, rather than waiting five minutes, the torpedoes would have been in the water before the Japanese were even aware of Wright's task force, and they might have found their targets.

As Wright's report traveled upward through the Navy's hierarchy, it became clear that Cole was being scapegoated. "The offensive action of the van destroyers was disappointing," wrote Halsey. "The van destroyers, after firing torpedoes, did not assist the cruisers, but turned away and retired to the northwest."[158]

Halsey later saw the Battle of Tassafaronga for what it was—a decisive tactical defeat. "For an enemy force of eight destroyers, as it was estimated, to inflict such damage on a more powerful force at so little cost is something less than a credit to our command."[159]

Wright and Halsey, however, failed to grasp Tassafaronga's primary lesson: that US warships, even with state-of-the-art radar and superior guns, were overmatched in night combat against Japan's superb destroyer fleet, whose tactics were shaped by its Long Lance torpedoes. The US Navy was strangely incurious about why Japanese torpedoes were so much more lethal than its own torpedoes, whose range was shorter and which often ran too deep and failed to detonate, nor did it ask why enemy destroyer tactics were more effective. "Big gun" admirals dominated the Navy hierarchy. It would take a former submariner to probe a little deeper, just as it had taken Halsey, a pilot, to improve carrier tactics.

Early in his career Admiral Chester Nimitz commanded a destroyer in the South China Sea (and accidentally ran her aground) and then a submarine. He later lectured and wrote about the future of submarines, which he envisioned sailing in fleets.[160]

In his report on the Battle of Tassafaronga to Admiral Ernest King, Nimitz generously praised Japan's efficient destroyer fleet and especially its "most damaging weapon," the torpedo. Nimitz acknowledged that the United States lagged behind Japan in its tactical use of destroyers—and its torpedoes were "not sufficiently deadly."

Although in the report Nimitz did not openly advocate developing better torpedoes, he did propose that Navy guns use flashless powder, hinting that the cruisers' gun flashes provided Japanese destroyer captains with vivid aiming points. As for the loss of four cruisers, one of them sunk, Nimitz went along with the conclusions of his subordinates, blaming it on Ironbottom Sound's "restricted waters," although cruisers—even battleships—had fought there many times before.

In conclusion, he said the answer for the Navy's shortcomings was "training, TRAINING and M-O-R-E T-R-A-I-N-I-N-G."[161]

The battle reports glossed over the more embarrassing elements of the defeat, but it would not matter so much, because Tassafaronga would be remembered as another turning point in the Guadalcanal campaign. Although the battle itself was a Japanese victory, Wright's cruisers had prevented Tanaka from landing reinforcements and most of his supplies.

Consequently, Tassafaronga further dampened Japanese enthusiasm for continuing large-scale efforts to reinforce and resupply the island. It would be the last major sea battle fought in the southern Solomons and would ultimately influence the escalating debate over whether the Japanese should continue fighting on Guadalcanal, or withdraw.[162]

6

December:
The Army Takes Charge

*All the soldiers wherever they are walking go staggering along.
This is hell's front line!*

—EXCERPT FROM A JAPANESE DIARY[1]

*And when he gets to Heaven
To St. Peter he will tell:
One more Marine reporting, sir—
I've served my time in hell.*

—DOGGEREL FOUND ON MARINE
GRAVES ON GUADALCANAL

FOUR MONTHS AFTER INVADING GUADALCANAL, Tulagi, Gavutu, and Florida Islands, the 1st Marine Division was being relieved. Officially, General Vandegrift's losses totaled 774 dead or missing and 2,736 wounded, but thousands of others were suffering from an array of tropical diseases—malaria being the most ubiquitous, with 3,200 hospitalizations and at least as many walking cases. The elite division was a ghostly simulacrum of the 19,000-man force that came ashore in the southern Solomons in August. The harsh environment, the scanty rations, and the malaria and dysentery had winnowed, on average, twenty to fifty pounds per man, but that wasn't all. When not in combat, where they were marvels of lethality, the Marines resembled old men grumpily attending to the business of eating, sleeping, and elimination while fastidiously keeping their weapons bright and clean.

The Marines were spent. "We were all exhausted," wrote Corpsman Louis Ortega. "We had no clothes. All I had was my shoes, no socks, no under clothes. All I had was a pair of torn dungarees and a khaki shirt." They were rail-thin, grimy—and enormously relieved that their long ordeal was over.[2]

Some Marines had been in the lines for several weeks, and when they came down from the hills, like Rip Van Winkle, they were dazzled by the changes that had occurred in their absence. Henderson Field, with its Spartan amenities, had blossomed into three airfields occupied by nearly two hundred planes and thousands of mechanics, clerks, cooks, warehousemen, and drivers. Four-engine bombers were parked on the airfield aprons. There were mountains of food, an outdoor movie theater, and roads clogged with truck traffic. The air was thick with dust and gasoline fumes.[3]

While welcoming their replacements, the Marines also eyed them narrowly, envying them their robust health and disapproving of their naivety. "They seemed not to show the proper respect for danger," observed Private Robert Leckie.[4]

The Marines were critical of the Army way of doing things, from their reliance on a large support network to their behavior in combat. When they came under fire, Army troops typically stopped await for reinforcements and artillery and air support; the Marines usually pressed stubbornly ahead. Facing strong resistance, the Army often pulled back; the Marines dug in. The schism between the two military branches became conspicuous on Guadalcanal, widened as the war proceeded, and endures today.

The Marines disparaged what they perceived to be the Army's excessive caution and slowness and deplored their occasional carelessness with their equipment. Private First Class Arthur Farrington scornfully observed that when soldiers left thirteen machine-guns unguarded near the front line, enemy soldiers used them to kill eleven Americans in a chow line.[5]

Replacements would quickly fill the void left by the 1st Marine Division's departure for Australia, where it would join General Douglas MacArthur's command and get some needed rest. Within weeks, more than three divisions would occupy the Marine division's lines: the 2nd Marine Division; the Americal Division; the regular Army 25th Infantry Division, on its way from Schofield Barracks in Hawaii; and the independent 147th Infantry Regiment, an Ohio National Guard unit. West of the perimeter, the front extended past the Matanikau River to Point Cruz; east of the perimeter, it stretched beyond Koli Point.

The replacements, many of them understandably nervous about the prospect of going into combat for the first time, were surprised by the unexpected beauty of the island, which would never appear so enchanting to them as it did when they first landed. "The whole little world we were living in was, in one way of thinking, no less than a fairy land of natural beauty, with its charm regrettably lost to the greater portion of us," wrote Lieutenant John George of the Americal's 132nd Infantry Regiment. George's Illinois National Guard unit landed December 8, the day Vandegrift's Marines began leaving.[6]

Arriving with the 25th Division three weeks later, Private James Jones thought Guadalcanal was "beautiful . . . the delicious sparkling tropic sea, the long beautiful beach, the minute palms of the copra plantation waving in the sea breeze, the dark green band of jungle, and the dun mass and power of the mountains rising behind it to rocky peaks." From the mountain slopes, the future novelist said, "you could look back down to the beach and off across the straits to Florida Island and one of the most beautiful views of tropic scenery on the planet. None of it looked like the pestilential hellhole that it was."[7]

WITH THE CHANGE IN GROUND forces came a change in command. Army Major General Millard Harmon appointed Major General Alexander "Sandy" Patch, the Americal's commander, to direct tactical operations on Guadalcanal after the Marines and Vandegrift departed. Although Admiral Halsey had unequivocally ordered Harmon to drive the Japanese from Guadalcanal, Harmon conceded that he could not vouchsafe "the ability of our naval surface forces and air to satisfactorily interdict the operation of Jap submarines and the Tokyo Express into Guadalcanal."[8]

The son of an Army cavalry captain, Patch, fifty-three, was tall, spare, and a man of nervous energy and drive. After graduating from West Point in 1913, he became aide-de-camp to General John J. Pershing during his campaign in Mexico against Pancho Villa. In France in 1918, Patch led a battalion during the Meuse-Argonne offensive.

He was known as plain, unassuming, and quick to act; some said that he resembled Gary Cooper. He rolled his own cigarettes from sacks of Bull Durham, drank bourbon, and wore riding breeches and boots when in the field.

As a member of the Infantry Board at Fort Benning, Georgia, Patch helped develop the three-regiment division model that was now the Army standard. A staff officer said Patch's hallmarks were his competitive drive and his abhorrence of wasting his men's lives. "He practically died a death every time a soldier was shot." When he left Guadalcanal, Patch said, "The American soldier does not like to fight and does not like to die."[9]

ALLIED SUPPLIES WERE NOW REACHING Guadalcanal in such profusion, gloomily observed Yamamoto's chief of staff, Vice Admiral Ugaki, "that it was rather too much trouble to make notes about them." The logistics pipeline would have flowed faster if Guadalcanal had docks; instead, ships had to transfer supplies to lighters, which brought them to the beach, to be moved inland by truck. Supplies piled up on the beach, presenting an inviting target for Japanese pilots, until Martin Clemens and the Marines organized a native labor battalion to speed up the process. By December, six hundred native laborers worked for the Americans as longshoremen, and lugged rations and supplies to troops in the field.[10]

Another systemic problem was the bottleneck at Noumea Harbor, which was the transfer port between the US mainland and Guadalcanal. Since Ghormley's days as South Pacific commander, the harbor had been congested with supply ships waiting to be unloaded. In early December, ninety-one of them were in line with 180,000 tons of cargo aboard. Noumea neither had the berthing capacity, nor the men, equipment, and storage to handle the tidal wave of materiel. Halsey suggested making the Army solely responsible for the unloading—rather than leaving it to a medley of work details from the Army, Navy, and Marines. His idea provided some relief.[11]

IN OBSERVANCE OF THE PEARL HARBOR attack's first anniversary on December 7, General Pedro del Valle, commander of the Eleventh Marines, organized a special artillery concentration against Japanese positions west of the Matanikau River. On the shells was etched, "Tojo. Dec. 7, 1942." Enemy artillery, now beyond the range of Henderson Field, did not attempt to retaliate.[12]

Two days later at 11:00 a.m. Vandegrift formally handed operational command of the island to General Patch. Before leaving Guadalcanal, the Marine general paid tribute to the dead at the island's cemetery, Flanders Field, a cleared area in the Lunga Point coconut groves. Gazing silently over his men's graves, Vandegrift, whose grandfather had fought in General Robert E. Lee's Army of Northern Virginia at Gettysburg, recalled Lee's words: "What a cruel thing is war; to separate and destroy families and friends, and mar the purest joys and happiness God has granted us in this world; to fill our hearts with hatred instead of love for our neighbors, and to devastate the fair face of the beautiful world." Vandegrift was later awarded the Medal of Honor for leading America's first offensive of World War II.

Most of the departing Marines also visited their dead comrades' resting places one last time. Simple palm fronds marked most of the graves, but rude crosses had been erected over others. To the crosses were nailed dog tags and mess gear. Epitaphs were carved in the wood: "Our Buddy," "He died fighting," "A big guy with a bigger heart." On many appeared a bit of doggerel that was a favorite of the Marines:

"And when he gets to Heaven
To St. Peter he will tell:
One more Marine reporting, sir—
I've served my time in hell."[13]

One of Vandegrift's last acts as commander of Guadalcanal ground forces was to convince Halsey to scuttle Admiral Turner's plan to build a bomber airfield at Aola, thirty-five miles east of the perimeter. The site was swampy and lay in an area of low ridges. For those reasons, engineers had rejected it, as had high-ranking Marine, Navy, and Army officers, but Turner had secured Halsey's support to keep the project alive. With Halsey's reversal, however, the airfield would be constructed south of Koli Point, fifteen miles east of Henderson, instead of at Aola.

When completed, it was christened Carney Field, in honor of Captain James Carney, commander of Naval Construction Battalion 14—the Seabees who built the airstrip. Carney made the first landing there on December 16 at the controls of a Dauntless dive bomber. After takeoff, the SBD stalled over Sealark Channel and crashed, killing Carney.[14]

THE FIFTH MARINES LEFT FIRST—THE self-anointed "raggedy-ass Marines," in filthy, frayed dungarees and boondockers run down at the heels. About one-third of them had been rated unfit for further combat. Before the regiment departed, five Army colonels interviewed some of the Marines for a training manual they were writing about jungle warfare; it would be titled *Fighting on Guadalcanal.* Sergeant Major B. Metzger articulated a common theme when he said, "Your men have to be rugged and rough, and to win they must learn to disregard politeness and must kill." The manual contained pointers on tactics, night combat (eliminate tracers), equipment and clothing, weapons, the use of grenades, and hand-to-hand fighting.

Higgins boats took the Fifth Marines to the transport ship *President Jackson,* where they climbed cargo nets to come aboard. Thin, exhausted, and ill, some were only able to wrap their arms around the nets and hang on. A few plunged into the sound with their packs and rifles and had to be fished out; others made it partway up and froze until sailors climbed down to help them. "Are we really as weak, gaunt, and decrepit as we seem to be?" a Marine asked rhetorically. Using ropes, sailors hoisted aboard those who were so weak they could not even begin to climb the nets; one them was Corpsman Ortega, whose weight had dropped from 150 pounds to 110.

Sergeant Ore Marion reached the deck unassisted, but it was a struggle because of his shocking weight loss. Five-foot-six, Marion normally weighed 130 pounds, but he was now 90 pounds. Marion claimed that no man in his platoon, large or small, weighed more than 135 pounds. Once aboard ship, the Marines were fed thick macaroni soup. Marion vomited up two bowls of it before he was able to hold down some of the unaccustomedly rich food.[15]

Those who could went topside to view Guadalcanal for the last time. It was beautiful, wrote Marion. When someone asked about the "strange smell," a comrade replied, "That's fresh, clean air, you dumb bastard."[16]

As the Eleventh Marines prepared for departure in mid-December, the artillerists witnessed a disturbing ceremony on the beach. A unit of the Seventh Marines had formed two ranks; both ranks had turned their backs on a man being escorted by guards between them. The prisoner and his guards boarded a landing craft and left. The artillerists learned that the man had left the line twice while under fire; the first time, he was sent back to the line; the second time, he was placed under guard. "Every man present realizes that some things are worse than death and this . . . is one of them," wrote William White.[17]

The First Marines, as motley and pitiable a sight as the Fifth Marines, boarded Higgins boats for the short trip to their transport ship. Clad in broken-down shoes, tattered utilities, and blue Navy shirts given them by the Seabees, they were as "skinny as starved cattle, our skin and eyes colored a deep golden from the months on atabrine." They had the same difficulty as the Fifth Marines in scaling the cargo nets, with some of them making it halfway to the deck and able only to hang there, "trembling and cursing."[18]

Before the First Marines left for Australia, Private Robert Leckie and some of his comrades met a soldier who was about to go ashore on Guadalcanal for the first time. The soldier asked the Marines how it was there. "Rough," they tersely replied.

Someone asked the soldier whether he had ever heard of Guadalcanal before being deployed there. Momentarily speechless, the soldier then replied, "Hell, yes! Guadalcanal. The First Marines—everybody's heard of it. You guys are famous. You guys are heroes back home."

Leckie and a companion looked away quickly so no one would see their tears; for months, they had believed that they had been written off. It was a pleasant surprise to learn otherwise. "They had not forgotten," Leckie wrote.[19]

THE MARINES WERE COMPELLED TO wear Australian or American Army uniforms until they received new Marine uniforms to replace their rags. In the meantime Vandegrift wanted them to wear a badge or a patch that would identify them as Marines. He directed Lieutenant Colonel Merrill Twining to design a shoulder patch.

Lieutenant Don Dickson, the former art editor at *Leatherneck* magazine who had designed the "Let George Do It" medal, had come up with some ideas for the patch that utilized the code names "Watchtower," "Cactus," and "Lone Wolf," but they were rejected. General Rupertus liked the British shoulder straps, but Vandegrift did not.

On the flight to Brisbane, Twining was doodling with a pencil on the fly of an old notebook and sketched a patch that incorporated the name "Guadalcanal" vertically through the center, with the Southern Cross as a backdrop. Vandegrift, who was looking over Twining's shoulder, liked it and initialed it, "A.A.V." "Now, get it done," the general said. Twining hired Australian Knitting Mills in Melbourne to make tens of thousands of the patches.[20]

THE STARVING JAPANESE TROOPS ON the front lines from Port Cruz to Mount Austen were now the ones wondering whether they had been forgotten. After the Naval Battle of Guadalcanal, food shipments became increasingly irregular and insubstantial. The vigilant Cactus Air Force curtailed the resupply runs to occasional nighttime dashes from Shortland Harbor. Combat troops were subsisting on one-fourth rations, and sick and wounded men on one-twelfth rations. The malnourished soldiers' weakened immune systems succumbed to malaria, dysentery, beri-beri, and other diseases and illnesses. Wracked by fevers and diarrhea, the men had no medicine to provide relief.

On December 3 ten destroyers set adrift enough steel barrels of food offshore to last a week. The Tokyo Express shipments continued sporadically, with one of the best nighttime runs resulting in fifteen hundred drums cast into the channel and three hundred reaching shore.

The Japanese navy tried to augment these efforts with submarine deliveries. The subs were stripped of torpedoes, shells, and guns, and loaded with food and supplies for the Guadalcanal troops. Japanese submariners disparagingly nicknamed the deliveries the "submerged freight service." They were initially successful, and up to thirty-eight subs attempted supply runs during December.

Radio intercepts began alerting US naval forces to the deliveries, and they became riskier. On December 9, two PT boats were waiting off Kamimbo when a resupply sub, the *I-3*, surfaced. *PT-59* sank it with one torpedo. Three nights later, PT boats sent the destroyer *Teruzuki* to the ocean bottom. More than a dozen Japanese submarines were lost attempting to bring food to the beleaguered soldiers.

Supplies were at times successfully air-dropped by bombers, but never in sufficient quantities. Less than 30 percent of the twenty thousand barrels cast overboard were recovered; the rest became snagged on the coral reefs, or were riddled by dawn air patrols and sunk. Destroyers and transports were also strafed, bombed, and torpedoed. Between November 16 and February 9, eleven Tokyo Express runs reached Guadalcanal, at a cost of ten destroyers lost and nineteen damaged. As the Americans became better at anticipating the supply runs, the Japanese attempted to air-drop supplies from bombers, but too few of them reached the soldiers.

"As even destroyer transportation has now become impossible," wrote Ugaki in early December after PT boats and American aircraft had turned back another destroyer resupply run, "the situation has undergone a sudden change. So the time for changing future policy might come sooner than expected"—alluding to the ongoing debate over whether to continue the campaign.

Yet, Ugaki dutifully ordered an all-out effort by destroyers to deliver men and food in December, in anticipation of a new offensive in January. Briefly elated over a report, which later proved to be mostly false, that twelve hundred drums of provisions had reached shore, Ugaki drily noted, "The enemy had eight transports enter the road under the protection of over a dozen destroyers and patrol boats. What a difference between them and us!"[21]

WHEN THE JAPANESE SOLDIERS RAN out of rice, they ate grass, roots, berries, and tree bark; they roasted and ate lizards; some gnawed on their belts and slings. A recovered Japanese diary described one soldier's physical decline during late November and December. Acute hunger set in November 22, when the diarist reported, "Due to hunger I don't have any strength in my stomach. I feel dizzy when I move around." Five days later he was suffering from malaria, followed by dysentery and beri-beri. The diary's last entry was on December 22.[22]

A Seventeenth Army staff officer's report on December 8 said that forty-two hundred effectives remained in the army, and that it was losing fifteen hundred fighting men each month. Both figures were surely deliberate exaggerations—the effectives being possibly three or four times the number cited—to persuade higher-ups of the urgent need for reinforcements. The report said that of three thousand men in one regiment, just sixty to seventy remained able to fight. Sixty wounded men were abandoned west of Mount Austen because the three hundred stretcher bearers needed to carry them out could not be spared. The officer characterized the Americans' fighting spirit as being "not good at all," but added, "we can hardly stand their firepower."[23]

A diary recovered from a dead Japanese truck driver, which was obtained by Lieutenant William Whyte of the First Marines, described how "all the soldiers, wherever they are walking go staggering along. This is hell's front line!"[24]

A soldier poet described the suffering of the Japanese troops:

(*Top*)
Rear Admiral
Richmond Kelly
Turner discusses
Operation
Watchtower with
Major General
Alexander Vandegrift,
commander of the 1st
Marine Division.
National Archives.

(*Right*) Rear Admiral
Frank Jack Fletcher,
Watchtower's tactical
commander.
National Archives.

(Top) Japanese "Betty" bomber that was splashed on landing day, August 7. *National Archives.*

(Center) *Enterprise* crewmen load bombs on a Dauntless dive-bomber. *National Archives.*

(Bottom) Fires burn on Tanambogo on landing day, August 7. *National Archives.*

1st Raider Battalion officers on Tulagi. Colonel Merritt "Red Mike" Edson is second from left, bottom row. Behind Edson is Brigadier General William Rupertus, who was in command of the landings on Tulagi, Gavutu, and Tanambogo. *Naval History and Heritage Command.*

Cruiser *Quincy* burning near Savo Island early August 9. *Naval History and Heritage Command.*

(Top) 1st Marine Division staff. Major General Alexander Vandegrift is fourth from left, front row. *US Marine Corps.*

(Left) Colonel Frank Goettge, 1st Marine Division intelligence officer, with captured enemy currency. *US Marine Corps.*

(Right) Major General Alexander Vandegrift, commander of the 1st Marine Division, at his desk on Guadalcanal. *US Marine Corps.*

(Top left) Vice Admiral Gunichi Mikawa, Japanese 8th fleet commander. *Naval History and Heritage Command.*

(Top right) Rear Admiral Raizo Tanaka, Japan's destroyer avatar. *Naval History and Heritage Command.*

(Bottom) Lieutenant General Harukichi Hyakutake, commander of the Japanese 17th Army. *Wikimedia Commons.*

Grumman F4F Wildcats parked at Henderson Field. *National Archives.*

F4F Wildcat on fire at Henderson Field. *US Marine Corps, Thayer Soule Collection.*

(Top) Japanese Zeros warming up on the carrier *Shokaku. National Archives.*

(Center) Bomb explodes on USS *Enterprise. National Archives.*

(Bottom) Henderson Field's air operations center, nicknamed the Pagoda. *US Marine Corps, Thomas Carcelli Collection.*

Marines wade river on Guadalcanal. *US Marine Corps, Frederick R. Findtner Collection.*

(Center) Marine Brigadier General Roy Geiger, Henderson Field's air operations commander. *US Marine Corps.*

(Bottom) Captain Martin Clemens of the British Solomon Islands Protectorate Defense Force and his scouts on Guadalcanal. *National Archives.*

Marines taking a break while patrolling on Guadalcanal. *National Archives.*

Marines bathing in the Lunga River. *US Marine Corps, Frederick R. Findtner Collection.*

USS *Wasp* burning after being torpedoed by a Japanese submarine. National *Archives*.

Admirals Chester Nimitz (left) and William Halsey.
National Archives.

Colonel Lewis "Chesty" Puller at his battalion command post on Guadalcanal. *US Marine Corps*.

Marines evacuate wounded comrade. *US Marine Corps, Frederick R. Findtner Collection.*

Marine aces John Smith, Robert Galer, and Marion Carl display their Navy Crosses. *US Marine Corps.*

Brothers Joseph, Francis, Albert, Madison, and George Sullivan of Waterloo, Iowa. All five were lost when their ship, the cruiser *Juneau*, was torpedoed. *Naval History and Heritage Command.*

Battleship *Washington* fires on the Japanese battleship *Kirishima*. *US Navy.*

Beached Japanese transport *Kinugawa Maru*. *Naval History and Heritage Command.*

Cruiser USS *Minneapolis* after a torpedo blew off her bow at the Battle of Tassafaronga. *National Archives.*

Rear Admiral John McCain (left) and his successor as South Pacific air commander, Rear Admiral Aubrey Fitch, on September 20, 1942. *National Archives.*

Admiral Chester Nimitz awards the Navy Cross to Lieutenant Colonel Evans Carlson following his 2nd Marine Raider Battalion's "long patrol." Looking on is Major General Alexander Vandegrift (left), and Brigadier General William Rupertus. *Naval History and Heritage Command.*

Admiral William Halsey awards the Navy Cross to Rear Admiral Willis Lee for his actions during the Naval Battle of Guadalcanal. *National Archives.*

Generals Alexander Patch, commander of the Americal Division; Millard Harmon, senior Army commander in the South Pacific; and Nathan Twining, Harmon's chief of staff. *Library of Congress.*

Guadalcanal Medal of Honor winners (left to right): Major General Alexander Vandegrift, Colonel Merritt Edson, and Sergeants Mitchell Paige and John Basilone. *US Marine Corps.*

Guadalcanal cemetery. *US Marine Corps.*

"Our rice is gone
Eating roots and grass
Along the ridges and cliffs
Leaves hide the trail. We lose our way
Stumble and get up, fall and get up.
Covered with mud from our falls
Blood oozes from our wounds
No cloth to bind our cuts
Flies swarm to the scabs
No strength to brush them away
Fall down and cannot move
How many times I've thought of suicide." [25]

On December 1 Lance Corporal Heicho Koto Kiyoshi of the 16th Infantry wrote a somber letter from west of the Matanikau to his older brother. Wounded in the arm by a shell fragment five days earlier, Kiyoshi had been released from a field hospital on December 1 and sent back to the lines. "I have not eaten properly since the 24th of November," he wrote. "Many days I have had nothing to eat at all. . . . I am holding my rifle with a right arm that doesn't move easily. . . . I must serve as long as I can move at all." His regimental and company commanders were dead; two platoon commanders had been wounded. Just four men were left in his squad, thirty in his company. "In conclusion, I am writing this as a farewell letter," he said. That night at midnight, Kiyoshi was killed. [26]

Although harrowed by disease and casualties and with one hundred men starving to death each day on average, General Hyakutake's army was still determined to fight, and its morale remained high. Vice Admiral Ugaki met at Truk with Colonel Taksuhiro Hattori of the Army General Staff after Hattori had toured the island. Hattori said the situation was much worse than he had anticipated. The army's fighting strength, he said, was just one-fourth of what it previously was. Yet a new offensive was planned for January 20, Hattori informed Ugaki, and before it was launched, the army would send ten thousand fresh troops, followed by two more divisions.

Yamamoto and Ugaki threw cold water on the plan, predicting that just half of the troops would reach Guadalcanal and only one-third would be equipped to fight. "Nothing can be done unless enemy air strength is destroyed," Ugaki said, and too few squadrons were being sent to achieve air superiority. While observing the first anniversary of the Pacific War, he wrote in his journal, "In looking over the past year, I regret that we have not gained what we wished." [27]

Hattori's pessimistic assessment of the army's condition reflected what the Americans were now seeing for themselves—an army that was beginning to unravel. Patrols had found Japanese soldiers living in isolation from the rest of the army; many of them had been ostracized for retreating rather than fighting to the death. "A great many Japs are wandering around in small bands, which are continually being killed off, both by our own and native patrols," said one report.[28]

As December began winding down, the Seventeenth Army urgently appealed for a "priority supply" to relieve food shortages so severe that many soldiers were subsisting on "tree buds, coconuts, and seaweed." Some units had become so badly incapacitated by lack of food that they were unable to send a single soldier on patrol, or to counteract enemy threats to their rear. Captured diaries reported the absence of rice and a shortage of coconuts, while "every day enemy planes dance in the sky, fly low, strafe, bomb, and numerous officers and men fall. . . . O friendly planes! I beg that you come over soon and cheer us up!"[29]

STILL-OPERATIONAL JAPANESE FORCES ON THE island in mid-December consisted of General Maruyama's Sendai Division remnants, the survivors of Kawaguchi's Ichiki Detachment, and General Tadayoshi Sano's 38th Division. They comprised twenty to twenty-five thousand soldiers, but fewer than one-half were combat capable. Most of them occupied strong defensive positions west of the American lines stretching from Point Cruz into the mountain foothills. But elements of two Sano regiments, the 124th and 228th, were dug in around Mount Austen between the upper Lunga and Matanikau rivers. Major Takeyosho Inagaki's 2nd Battalion of the 228th held Mount Austen's northeastern slopes; Colonel Akinosuke Oka, whose attack during October's big push had failed, commanded the remnants of the 124th Infantry Regiment and other units between Mount Austen and the Matanikau.

JUST AS THE JAPANESE WERE making plans for a new offensive in January to drive the Americans from Guadalcanal, Generals Harmon and Patch were preparing the groundwork for their own January campaign. As a prelude, they intended to clear Mount Austen of enemy soldiers in December so that in January they could advance to the west along a broad front.

The January plan ignored western Guadalcanal's challenging topography of accordion ridges separated by plunging jungle valleys. Patch and Harmon rejected an unorthodox plan to land troops in the enemy's rear on the island's southwest coast. It would cost minimal casualties, proponents said, and troops could be easily resupplied. But Patch and Harmon said the plan was unworkable because not enough shipping was available.[30]

When he commanded Guadalcanal's ground forces, Vandegrift had decided to not attempt to drive the Japanese from Mount Austen. Limited manpower was a factor, but his main reason was that the enemy there, although just six miles south of Henderson Field and the Marine perimeter, posed such a small threat. From their commanding positions, the Japanese could see practically everything that went on inside the perimeter and, in fact, all the way to Kokumbona, five miles to the west. But because of poor radio communications, the enemy had been unable to utilize this potent advantage to summon timely artillery barrages or air raids. Consequently, the northern areas of Mount Austen had become a warehouse for Japanese units in disfavor, such as Colonel Oka and the survivors of his 124th Regiment.[31]

FOR THE MOUNT AUSTEN OPERATION the US Army stuck to its dubious practice of assigning new, untried units to spearhead attacks. In November at Point Cruz it had been the Americal's 182nd Regiment from Massachusetts; this time it would be another green Americal regiment, the 132nd from Illinois.

Ten days after first setting foot on Guadalcanal the 3rd Battalion of the 132nd began toiling up the mountain in the predawn darkness. The blackness was so complete that the troops were ordered to grasp the packs of the men ahead of them so they would not stray from the path and become lost in the jungle. As if that were not enough, the skies opened up, soaking them with torrential rain, and they came under enemy rifle and machine-gun fire for the first time and sustained their first casualties. When the sun appeared, they sweltered in the suffocating heat and humidity.

Exhausted by its uphill march, the battalion went into bivouac. The soldiers remained confident, however, that with artillery and air support they could quickly drive the Japanese into the Matanikau River. Its faith in an easy victory made the battalion complacent, and its reconnaissance of the enemy position was brief and perfunctory.[32]

If it had thoroughly scouted the area, the battalion would have learned that it had struck the core of the enemy's Mount Austen defense—the "Gifu," a nearly mile-long warren of forty-five log bunkers built by Japanese engineers. The positions were well camouflaged, with some of them hidden beneath the roots of trees, and their fields of fire interlocked. Inside the Gifu were two to three hundred veteran soldiers who were slowly starving, without medical supplies, and resigned to dying behind their guns. They belonged to the 228th Infantry and had named their nearly impregnable position after a district on Honshu that was home to many of them. The Gifu was the strongest defensive position constructed by the Japanese on Guadalcanal.[33]

Colonel LeRoy Nelson, the 132nd's commander, reinforced the 3rd Battalion with its sister 1st Battalion, and from December 19–21 the soldiers attempted, with mounting frustration, to eliminate the enemy stronghold. On December 19, the 3rd Battalion's commander, Lieutenant Colonel William Wright, who was inadvisably wearing plainly visible insignia denoting his rank, was wounded during his battalion's first hour in combat. Then he was hit again while throwing a grenade.

Five men were wounded trying to rescue Wright; the colonel died before medics could reach him. His inexperienced battalion was "shaken by the loss of a brilliant leader" in its first action. Major Louis Franco took command and continued the attack. American artillery fire plastered the area with no observable effect. Dive bombers could not find the Japanese positions, but P-39s had better success when they dropped depth charges into the nearby ravines, inflicting casualties in the confined spaces.

Nelson asked General Sebree, the Americal's commander, to send him the 132nd's 2nd Battalion, which had been assigned to perimeter security. Sebree refused, claiming the impasse was due to Nelson's faulty leadership, not insufficient troops. "Make no more requests for 2nd Battalion. Final decision," snapped Sebree.[34]

On December 22 the heaviest artillery barrage of the Guadalcanal campaign rained down on the Gifu, but Nelson's men made no headway in cracking open the stronghold.

A Tenth Marines forward observer, William Paull, was assigned to direct artillery fire supporting the 132nd. Paull and two Army radiomen found themselves on one side of a ridge whose reverse slope was held by the Japanese. Snipers made their lives miserable. "At night, we could hear the Japs shout, 'Maline, you die!'" said Paull. Sent to another ridge where enemy troops also occupied the reverse slope, Paull called in artillery fire that passed so close to him, "I felt I could reach up and caress a projectile as it whispered over our heads."[35]

On Christmas Day, the 132nd ate cold beans and planned a new attack while soldiers inside the perimeter feasted on turkey, mashed potatoes, cranberries, and nuts. A patrol led by a newly commissioned second lieutenant probed a thousand yards ahead before turning back. Violating a cardinal rule of jungle warfare, the exhausted lieutenant ordered his men to return by the same route—and, predictably, they walked into an ambush. Grenades and rifle and machine-gun fire killed the lieutenant and four others. Another man was wounded, and a sergeant went berserk and had to be forcibly restrained.[36]

Two days later, Nelson's 1st Battalion led a fresh attack, but was unable to advance beyond its starting point.

Patch released the 2nd Battalion from perimeter duty and assigned it to protect the muddy Jeep road that was the regiment's supply lifeline. Enemy snipers harassed stretcher bearers attempting to evacuate the wounded. Skids were used to slide wounded men down steep hills, and pulleys and cables helped pass them across the yawning ravines.

On December 31, Nelson's soldiers captured Hills 27 and 31, hemming the Gifu between them, and that night the Japanese tried to drive them off the high ground. Six enemy counterattacks, led by sword-wielding troops shouting "Banzai! Banzai!" and supported by mortars, field artillery, and machineguns, failed to dislodge the Americans from the two hills during the night of January 2–3.

Lieutenant John George of the 2nd Battalion, experiencing one of his first combat actions, never forgot the attackers' hoarse voices—"blood-curdling; croaking with fanaticism, savagery, hate." Their leader, an officer with a peaked cap and brandishing a sword, was shot just above the belt buckle. Staggering backward, he tossed his sword aside as he fell.

"Machineguns and rifles pinged from all directions," wrote forward artillery observer Captain John Casey Jr. "Snipers fired from trees. Cross fire cut down our boys who were over the hill." The 2nd Battalion reported seventy-eight casualties in forty minutes.

The guns of the Tenth Marines' 3rd Battalion helped keep the enemy at bay. Sixty to seventy Japanese died in the attacks.

The Mount Austen offensive was suspended on January 3 pending the 132nd's replacement by the just-arrived 25th Infantry Division. The regiment dug a perimeter partway around the Gifu and reinforced its positions with machine-gun platoons. In a little more than two weeks the Illinois Guardsmen reported 112 men killed in action, 268 wounded, and three missing. Hundreds of others were evacuated as a result of illness or exhaustion; regimental morale was at a nadir. Colonel Nelson, malarial and stressed, asked to be relieved. Seventeen days of poorly conceived and executed attacks had failed to eject the Japanese from the Gifu.[37]

AS 1942 ENDED, BOUGAINVILLE COAST watcher Jack Read, presciently foreseeing a large Japanese military presence on Bougainville during 1943, gathered the island's missionaries, sisters, white women, and plantation owners for evacuation. On December 31, the submarine USS *Nautilus* surfaced in Teop Harbor off northern Bougainville and took aboard seventeen women, three girls, and nine men.[38]

ON NEW YEAR'S DAY 1943, US forces on Guadalcanal were more numerous than at any previous time during the campaign. In late August 1942, just fourteen thousand Marines and the Cactus Air Force's two and a half dozen aircraft had precariously clung to Henderson Field as the Japanese battered them from the air, land, and sea.

The doubting times were now over. The Naval Battle of Guadalcanal had sent a clear message to the Japanese that the US Navy was ready to risk everything to hold Guadalcanal. As 1943 began, Admiral Halsey commanded five naval task forces—one of battleships and destroyers; another of heavy cruisers, light cruisers, destroyers, and auxiliary carriers; two task forces composed of carriers, cruisers, and destroyers; and one of light cruisers and destroyers. The repaired carriers *Enterprise* and *Saratoga* returned, as did the battleships *Washington* and *North Carolina*, joined by three new battleships armed with sixteen-inch guns and two older ones with fourteen-inchers. Believing that the Guadalcanal campaign was "past the most critical period," Nimitz recalled seventeen submarines from the South Pacific for duty elsewhere in the Pacific.

The island itself throbbed with the purposeful activity of three infantry divisions totaling more than forty thousand men, plus support and auxiliary forces, and up to two hundred aircraft flying from Henderson Field, Fighter One, and Fighter Two. Guadalcanal's fourth airstrip, Carney Field, was close to being operational near Koli Point. Based at the airfields were the 2nd Marine Air Wing and five Army fighter squadrons of P-40s, P-400s, P-39s, and the coveted P-38s, as well as elements of three bomber groups. Brigadier General Louis Woods stepped down as Cactus's air commander, and Marine Brigadier General Francis Mulcahy, a close air support pioneer and World War I veteran, succeeded Woods.

The Army's service troops and engineers rapidly improved the squalid living conditions that the 1st Marine Division had endured for four months. Tents with wooden floors went up at Fighter Two. New mess tents were erected on concrete floors, with tables and benches. There were new showers, latrines, and wash stations. A Jeep-towed water trailer made deliveries to the pilots' bivouacs.[39]

The Army established the 13th Air Force as an overarching framework for its squadrons. After Admiral Lee's victory, the Army Air Force had begun flying missions against the Japanese-held Central Solomons, New Georgia, and Kokumbona. The American squadrons controlled the skies over Guadalcanal and its sea approaches, which they patrolled assiduously, choking off supply and reinforcement deliveries to the beleaguered Japanese on the island. Flight operations, which consumed forty-five thousand gallons of gasoline each day, occupied two hundred men twenty-four hours a day, seven days a week. They ceaselessly transferred gasoline drums to the airfield from hidden dumps in the jungle and refueled planes.[40]

On November 18, eleven B-17s staged through Henderson and joined four B-26s for a mission against Buin; eight P-38s from Fighter Two escorted them.

After two sorties against their targets, the B-17s turned back to Guadalcanal. The P-38s were nowhere in sight when, without warning, eighteen Zeros swarmed the bombers head-on. Enemy gunfire killed the lead bomber's pilot, badly wounded the copilot, and knocked out the plane's left engine, setting the wing on fire. Colonel LaVerne "Blondie" Saunders, the commander of the 11th Bomber Group and a passenger on the plane, took the controls and guided the plane to a soft landing in the sea near Vella Lavella. The colonel and all the surviving crewmen reached shore in rubber rafts, although the injured copilot died en route. Shuttled from island to island by a coast watcher and assorted natives and missionaries, the airmen were finally picked up by a PBY and flown to Guadalcanal. Saunders was awarded the Navy Cross.

Marine Captain Joe Foss returned to Guadalcanal on January 1 after spending six weeks in Australia recovering from malaria. Exactly two weeks later, Foss shot down three enemy planes to raise his total to twenty-six, equaling Eddie Rickenbacker's record from World War I.[41]

ON THE FIRST ANNIVERSARY OF the Pearl Harbor attack, Major Joe Sailer, VMSB-132's skipper, took off from Henderson Field on his twenty-sixth mission since arriving on Guadalcanal on November 1. During the Naval Battle of Guadalcanal on November 13–15, Sailer had scored five direct hits during six dive-bombing runs. Five-foot-eleven and 155 pounds in good times, Sailer, as did practically everyone who served for long on Guadalcanal, had dropped a lot of weight, even though his mostly abstemious squadron bartered its rum ration for extra food.

Sailer had been a Marine Reserves pilot since 1930, the year he graduated from Princeton with an engineering degree. He later acquired a master's degree and, between active duty tours, worked for Sperry Gyroscope Corporation, where he helped perfect the Sperry autopilot and bombsight. He tested the bombsight in England in 1940.

On December 7, Sailer and his squadron of Dauntless dive bombers swooped down on a formation of Japanese destroyers. The flaps of Sailer's SBD became stuck when he attempted to recover from his dive, and the plane was unable to rise above a thousand feet. It became an easy target. A Japanese float biplane pilot spotted the stricken aircraft and riddled it with machine-gun fire, sending it plummeting into the water. Sailer and his gunner died.[42]

7

January–February:
Operation KE and US Victory

Guadalcanal is under observation of the whole world. Do not expect to return, not even one man, if the occupation is not successful.

—JAPANESE OFFICER'S REMARKS TO HIS MEN[1]

Total and complete defeat of the Japanese forces on Guadalcanal effected 1625 today. . . . Am happy to report this kind of compliance with your orders. . . . "Tokyo Express" no longer has terminus on Guadalcanal.

—GENERAL ALEXANDER PATCH MESSAGE TO
ADMIRAL HALSEY ON FEBRUARY 9[2]

Old Glory flies unchallenged over all the island. Her navy smashed repeatedly at sea, her Zeros and Mitsubishis erased from the skies and her proudest regiments now masses of rotting corpses, Japan has tasted defeat for the first time in a thousand years.

—INS REPORT OF FEBRUARY 10[3]

IN EARLY DECEMBER HALSEY HAD ordered Major General Millard Harmon to drive the Japanese from Guadalcanal, and on January 2 Harmon activated XIV Corps for that purpose under Major General Alexander "Sandy" Patch. XIV Corps's principal elements were the Americal, 25th, and 2nd Marine Divisions, and the independent 147th Infantry Regiment—in all, ten infantry regiments, along with artillery, tank, medical, transportation, and antiaircraft units. Brigadier General Edmund Sebree, formerly the Americal's assistant commander, became its new commander.

Major General Lawton "Joe" Collins reported to Patch on December 11, a week before his 25th Division began arriving from Pearl Harbor. The 25th had been part of the regular Army's "Hawaii Division" until October 1941, when the division's four regiments were divided into the 24th and 25th Divisions, based at Schofield Barracks. While the 24th remained in Hawaii, the 25th was on its way to the Solomons with its two regiments of regulars, the 27th and 35th, and a National Guard regiment, the 161st from Washington state. For the past six months Collins had rigorously trained his men in Hawaii's hills; he was now satisfied that they were physically and mentally prepared for combat.[4]

Collins's father, an Irish immigrant, had been a drummer boy with the Ohio volunteers during the Civil War. Later, the Collinses settled in Algiers, Louisiana, where Joe was born in 1896, the tenth of eleven children. He learned algebra and astronomy from a blind summer tutor and entered West Point when he was seventeen, graduating in 1917.

Collins reached France after World War I ended. He spent twelve years as a West Point instructor and as a student in various Army schools. After duty tours in Philadelphia and the Philippines, he became chief of staff of VII Corps, and following the Pearl Harbor attack, he was responsible for defending Hawaii.[5]

Rapid flanking movements, Collins firmly believed, were more effective and stingier with men's lives than frontal attacks. When his division went into action, Collins intended to emphasize maneuver over direct force, isolating the enemy in scattered pockets that could later be eliminated.

THE STALEMATE WEST OF THE Matanikau that began November 23 was now nearing its end. Throughout December, American patrols had reported ebbing Japanese resistance and even troop withdrawals from the enemy lines. When the Americal Division reached full strength and the 25th Infantry Division was in place, Patch would have the manpower—close to fifty thousand troops on the island—to launch a powerful offensive.

He and his aides drafted a plan to push the American lines a mile and a half to the west during the attack's first phase beginning January 10. While the 2nd Marine Division advanced along the northern coastline toward Cape Esperance, the 25th Division would tackle the more problematic southern sector—a complex landscape of jagged ridges separated by deep ravines and rivers. The Army would continue its practice of leading off major operations with units lacking combat experience—although in the 25th Division's case, the soldiers were well-trained regulars.

Collins's men were to take over for the America's bloodied 132nd Regiment and clear out the Gifu. The 25th was also assigned to capture two other important features in the southern end of the attack axis: the "Sea Horse," which consisted of Hills 43 and 44, and the "Galloping Horse," less than a mile northwest of the Sea Horse. The Galloping Horse was a cluster of five hills that, when seen together, inspired the nickname.

To the 25th's 35th Regiment fell the task of securing the Gifu and Sea Horse; the 27th Regiment would seize the Galloping Horse. The 161st Infantry was placed in reserve, and the 2nd Battalion of the America's 182nd Regiment was ordered to plug the gap between the 25th Division's two attacking regiments.[6]

Three forks of the upper Matanikau carved up the 25th Division's area of operations. The Gifu lay east of the southeast fork, the southeast and southwest forks bracketed the Sea Horse, and the southwest and northwest forks bounded the Galloping Horse. Because of the extremely difficult terrain, each objective had to be approached in its own way—the Gifu from the north, the Sea Horse from the south, and the Galloping Horse from the north.[7]

The Army was better equipped than Vandegrift's Marines had ever been, and it faced Japanese units that were being inexorably ground down by casualties, starvation, and disease. None of this made adapting to Guadalcanal's harsh environment any easier for the new men. James Epperson's poem "Life in Guadalcanal" described their difficulty in becoming acclimated:

"Down in these muddy valleys.
We sure are in a spot,
Battling in the terrific heat,
In the land that God forgot."

Robert Kennington, a 25th Division infantryman, had grown up in Florida and lived in North Carolina, but "Guadalcanal put both of them to shame. In the jungle the trees block any breeze. You don't get any air at all. You can cut the humidity with a knife." Some of his comrades fainted from the heat. "They just passed out along the trail," he wrote.[8]

A lieutenant described the shallow foxholes as "ovens." Heat waves blurred distant objects. "With that kind of heat there was no use for binoculars," he wrote. "The images would be so distorted by mirage that you couldn't see a thing."[9]

The 25th Division launched its triple-headed operation on schedule January 10. The 35th Infantry's 2nd Battalion, given the thankless job of clearing the Gifu, conducted a reconnaissance in force and surrounded the enclave. This was not a major tactical achievement because the Japanese had no intention of escaping and leaving behind their many ill and wounded comrades; they were determined to starve together and die together.

The 35th's other two battalions approached the two hills of the Sea Horse without artillery preparation, hoping to achieve surprise, but they were the surprised ones—when the Japanese suddenly attacked and nearly broke their lines.

Sergeants William Fournier and Lewis Hall teamed up to help crush the assault, with Fournier cradling a machine-gun and tripod and Hall pulling the trigger. Both men were killed and posthumously awarded Medals of Honor. The battalions dug in for the night just south of Hill 43.

The next day, January 11, the 35th Regiment drove the Japanese from the hill, captured the Sea Horse's other promontory, Hill 44, and advanced four miles. When the area was pronounced secured on January 16 and the soldiers occupied high ground overlooking the Matanikau River, the 35th claimed to have killed 558 Japanese.[10]

FOR THIRTY MINUTES EARLY JANUARY 10, field artillery batteries bombarded a water hole near the Galloping Horse where Japanese soldiers were believed to be entrenched. The hundred-gun barrage with fifty-seven hundred 105mm and 75 mm howitzer rounds was coordinated to the split second—a new technique known as "Time on Target." Its first use during the Pacific War was by American units at the water hole. All initial rounds hit their targets simultaneously, like a cloudburst, without preliminary aiming fire. With no warning and no time to seek cover, the thinking went, enemy troops would die in shockingly high numbers. The artillery fire was delivered in short, intensive bursts, followed by intervals of silence—so that the Japanese would believe the bombardment had ended and it was safe to come into the open, where they could be shelled again. Following the artillery onslaught near the Galloping Horse, P-39s and dive bombers dropped bombs and depth charges on Hill 57's reverse slopes and ravines. The 27th Infantry's 1st and 3rd Battalions raced to the crests of Hills 57 and 52.

A water shortage delayed the 3rd Battalion's attacks on Hill 53 on January 11. When the battalion resumed its advance, Japanese strongpoints barred its way. The exhausted battalion was taken out of the line and replaced with the 2nd Battalion on January 12. It too failed to capture the hill, stubbornly defended by Japanese on Sims Ridge.

On January 13 Major Charles Davis unholstered his pistol and, with four other men, rushed Sims Ridge, where they killed the remaining defenders and broke the logjam. Private James Jones described the small party's sanguine fight for the ridge in his novel The Thin Red Line. The "electrifying effect" of Davis's attack inspired the battalion to capture Hill 53, the final Galloping Horse stronghold. Davis was awarded the Medal of Honor.[11]

Early January 13, the 2nd Marine Division, led by Brigadier General Alphonse DeCarre, its assistant commander, and operating for the first time as a complete division, began advancing along the mile-and-a-half corridor between Point Cruz and Hill 66, the end point of the 182nd Regiment's November attack. Ranged against them were the strongest remaining Japanese units: the survivors of the 38th and Sendai Divisions. The Second Marine Regiment advanced on the left from Hill 66, while the Eighth Marines pushed along the coast. In reserve was the untried Sixth Marine Regiment of World War I Belleau Wood fame that had arrived on January 4.

The Marines' progress was slow because enemy troops occupied fortified, cleverly camouflaged positions on the nearby hilltops. On January 15 a tank-supported attack failed to break up the enemy defenses, although tanks were often effective at flushing Japanese, who could then be "shot down like running quail," observed news correspondent Ira Wolfert. At one point, with the attack stalled, Captain Henry Crowe, a fierce redhead, rallied a half-dozen dazed Marines who had taken cover in a shell hole. "Goddamn it," Crowe said, "you'll never get a Purple Heart hiding in a foxhole! Follow me!" The Marines joined Crowe in a rifle-grenade attack that wiped out a Japanese position.

On this day, two Marines trained by the Army Chemical Warfare Service used a flamethrower for the first time during the Pacific War. Covered by automatic weapons fire, they crawled to within twenty-five yards of a Japanese bunker and unleashed a fiery arc of gasoline on the occupants. Five enemy soldiers died and two escaped, injured. The results so encouraged the Marines that, minutes later, they used the flamethrower to destroy two more bunkers. Flamethrowers quickly became indispensable tools for clearing caves and bunkers, but their operators just as quickly became prime targets—their casualty rates often exceeded 50 percent. When flamethrowers were modified so they could be used by tanks, operator casualties dropped sharply.[12]

GENERAL PATCH GRUMBLED TO ARMY Chief of Staff George C. Marshall that the Army had not gotten due credit for the fighting it had done since December. "The Army made a larger contribution to the operations here on the island than is popularly understood," he wrote. Reports that there were "only a few starving Japs left on the island may give a false impression" because at the moment "we are closed with him in the most desperate form of fighting," he said with a touch of hyperbole. Patch's plaints notwithstanding, the 1st Marine Division's accomplishments on Guadalcanal would always overshadow the Army's.

On January 18, the advance along the coast paused while units from the Army's unaffiliated 147th Regiment and from the American's 182nd Regiment took the point from the Second and Eighth Marines. The Sixth Marines, formerly in reserve, was now the only 2nd Marine Division infantry unit still on the line. The Eighth Marines had gone into reserve after having killed 643 Japanese between January 13 and 17, with the 3rd Battalion accounting for more than half of those deaths.[13]

WHEN THE OFFENSIVE BEGAN ON January 10, US aircraft dropped eighteen thousand leaflets urging the Japanese to surrender. The leaflets extolled the comparatively pleasant life the Japanese soldiers would enjoy as war prisoners. Two days later, there rained down from the skies twenty-five thousand copies of a poem written by Emperor Hirohito in 1941 expressing his desire for peace. Japanese soldiers did not lay down their weapons.[14]

Besides trying its hand at psychological manipulation, the Army also attempted to use mules to tow 75mm pack artillery belonging to the 97th Field Artillery Battalion. It seemed like a good idea to use pack animals to negotiate Guadalcanal's rough terrain. It proved not to be.

With 182 mules needed to pull each battery of four guns, the slow-moving animal convoys caused traffic bottlenecks. Moreover, mules refused to cross stream beds or swamps, and each mule ate eight pounds of oats and fourteen pounds of hay each day; two tons of feed had to be hauled to the front daily to provision a battery of mules. The experiment was a failure.[15]

The leaflets and the mules were inarguable flops, but using boats to transport wounded men downriver from Mount Austen and the adjoining high country was not. The boat line on the Matanikau—it was nicknamed the "Pusha Maru"—carried supplies upriver and wounded men downriver. However, Jeeps still transported most of the wounded men to hospitals after they had been laboriously hand-carried on litters, swung on cables over chasms, and skidded down steep hills to the roads.[16]

THE STARVING FRONTLINE JAPANESE SOLDIERS dreamed of food and obsessively discussed their favorite dishes as they lay on their straw mats, scarcely able to stand. "Lately more and more of us have started to eat lizards," a Sergeant Murayama wrote in his diary in late December. They were best eaten broiled. When the soldiers ran out of lizards, they ate leaves.

Murayama, who had been on Guadalcanal from the beginning, was in one of Colonel Oka's battalions along the upper Matanikau. No food reached Murayama's men during late December, and starvation set in. "Day after day, we have done nothing except drink water and get up and lie down just like a sick man," Murayama wrote on January 1. Incessant US artillery barrages and air strikes robbed them of sleep and spoiled their attack plans. Murayama's great fear was that his men would die without getting a chance to fight. "Every one of us is as good as dead now," he wrote. "Our struggles to keep alive are worse than death itself."

In his last diary entry, on January 9, he reported, "Exploding shells burn up the field and jungle, so that gradually the area in which we can conceal ourselves becomes smaller and smaller." Murayama did not survive; an American soldier recovered his bloodstained journal.[17]

Another Seventeenth Army frontline soldier, Second Lieutenant Yasuo Ko'o, devised a morbid system that estimated a man's life expectancy by his ability to stand or sit. If a man could stand, he might live thirty days; if he could sit up, three weeks; if he could only lie down, one week. If he urinated lying down, he had three days to live; if he stopped speaking, two days; and if he stopped blinking, just one day.[18]

IN SEPTEMBER, IMPERIAL GENERAL HEADQUARTERS had sent Lieutenant Colonel Masanobu Tsuji to Guadalcanal to analyze General Kawaguchi's debacle on Bloody Ridge, and he was still on the island in October when the Sendai Division was demolished at the same place. Reporting to his superiors in Tokyo in November on the Guadalcanal situation, Tsuji confessed that he had underestimated the Marines' firepower and fighting ability. His somber report inspired a broader review by Japan's top military leaders. Revealingly, none of the admirals or generals in the Eighth Fleet and Eighth Area Army appeared to be confident that a new offensive in January would succeed.

The heretofore-taboo word *withdrawal* began surfacing in confidential discussions at the highest levels of the army and navy. Colonel Sako Tanemura of the Army General Staff, who strongly believed that Guadalcanal was the Pacific War's pivotal battle, was present for the talks in Tokyo. "Today there is the impression that Japan is on the verge of rise or fall. . . . If we should be defeated on Guadalcanal, it is certain we will lose the Pacific war itself," Tanemura wrote in his diary.

Imperial Headquarters began to waver in its commitment to Guadalcanal, diverting the 51st Division from its intended reinforcement of the island and sending it instead to New Guinea.

The Japanese military leadership convened an emergency meeting on Christmas Day at the Imperial Palace. The session followed General Hyakutake's message of two days earlier advising, "No food available and we can no longer send out scouts. We can do nothing to withstand the enemy's offensive. Seventeenth Army now requests permission to break into the enemy's positions and die an honorable death rather than die of hunger in our own dugouts."[19]

The immediate obstacle to a new offensive in January was a shortage of troop transports. The Japanese Navy had lost twenty transports in the Solomons, and too few remained to bring to Guadalcanal the fifty thousand men the Eighth Area Army planned to assemble at Rabaul for the new operation.

Moreover, overwhelming American air power was squeezing the supply line to Guadalcanal to the extent that the army was "bound hand and foot," powerless to mount major attacks, wrote Major General Shuichi Miyazaki, the Seventeenth Army's chief of staff. American aircraft at the same time were safeguarding the ocean transit of US reinforcements and supplies that were now pouring onto the island. There could be no January offensive unless Imperial General Headquarters in Tokyo committed more shipping and warplanes to the Solomons, the army said.[20]

Hideki Tojo, Japan's prime minister and war minister, balked at the army's request for an additional three hundred thousand tons of shipping. The tonnage, he said, was essential to sustaining Japan's war production; steel and aluminum production were already slipping because of a shortage of ships' bottoms and US submarine attacks; Tojo said Japan had no more to spare. The debate over shipping and the proposed January offensive at times grew so heated at Tokyo headquarters that staff officers came to blows. Tojo won the argument—the army did not get the increased tonnage. Withdrawal remained the only option on the table.

Informed that evacuation was being contemplated, Emperor Hirohito requested details. On December 31, Tojo and Japan's army and navy chiefs went to the Imperial Palace to present their new Solomon Islands plan to Hirohito.

The plan, called Operation KE, ended efforts to recapture Guadalcanal while readying soldiers on the island for evacuation in early February. Afterward, Japanese forces would defend the Solomon Islands north of Guadalcanal and capture Port Moresby.

At the end of the one-hour, forty-minute meeting, Hirohito approved the evacuation plan and issued a new rescript praising the army for its sacrifices on Guadalcanal.[21]

In his diary that day, Admiral Ugaki summed up 1942 as a year whose "brilliant" early months had been tarnished by "miserable setbacks" after Midway in June. "The invasions of Hawaii, Fiji, Samoa, and New Caledonia, liberation of India and destruction of the British Far East Fleet have all scattered like dreams . . . it's most regrettable."[22]

AT THE END OF DECEMBER the Japanese switched to a new communications codebook, "RO." The change was strictly procedural, but it could not have come at a worse time for the American code breakers; it effectively cloaked the enemy's plans and actions in January. US intelligence analysts had made progress in deciphering the old codes, but now they could only try to divine the enemy's intentions by tracking the movements of troops, ships, and headquarters. They still assumed that the Japanese planned to launch a major offensive in January.[23]

The fact that Tokyo Express runs resumed in January after a nearly three-week hiatus—during the interim, submarines attempted to shuttle supplies to Guadalcanal—supported the Allies' presumption that a new buildup had begun, prefatory to a new offensive. Seaplanes from Rekata Bay and dive bombers flew cover for the nighttime convoys, which the Americans tried to disrupt with PT boats and a "Black Cat" squadron of night-flying PBY Catalinas.

During the night of January 2, linked supply drums were cast into the sea off Cape Esperance amid swarming PT boats. US fighter planes shot up the drums. On January 10 enough supplies were landed to last the Seventeenth Army a week, but little food reached the frontline troops. Also put ashore were twenty-three days' rations for the Japanese rearguard battalion that was scheduled to land on January 15.

Between January 14 and February 9, Japanese submarines made twenty-eight trips to Guadalcanal with fifteen hundred tons of supplies. One large submarine might carry enough food to feed Japanese troops on the island for two days, but the growing presence of small Allied craft offshore made the submarines' task increasingly perilous. Two subs were lost during the January resupply operation. One of them, the *I-1*, surfaced off Kamimbo on January 29, immediately drawing the attention of a New Zealand antisubmarine corvette, *Kiwi*. Manning deck guns and machine-guns, *Kiwi*'s crewmen wiped out the *I-1*'s gunners, and the corvette proceeded to ram the *I-1* three times. Brandishing a sword, *I-1*'s navigator attempted to board the *Kiwi*, but fell between the two vessels and was made a prisoner instead.

The New Zealand gunners' intensive firing caused the *Kiwi*'s deck guns to overheat and fall silent, but a sister corvette, the *Moa*, raced to the scene and continued to pummel the submarine. *I-1*'s senior surviving officer issued orders to beach the sub, which was hopelessly outgunned and no longer submersible. Grabbing handfuls of documents, fifty officers and crewmen escaped to join Guadalcanal's ground troops. Thirty men died on the submarine.[24]

Navy divers later searched *I-1* for classified material, finding old codebooks and call signs, as well as charts suggesting future targets. Also left behind during the crew's hasty exit were communication codes to be used during the coming months, and documents describing the *I-1*'s radio and sonar ranges, the sub's specifications and capabilities, and the different classes of Japanese submarines.[25]

CONTRIBUTING TO THE ILLUSION OF a new Japanese offensive was the completion on December 29 of a new Japanese airfield at Munda Point, New Georgia Island, 175 miles from Guadalcanal, despite nearly daily air raids by SBDs and

B-17s. Operating from Munda, Zeros could remain over Guadalcanal even longer than when they flew from the new airfields at Buin or Kolombangara; Bettys could double their bomb loads. When the Guadalcanal evacuations began, Japanese squadrons could rise from these airstrips and disrupt Cactus Air Force operations.

New Japanese runways notwithstanding, the Americans were now giving the enemy a taste of what they had endured for months. On Christmas Eve, Dauntless dive bombers destroyed ten Zeros on the ground at Munda while Army fighters and Wildcats knocked enemy planes out of the air. A week later, PBY "Black Cats" dropped small bombs at fifteen-minute intervals with rubber bands attached to their fins to make them whistle, and milk bottles that also made annoying sounds while falling from the sky.

On January 5, Rear Admiral Walden Ainsworth's cruiser-destroyer Task Force 67 bombarded Munda Airfield for an hour, firing 3,000 six-inch shells and 1,400 five-inch projectiles at the airfield. The extent of the damage was unknown, but it could not have been devastating—the airfield was back in operation eighteen hours later.[26]

In response to increasing numbers of Japanese ships seen in Rabaul's Simpson Harbor, B-17s bombed the harbor every night for a week, and US submarines roved the sea lanes between Rabaul and Guadalcanal. American subs had played a small role in the battle for naval supremacy, but they now went on a small tear. *Wahoo* sank a five-hundred-ton supply ship, and *Grouper* put torpedoes into the four-thousand-ton transport *Bandoeng Maru* and sent her to the bottom. *Albacore* sank the light cruiser *Tenryu*, which had fought at Savo Island on August 9 and bombarded Henderson Field early November 14. *Sea Dragon* and *Grayback* each sank a Japanese submarine.[27]

The Japanese attempted to conceal their true purposes by creating a spike in radio traffic on Java, initiating a faux naval operation east of the Marshall Islands, and launching nighttime air raids against Port Darwin, an important Allied base in northwest Australia.[28]

LIEUTENANT COLONEL KUMAO IMOTO, AN operations staff officer in the Eighth Area Army, volunteered to hand-carry the evacuation order to General Hyakutake on Guadalcanal. During the night of January 14–15, a destroyer squadron landed Imoto at Cape Esperance with six hundred troops—most of them from the Yano Battalion and misleadingly described as a "reinforcement unit"—to act as the evacuation rear guard.

"The troops in the Solomon Islands will give up the task of recapturing Guadalcanal Island and will withdraw to the rear. After withdrawal, they will hold New Georgia Island and the Solomon Islands from Santa Isabel north, including the Bismarck Archipelago," the evacuation order said. The stiff language masked the order's enormous implication: a humiliating defeat for Japan, the first of the Pacific War.[29]

Imoto hiked eighteen hours through the jungle to deliver the evacuation order to Hyakutake's Seventeenth Army headquarters. On the trail he passed the remains of soldiers who had died from hunger and disease—persuasive evidence, if Imoto needed any, that withdrawal was the correct decision.

Imoto found Hyakutake living in a cave beneath the roots of an enormous tree, and as he explained the reasons for the evacuation order, the general closed his eyes. He needed time to think before he could respond, he said. His chief of staff, Major General Shuichi Miyazaki, and other high-ranking Seventeenth Army officers vehemently opposed withdrawal. "We cannot execute it," declared Miyazaki. "Therefore, we must attack and die, and give everyone an example of Japanese Army tradition." Colonel Haruo Konuma was even more adamant. "It's impossible, so leave us alone!"

But after consideration Hyakutake agreed to obey the order. He told Imoto that withdrawal would be difficult—indeed, retreating from a contested battle-field is one of the most dangerous tactical maneuvers—but it "must be carried out at any cost. . . . I will do my best." Imoto and Hyakutake calmed the agitated Seventeenth Army staff officers and convinced them to comply. Orders sent to Generals Maruyama and Sano at the battlefront said the withdrawal of able-bodied soldiers to the island's western coast must begin in a week. Critically ill and wounded men were to be left behind.[30]

FEW SOLDIERS ARE AS DANGEROUS as cornered combat veterans who have vowed to die fighting. Examples include Leonidas's 300 at Thermopylae, the 182 Americans at the Alamo, and, more relevantly to the Gifu's defenders, the 300 rebel samurai warriors surrounded in 1877 by 30,000 imperial troops at Shiroyama, Japan.

Although they were starving and ill, emaciated and wounded, the two to three hundred Japanese soldiers in the Gifu were better-armed and -entrenched than all of their doomed predecessors. They manned forty well-camouflaged pillboxes whose fields of fire overlapped. There were also small groups of snipers and light machine-guns in shallow foxholes. The defenders had plenty of ammunition, and they were making the 2nd Battalion, 35th Infantry pay dearly for every yard it advanced.

The battalion had reached Mount Austen on January 10, relieving the Americal's 132nd Infantry after its failure to capture the Gifu in December, while suffering 112 battle deaths. On January 12 the 2nd Battalion attempted to advance, but dozens of buzzing Nambu machine-guns drove them back.

Two days later the battalion rated itself just 75 percent battle-effective—its strength eroded by casualties and illness—and the 35th Infantry's antitank company was sent to reinforce it.

From his headquarters on the Matanikau, Colonel Oka, commander of the 228th Regiment, ordered his men to leave the Gifu, slip through the American lines, and march to the coast. Oka and his staff then left their command post and hiked through the jungle to the Seventeenth Army's rear.

Major Takeyosho Inagaki's soldiers in the Gifu, however, refused to abandon their sick and wounded comrades. They ate their last rations and braced for further American assaults.

On January 15, the 2nd Battalion again attacked, and was again repelled. A withdrawal order sent to a shaken American platoon was misconstrued as being intended for the entire battalion; it pulled back in disarray. The next day, the battalion commander was relieved, and Lieutenant Colonel Stanley Larsen succeeded him.[31]

After envelopment and direct attacks failed to dislodge the defenders, XIV Corps intelligence officers broadcast a surrender appeal in Japanese over a loudspeaker. Five emaciated enemy soldiers straggled in on January 16, but additional broadcasts yielded no more prisoners. A Japanese company commander wrote in his diary, "I heard one of the enemy talking busily in Japanese using a loud speaker. He was probably telling us to come out. What fools the Americans are. The Japanese army will stick it out to the end. This position must be defended with our lives. . . . We have no fear." An entry in another Japanese diary scorned the speaker's "very, very poor Japanese. We could hardly understand him . . . how in the world do the Americans expect to have us respect their propaganda when they speak such terrible Japanese?"[32]

On January 17, forty-nine howitzers shelled the Gifu with seventeen hundred rounds, and over the next two days soldiers knocked out a pair of pillboxes and pounded the stronghold with heavy weapons.

Three Marine light tanks driven by 25th Division reconnaissance troops churned up the Jeep trail leading to Mount Austen's 1,514-foot summit on January 22. Two broke down, but the third reached the top. With sixteen infantrymen accompanying it, the lone tank, manned by Captain Teddy Deese and two volunteers, entered the Gifu's northeast side and destroyed three pillboxes with 37mm high-explosive shells, canister, and machine-guns before exiting. Re-entering the stronghold, the tank shattered five more pillboxes and carved a two-hundred-yard-wide gap in the enemy defenses. Army infantrymen moved in.

At 2:30 a.m. on January 23, Major Inagaki and about a hundred men, with high-pitched shrieks of "Banzai!," attacked the entrenched US infantrymen and antitank guns. In just twenty minutes the Americans wiped out the attackers almost to the last man. At daybreak eighty-five gore-caked bodies could be seen sprawled in front of the American positions. Among the dead were Inagaki, a Major Nishihata, eight captains, and fifteen lieutenants.[33]

That morning the battalion swept the Gifu of remaining enemy troops against light opposition. Lieutenant Colonel Larsen reported that his men found the partially cannibalized bodies of several US officers killed earlier in the battle. "Meat had been cut off the thighs right down to the bone and had been eaten. Obviously, it must have been the only food they had." A dead Japanese warrant officer's mess kit yielded a human liver.[34]

The operation cost the 2nd Battalion 64 killed and 42 wounded. It reported having killed 518 Japanese soldiers, including Inagaki and his staff, and capturing forty machine-guns and twelve mortars; 29 prisoners were taken, one of whom said the defenders had eaten nothing for a week.[35]

The enemy dead were bulldozed into a mass grave.[36]

THE GIFU'S CAPTURE COINCIDED WITH a fresh XIV Corps drive westward from the Sea Horse and Galloping Horse areas. A Composite Army-Marine (CAM) division—the Sixth Marines, two battalions of the Americal 182nd, and two battalions from the 147th Regiment—attacked along the coastline while the 25th Division advanced on its left, farther inland. On January 22, CAM gained a thousand yards against fierce resistance.

The 25th Division scaled a sinuous ridge nicknamed "the Snake," which poked above the jungle canopy and was the main approach to Hills 87, 88, and 89. Four artillery batteries shelled Hill 87 with 75mm, 105mm, and 155mm guns as a prelude to an assault by the 1st Battalion, 27th Infantry. The soldiers swarmed up the hill, but the Japanese were no longer there. The 1st Battalion went on to capture Hills 88, 89, 90, and 98 east and south of Kokumbona.[37]

The next day, January 23, the 1st Battalion entered Kokumbona—for months the elusive object of Vandegrift's Marines—while CAM resumed its march westward. Stalled by Japanese forces at a ravine east of Hill 99, CAM's Sixth Marines stormed the ravine and killed more than two hundred enemy soldiers.

The 2nd and 3rd Battalions of the 27th Regiment spearheaded the drive west on January 25 toward the Poha River, a mile and a half northwest of Kokumbona. The infantrymen reached the river late that afternoon. Cape Esperance was less than twenty miles away.[38]

As the Americans drove the Japanese inexorably westward, the January campaign appeared to be winding down. American generals did not suspect that their swift progress was because the enemy was simultaneously conducting a phased withdrawal.

PATCH AND HIS STAFF STILL believed that the Japanese planned to soon send fifty thousand reinforcements to Guadalcanal from Truk and Rabaul. In the backs of their minds lurked the nightmare scenario that had haunted Vandegrift—a massive Japanese amphibious landing at Lunga Point that would overwhelm the perimeter and Henderson Field.

Taking counsel from his fears, Patch recalled two of the 25th Division's three regiments to the perimeter while praising Collins's division for having broken "the enemy's power to offer further effective defense by fighting its way into Kokumbona." Patch evidently still believed the Army's efforts on Guadalcanal were unappreciated when he wrote to his wife in early February: "What is not known in the US is that our forces have given the enemy on this front a genuine licking. But he is right now coming back with bigger and bigger stuff. And a fight on a grand scale is just in the offing."

Based on the intelligence reports of ships gathering at Rabaul and Shortland, Admiral Halsey also anticipated a Japanese offensive. He began deploying dozens of battleships, carriers, escort carriers, cruisers, and destroyers to the Guadalcanal area, bracing for an onslaught by more than fifty Japanese warships and 175 aircraft.[39]

DETERMINED TO DESTROY ENEMY TROOPS on the island and block their escape into the southwestern mountains, Patch in early January sent I Company of the 147th Infantry by boat to Beaufort Bay in southwest Guadalcanal. The soldiers marched north over the mountains to Tatamoili on the Kokumbona-Beaufort Bay Trail and occupied defensive positions. But no Japanese troops appeared on the trail.

A few weeks later, the reinforced 2nd Battalion of the American's 132nd Infantry under Colonel Alexander George was loaded onto landing craft and taken to a beach near Verahue, ten miles southwest of Cape Esperance and behind enemy lines, in the hope of trapping retreating enemy troops. Japanese aircraft spotted the landing craft and their destroyer escorts. Six enemy dive bombers attacked and sank the destroyer *DeHaven* with two bombs; she went down with 167 crewmen.

Ashore, the 2nd Battalion trapped no one, but did experience the frustration of watching several hundred enemy soldiers board ships without being able to stop them. Poor radio communication prevented the battalion from contacting headquarters and calling down artillery fire on the beach. During the next two days, the battalion advanced three and a half miles to Titi, and then cautiously patrolled the area during the following two days without encountering any Japanese. Unable to contact George's battalion, Patch dispatched a staff officer by boat with orders for George's men to march northeast and rendezvous with CAM. On February 7, the battalion was at last ready to move out.[40]

CAM, which had been advancing westward along the coast without encountering serious resistance, ran into stiff opposition on January 30 along the Bonegi River. Led by the 147th Infantry and commanded personally by General Sebree, the drive ground to a standstill. The Americans had met the Japanese rear guard— Major Keiji Yano's battalion—dug into well-concealed positions west of the river. The stubborn Japanese defenders caught the Americans by surprise and held up their advance for two days. After the rear guard withdrew, the 147th was able to cross the Bonegi and reach Tassafaronga Point.[41]

The stench of decomposing Japanese corpses hung heavily in the hills and valleys as the American troops drew nearer to Cape Esperance. To counteract the sickening smell, some soldiers adopted the practice of breaking Pall Malls in half and sticking the ends in their nostrils.

Along the Tambalego River, Army units encountered live, incapacitated enemy soldiers, which was even worse. Lieutenant John George was appalled by the "intense human suffering and starvation . . . their maggoty bodies breeding clouds of flies. The insects swarmed onto our food during meals and prevented any rest during daylight hours."[42]

ON JANUARY 31, THE 2ND Marine Regiment, which had fought on Guadalcanal, Tulagi, and Florida Islands longer than any other regiment, left Lunga Point for a rest area in New Zealand. They were the first Marines to land on August 7, and their experiences during six months of campaigning were etched in their wizened features and gaunt bodies; some were in such poor shape, due to illness, that they had to be hoisted in slings to the deck of their transport ship.[43]

AS PLANNED, THE JAPANESE HAD begun withdrawing from their lines during the night of January 22–23. General Hyakutake had rescinded his orders to fight to the last man, and had issued a new directive: fall back to Cape Esperance and there offer "desperate resistance." The emaciated, exhausted men of the 38th Division passed through the Yano rear guard and the Sendai Division, which were both also pulling back. Scouts screened the rearward movement, offering enough resistance to slow the Americans. The Japanese destroyed artillery, tractors, and trucks, and buried or threw into the sea excess ammunition.

Senior commanders had been told the truth about the withdrawal—that it was a prelude to evacuation by sea—but the fighting men believed they were regrouping for a new offensive. One officer reportedly told his men, "From now on the occupying operation of Guadalcanal is under observation of the whole world.

Do not expect to return, not even one man, if the occupation is not successful." Throughout the Japanese withdrawal, Americans and Japanese continued to die daily.[44]

Wounded and ill Japanese soldiers who had the good fortune to be transported to Cape Esperance were evacuated in late January. The evacuees' condition shocked soldiers at Shortland Island. "Hardly human beings, they were just skin and bones dressed in military uniform, thin as bamboo sticks," wrote Ishida Yahachi. "They were so light, it was like carrying infants. Only their eyes were bright. . . . When I put a spoon with some lukewarm rice gruel to their mouths, large teardrops rolled down their faces, and they said thank you in tiny mosquito-like voices."[45]

FOR THE FIRST TIME IN two months dozens of Bettys and Zeros appeared over Henderson Field at Tojo time on January 25. Thus began a campaign to temporarily wrest air superiority from the Americans. The Japanese hoped Americans would also misconstrue the air campaign to be a prelude to the phony offensive the Japanese had conceived from false radio transmissions and misleading naval maneuvers. The January 25 raid and another one two days later did not alter the balance of air power, much less establish the air superiority that the Imperial Japanese Navy believed was essential. Yet the Eighth Area Army insisted that Operation KE go forward anyway.[46]

Meanwhile, US fighter and bomber squadrons continued to carry out raids farther up the Solomon Islands chain. On January 31, Lieutenant Jefferson DeBlanc led six VMF-112 Wildcats escorting a flight of dive bombers near Kolombangara, about two hundred miles northwest of Guadalcanal. Their mission was to disrupt the Tokyo Express. DeBlanc was in "perfect control" on this day, he later wrote. Indeed, he quickly shot down two Japanese "Rufe" float planes before ten Zeros suddenly swarmed the Wildcats. DeBlanc's machine-guns damaged the enemy flight leader's plane, and he shot up another Zero, which exploded.

Leaking fuel, DeBlanc turned back, but two Zeros closed in on the American formation and he took them on to lure them away from the dive bombers. Attacking one of them head-on, DeBlanc machine-gunned its gas tank and it exploded, pelting DeBlanc's plane with debris. He then shot down the second Zero. More Zeros converged on DeBlanc's Wildcat from behind, riddling his plane.

When his Wildcat became unflyable, DeBlanc bailed out, and he and another Marine pilot shot down about the same time, Staff Sergeant James Felton, swam to shore on Kolombangara, in enemy territory. Friendly natives found them and brought them into their village. A coast watcher bartered a sack of rice for them and brought them to Vella LaVella, where a PBY Catalina picked them up on February 12. DeBlanc's willingness to shield the SBDs while his own plane was leaking fuel, along with his five kills in a single day earned the Louisiana Cajun the Medal of Honor.[47]

ON FEBRUARY 1, TWENTY JAPANESE destroyers led by Rear Admiral Shintaro Hashimoto and escorted by forty Zeros and a dozen dive bombers left Shortland Harbor to retrieve the first evacuees from Guadalcanal. Ninety American fighters, dive bombers, and torpedo bombers attacked the Japanese warships in the Slot, damaging two destroyers, forcing them to turn back. They also shot down several Zeros. But the rest of the task force proceeded to Guadalcanal. That night, the destroyers reached Cape Esperance and Kamimbo Bay, where they were met by a swarm of American PT boats. Destroyer gunfire and a float plane bomb sank three PT boats.

Around midnight, the gaunt, ragged remnants of General Tadayoshi Sano's 38th Division—once eight thousand strong but now just twenty-three hundred men—were ready to leave what they now called "the island of death." Left behind at their former battle lines were comrades who stared sightlessly into the sky and would never be hungry again. Other comrades, still alive but unable to walk, were given ammunition to fight to the death, and were told to save a bullet for themselves. Each also received two tablets of bichloride of mercury—poison pills to hasten death.

Motorized rubber boats launched from the destroyers appeared offshore, the soldiers waded to them, and they were taken to the ships five to six hundred yards offshore. They clawed their way up the rope ladders to the ship decks, or were helped aboard by sailors. Two hours later, the destroyer squadron was on its way to Shortland, where the evacuees, wasted by starvation and disease, were initially able to eat only small portions of porridge.[48]

THE HEAVY CRUISER *CHICAGO* HAD limped away from the Battle of Savo Island without her bow—it had been blown off by an enemy torpedo—and was lucky to remain afloat. After repairs were made at Mare Island Navy Yard near San Francisco, *Chicago* returned to the South Pacific in late December with many new crewmen and a new skipper, Captain Ralph Davis. Davis succeeded Captain Howard Bode, whose actions at Savo Island were under official review.[49]

Chicago was now the flagship of Rear Admiral Robert Giffen's Task Force 18, one of six task forces that Admiral Halsey had sent to the Guadalcanal area to counter the enemy offensive believed to be imminent. Giffen's sixteen ships—two escort carriers, six cruisers, and eight destroyers—departed Efate, New Hebrides, for Guadalcanal on January 27 in the company of four troop transports.

Before reaching the island, TF-18 peeled away from the transports and their four destroyer escorts and swung around the island's south side. Giffen planned to rendezvous with a four-destroyer strike force southwest of Guadalcanal on January 30. Impatient with the slower escort carriers, which bristled with fifty-three warplanes, Giffen left two destroyers with the carriers on January 29 and put on speed for the rendezvous point.[50]

A Japanese plane spotted the task force south of Guadalcanal. Its six cruisers traveled in two parallel columns two miles behind the six destroyers, which were arrayed in a semicircle. Thirty-one torpedo-armed Bettys rose from the new Munda Airfield, from Buin, and from Rabaul to strike them.[51]

Thirty minutes after sunset, the Japanese warplanes, led by Lieutenant Commander Joji Higai, located Giffen's task force 50 miles north of Rennell Island, a large coral atoll 140 miles south of Guadalcanal. The enemy planes dove at TF-18 out of the still-bright western sky.

"Every ship in the force was under attack," wrote seaman James Fahey, who manned a 40mm machine-gun aboard the light cruiser *Montpelier*. "Bombs were exploding very close to the ships and torpedoes were cutting through the water as the ships twisted and turned."[52]

Antiaircraft fire sent flight leader Higai's plane plummeting toward the sea, and in its blazing last moments the bomber illuminated *Chicago* for Higai's comrades.

At 7:40 p.m. torpedoes smashed into *Chicago*'s starboard side and her number-three engine room. Marine Tom Sheble, firing a 20mm gun, felt the ship rise up and crash back down on the water with a great slap. Seawater poured into the forward and after engine rooms. Her decks awash, the cruiser lost power.

Her generator-powered pumps working furiously, *Chicago* stayed afloat through the night as the cruiser *Louisville* towed her toward Espiritu Santo. The fleet tug *Navajo* took over at 7:40 p.m. on January 30, while the two escort carriers and *Enterprise* provided air cover. Six destroyers formed a protective ring around *Chicago*.[53]

THAT AFTERNOON, A DOZEN JAPANESE torpedo planes appeared, looking for the *Enterprise*. The carrier's combat air patrol drove them off, and the intruders then stumbled upon the *Chicago* and her escorts. At 4:20 p.m., with every escort ship firing at the enemy planes, four torpedoes plowed into the stricken cruiser. There was now no longer any question of saving her, and Captain Davis gave the order to abandon ship. At 4:43 p.m., as sailors scrambled off her, *Chicago* rolled over and took the plunge by the stern. Bobbing in the water in his Mae West life jacket, crewman Charles Goldsmith sadly watched his ship go down with 62 men aboard. It was "the dying of a beautiful friend." Other ships picked up 1,049 survivors.[54]

Radio Tokyo wildly exaggerated the outcome, claiming that two battleships and three cruisers had been sunk, and that a third battleship and four other cruisers had been damaged.[55]

DURING THE NIGHT OF FEBRUARY 3–4, twenty-one Japanese warships appeared off Cape Esperance and disgorged boats that chugged through the dark shallows to the beaches, where five thousand wraith-like soldiers quietly waited to board. These men belonged to General Maruyama's Sendai Division and included General Hyakutake and his senior staff. A few miles inland, the rearguard Yano Battalion, some Seventeenth Army soldiers, and an assortment of service troops, sailors, and rescued pilots—twenty-six hundred in all—continued to harass Patch's cautiously advancing soldiers.[56]

Patch, Sebree, and Halsey remained convinced that the spike in enemy naval and air activity presaged a massive reinforcement effort and offensive. The Americans' inability to discern what the Japanese were actually up to was the most profound intelligence failure of the Guadalcanal campaign. But the lapse was also understandable, for this type of enemy activity had always signified a new offensive.

Warships spotted by air patrols as they sailed toward Guadalcanal supported the American supposition. "Some observers think the Japs hope to bolster their tottering Guadalcanal ground forces with reinforcements," a February 5 news dispatch said.

After days of cautious patrolling behind enemy lines on Guadalcanal's western coast, the 2nd Battalion, 132nd Infantry was marching to the northeast to rendezvous with the 161st Infantry, now leading the CAM division's slow advance along the northern coastline toward Cape Esperance. When the pincers closed, the Americans believed, the trapped Japanese could only surrender or die.

On February 7, the 132nd's 2nd Battalion encountered enemy resistance at Marovovo, just three miles from Kamimbo Bay. The next morning, February 8, the Illinois Guardsmen entered the village of Kamimbo. They found hospitals full of sick and wounded Japanese troops and others who evidently had taken poison rather than be captured alive.[57]

If Colonel George's men had reached Kamimbo Bay twelve hours earlier, they might have seen the last Japanese evacuees leave Guadalcanal. During the rainy night of February 7–8, eighteen destroyers lay off the coast and sent landing craft to the beaches to bring off about three thousand soldiers, including the Yano Battalion.

The soldiers were taken to Shortland and Rabaul. Some of them carried small wooden boxes containing the ashes of comrades for whom they had performed last rites. Left on the beach were hundreds of men too ill to survive the trip. They clasped grenades with which to blow themselves up when American soldiers approached them.[58]

DURING THE MORNING OF FEBRUARY 9, the two American Army pincers, just eleven miles apart, began closing. They encountered only small groups of diehards firing machine-guns.

At 2:00 p.m. the 1st Battalion of the 161st Infantry reached Tenaro on the Tenamba River; forty-five minutes later the 2nd Battalion, 132nd Infantry arrived at the village.

"Boy, am I glad to see you!" cried Lieutenant Colonel James Dalton, commander of the 161st's advance unit as he grasped the hand of Major H. Wirth Butler of the 2nd Battalion, 132nd Infantry. Their men cheered, believing the handshake meant organized resistance on Guadalcanal would soon be over.

In fact it was over quicker than they realized: the enemy troops the Americans believed they had trapped were not there. Instead, they found decomposing corpses—victims of suicide, starvation, and disease—and a few men who were barely alive, "living among their own diseased and unburied dead." They were "so weak they could barely lift their heads or hands. Their ribs showed under their shrunken skins." In the tents of a Japanese field hospital, the guardsmen found patients dead on their cots, some of them still warm, probably suicides by poison.[59]

Discarded gear was strewn everywhere, and the Americans were surprised to find that some of it—Japanese rifle-cleaning kits, mess gear, and shovels—was superior to their own. "Our own shovel . . . was a ridiculous toy by comparison," wrote Lieutenant John George. The oval-bottom mess kits were excellent for field cooking. Many soldiers appropriated the enemy field kits and threw away their own. They were fascinated by the compact rifle-cleaning kits, which were tucked into small canvas rolls "with a short-jointed cleaning rod cleverly enlarged at the joints to prevent buckling." But the Japanese clothing, bedding, and rifles were considered inferior to American issue—and useful as souvenirs only.[60]

The dawdling march on Cape Esperance and Patch's mistaken assumptions about the enemy's intentions abetted the Seventeenth Army's escape. Thousands of Japanese soldiers had slipped away to fight again.

Hyakutake expressed mock gratitude to the Americans for their plodding advance—if they had moved quickly to Cape Esperance, they would have destroyed his Seventeenth Army. Even so, the evacuation, to the credit of the Japanese, resembled a miniature Dunkirk or Gallipoli in planning, deception, and execution.

General Collins suggested that the Japanese would not have gotten away if his 25th Division had spearheaded the final offensive instead of being withdrawn to the perimeter to counter the phantom enemy offensive. He was probably right—Collins and the 25th Division were already acquiring a reputation for rapid movement; Halsey said Collins was "quick on his feet and even quicker in his brain." Fighting farther up the Solomon Islands chain in 1943, the 25th would become known as the "Tropic Lightning Division," and Collins would acquire the nickname "Lightning Joe."[61]

PATCH TRIUMPHANTLY MESSAGED HALSEY ON February 9: "Total and complete defeat of the Japanese forces on Guadalcanal effected 1625 today. . . . Am happy to report this kind of compliance with your orders. . . . 'Tokyo Express' no longer has terminus on Guadalcanal."

Navy Secretary Frank Knox informed reporters that day in Washington of Tokyo's announcement that Japanese troops had been evacuated from the island. It was true, he said. "All enemy resistance on the island apparently has ceased, except there may be a few little groups left."

The Japanese report described the withdrawal in a surprisingly positive light: troops had "succeeded in cornering strong enemy forces. . . . However, having attained their objective, these troops were removed to another strategical [sic] part of the islands in February." The Tokyo report also said troops in Buna were transferred after having "completed their duties," when in fact MacArthur's men had wiped them out three weeks earlier.

Many Japanese people, however, might have suspected there was more to it than that. And during the same week that they learned of Guadalcanal's abandonment there came news of the German Sixth Army's surrender at Stalingrad.[62]

"Old Glory flies unchallenged over all the island. Her navy smashed repeatedly at sea, her Zeros and Mitsubishis erased from the skies and her proudest regiments now masses of rotting corpses, Japan has tasted defeat for the first time in a thousand years," read a triumphal INS report. It observed that the American victory was the consequence of combined operations under a unified command. "The Navy alone, or the Marine Corps without aid, or the Air Force without land troops, could not have captured this strongly held Japanese base and airfield."

Admiral Chester Nimitz gave the Japanese due credit for hoodwinking the Americans and flawlessly executing their evacuation plan. "Until the last moment it appeared that the Japanese were attempting a major reinforcement effort," he wrote. "Only skill in keeping their plans disguised and bold celerity in carrying them out enabled the Japanese to withdraw the remnants of the Guadalcanal garrison. Not until all organized forces had been evacuated on 8 February did we realize the purpose of their air and naval dispositions."[63]

Halsey wittily praised Patch and his divisions for securing the island. "Having sent General Patch to do a tailoring job on Guadalcanal, I am surprised and pleased at the speed with which he removed the enemy's pants to accomplish it."[64]

Japan's abandonment of Guadalcanal meant that US air forces were now "within striking distance of some of the most important bases of the Japanese," said Navy Secretary Knox. "The Southwest Pacific would have been a vastly different story for the last three or four months if we had not established our position in the Solomons."[65]

Retaining Guadalcanal and New Guinea was the first stage of the joint chiefs of staff's Pacific strategy. Now Stage Two could be undertaken: a drive by US, New Zealand, and Australian forces through the Solomons and New Guinea, culminating in the capture of the Bismarck Archipelago, including Rabaul, and the Admiralty Islands north and northeast of New Guinea.[66]

Epilogue

Guadalcanal is "no longer merely a name of an island in Japanese military history. It is the name of the graveyard of the Japanese Army."

—MAJOR GENERAL KIYOTAKE KAWAGUCHI[1]

There is no question that Japan's doom was sealed with the closing of the struggle for Guadalcanal.

—REAR ADMIRAL RAIZO TANAKA[2]

AT 5:55 P.M. ON APRIL 13, 1943, US naval intelligence intercepted a Japanese radio message that detailed Admiral Isoroku Yamamoto's travel itinerary for the coming days. Message No. 131755 began, "Commander in Chief Combined Fleet will personally inspect Ballale, Shortland, and Buin on April 18. Schedule as follows."

The information was invaluable—it could be used to eliminate one of Japan's top military leaders.

At US Navy headquarters in Hawaii, Admiral Chester Nimitz and his staff debated whether to act on the information. The United States had never targeted enemy leaders during wartime, but the Pacific War was in many ways unprecedented. It had begun with a surprise attack—planned by Yamamoto—and had evolved into a war without mercy, closer in spirit to the no-quarter-given American Indian wars than to any other US conflict, including the Civil War.

Admiral Nimitz approved the mission, and the centuries-old tradition of military chivalry died a little more.

At 6:00 a.m. on April 18, 1943, Yamamoto, chief of staff Vice Admiral Ugaki, and staff officers boarded two Betty medium bombers at Lukanai Field in Rabaul. Yamamoto periodically toured bases within his command to raise morale, and today, wearing khakis, airman's shoes, and all his insignia and medals, he was embarking on a two-hour, forty-five-minute flight to southern Bougainville, three hundred miles away. Escorted by six fighters from the 204th Squadron, the two bombers flew over the Solomon Sea and the southern half of Bougainville.

Without warning, sixteen P-38s appeared and opened fire on Yamamoto's fighter escorts and the two bombers. Yamamoto's plane was hit, and it plunged into the dense jungle, spitting smoke and flames. Ugaki, who was a passenger in the second bomber, saw a pillar of black smoke rise from the crash site.

Ugaki's plane flew out to sea in an attempt to evade the attackers. But the bomber was strafed by a P-38 and crash-landed in the water. Ugaki and a crewman managed to reach shore, but the others died.

An army search found the wreckage of Yamamoto's plane the next day. All eleven people on the plane were dead. The Combined Fleet's commander in chief was found strapped into his seat a short distance from the wreckage, his gloved left hand still grasping his sword. Machine-gun rounds had shattered his jaw and pierced his shoulder. The American mission to kill Japan's most famous admiral was a success.[3]

The Japanese people learned of Yamamoto's death on May 21. "We were aghast," wrote journalist Kiyosawa Kiyoshi, who was in Tokyo that day. The admiral had opposed war with America, but when it became settled national policy, he threw all his energy into winning, despite his grave misgivings.

There was a state funeral at Hibiya Park in the center of Tokyo on June 5; a naval band played Chopin's "Funeral March." A plan to erect a monument was thwarted by the admiral's friends, who knew he believed that "to make a god of a military man is absurd." Yamamoto would have been embarrassed, they said.[4]

THE CATASTROPHE THAT YAMAMOTO HAD foreseen, but would never see fully realized, was beginning to come to pass: Japan faced defeat unless it could drive America out of the war before mid-1943. Clearly this was not going to happen. "There is no question that Japan's doom was sealed with the closing of the struggle for Guadalcanal," wrote Rear Admiral Raizo Tanaka.[5]

Although the Japanese quixotically described Operation KE as a "tenshin"—a "turned advance," or an attack in another direction—it was in fact the final act of a devastating military defeat. Japan had ceded the Guadalcanal battlefield to the Allies.[6]

Yet the Japanese deserve credit for Operation KE and its calculated deceptions that misled the Allies. In planning and execution, although not in scale, it was comparable to the brilliant evacuations of Dunkirk and Gallipoli. A total of 10,652 Japanese soldiers were withdrawn from the battleground and transported to safety under the noses of Patch's XIV Corps, six naval task forces, and the powerful Cactus Air Force, now flying from four Guadalcanal airfields.[7]

Nearly all the evacuees, said Major General Shuichi Miyazaki, the Seventeenth Army's chief of staff, suffered from severe malnutrition, malaria, or amoebic dysentery. About six hundred of them later died, but the rest—more than ten thousand soldiers—lived to fight again. They were all that remained of the thirty-two thousand men sent to Guadalcanal. More than twenty thousand had been killed in action, or had died of wounds, disease, or starvation. Several hundred had become war prisoners. An additional four thousand were lost at sea aboard transports that were bombed, machine-gunned, and sunk before reaching Guadalcanal.[8]

American infantry losses were considerably lower: about 1,600 killed in action and 4,245 wounded. Because of its participation in the campaign's bloodiest battles, the 1st Marine Division reported the highest losses of the four US divisions that fought on the island: 774 killed and 1,962 wounded, plus many others incapacitated by disease. The Americal and 2nd Marine divisions, with the next-longest tenures, reported, respectively, 334 killed and 850 wounded, and 268 killed and 932 wounded (the 2nd Division's losses on Tarawa would exceed its Guadalcanal casualties by a factor of three). The Army's 25th Division, on the island for the briefest period and against a diminished enemy, lost 216 killed and 439 wounded.[9]

Historian Richard Frank, who analyzed air losses between August 1 and February 9, reported that 615 Allied planes and 683 Japanese aircraft were destroyed. Japanese historian Masanori Ito, however, said Japanese aircraft losses totaled 893.

This is a remarkable figure considering the inferiority of the Cactus Air Force's F4F Wildcat to the Japanese Zero. For months the outnumbered American pilots avoided taking on the faster-climbing, more maneuverable Zeros in one-on-one aerial combat. The Thach Weave provided an interim solution to the disparity in aircraft capabilities, until the steady attrition of Japan's best fighter pilots brought inexperienced replacements into the air war. Cactus pilots then confidently took on the Japanese second team in single combat. Five Marine pilots were awarded Medals of Honor: Captains Joe Foss and Jefferson DeBlanc and Majors Robert Galer, John L. Smith, and Harold Bauer.

Aircraft losses alone do not tell the entire story, for they do not take into account the ability to replace aircraft and, especially, airmen. Frank estimated that 420 Allied air crewmen died during the six-month campaign, while between 800 and 1,700 Japanese airmen perished (Ito reported 2,362 deaths). The losses cut deeply into Japan's cadre of experienced Imperial Navy pilots, claiming at least one-third of the 600 who were flying at the campaign's beginning.

Besides being hundreds of miles from base and the possibility of rescue, Japanese airmen were often indifferent to their fate. Many did not bother to even open their parachutes after bailing out of their stricken planes, fearing captivity more than death.

US losses were smaller because the aerial battleground was relatively close to Guadalcanal and potential air or sea rescue. Coast watchers and friendly Solomon islanders rescued more than two hundred Allied airmen between August and the end of November, according to Martin Clemens.

Each side lost twenty-four warships between August and February. Although the Imperial Japanese Navy had won important naval battles, Japanese leaders sensed that they were being drawn into an attritional battle that they could not win.

Indeed, new US ships were being sent down the shipways faster than Japanese sailors could sink them. The United States, with nearly twice Japan's population and with an enormous industrial infrastructure, could more easily absorb losses and make good on them. Its defense factories were increasing output monthly; production would not peak until late 1944. America's 1939 GNP of $91 billion would reach $166 billion in 1945. During the war years the economy would create 17 million new jobs, sharply raise average incomes, and, in the process, lift the United States out of the Great Depression. Conversely, Japan struggled to sustain its 1941 production levels.

A shocking five thousand US sailors and naval officers were killed during the Guadalcanal campaign—fourteen hundred at the Naval Battle of Guadalcanal in November and more than one thousand at the Battle of Savo Island in August—surpassing the Navy's accumulated losses during all previous wars. Although lacking comparable Japanese figures, it is fair to say they at least equaled and probably surpassed American losses.[10]

TANAKA, THE BRILLIANT DESTROYER SQUADRON leader, said the great flaw in his countrymen's Guadalcanal strategy was the piecemeal reinforcement of its ground forces. "Gradual reinforcement of landing forces by small units is subjecting all of the troops involved to the danger of being destroyed bit by bit. Every effort must be made to use large units, all at once!" said one of his critiques.

The same incremental approach contributed to the heavy attrition of Japanese planes and pilots that Captain Toshikazu Ohmae of the Southeastern Area Fleet believed cost Japan the battle and many of its best pilots. "We had three or four squadrons at Rabaul, but they were sent down one at a time. The constant attrition was very expensive. The 21st, 24th, 25th, and 26th air groups were lost," and their absence was felt later in the Central Pacific.[11]

Even more than Japan's piecemeal air and ground force deployments, strategic failures by the Imperial Japanese Navy doomed the effort to recapture Guadalcanal. After the US Navy sailed away on August 9 the Japanese had a superb opportunity to consolidate its naval power, seize the island, and crush Admiral Ghormley's scattered forces. Had the entire Combined Fleet struck Ghormley's South Pacific forces, the campaign's outcome might have been different.

Instead, the Imperial Navy's episodic forays reflected the same incremental policy that governed the deployment of ground troops and aircraft. It enabled the plucky Cactus Air Force to keep disaster at arm's length by disrupting enemy resupply and reinforcement efforts, while grinding down the Japanese navy's aircraft and pilots. It created breathing room for the Marines until the Navy at last came to Guadalcanal's defense.

After squandering opportunities to land large numbers of reinforcements in August and September—when Japan enjoyed air and naval superiority—the Japanese attempted to make up for it in October and November. It was too late; by then American air and naval forces had become too formidable.

The Japanese also failed to build new airstrips closer to Guadalcanal in time to overcome their air fleets' greatest disadvantage—the 560-mile distance between Rabaul and Guadalcanal—during the months when it mattered. Buin Airfield was completed in late October, reducing the flying distance to 300 miles. Munda Airfield in the New Georgia Islands, 125 miles closer, became operational in mid-December; Ballale Airfield on Shortland Island was completed in January 1943. By December, powerful Allied air and naval forces were able to bomb and shell the airfields even as they were being built. Quicker to grasp the importance of airstrips and to build them, the Allies operated three airfields on Guadalcanal by December and that month completed a fourth one.[12]

Wounded in December when his destroyer was torpedoed during a resupply run, Tanaka was sent to Singapore to recover. The admiral was unpopular with his superiors because of his outspokenness—and for often being right. He was made one of the scapegoats for Japan's failure on Guadalcanal; his punishment was not receiving another seagoing command. For the rest of the war, the Tokyo Express's guiding spirit and the hero of the battles of the Java Sea and Tassafaronga was assigned to shore commands in Singapore and Burma.[13]

MORE THAN ANY OTHER PACIFIC campaign, Guadalcanal was a laboratory for testing strategy, tactics, and decision-making over a period of months. Because it was not fought near population centers, the Guadalcanal battleground retained a strange purity. It bore more of a resemblance to eighteenth-century European warfare, which was usually waged in the countryside, than it did to the contemporary fighting in China, Europe, and Russia that consumed civilians and soldiers alike. There would be further examples of this anachronistic type of fight-ing—on Tarawa, Iwo Jima, and Peleliu—but none for so long a period as Guadalcanal.

The Americans' decisive victory shattered the "Japanese superman" myth that prevailed in the wake of Japan's earlier victories over weaker foes. After Guadal-canal, the Japanese were no longer presumed to be superior jungle fighters; the Marines had proved to be their equals or betters. Replacing the superman myth was the image of Japanese cruelty, treachery, and willingness to slaughter prison-ers. Thus, the Marines felt justified in extending no mercy in turn. "Emotions forgotten since our most savage Indian wars were reawakened by the ferocities of Japanese commanders," historian Allan Nevins wrote.[14]

With few heavy weapons and inadequate close air or naval support, Japanese ground forces reverted to the nighttime bayonet attacks that had worked for them in China and Southeast Asia. Their failure on Guadalcanal demonstrated that morale, fighting spirit, and so-called bamboo spear tactics were not enough to defeat a determined enemy armed with overwhelming firepower. "Each attack was a hurried night attack, which left little time for the soldiers to rest, and rap-idly diminished the physical fitness of the men," wrote Major General Miyazaki. Moreover, almost invariably after breaching one barbed-wire barrier, they charged blindly into the second one, "becoming a fine target for our automatic fire," as one Marine observed. "They have been slaughtered repeatedly in this manner."[15]

One reason was that the Japanese lacked good intelligence about the Ameri-cans and seldom reconnoitered the targets of their attacks. They consistently un-derestimated the Marines—their numbers, fighting ability, determination, and especially their firepower—initially believing they were like the soldiers they had faced and beaten in Java and Burma. The hard lessons learned by the Japanese were paid for in blood and suffering.

Vandegrift and Lieutenant Colonel Evans Carlson highly respected the ene-my's courage. "I have had wounded men get up and assault my men who were attempting to take them prisoner," Carlson wrote with mingled awe and alarm.[16]

The Japanese soldier's tenacity of purpose may have been admirable, but it was also a weakness, Vandegrift's final report said. When a plan failed, the Japa-nese stuck to it and tried harder to make it work—rather than attempt to impro-vise a new plan. When their officers were killed, Japanese soldiers, drilled in absolute obedience, were incapable of taking "independent action to redeem [their] situation," wrote Vandegrift. A Seventh Marines NCO put the matter more bluntly: "If you shoot their officers, they mill around. Their NCOs were poor." Their fallback was the "tactically dramatic 'bushido'" and its ultimate manifestation, the banzai attack, which the Marines sometimes goaded the Japanese into launching.

GENERAL GEORGE KENNEY, THE ALLIED Air Forces commander in the Southwest Pacific, warned that the American people continued to underrate the Japanese and that defeating them would exact a higher cost than they knew. "I'm afraid that a lot of people who think this Jap is a 'pushover' as soon as Germany falls, are due for a rude awakening," he wrote to General H. H. "Hap" Arnold, head of the US Army Air Forces. "No amateur team will take this boy out. We have got to turn professional."[17]

Indeed, the Guadalcanal campaign was by necessity an amateur production in its earliest stages. The 1st Marine Division's final report on the campaign drily observed, "Seldom has an operation been begun under more disadvantageous circumstances." Operation Watchtower's planning, rehearsal, and execution were completed in a breathtakingly short six weeks. Haste was required, though, to stop the nearly completed Japanese airfield from becoming operational and menacing the US-Australian sea lanes.

Vandegrift acknowledged that there was no time for adequate reconnaissance or planning, to properly combat-load the ships at Wellington, or for even "a complete meeting of the minds of the commanders concerned." In his final report he described the landing's rehearsal as "dubious," and Koro "a poor site for the practice landing because it was fringed in coral"—while Guadalcanal was not. The Marines believed it was essential that the Navy establish "firm control of sea and air," but the Navy viewed the operation "more in the nature of a large scale raid or hit and run operation," Vandegrift wrote. The Navy left the Marines to contend for two months with Japanese air, naval, and ground attacks. Yet they somehow managed to carry out Operation Shoestring with the help of warehoused Japanese rice, supplies landed fitfully by the Navy, and the indispensable Cactus Air Force.[18]

A JAPANESE MILITARY COMMENTARY FLATTERINGLY portrayed the Marines as "a first-line fighting unit, possessing considerable fighting strength. . . . It is said the caliber of men and equipment is the highest of the US Armed Forces." Even from defensive positions the Marines made daring counterattacks, the Japanese report said, and quickly sealed breaches and isolated penetrating units. It rated American artillery as effective and accurate; concentrated artillery fire, even in the jungle, inflicted "considerable losses." American soldiers were good marksmen, they used tanks well, and their communications were superior, the analysis said.

But US soldiers and their leaders lacked "tenacity," the Japanese believed. If a plan failed, the Americans would discard it and try a new one. To the Japanese, improvisation bespoke weakness when it was in fact a great asset. With better justification, the Japanese criticized Americans' inability to maneuver at night and noted their "dislike for hand to hand combat. Indeed, they fear it."[19]

Vandegrift did not need for the Japanese to tell him that his Marines were superior combat troops—he knew that. It was their lack of "adequate physical training, and hardening prior to combat" that concerned him. However, the already rigorous training regimen did not appear to be the problem; rather, it was the long weeks cooped up on troop transports that had eroded the Marines' fitness, causing them to struggle during their first days ashore.

But Vandegrift, who would soon become the Marine Corps commandant, wanted infantry training made tougher. "Troops in training must be made to live hard and to march long distances by day and night through unfavorable terrain"—as Merritt Edson and Evans Carlson had required their Raiders to do. "Ease and comfort in training periods will lead to excessive losses in combat," Vandegrift wrote.[20]

On Guadalcanal, American officers often got their first taste of combat after years of peacetime service—and many failed the test. The weeding-out process was especially severe in the Americal Division, where National Guard officers accustomed to weekend musters, summer exercises, and steady promotions were suddenly thrown into battle. Colonel Bryant Moore, commander of the 164th Regiment, sacked twenty-five officers. "They just weren't leaders," he said. Enlisted Guardsmen resented the replacement of their officers and longtime Guard friends by regular Army officers, many of them West Pointers like Moore. Of course, Moore was right—in combat, leadership was more important than friendship—but his dismissals only partly addressed a broader problem that he had observed: "The good leaders seem to get killed; the poor leaders get the men killed."[21]

PERCEPTIVE JAPANESE LEADERS SENSED THAT the defeat on Guadalcanal foreshadowed future reversals as well. Guadalcanal, wrote General Kawaguchi, was "no longer merely a name of an island in Japanese military history. It is the name of the graveyard of the Japanese Army."[22]

Guadalcanal was the turning point of the Pacific War. In its jungles, on its coral ridges, in the tropical skies above, and in the seas surrounding the island, US forces defeated the vaunted Japanese military machine, stopped Japanese expansionism, and placed Japan permanently on the defensive. Just as Ulysses Grant's Overland Campaign of 1864 was the beginning of the end for the

Confederacy, so was Guadalcanal for Japan—although the end lay years away, after a succession of increasingly bloody battles.

MANY OF THE JAPANESE SOLDIERS, seamen, and airmen who fought to recapture Guadalcanal joyfully anticipated the day when their names—and their *kami*, or spirits—would reside at the Yasukuni Shrine, which was a short distance from the Imperial Palace in Tokyo. When Japanese pilots bade one another farewell before going on a mission, they often parted with the fatalistic words, "See you at Yasukuni!" At Yasukuni the Japanese pray to their Shinto gods for those who died in the Empire of Japan's service between 1868 and 1951.

Erected in 1869 to honor the 6,971 Japanese who died establishing the Meiji Restoration, the shrine's list of war dead exploded during and after World War II. Today it contains the names of more than 2.4 million kami—2.1 million of them killed during the Pacific War.

There is a song about an aged mother visiting her dead son's spirit at Kudanzaka, the hill where the shrine is located:

> *"It has taken me all day, leaning on my cane*
> *To come and see you, my son, at Kudanzaka*
> *The great torii [gate] looming up in the sky*
> *Leads to a magnificent shrine*
> *That enrolls my son among the gods.*
> *Your unworthy mother weeps in her joy.*
> *I was a black hen who gave birth to a hawk.*
> *And such good fortune is more than I deserve.*
> *I wanted to show you your order of the Golden Kite [a combat medal],*
> *And have come to see you, my son, at Kudanzaka."*[23]

IN JULY 1978 RETIRED GENERAL Samuel B. Griffith, the former 1st Raider Battalion leader and historian, returned to Guadalcanal for the celebration of the newly sovereign and independent Solomon Islands, no longer a British protectorate. The Solomons encompassed six major islands and hundreds of smaller ones east of Papua New Guinea. Honiara (pronounced *naho naira* and meaning "the face of the east wind"), a postwar city on the Matanikau River, is the Solomon Islands' capital.

Griffith and the other Americans invited to the celebration landed at Henderson Field (now called Honiara International Airport), evoking memories of desperate air battles and furious bombardments. Gray-haired octogenarian Jacob

Vouza met them on the tarmac in his Marine Corps blues and honorary sergeant major rank insignia. He wore all of his medals, including the Silver Star that he earned for his ordeal at Alligator Creek, where he escaped his Japanese tormentors and warned the Marines of the imminent attack. Vouza was the island's most famous war hero. Sent to London as Guadalcanal's representative in 1953 to attend Queen Elizabeth II's coronation, he would be knighted in 1979.

"You write me and tell me you come back. Long time. Many years. Me old man now," Vouza said to Griffith. Yet Vouza stood tall with his chest proudly thrust out. The American visitors dined at a Chinese restaurant on the east bank of the Matanikau, where four battles had been fought. There was a nine-hole golf course at Kukum, the onetime US bivouac. Australian cruise ships docked at Point Cruz, another former battleground. Dizzying changes had occurred over thirty-six years.

Griffith and his former comrades toured the old battlefields. At Tulagi, the one-time British protectorate capital where the Raiders had fought their short, violent battle, Japanese tuna boats skimmed across the harbor, bringing in their daily catches for processing and packing. Distasteful though it might have been to some of the aging combat veterans, the irony did not escape them.

On Red Beach, where thousands of Marines had streamed ashore on August 7, 1942, the veterans' eyes fell on a more agreeable sight: rusted amphibian tractors overgrown with vines, a fitting monument to the beginning of America's first offensive of World War II.[24]

ACKNOWLEDGMENTS

I AM INDEBTED TO THE many libraries and individuals that helped inform me about the complex Guadalcanal campaign.

Foremost is my home research library, Davis Library at the University of North Carolina–Chapel Hill, whose World War II shelves laid a foundation for writing about the unique problems faced by American and Japanese forces on this remote South Pacific island. This library has been my touchstone for the past fifteen years.

Dr. Fred Allison (major, USMC, retired) aided me at the Marine Corps Archives and Special Collections in Quantico, Virginia, by opening up the archives' oral histories on Guadalcanal. Because of the Marine Corps' predominance in ground operations during the campaign's first months, Dr. Allison's assistance was indispensable.

The archivists and librarians at the Navy History Center and the Navy Department Library assisted me at the Washington, DC, Navy Yard. There, and through the impressive online resources provided by the Naval Historical and Heritage Command, I was able to leaven the naval war narrative with eyewitness accounts from sailors, carrier pilots, and ship commanders, and with ship battle reports.

The documents and eyewitness reports at the Army's Heritage and Education Center at Carlisle Barracks, Pennsylvania, sharpened my understanding of the roles played by the Americal and 25th Infantry divisions, the 147th and 161st regiments, and their supporting elements.

Aided by the helpful librarians in the reference department of the University of Wyoming's American Heritage Center, I was able to study the papers of International News Service correspondent Richard Tregaskis. His *Guadalcanal Diary* was the first popular narrative of U.S. land warfare during the Pacific war.

I am grateful to the National Archives and Research Administration and the Library of Congress for permitting access to their collections of photographs from the campaign.

A special thanks goes to David Streetman of Durham, North Carolina, who, unasked, contributed video and print sources that aided my research.

Bob Pigeon, executive editor of Da Capo Press, has my gratitude for strongly supporting my work down through the years, as does my agent, Roger Williams of Roger Williams Agency, for his encouragement and advice.

My wife Pat not only provided moral support as I learned and wrote about this subject, but she aided my archival research. For this I am grateful.

NOTES

PROLOGUE

1. "The Cruise of the Snark by Jack London," Project Gutenberg, www.gutenberg.org /files/2512/2512-h/2512-h.htm.
2. Loxton, xxiii; Lundstrom, *First Team*, 33; *First Marine Division Commander's Final Report*, 41; Toland, 400; Morison, 15–16.
3. Groft, 37–38; Ambrose, 74–75; Tregaskis, *Guadalcanal Diary*, 15–16, 22; Bergerud, *Touched with Fire*, 153.
4. Phillips, 71–72, 92; Lord, 38; Hart, 120.
5. Morison, 3–5; Groft, 33; Merillat, *Island*, 49–50; Michael Smith, *Bloody Ridge*, 18.
6. Clemens, 3–7; Rogal, 103; White, 67; Morison, 8.
7. Griffith Papers, Box 2, Folder 4; *First Marine Division Commander's Final Report*, 2.

CHAPTER 1
AUGUST PART I:
MARINE INVASION AND NAVAL DISASTER

1. Ohmae, 1268.
2. Zimmerman, 24–26.
3. McMillan, 23.
4. Toland, 401; Phillips, 73; McEnery, 2–5.
5. Lundstrom, *First Team*, 35–38, 41; Zimmerman, 26–27.
6. Buell, 98; Tregaskis, *Guadalcanal Diary*, 35–39; Ambrose, 77; Calhoun, 52–53.
7. Clemens, 3–5, 101–102, 176, 184, 189.
8. Shaw, ii; McEnery, 4–5, 8; Tregaskis, *Guadalcanal Diary*, 39–41; Schom, 316–317; Leckie, *Helmet*, 58; Phillips, 73; Buell, 98.
9. Zimmerman, 26; Hoffman, *Once*, 135; Groft, 32; Leckie, *Challenge*, 91, 96.
10. Ohmae, 1268; Zimmerman, 28.
11. Alexander, 76; Zimmerman, 26–27, 31; Griffith, *Oral History*, 97–98.
12. Thomas, 109; Thomason, 667.
13. McEnery, 10–11; Schom, 328; Zimmerman, 18–19; Whyte, *Time of War*, 27.
14. Leckie, *Helmet*, 60.
15. Whyte, *Time of War*, 27–28; Zimmerman, 44–45; Thomas, 109.
16. Leckie, *Challenge*, 102–103; William White, 44.
17. Thomas, 112; Leckie, *Challenge*, 103–104; Hammel, *Starvation*, 59–60; Schom, 328.
18. Hayashi and Coox, 58.
19. Agawa, 2, 217, 180, 72–74.
20. Toland, 414–415; Griffith, *Papers*, Box 4, Folder 12; Hayashi and Coox, 58.

21. Lord, 45–46; Tillman, 70–71; Griffith, *Papers*, Box 2, Folder 9; Hara, 104; Frank, 64–65; "The Lost Fleet of Guadalcanal"; Sakai, 207–210; Lundstrom, *First Team*, 46, 71–72; Hoyt, *Guadalcanal*, 22–23.

22. Thomas Miller, 4–5; Frank, 65.

23. Smoot, 90–97; Petty, *At War*, 118; Sherrod, 75–76.

24. Leckie, *Challenge*, 7–8.

25. Sakai, 210–237; Cook, 141.

26. Thomas Miller, 4–6; Tillman, 70–71; Smoot, 90–2; Lundstrom, *First Team*, 71–72; Young, 43.

27. Lundstrom, "Frank Jack Fletcher"; Thomas Miller, 7; William White, 45; Ohmae, 1272; Navy History and Heritage Command.

28. *First Marine Parachute Battalion Report*, August 7–9; Hough, 266–7; *1st Marine Division Commander's Final Report*, 74–75; Christ, 58, 63–68, 74; Hersey, 78–79; McMillan, 36–7; Zimmerman, 35.

29. Griffith, *Battle for Guadalcanal*, 66–67; Christ, 106–107.

30. *1st Marine Division Commander's Final Report*, 74–77; Christ, 113; *First Marine Parachute Battalion Report*, August 7–9; Zimmerman, 35–36; John Miller, 67; Hough, 269–270.

31. Hough, 270–273; Frank, 79.

32. Griffith, *Oral History*, 80; Alexander, 80.

33. *1st Marine Division Commander's Final Report*, 70–72; Christ, 160; MacMillan, 34–35.

34. *1st Marine Division Commander's Final Report*, 72–73; Griffith, *Oral History*, 91; Hoyt, *Guadalcanal*, 19–20; Groft, 54. Ironically, "banzai," a common refrain during suicidal Japanese frontal attacks, originally meant "10,000 years"—as in "have a long life."

35. Walt, *Oral History*; Richter, 126–127; *Raider Patch*, 1st Quarter 2014, 14–15; Berry, 116.

36. Alexander, 84–102; Frank, 78–79, 663; Groft, 60.

37. Owens, 50–551; Leckie, *Helmet*, 73.

38. Lord, 38–39; Lundstrom, *First Team*, 39.

39. Lord, 38–39; Orita, 116; Lundstrom, *First Team*, 39; Merillat, *Island*, 86; Zimmerman, 49; Griffith, *Papers*, Box 2, Folder 4; Tregaskis, *Guadalcanal Diary*, 56.

40. Tregaskis, *Guadalcanal Diary*, 55–56.

41. McMillan, 50; Hammel, *Starvation*, 63; Whyte, *Time of War*, 43; Leckie, *Helmet*, 67–68; Tregaskis, *Guadalcanal Diary*, 58.

42. Tregaskis, *Guadalcanal Diary*, 54.

43. Vandegrift, 103–104, 109; Michael Smith, *Bloody Ridge*, 3–4; Zimmerman, 10; Young, 39; Schom, 320; Feuer, xi; Layton, 457; Toland, 394–395; Lundstrom, "Frank Jack Fletcher"; Lundstrom, *First Team*, 4–5, 18–19, 28–29.

44. Thomas, 100; Vandegrift, 113; Twining, 35–37; Hammel, *Starvation*, 34–36; *1st Marine Division Commander's Final Report*, 24–25; Clemens, 14–15; Zimmerman, 14–17. The Army's reconnaissance photos turned up in December, after the 1st Marine Division had left Guadalcanal. Griffith, *Battle for Guadalcanal*, 292.

45. McMillan, 4–6.

46. Twining, 9.

47. Moskin, 219–226; Leckie, *Challenge*, 17–18; McMillan, 4–5.

48. Thomas, *Oral History*, 99; Zimmerman, 20–22; Phillips, 58; Griffith, *Battle for Guadalcanal*, 37–38; *1st Marine Division Commander's Final Report*, 51–53.

49. Layton, 96; Vandegrift, 120–121; Asprey, 243; Loxton, 99; Griffith, *Battle for Guadalcanal*, 41–42; Lundstrom, *Black Shoe*, 27–29; Lundstrom, "Frank Jack Fletcher"; Nathan Miller, 262–263; Hoyt, *Guadalcanal*, 8.

50. Marion, 18–22; Griffith, *Oral History*, 81–82; Vandegrift, 121; Asprey, 243.

51. Zimmerman, 49; Lundstrom, "Frank Jack Fletcher"; Morison, 28; Vandegrift, 128.

52. Zimmerman, 50fn.

53. Asprey, 253; Loxton, 109, 114, 117; Frank, 97.

54. Loxton, xxiv, 111; Leckie, *Challenge*, 110; Morrison, 26, 31; *Combat Narratives: Savo*, 2; Warner, 10–23.

55. Morison, 18; Leckie, *Challenge*, 136–137; Ohmae, 1270–1271.

56. Orita, 117–118; Winton, 69–71; Loxton, 120–121, 126, 129–130; Dull, 104.

57. Willmott, 7–8 and fn; Leckie, *Challenge*, 108–109; Friedman, 169–170; Campbell, 202, 207; Koburger, 69; Tanaka, 699.

58. Loxton, 132.

59. Ohmae, 1273–1275, Leckie, *Challenge*, 113; Warner and Warner, 114.

60. *Combat Narratives: Savo*, 2–5; Loxton, 165.

61. Ohmae, 1275; Loxton, 177–178.

62. Loxton, 180–181.

63. Warner, 114, 123–131; Loxton, xxv–xxvii, 180–190, 195; Petty, *At War*, 103–105; *Combat Narratives: Savo*, 6, 9.

64. *Combat Narratives: Savo*, 7; Warner, 119–122, 133–134, 141–143; Morison, 39; Domagalski, 89–93.

65. Frank, 109.

66. Griffith, *Battle for Guadalcanal*, 83–84.

67. *Combat Narratives: Savo*, 15–16; Warner, 144,150–153; Ohmae, 1275.

68. Warner and Warner, 153–155; Dorris, 259, 261, 324, 331, 334.

69. "The Lost Fleet"; Warner and Warner, 162–169; *Combat Narratives: Savo*, 15–22; Ohmae, 1275–1276.

70. Domagalski, 130; Petty, *Voices*, 77.

71. Hornfischer, 71; Domagalski, 104–109, 110–119, 120, 130,141; *Combat Narratives: Savo*, 16–19; Warner and Warner, 170–180.

72. Ohmae, 1278.

73. Ibid., 1278; Winton, 72–74; Frank, 116; Dull, 203; Morison, 61; Griffith, *Battle for Guadalcanal*, 81.

74. Frank, 119.

75. Morison, 58.

76. Ibid., 61; Blair, 298.

77. Warner and Warner, 195–201.

78. Domagalski, 132, 150–155; Petty, *Voices*, 78.

79. Laing, 63–64; Warner and Warner, 206; Hornfischer, 86; Morison, 168fn; Dorris, 335.

80. Lundstrom, *Black Shoe*, 398; Morison, 62–63.

81. Warner and Warner, 198.

82. *New York Times* archives, September–October 1942.

83. Leckie, *Challenge*, 127; Griffith, *Battle for Guadalcanal*, 81.

84. Whyte, *Time of War*, 33; Warner and Warner, 193–195; Morison, 52; Tregaskis, *Guadalcanal Diary*, 62; Hornfischer, 80; *Combat Narratives: Savo*, 40.

85. Thomas, 117; Vandegrift, 129.

86. Christ, 144–145, 199; Koburger, 31; Michael Smith, *Bloody Ridge*, 13–17; Merillat, *Guadalcanal Remembered*, 77–78; *1st Marine Division Commander's Final Report*, 41; Rogal, 58.

87. Asprey, *Vandegrift Oral History*; Dupuy, et al, 770.

88. Vandegrift, 131; Asprey, 260; McMillan, 48–49; Phillips, 100.

89. Morison, 36n, 52n.

CHAPTER 2:
AUGUST PART II: JAPAN STRIKES BACK:
TOJO TIME AND ALLIGATOR CREEK

1. Vandegrift, 142.
2. Mears, 114–115.
3. Thomas Miller, 68-70.
4. Twining, 105–108; Zimmerman, 56–57, map; *Guadalcanal Echoes*, Winter 2012, 11; Frank, 150; Asprey, 260; Vandegrift, 132.
5. Vandegrift, 133.
6. George W. Smith, *Do-or-Die Men*,195–196; Tregaskis, *Guadalcanal Diary*, 164–165; Vandegrift, 134.
7. Vandegrift, 134; Tregaskis, *Guadalcanal Diary*, 99; Asprey, 718.
8. Fox, 28.
9. Zimmerman, 73, 64; Griffith, *Battle for Guadalcanal*, 86–87; Vandegrift, 132–133; Thomas Miller, 28; Twining, 75.
10. Richter, 151–153; Griffith, *Battle for Guadalcanal*, 87–88; Zimmerman, 58–59.
11. Richter, 153–157; Griffith, *Battle for Guadalcanal*, 87–88, 94; Merillat, *Island*, 87–88; Zimmerman, 59–60, 77–79; McMillan, 52–56; Leckie, *Challenge*, 131–132; Laing, 81; *1st Marine Division Commander's Final Report*, 159–160, 218–219; Marion, 98–101.
12. Zimmerman, 60; Thomas, 123; Marion, 93–94.
13. *1st Marine Division Commander's Final Report*, 157–158; Morison, 69; Marion, 79.
14. Thomas, 124; Clemens, xv, 7–8, 19, 41, 159; Feuer, xi–xiii, xix–xx; Lord, 7–10, 22–23; Richter, 160, 213–214.
15. Feuer, xix, 62–64; Lord, 61–62. Mason and Read were awarded US Distinguished Service Crosses in recognition of their contributions.   Feuer, xiii.
16. Clemens, 20–21, 221, USAFISPA, 3, Box 6, Folder 37; Richter, 159–161, 213–214, 217–219; Davis, 143; Feuer, 63–64.
17. Leckie, *Challenge*, 132.
18. Griffith, *Battle for Guadalcanal*, 96; Griffith, *Papers*, "Miyazaki Manuscript," Box 2, Folder 9; Ugaki, 183.
19. Griffith, *Battle for Guadalcanal*, 99; Michael Smith, *Bloody Ridge*, 28.
20. Toland, 416; Griffith, *Battle for Guadalcanal*, 98–99; Leckie, *Challenge*, 127–129; Griffith, *Papers*, "Miyazaki Manuscript," Box 2, Folder 9.
21. Walker, 60, 145, 159–164; Hoyt, *Japan's War*, 7–8; Drea, *Japan's Imperial Army*, 1–10, 16–20; Toland, 66; Griffith, *Papers*, "Miyazaki," Box 2, Folder 6.
22. Gailey, 4; Toland, 172.
23. Dull, 3–4; Toland, 46–52, 68–74, 98–103; Ienaga, 153–154; Dower, *War Without Mercy*, 67–68; F. C. Jones, 2–4, 353–368; Willmott, 5; Hayashi and Coox, 4, 21–22; Drea, *Japan's Imperial Army*, 199, 235; Shillony, 141, 143–150.
24. Hayashi and Coox, 1–3; Cook, 264; F. C. Jones, 7–12; Bergerud, *Touched with Fire*, 125–127, 130–131; Dull, 3; Ellwood, 146; Ugaki, 280; Drea, *In the Service*, 76–87; Toland, 296.
25. Drea, *Nomonhan*, ix–x, 4–11; Hayashi and Coox, 15.
26. Hayashi and Coox, 16; Drea, *Nomonhan*, 87, 90.
27. Griffith, *Papers*, "Miyazaki Manuscript," Box 2, Folder 9.
28. Richter, 189; Dull, 205; Lane, 191–192; Hara, 109.
29. Zimmerman, 61–62; Richter, 170.
30. Bartsch, 89–96.
31. Hough, 285; Bergerud, *Touched with Fire*, 167; Bartsch, 89–96.
32. Bartsch, 96–98; Bergerud, *Touched with Fire*, 167–168; Hough, 285; *1st Marine Division Commander's Final Report*, 161–163; Leckie, *Challenge*, 134.

33. Richter, 47–62; 84–85; Clemens, 12–13.

34. Richter, 171.

35. Bartsch, 117–120, 144; Richter, 172–180; *Guadalcanal Echoes*, Winter 2012, 8–11; Leckie, *Challenge*, 141.

36. Leckie, *Helmet*, 74–75; Bartsch, 120–125, 222; Cates, 5–7.

37. Zimmerman, 68; MacMillan, 61; *1st Marine Division Commander's Final Report*, 215; Bartsch, 131–137, 156, 228.

38. Zimmerman, 68; Bartsch, 142–143, 154, 156; Bartlett, 40; Phillips, 105; Leckie, *Strong Men*, 46; Pintwala, 3–6. Years later Schmid regained partial sight.

39. Leckie, *Helmet*, 80–81; Hixon, 61.

40. Clemens, 209–210; Laing, 109–110. Vouza was awarded the Silver Star and the honorary rank of sergeant major in the Marine Corps. Richter, 194.

41. Cates, 5–7; Bartlett, 40–41; Tregaskis, *Guadalcanal Diary*, 142; Bartsch, 190–203; Bergerud, *Touched with Fire*, 174; Leckie, *Challenge*, 148.

42. Hough, 290–291; Tregaskis, *Guadalcanal Diary*, 145; Leckie, *Helmet*, 83; Cates, 5–7.

43. Bartsch, 218; Richter, 187–188; Zimmerman, 69; Cates, 5–7.

44. Laing, 107–108; Bergerud, *Touched with Fire*, 410–411.

45. Tregaskis, *Guadalcanal Diary*, 146–147; Merillat, *Guadalcanal Remembered*, 106.

46. Clemens, 211; Cameron, 126; Tregaskis, *Guadalcanal Diary*, 148; Shoptaugh, 214, 222; Leckie, *Helmet*, 84–87.

47. Bartsch, 214; Phillips, 108–109.

48. Owens, 128; Vandegrift, 141–142; Lane, 192–193.

49. Vandegrift, 142; Asprey, 272.

50. Ugaki, 187; Griffith, *Papers*, "Miyazaki Manuscript," Box 2, Folder 9.

51. McEnery, 77; Merillat, *Guadalcanal Remembered*, 102; Phillips, 101; Bartsch, 128–129; *1st Marine Division Commander's Final Report*, 211; Thomas Miller, 25.

52. Sherrod, 77; Tillman, 72–75; Thomas Miller, 24–28.

53. Hoyt, *Guadalcanal*, 59–60; Young, 28–29; Hixon, 112.

54. DeChant, 72.

55. Twining, 75; Clemens, 233; *1st Marine Division Commander's Final Report*, 170–171.

56. Wolf, 272–273; Sherrod, 82, 96–97; Leckie, *Challenge*, 168–169; Merillat, *Guadalcanal Remembered*, 102–103; Young, 61–62; Thomas Miller, 33, 71; *1st Marine Division Commander's Final Report*, 229; Galer Interview.

57. Cook, 139; Lundstrom, *First Team*, 192; John Smith; Brand, 80; Hixon, 115; Thomas Miller, 75–76.

58. John Smith; Gunston, 428–430, 268, 298; Bergerud, *Fire in the Sky*, 206, 213.

59. Gunston, 116, 284; Tillman, 6–7; Young, 20–23; Toland, 236fn.

60. Lundstrom, *First Team*, 191–192.

61. Thach, 148.

62. Bergerud, *Fire in the Sky*, 200–202.

63. Cook, 135–136.

64. Thach, 148–153; Young, 53–56, 70. Thach received the Navy Cross for the Thach Weave. Thach, 208–209.

65. Lundstrom, *First Team*, 533–535; 455; Toland, 566fn.

66. Brand, 113.

67. Cook, 139; *1st Marine Division Commander's Final Report*, Aviation Chronology, 229.

68. Sherrod, 85.

69. Thomas Miller, 68–70; Merillat, *Island*, 271.

70. Hoyt, *Yamamoto*, 177.

71. Thomas Miller, 72–73; Tillman, 76.

72. Thomas Miller, 29.

73. Ugaki, 186.
74. Dull, 196.
75. Thomas Miller, 39–40; Dull 208.
76. Winton, 67–69; Holmes, 48, 53–54, 110; Drea, *MacArthur's ULTRA*, 12–13, 33, 37–39.
77. Griffith, *Battle for Guadalcanal*, 111; Thomas Miller, 38.
78. Griffith, *Battle for Guadalcanal*, 111; Frank, 172–174.
79. Hara, 97–98; Griffith, *Battle for Guadalcanal*, 111–112; Morison, 82; Hixon, 67, 74–75; Gailey, 150; Buell, 104.
80. Hoyt, *Guadalcanal*, 67–70; Felt, 106–107; Thomas Miller, 45–47.
81. Hixon, 71–72; Frank, 177; Hoyt, *Guadalcanal*, 69–70; Ugaki, 192; Hara, 100–103; Dull, 212.
82. Thomas Miller, 44, 47–49.
83. Thomas Miller, 50; Frank, 180–181.
84. Mears, 114; Frank, 182–183; Petty, *At War*, 83.
85. Leckie, *Challenge*, 157–158; Frank, 184–185.
86. Mears, 114–116.
87. Buell, 108–110.
88. Frank, 189.
89. Griffith, *Battle for Guadalcanal*, 112–113; Hoyt, *Guadalcanal*, 79; Winton, 80; Thomas Miller, 60–61, 63; Sherrod, 81; Tanaka, 693–696.
90. Ugaki, 192–194.
91. Tanaka, 697; Hammel, *Decision*, 363–364; Buell, 116–117, 123–124; Ugaki, 193, 207.
92. Mears, 116; Petty, *At War*, 83.
93. Buell, 118.
94. Tillman, 121, Buell, 120–122.
95. Hammel, *Aces*, 17, 22.
96. Brand, 72–75.
97. Richter, 232–235; Leckie, *Challenge*, 222.
98. Clemens, 223.
99. D'Albas, 190; Hoyt, *Yamamoto*, 142–143.
100. Orita, 129; Morison, 110–112; Hixon, 79–80; Hornfischer, 121; Thomas Miller, 70.
101. Orita, 131, Lundstrom, *First Team*, 223; Nathan Miller, 278; Leckie, *Challenge*, 217.
102. Morison, 132–136; Lundstrom, *First Team*, 223; Weschler, 93–96; Hornfischer, 133–135.
103. Lundstrom, *First Team*, 231.

CHAPTER 3
SEPTEMBER: "LET GEORGE DO IT"

1. *New York Times*, GenealogyBank.
2. Alexander, 145, 148–149.
3. Ugaki, 209–210.
4. Hornfischer, 119.
5. Morison, 113–114.
6. *1st Marine Division Commander's Final Report*, 160; Sherrod, 86; Vandegrift, 147.
7. Thomas Miller, 68–70.
8. Ibid., 78–79, 104; Thomason, 661; "Guadalcanal, Island of Death" video; DeChant, 2–16; Vandegrift, 149 [Geiger brought Vandegrift a package from Nimitz marked "fan mail." It was a case of scotch.   Knowing that Vandegrift preferred bourbon, Geiger offered to trade a case of his bourbon for the scotch. Vandegrift readily agreed,

but then Geiger discovered that someone had stolen the bourbon. Vandegrift kept the scotch, but gave a few bottles to Geiger.]

9. Mears, 130.

10. Lundstrom, *First Team*, 188–190; Thomas Miller, 73; Michael Smith, *Bloody Ridge*, 94.

11. Laing, 112; Thomas, 138; Tregaskis, *Guadalcanal Diary*, 243; Woods, 157; DeChant, 69–71; Morison, 78; McEniry, 87; Buell, 130; Thomas Miller, 74, 85.

12. Ugaki, 199; Bergerud, *The Land War*, 134; Griffith, *Battle for Guadalcanal*, 113–115; Toland, 422.

13. Sherrod, 87; Griffith, "Kawaguchi Interview," 9–11; Griffith, *Papers*, "Miyazaki"; Hoyt, *Yamamoto*, 180; Ugaki, 202–203; Thomas. Miller, 82; Alexander, 115.

14. Toland, 422; Griffith, *Battle for Guadalcanal*, 115–116; Thomas Miller, 63.

15. Ugaki, 217; Griffith, "Kawaguchi Interview, 12, 4–5; Richter, 226–228; Miller, 222; Michael Smith, *Bloody Ridge*, 132–133; Griffith, *Battle for Guadalcanal*, 122, 124; Hixon, 78.

16. Lundstrom, *First Team*, 196.

17. Mears, 129; Farrington, 94–95.

18. Wolf, 39; Morison, 75–77; Thomas Miller, 86; Hixon, 87; Leckie, *Challenge*, 182.

19. *1st Marine Division Final Report*, Annex V, 506–510; Leckie, *Helmet*, 29, 96; Groft, 63; McMillan, 45–46.

20. Clemens, 311; Shaw, 48; www.nps.gov/parkhistory/online_books/npswapa/extContent/usmc/pcn-190-003117-00/sec6.htm.

21. Wyant, 50.

22. *1st Marine Division Commander's Final Report*, 165; Associated Press story in Dallas *Morning News*, September, GenealogyBank; Lane, 186–188; Bergerud, *Touched with Fire*, 291–295; Griffith, *Oral History*, 99–100.

23. Hixon, 86–87.

24. Marion, 110–112; Reeder, 1.

25. John Miller, 317.

26. Alexander, 109; Michael Smith, *Bloody Ridge*, 102–103.

27. Updegraph, 36–40; Michael Smith, *Bloody Ridge*, 104–105.

28. Gilbert, 9–11; Alexander, 13–14, 20, 29–30, 41, 43, 60–61; Clemens, 224; Hoffman, *Once*, xv, 36, 55, 96, 104, 114–119, 143, 155–162, 166–168; Wukovits, *American Commando*, 44–45; Tregaskis, *Guadalcanal Diary*, 80; Berry, 112; Griffith, *Oral History*, 51, 86–88, 91; Twining, 141; Groft, 30.

29. Christ, 175, 182.

30. George W. Smith, *Do-or-Die Men*, 189–193; Leckie, *Challenge*, 185–186; Hoffman, *Once*, 186.

31. Torgerson; *1st Marine Division Commander's Final Report*, 257, 220; Alexander, 45, 200, 203–206; Tregaskis, *Guadalcanal Diary*, 206–208; Michael Smith, *Bloody Ridge*, 122–127; Griffith, *Oral History*, 103; Hoffman, *Once*, 189–190; Griffith, *Battle for Guadalcanal*, 131; Griffith, *Papers*, "Kawaguchi Interview," 14; George W.   S m i t h, *Do-or-Die Men*, 203–206, 212; Leckie, *Challenge*, 193; Groft, 90; *Raider Patch*, 4th quarter 2013, 20–21; Clemens, 295.

32. Michael Smith, *Bloody Ridge*, 138; Twining, 95; Hoffman, *Once*, 192–193.

33. Merillat, *Guadalcanal Remembered*, 133; Frank, 226; Richter, 228–229.

34. Winton, 81; Christ, 200; Sledge, 92.

35. Griffith, *Battle for Guadalcanal*, 132–133.

36. George W. Smith, *Do-or-Die Men*, 311.

37. Vandegrift, 152–154; Leckie, *Challenge*, 202; Twining, 96–98, 156; Asprey, 659–661; Thomas, 135–136.

38. Morison, 116.

39. Baldwin, Vol. 2, 347–349; Baldwin, *New York Times* interview of Vandegrift Sept 1942, published 3 November 1942 in the Omaha *World-Herald*, GenealogyBank. Hanson Baldwin, a 1924 Naval Academy graduate, won a Pulitzer Prize for his reporting on Guadalcanal. George W. Smith, *Do-or-Die Men*, 311, 314.

40. Hough, 303–304.

41. Hixon, 82.

42. George W. Smith, *Do-or-Die Men*, 227–228; Richter, 240; Alexander, 144.

43. Griffith, *Battle of Guadalcanal*, 134; Alexander, 141.

44. Hoffman, *Once*, 194; Zimmerman, 85–86.

45. George W. Smith, *Do-or-Die Men*, 224–225; Zimmerman, 84–86.

46. Owens, 106.

47. Alexander, 145, 148–149.

48. Griffith, *Papers*, "Kawaguchi Interview," 13–15, 21; Hashiba Manuscript; *Translated Captured Japanese Documents*; Frank, 225; Michael Smith, *Bloody Ridge*, 161–162; Griffith, *Papers*, "Miyazaki"; Ugaki, 209–210.

49. Alexander, 149.

50. Griffith, *Battle for Guadalcanal*, 140; Michael Smith, *Bloody Ridge*, 151–152.

51. Zimmerman, 86; Alexander, 152–154; George W. Smith, *Do-or-Die Men*, 238–239, 242; Youngdeer, *Oral History*.

52. *1st Marine Division Commander's Final Report*, 221–223.

53. Hoffman, *Once*, 199; Zimmerman, 186; Griffith, *Battle for Guadalcanal*, 140–141.

54. Griffith, *Battle for Guadalcanal*, 141; Hoffman, *Once*, 199–200; Michael Smith, *Bloody Ridge*, 153; George W. Smith, *Do-or-Die Men*, 259.

55. Lundstrom, *First Team*, 207–210; Griffith, *Battle for Guadalcanal*, 141–142; Leckie, *Challenge*, 207–208; Frank, 233–234.

56. Vandegrift, 152–154.

57. Griffith, *Papers*, Box 2, Folder 16; Twining, 98, 101–102.

58. George W. Smith, *Do-or-Die Men*, 253; O'Donnell, 48.

59. Griffith, *Battle for Guadalcanal*, 142; Tillman, 131; Buell, 125.

60. Michael Smith, *Bloody Ridge*, 158.

61. Toland, 431–432.

62. Toland, 433; Groft, 117, 134; Christ, 221; George W. Smith, *Do-or-Die Men*, 261–263; Carroll, 197–198.

63. Alexander, 233, 246; *First Marine Parachute Battalion Report*, 1–5, Enclosure; Christ, 231–232; McMillan, 78; *1st Marine Division Commander's Final Report*, 222–224; Michael Smith, *Bloody Ridge*, 163–166.

64. Owens, 115.

65. O'Donnell, 49; Twining, 101.

66. *First Marine Parachute Battalion Report*, 9–11; Groft, 120, 137, 145; Thomas, 137.

67. Zimmerman, 91; Del Valle, 4; Tregaskis, *Guadalcanal Diary*, 227–228; Groft, 144, 146; Merillat, *Guadalcanal Remembered*, 140–141; Christ, 286; Alexander, 255; Leckie, *Helmet*, 94; *1st Marine Division Commander's Final Report*, 222–224.

68. Twining, 100.

69. Alexander, 183; Christ, 240–242; O'Donnell, 54–55.

70. Tregaskis, "The Best Soldier"; Alexander, 184–187; Christ, 252–253; Richter, 246; Michael Smith, *Bloody Ridge*, 167–168.

71. Twining, 100.

72. Laing, 137–138, 141–144, 149.

73. George W. Smith, *Do-or-Die Men*, 283–284; Tregaskis, *Guadalcanal Diary*, 239–240; Michael Smith, *Bloody Ridge*, 171.

74. Christ, 254–255; Thomas, 137; Hoffman, *Once*, 31.

75. Michael Smith, *Bloody Ridge*, 172–173; Hixon, 94, 98; Buell, 126.
76. Tregaskis, *Guadalcanal Diary*, 232; Vandegrift, 159; Lane, 169.
77. Thomas, 137; Griffith, *Oral History*, 109–110.
78. Wolf, 50–51; Lundstrom, *First Team*, 214; Thomas Miller, 96; George W.   S m i t h , *Do-or-Die Men*, 282.
79. Michael Smith, *Bloody Ridge*, 177–181; Whyte, *Time of War*, 47–48; Christ, 250; *1st Marine Division Commander's Final Report*, 225.
80. Christ, 250; Michael Smith, *Bloody Ridge*, 181; *1st Marine Division Commander's Final Report*, 226.
81. Tregaskis, *Guadalcanal Diary*, 247–248; Toland, 435; Christ, 277; O'Donnell, 54–55.
82. Michael Smith, *Bloody Ridge*, 170.
83. Ibid., 184–185; Zimmerman, 90; Griffith, *Papers*, "Kawaguchi Interview." The Parachutists later fought on Bougainville. In 1944 they were absorbed into the new 5th Marine Division, which fought on Iwo Jima. Two of the Mount Surabachi flag raisers in the iconic Joe Rosenthal photograph—Corporal Harlon Block and Private First Class Ira Hayes—were former Parachutists. Christ, 295.
84. Tregaskis, *Guadalcanal Diary*, 230, 233–234.
85. Richter, 248; McEnery, 98; *1st Marine Division Commander's Final Report*, 226–227; McMillan, 82.
86. George W. Smith, *Do-or-Die Men*, 289; Michael Smith, *Bloody Ridge*, 186–187; Hoffman, *Once*, 208–209, 213.
87. Toland, 435; Hoyt, *Yamamoto*, 183–184; Ugaki, 214; Griffith, *Battle for Guadalcanal*, 147.
88. Griffith, *Battle for Guadalcanal*, 147; Toland, 438; Michael Smith, *Bloody Ridge*, 195; Hashiba; Hoyt, *Guadalcanal*, 270.
89. Agawa, 326–328; Hoyt, *Yamamoto*, 184–185, 188; Richter, 283–284, 286.
90. Toland, 439; Twining, 104; Ortega; William White, 92–93; Leckie, *Challenge*, 221; Groft, 156; Christ, 295.
91. Davis, 115–116; Leckie, *Challenge*, 221.
92. Twining, 105.
93. *1st Marine Division Commander's Final Report*, 337–338.
94. Moskin, 184–186; Merillat, *Island*, 219.
95. Owens, 122; Davis, 118–120.
96. Davis, 121–122, 125–126.
97. Asprey, 704.
98. Zimmerman, 96–97; Leckie, *Challenge*, 233–235; *1st Marine Division Commander's Final Report*; Twining, 108.
99. Lane, 211–214; Griffith, *Battle for Guadalcanal*, 161; *1st Marine Division Commander's Final Report*, 328; Davis, 133–134; Hoffman, *Once*, 215–216; Zimmerman, 93.
100. Zimmerman, 98; Griffith, *Battle for Guadalcanal*, 162.
101. Lane, 215; Davis, 136; Griffith, *Battle for Guadalcanal*, 163; Berry, 120; Morison, 141; Zimmerman, 99.
102. Zimmerman, 99; Griffith, *Battle for Guadalcanal*, 163.
103. Davis, 138; Hoffman, *Chesty*, 165.
104. Lane, 216; Davis, 138–140; Hoffman, *Chesty*, 165.
105. Williams, xiii–xviii, 98.   Munroe was posthumously awarded the Medal of Honor, the only member of the Coast Guard to receive the nation's highest military honor.
106. Griffith, *Battle for Guadalcanal*, 163; Davis, 140–141; *1st Marine Division Commander's Final Report*, 329–331; Hoffman, *Chesty*, 165–167.
107. Twining, 111–112; Griffith, *Oral History*, 113–114, 118–119; Groft, 162–163; Hoffman, *Once*, 218–219; *1st Marine Division Commander's Final Report*, Part V, 21–22.

108. Vandegrift, 168–169.
109. Thomas, *Oral History*, 142; McMillan, 86–87; Twining, 108.
110. Hoyt, *Guadalcanal*, 151–152; Leckie, *Challenge*, 219; Ugaki, 228; Thomas Miller, 97–98; Michael Smith, *Bloody Ridge*, 196–197; Griffith, *Papers*, "Kawaguchi Interview," 27; Lundstrom, *First Team*, 241–242; Twining, 127–128. Twining wrote that the 29th Regiment was regarded as the Japanese army's "premier unit," priding itself on its physical conditioning and its ability to fight under harsh conditions. Every December, he wrote, the regiment climbed Mount Fujiyama with their weapons, with full packs—and wearing only their underwear.
111. Thomas Miller, 112.
112. Sherrod, 92; Griffith, *Papers*, "Miyazaki Manuscript."

CHAPTER 4
OCTOBER: PLAN X SHOWDOWN

1. Morris, 34.
2. Hixon, 157.
3. Lundstrom, *First Team*, 456.
4. Griffith, *Papers*, "Arnold"; Morison, 115–116; Hixon, 133; Hornfischer, 151–152.
5. Hayes, 183–187; Wolf, 53; Morison, 116.
6. Asprey, 730–734; Vandegrift, 171.
7. Hixon, 133–134; Hornfischer, 153–155.
8. Borneman, 53–57, 60–65, 83, 215, 220–221; Harris, 107.
9. Tillman, 85; Lundstrom, *First Team*, 238; Hixon, 110.
10. Tillman, 85–86; Lundstrom, *First Team*, 250.
11. Thomas Miller, 107–108; Feldt, 96.
12. Tillman, 86–87; Ugaki, 220; Young, 69; Sherrod, 92; DeBlanc, 83.
13. Tregaskis, *Guadalcanal Diary*, 220–222; William White, 99.
14. Cook, 138; Brand, 73.
15. Fox, 2; *1st Marine Division Commander's Final Report*, 170; Wolf, 38; Morison, 77.
16. Young, 69; Thomas Miller, 115; Sherrod, 431–432.
17. Thomas Miller, 115.
18. Tillman, 85.
19. Owens, 124; Whyte, Time of War, 55.
20. Leckie, *Challenge* 255–257; Griffith, *Battle for Guadalcanal*, 170–171.
21. Hersey, 64–65, 80–92.
22. Zimmerman, 102; *1st Marine Division Commander's Final Report*, 332–335; Reeder, 21–23; George W. Smith, *Do-or-Die Men*, 329–338; Griffith, *Battle for Guadalcanal*, 174; Marion, 159–161; Groft, 181–184.
23. Hoffman, *Chesty*, 172–174; *1st Marine Division Commander's Final Report*, 332–336; Davis, 143.
24. *1st Marine Division Commander's Final Report*, 332–336; Twining, 115–118; Hoffman, *Once*, 225–226; Thobaben, 36; Hoffman, *Chesty*, 175–176; Owens, 135; Davis, 145–147; McMillan, 96.
25. Griffith, *Battle for Guadalcanal*, 175–176; Toland, 446.
26. Richter, 266–267; Richard Johnston, 44–45.
27. Dull, 225; Cronin, 28–31; John Miller, 141–142, 220.
28. John Miller, 140; Griffith, *Battle for Guadalcanal*, 168.
29. John Miller, Appendix A, 357–359; Griffith, *Battle for Guadalcanal*, 169.
30. Morison, 148–151; Thomas Miller, 116–117; Carmichael, 67.
31. Morris, 34.

32. *Combat Narratives: Cape Esperance*; Morison, 154–155.
33. Morison, 156–157.
34. Ibid., 157; Chew, 57–60; Morris, 47; Yarbrough, GeneaologyBank; *Combat Narratives: Cape Esperance*, 12.
35. Hoyt, *Yamamoto*, 204–205; Hara, 126–127; Dull, 228; Morison, 160–165; *Combat Narratives: Cape Esperance*, 12–17.
36. Yarbrough, GenealogyBank; Morison, 166–168.
37. Nelson; Brand, 116.
38. Hoyt, *Yamamoto*, 205, 190; Ugaki, 226; Toland, 542; Hornfischer, 185.
39. Morison, 168–169.
40. D'Albas, 183–189; Tanaka, 699.
41. Thomas Miller, 74–75; Wolf, 111; Tillman, 79; Ugaki, 229.
42. Tillman, 90–91; Brand, 122–123; Leckie, *Challenge*, 226–227.
43. Hoyt, *Guadalcanal*, 131–132; Hara, 111; Lundstrom, *First Team*, 293–294; Frank, 315.
44. Hara, 107; Ito, 18–19; Agawa, 286; Hornfischer, 195.
45. Wyant, 53; Leckie, *Helmet*, 106.
46. George W.   Smith, *Do-or-Die Men*, 343; Leckie, *Challenge*, 275; Toland, 451; Davis, 134; Merillat, *Island*, 140.
47. Griffith, *Battle for Guadalcanal*, 181; Richter, 273–274; *1st Marine Division Commander's Final Report*, 339; William White, 112.
48. William White, 110–112.
49. Lane, 164–165; Foss, *Flying Marine*, 37–38; Phillips, 114–115; Leckie, *Helmet*, 90; Merillat, *Guadalcanal Remembered*, 179–180; Thomas Miller, 122; Vandegrift, 175; Thomas, 155.
50. *1st Marine Division Commander's Final Report*, 401; Clemens, 257; William White, 113–114; Brand, 128.
51. Thomas Miller, 123, 222; Sherrod, 100; Frank, 319.
52. Hixon, 146–147; Mears, 144–145; Mrazek, 351, 356.
53. Thomas, 155; Frank, 319; Hixon, 145; Merillat, *Guadalcanal Remembered*, 180–182.
54. DeChant, 80–81; Foss, *Flying Marine*, 40.
55. Owens, 145.
56. Shoptaugh, 97, 101.
57. Merillat, *Guadalcanal Remembered*, 191; GenealogyBank, Dallas *Morning News*, October 16, 1942; *New York Times* editorial October 16, 1942, *New York Times* Archives.
58. Thomas, 156; Thomas Miller, 125.
59. Hixon, 147.
60. Hoffman, *Chesty*, 179; Morison, 176.
61. Twining, 121–122; Clemens, 258.
62. Thomas Miller, 128–129, 133–134.
63. DeChant, 82–84; Thomas Miller, 129–132.
64. Twining, 121–122; Frank, 323–324; Agawa, 335.
65. Lundstrom, *First Team*, 305–307; Merillat, *Guadalcanal Remembered*, 189–190; Hornfischer, 188–189; Morison, 178; Layton, 461; Wolf, 65; Thomas Miller, 126–127; Brand, 117.
66. Morison, 178–180.
67. Ibid., 181.
68. Hornfischer, 198; Frank, 326.
69. Kunevicius, 141.
70. Merillat, *Guadalcanal Remembered*, 181–182; Lundstrom, *First Team*, 311; Hornfischer, 203.

71. Brand, 38, 102–104; "A. C. Bauer," Who's Who, US Marice Corps University, www. mcu.usmc.mil/historydivision/Pages/Who's%20Who/A-C/Bauer_HW.aspx.
72. Brand, 127–128.
73. Ibid., 82–84.
74. Foss, *Oral History Presentation*.
75. Hanson Baldwin, *New York Times*, September 27, 1942, *New York Times* archives.
76. "Search Our Collections," Franklin D. Roosevelt Presidential Library and Museum, www.fdrlibrary.marist.edu/archives/collections.html; Hayes, 193; Merillat, *Island*, 212–213.
77. Dull, 225; Winton, 83, 85.
78. Hoffman, *Once*, 227.
79. Richter, 251–257; Clemens, 251.
80. *Guadalcanal Echoes*, Winter 2013–2014, 4–8; Leckie, *Challenge*, 251–252.
81. Clemens, 251.
82. Ugaki, 226–227; Letourneau, 55–56; Cronin, 47; Hoyt, *Yamamoto*, 196; Clemens, 252–253.
83. William White, 103–104.
84. Morison, 182; Thomas Miller, 138–139; *1st Marine Division Commander's Final Report*, Annex J, 383–387.
85. Thomas Miller, 135.
86. Layton, 461–462.
87. Morison, 182–183; Hornfischer, 205; Frank, 333–334.
88. Harris, 119.
89. Halsey, 107.
90. Bourneman, 42–47; Halsey, 56–60.
91. Halsey, 108–109.
92. Schom, 408–410.
93. Morison, 183; Asprey, 725; Thomas Miller, 103.
94. Twining, 125; William White, 127; Hailey, 240; Asprey, 738.
95. Halsey, 117; Vandegrift, 184.
96. Lundstrom, *First Team*, 337.
97. Hornfischer, 211; Frank, 335–336.
98. Sherrod, 123; Twining, 125; Schom, 392; Morison, 187; Dower, *War Without Mercy*, 81; Dower, "Race, Language," 169–170.
99. Richter, 268–270; Brand, 136, 140–144; Thomas Miller, 141.
100. Brand, 149, 150–153.
101. Thomas Miller, 143, 145; Frank, 345–346; Brand, 161–164.
102. Merillat, *Guadalcanal Remembered*, 188–189; Lane, 223; Hixon, 149, 157; Frank, 330; *1st Marine Division Commander's Final Report*, Annex J, 386; Richter, 279–281; Sherrod, 95.
103. Leckie, *Challenge*, 287; Hixon, 157; Hoffman, *Chesty*, 180.
104. Hara, 114; Leckie, *Challenge*, 247–249; Griffith. *Papers*, Box 2, Folder 18; Hoffman, *Chesty*, 194; Ugaka, 259; "Imperial Rescript for Soldiers and Sailors (1882)," www.facstaff .bucknell.edu/jamesorr/ImpResSoldSailors1882webBOLD.htm.
105. *1st Marine Division Commander's Final Report*, 349; Richter, 265, 278–279.
106. Griffith, *Battle for Guadalcanal*, 187, 193–194; Frank, 339–340: Zimmerman, 115–117.
107. Ugaki, 242–244; Griffith, *Battle for Guadalcanal*, 194–195, 205; Griffith, *Papers*, "Miyazaki Manuscript."
108. *1st Marine Division Commander's Final Report*, 344; Clemens, 266; Whyte, *Time of War*, 73–74.

109. Whyte, *Time of War*, 73–75; Thomas, 161–162; Twining, 130; Leckie, *Challenge*, 304–305.
110. Leckie, *Challenge*, 310–311; Shoptaugh, 107; Davis, 152–155; Hoffman, *Chesty*, 182–184.
111. Leckie, *Challenge*, 309; *1st Marine Division Commander's Final Report*, 346; Morison, 191–192.
112. Shoptaugh, 110, 111.
113. Hixon, 154–155; Davis, 153–156.
114. Davis, 156–159; Hoffman, *Chesty*, 186–189; Moskin, 272–273.
115. Brady, 48–52, 111–113; Leckie, *Challenge*, 313; Moskin, 273; Twining, 135; Leckie, *Strong*, 100–101; Davis, 156–157.
116. Del Valle, 40–41; Hoffman, *Chesty*, 187; Shoptaugh, 116–117; Farrington, 112.
117. Shoptaugh, 118; Cronin, 53–56.
118. Frank, 366; Zimmerman, 119; Hoffman, *Chesty*, 189–190.
119. Shoptaugh, 134.
120. Ibid., 120, 125.
121. Griffith, *Battle for Guadalcanal*, 198–199; Hoffman, *Chesty*, 190; Davis, 160–162.
122. Hoyt, *Yamamoto*, 213–215; Thomas Miller, 145–146.
123. *1st Marine Division Commander's Final Report*, 347; Lundstrom, *First Team*, 343; Richter, 291–292; Hoyt, *Yamamoto*, 215–216.
124. Lundstrom, *First Team*, 246; Griffith, *Battle for Guadalcanal*, 200; Merillat, *Island*, 177–178, 200–206; Thomas, 162.
125. Brand, 167–169, 173–176; Thomas Miller, 147–151; Clemens, 266–267.
126. Thomas Miller, 151; Frank, 361.
127. Lundstrom, *First Team*, 346; Thomas Miller, 157; Richter, 295; Frank, 366.
128. Griffith, *Battle for Guadalcanal*, 298; Merillat, *Island*, 182.
129. Hoffman, *Chesty*, 191–192; Griffith, *Battle for Guadalcanal*, 203.
130. Morison, 193; Leckie, *Strong*, 109–110; Paige, 148.
131. Paige, 148–149.
132. Ibid., 150–151.
133. Ibid., 151–154; Morison, 193; Leckie, *Strong*, 110; Cameron, 127.
134. Thomas, 163; Merillat, *Island*, 183.
135. Paige, 158; *Los Angeles Times* obituary, November 18, 2003. Beginning in the 1950s Paige made it his mission to track down hundreds of men who falsely claimed to be Medal of Honor recipients. He lobbied Congress to increase the maximum penalty for such spurious claims to a $100,000 fine and a year in prison. In the 1990s Hasbro released a GI Joe action figure modeled upon Paige as a young man.
136. Griffith, *Battle for Guadalcanal*, 205.
137. Twining, 138; *1st Marine Division Commander's Final Report*, 350; Hoffman, *Chesty*, 193; Davis, 162; McEnery, 117; Thomas Miller, 134; Toland, 468.
138. Hoyt, *Yamamoto*, 218.
139. Frank, 407; Hashiba.
140. Johns, 60–62.
141. Ugaki, 258.
142. Whyte, "Hyakutake Meets," 42; Leckie, *Strong*, 112; *1st Marine Division Commander's Final Report*, 349; *Final Report*, Annex I, 376–380.
143. Thomas Miller, 152–153; Brady, 38; Hoyt, *Yamamoto*, 209, 212–215.
144. Okumiya and Horikoshi, 255–256.
145. Griffith, *Battle for Guadalcanal*, 207; Thomas Miller, 155.
146. Lundstrom, *First Team*, 354; Thomas Miller, 155.
147. Griffith, *Battle for Guadalcanal*, 207; Dull, 237.

148. Halsey, 121; Leckie, *Challenge*, 335.
149. Thomas Miller, 158.
150. Ibid., 160–161.
151. Jurika, 528.
152. Thomas Miller, 165.
153. Hornfischer, 228.
154. Hooper, 362–383.
155. Ibid., 362–383; Jurika, 516–528.
156. Charles McMurtry, Associated Press, *Cleveland Plain Dealer*, November 30, 1942 GenealogyBank.com.
157. D'Albas, 200.
158. Okumiya and Horikoshi, 260; Thomas Miller, 163–164; Frank, 388.
159. Dull, 241; Morison, 215.
160. Stafford, 165; Hornfischer, 231.
161. Morison, 217.
162. Ibid., 215; Hornfischer, 230; Frank, 388; *Combat Narratives: Santa Cruz*, 53.
163. Okumiya and Horikoshi, 268; Thomas Miller, 169–170.
164. Thomas Miller, 170; Stafford, 175.
165. Nathan Miller, 283; Thomas Miller, 170.
166. Okumiya and Horikoshi, 275; Thomas Miller, 170–171.
167. Thomas Miller, 174; Hooper, 362–383.
168. Morison, 220–221; *Combat Narratives-Santa Cruz*, 50–51.
169. Lundstrom, *First Team*, 447–448; Jurika, 516–528; D'Albas, 203.
170. Thomas Miller, 174; D'Albas, 204.
171. Okumiya and Horikoshi, 272–273; Winton, 87–88; Hara, 138.
172. Thomas Miller, 176; Okumiya and Horikoshi, 265–268.
173. Frank, 403.
174. Griffith, *Battle for Guadalcanal*, 210; Lundstrom, *First Team*, 453–454; Ugaki, 253.
175. Sakai, 240.
176. GeneaologyBank.com.
177. Lundstrom, *First Team*, 456.

CHAPTER 5
NOVEMBER: HALSEY'S NAVY TRIUMPHS

1. Chew, 57–60.
2. Leckie, *Helmet*, 122.
3. Agawa, 342.
4. Hixon, 84.
5. Wukovits, *American Commando*, 229–230; Laing, 59–60; Wolf, 30–31; *1st Marine Division Commander's Final Report*, Annex T-Medical, 457–459; Rogal, 61; Tregaskis, *Guadalcanal Diary*, 170; Hixon, 182; Hoffman, *Chesty*, 204; John Miller, 227; Twining, 147.
6. Tregaskis, *Guadalcanal Diary*, 170–174.
7. Bergerud, *Land War*, 92.
8. Laing, 68–69; *1st Marine Division Commander's Final Report*, Annex T-Medical, 459–460.
9. Wolf, 30.
10. Merillat, *Island*, 51; William White, 95; Hixon, 83.
11. Rogal, 99; Merillat, *Island*, 130.

12. Michael Smith, *Bloody Ridge*, 20–21, 92–93; William White, 92–93; Laing, 184–185; Twining, 149; Farrington, 113; Leckie, *Helmet*, 118–119, 83.
13. Twining, 155.
14. Merillat, *Island*, 369.
15. John Miller, 212; Twining, 148; *Guadalcanal Echoes*, Summer 2014, 8–9; William White, 95; Bergerud, *Land War*, 85–86.
16. *1st Marine Division Commander's Final Report*, 350–351; Zimmerman, 130; Merillat, *Island*, 187–188.
17. Zimmerman, 130–131; Wolf, 73; *1st Marine Division Commander's Final Report*, 350–351.
18. *1st Marine Division Commander's Final Report*, 350–351.
19. Merillat, *Island*, 190–191.
20. Zimmerman, 132–133; Leckie, *Challenge*, 357; Griffith, *Battle for Guadalcanal*, 215–216; Merillat, *Island*, 217.
21. Hoffman, *Once*, 227–228; Griffith, *Battle for Guadalcanal*, 216.
22. Rogal, 86–88.
23. *1st Marine Division Commander's Final Report*, 350–351; Merillat, *Island*, 226.
24. Dallas *Morning News*, November 7, 1942, GenealogyBank.com.
25. Hoyt, *Guadalcanal*, 199–200.
26. Paige, 162–164; Merillat, *Island*, 195–196; US Army, "XIV Corps Intelligence Memorandum," 3.
27. Merillat, *Island*, 195–196; Paige, 165.
28. Zimmerman, 136–137; Leckie, *Strong*, 117.
29. Griffith, *Battle for Guadalcanal*, 219.
30. Zimmerman, 138.
31. Ibid., 138–139.
32. Ibid., 138–139; Hoffman, *Chesty*, 201–202.
33. Griffith, *Battle for Guadalcanal*, 223; Shoptaugh, 151–162; Thomas, 166; Zimmerman, 140–141. Lieutenant Colonel Arthur Timboe, the commander of the 2nd Battalion, 164th Infantry, was sacked by Sebree when he refused Sebree's order to fire subordinates for letting Shoji escape.
34. Griffith, *Battle for Guadalcanal*, 223; Davis, 166.
35. Davis, 166–168; Hoffman, *Chesty*, 201–202; Zimmerman, 138–139. Puller wryly referred to his fragmentation wounds as "a fanny full of shrapnel."
36. Twining, 139–140; Griffith, *Battle for Guadalcanal*, 218.
37. Merillat, *Island*, 247.
38. Blackfort, 143–186; Wukovits, *American Commando*, 8–10; Griffith, *Oral History*, 50.
39. Blackfort, 220, 250, 268; Gilbert, 17; Wukovits, 17–18.
40. Hoffman, *Once*, 151–152.
41. Hoffman, *Once*, 156–158; Quirk, 58–61; Blankfort, 8–12; Wukovits, 44–45.
42. Griffith, *Oral History*, 53–54.
43. Richter, 331; Wukovits, *American Commando*, 46, 53; Gilbert, 14.
44. Wukovits, *American Commando*, 105–109; Gilbert, 29–31.
45. Wukovits, *American Commando*, 133.
46. George Smith, *Carlson's Raid*, 147, 153–156, 168–170. The Japanese later recovered the surrender note, and Tokyo Rose read excerpts from it on the air. The American public was unaware of its existence for fifty years.
47. Wukovits, *American Commando*, 170–171; Hillenbrand, 175, 179–180.
48. Blankfort, 295; Carlson, *Second Marine Raiders Report*, 14–15; Wukovits, *American Commando*, 212–213; Twining, 142.

49. Wukovits, *American Commando*, 194, 200–201; Thomas, 167; Keene, 68–74; Merillat, *Island*, 247; Richter, 335–336; Griffith, *Battle for Guadalcanal*, 246.

50. Clemens, 265, 277–278; Richter, 332–333, 355–356.

51. Keene, 68–74; Zimmerman, 142; Leckie, *Strong*, 120; Twining, 142; Wukovits, *American Commando*, 214.

52. Quirk, 58–61; Wukovits, *American Commando*, 204–205.

53. Zimmerman, 143.

54. Hixon, 184; Blankfort, 296–297.

55. Keene, 68–74; Carlson, *Second Marine Raiders Report*, 9–11; Whyte, *Time of War*, 61–62.

56. Merillat, *Island*, 247–249; Peatross; Carlson, *Second Marine Raiders Report*, 10–11; Frank, 424.

57. Carlson, *Second Marine Raiders Report*, 11–12, 16; Richter, 348–355; Wukovits, *American Commando*, 249–251, 258; Millett, "Guadalcanal and Martin Clemens," 24; Blankfort, 300.

58. Lundstrom, *First Team*, 470; Shillony, 135–136; Leckie, *Challenge*, 352, 359–364; Sherrod, 113–114; Stille, 12.

59. Drea, *MacArthur's ULTRA*, 37–39, 40; Lord, 104; Lundstrom, *First Team*, 467.

60. Richter, 361–362; Feuer, 76–77, 79–80; Leckie, *Challenge*, 375–376, 381.

61. Frank, 432.

62. Winton, 89.

63. Whyte, *Time of War*, 81; Vandegrift, 190.

64. Morison, 226–231, 247–249; Tillman, 94–96; Young, 71; Calhoun, 72–73; Hammel, *Decision*, 41–43, 61–63, 95; D'Albas, 209–210.

65. Hammel, *Decision*, 106.

66. *Combat Narratives: Battle of Guadalcanal*, 20; Musicant, 107–108; Hammel, *Decision*, 120.

67. Chew, 57–60; *Combat Narratives: Battle of Guadalcanal*, 15–18; Hara, 130–131; Dull, 247–248.

68. Chew, 57–60; Hornfischer, 172; *Combat Narratives: Battle for Guadalcanal*, 19.

69. Thomas Miller, 186–187; Leckie, *Helmet*, 121–122; Phillips, 133.

70. Hammel, *Decision*, 167–168, 171–174; Frank, 443–444fn. Historian Richard Frank, who studied documents cataloguing the forty-nine gunfire strikes on the *Atlanta*, said seven shells that landed near Scott and his officers left traces of the green dye routinely loaded with *San Francisco*'s shells.

71. *Combat Narratives: Battle of Guadalcanal*, 22; Richter, 365.

72. Hammel, *Decision*, 183–187; Ugaki, 265; McCandless; *Combat Narratives: Battle of Guadalcanal*, 29–30; *USS* San Francisco *Gunfire Damage*. McCandless and Schonlan were later awarded Medals of Honor.

73. Hammel, *Decision*, 209.

74. Ibid., 155–156; Morison, 246.

75. Becton, 9; *Combat Narratives: Battle of Guadalcanal*, 30.

76. *Combat Narratives: Battle of Guadalcanal*, 23.

77. Ibid., 30; Hammel, *Decision*, 159–164; Calhoun, 77–87.

78. Hara, 134–136; *Combat Narratives: Battle of Guadalcanal*, 30–31.

79. Hara, 139–141; Hammel, *Decision*, 199–200, 262.

80. Hailey, 271–273.

81. Hammel, *Decision*, 192–197; McCandless.

82. Hixon, 175; *Combat Narratives: Battle of Guadalcanal*, 33.

83. Thomas Miller, 187–188; *Combat Narratives: Battle of Guadalcanal*, 32–33, 40.

84. Thomas Miller, 188–191, 180–181; Sherrod, 115; William White, 94–95; Morison, 259–260; Hornfischer, 325; Hammond, *Decision*, 342; *Combat Narratives: Battle of Guadalcanal*, 39–41. When Woods was promoted from colonel to brigadier no stars were available, so an Army sergeant soldered together two pairs of dimes and filed them down into five-point stars. Thomas Miller, 114–115.

85. Petty, *At War*, 110; Hornfischer, 331; Morison, 256–257.

86. Orita, 137; Morris, 95–96; McCandless; Petty, *At War*, 110.

87. Kurzman, 1–5, 170–181; Morison, 257.

88. Satterfield, xi, 181–182, 189.

89. Halsey, 134.

90. Calhoun, 97.

91. William White, 95; Koburger, 63; Hammel, *Decision*, 348–352; Thomas Miller, 194; Frank, 464.

92. Morison, 263.

93. Thomas Miller, 194–195.

94. *Combat Narratives: Battle of Guadalcanal*, 49.

95. Ibid., 50–51; Morison, 264–267; Thomas Miller, 196–198.

96. Buell, 154–155.

97. Ibid., 155; Alexander White, 97–99; Frank, 465–466; *Combat Narratives: Battle of Guadalcanal*, 52–53.

98. Griffith, *Battle for Guadalcanal*, 236; *Combat Narratives: Battle of Guadalcanal*, 56; William White, 99; McEnery, 68–69; Leckie, *Strong*, 123–125; Stanley Johnston, 181; US Army, "XIV Corps Intelligence Memorandum," Box 6, Folder 8.

99. Buell, 156; Richter, 371; *Combat Narratives: Battle of Guadalcanal*, 54–55.

100. Buell, 159.

101. *Combat Narratives: Battle of Guadalcanal*, 57–58.

102. Frank, 467.

103. Brand, 201, 209–210; Sherrod, 425; Thomas Miller, 202–204; Foss, *Flying Marine*, 102.

104. Hooper, 73–80; Musicant, 78; Morison, 270; "Willis Lee," SR?Olympic Sports, www.sports-reference.com/olympics/athletes/le/willis-lee-1.html; *Naval Institute Proceedings*, May 2006; Pacific War Online Encyclopedia, pwencycl.kgbudge.com/L/e/Lee_Willis.htm.

105. Morison, 270; Hornfischer, 347–348; Musicant, 84–85.

106. Morison, 271–272; Hammel, *Decision*, 387–388.

107. Morison, 272–273.

108. *Combat Narratives: Battle of Guadalcanal*, 63–64; Hammel, *Decision*, 399–400; Morison, 270–278; Musicant, 118–119.

109. *Combat Narratives: Battle of Guadalcanal*, 67–69.

110. Ibid., 70–71; USS South Dakota *Gunfire Damage*; Hornfischer, 357–358; Musicant, 127–128.

111. *Combat Narratives: Battle of Guadalcanal*, 73–74; Backus, 154–163.

112. USS Washington *Damage Report*; Hooper, 73–80.

113. Morison, 278–281; Frank, 479–480; *Combat Narratives: Battle of Guadalcanal*, 74–75.

114. Ugaki, 271, 275–276; Dull, 253–254. In February 1945 Iwabuchi was killed in Manila while leading naval ground troops in a futile attempt to hold the city.

115. *Combat Narratives: Battle of Guadalcanal*, 75–77.

116. Hoyt, *How They Won*, 187; Halsey, 131.

117. Vandegrift, 198–199.

118. Wolf, 67; Halsey, 132.

119. Morison, 283; Hoyt, *Guadalcanal*, 231–232.

120. Twining, 162; Wolf, 82.
121. Alexander White, 99; Hailey, 283.
122. Morison, 283–284.
123. Leckie, *Helmet*, 122.
124. Morison, 284–285.
125. Hoyt, *Guadalcanal*, 233–234, 252.
126. Dull, 255; Griffith, *Battle for Guadalcanal*, 238; Ugaki, 275–276.
127. Clemens, 287–289; Halsey, 130.
128. Hara, 146.
129. Dull, 256; Associated Press, Omaha *World Herald*, November 17, 1942, Genealogy-Bank; Ugaki, 281–283.
130. Winton, 94; Hayashi and Coox, 61–62.
131. Morison, 289–290; Zimmerman, 150–152; Griffith, *Battle for Guadalcanal*, 248–249; Thomas, 170–171; Shoptaugh, 167–169, 190–191, 182; Farrington, 135; Frank, 494–495, 636, Appendix 2; Cronin, 65–70.
132. Morison, 316.
133. Hayashi and Coox, 61–62; Agawa, 342; Ugaki, 286.
134. Griffith, *Battle for Guadalcanal*, 247.
135. Merillat, *Island*, 237.
136. Hoffman, *Chesty*, 206; Clemens, 301–302; Farrington, 124; Sherrod, 111.
137. Morison, 292.
138. Ibid., 291.
139. Ugaki, 277–279.
140. Winton, 93.
141. *Combat Narratives: Tassafaronga*, 2–3; Griffith, *Battle for Guadalcanal*, 252; Friedman, 170–171.
142. Frank, 503–504; Winton, 93; Crenshaw, *Battle of Tassafaronga*, 111–112.
143. D'Albas, 227–232; Morison, 295; Lord, 121; Griffith, *Battle for Guadalcanal*, 253–254.
144. D'Albas, 231–232; Morison, 298.
145. *Combat Narratives: Tassafaronga*, 4; Griffith, *Battle for Guadalcanal*, 254.
146. *Combat Narratives: Tassafaronga*, 6–7; Morison, 295, 298.
147. Campbell, 156–157; Blair, 198, 436–437; *Combat Narratives: Tassafaronga*, 8–9, 18–19.
148. Griffith, *Battle for Guadalcanal*, 255; Morison, 301; Crenshaw, *Battle of Tassafaronga*, 145–146.
149. *Combat Narratives: Tassafaronga*, 20; Morison, 299–301; Dull, 265.
150. Morison, 303–304; *USS New Orleans Damage Report*, 2; Forgy, 217; Crenshaw, 56; *Combat Narratives: Tassafaronga*, 13; Dull, 265–266.
151. Morison, 305–306; *Combat Narratives: Tassafaronga*, 16.
152. Frank, 513.
153. *USS New Orleans Damage Report*, 3–4; *Combat Narratives: Tassafaronga*, 15; Forgy, 191–192.
154. Morison, 309–310; Forgy, 212–213; Hornfischer, 390–391; Frank, 514.
155. Wylie, 51–56; *Combat Narratives: Tassafaronga*, 10–17; *USS New Orleans Damage Report*, 1; Morison, 311.
156. *USS New Orleans Damage Report*, 4–5; *Combat Narratives: Tassafaronga*, 17–18.
157. Morison, 313, 306.
158. Crenshaw, *Battle of Tassafaronga*, 90, 107.
159. Ibid., 90; Halsey, 135.
160. Borneman, 83, 215.
161. Crenshaw, 98–106.
162. Morison, 315.

CHAPTER 6
DECEMBER: THE ARMY TAKES CHARGE

1. Whyte, *Time of War*, 84.
2. Merillat, *Island*, 255; Ortega; Zimmerman, 169.
3. Leckie, *Strong*, 128–129.
4. Leckie, *Helmet*, 106.
5. Cameron, 139; Farrington, 146.
6. George, 59; Muehrcke, 82.
7. James Jones, *WWII*, 48.
8. John Miller, 210–214, 232.
9. Collins, 145; Wyant, 1–2, 23–32; Dupuy, 575–576.
10. Hoyt, *Yamamoto*, 233; *1st Marine Division Commander's Final Report*, 545–546, 410.
11. John Miller, 223–224.
12. Merillat, *Island*, 246; Wolf, 95.
13. Twining, 168; Vandegrift, 203–204; Leckie, *Helmet*, 92–93; McMillan, 136–137.
14. Merillat, *Island*, 221–222, 242.
15. Ibid., 249; Reeder, 1–2, 10–30; William White, 6–7; Lane, 269; Ortega; Marion, 209–210, 217–220.
16. Bergerud, *Land War*, 87.
17. William White, 4–5.
18. Phillips, 137.
19. Leckie, *Helmet*, 138.
20. Twining, 170, 172, 175.
21. US Army, "XIV Corps Intelligence Memorandum," 82; Hayashi and Coox, 61–62; Lord, 121; Prados, *Combined Fleet Decoded*, 394; Winton, 95; Ugaki, 299–300, 310–313, 303–306; D'Albas, 232–233; John Miller, 230.
22. Griffith, *Papers*, Japanese diary, Box 2, Folder 8; Johns, 70–76.
23. Ugaki, 301.
24. Whyte, *Time of War*, 84.
25. Ienaga, 144.
26. USAFISPA, Office of AC of S, G-2, Box 6, Folder 36.
27. Toland, 477–478; Ugaki, 259–260, 298–299; Hoyt, *Yamamoto*, 234–235.
28. USAFISPA, "Enemy Morale and Supply."
29. Ugaki, 313–314; Morison, 316–317.
30. Griffith, *Battle for Guadalcanal*, 263–265.
31. Twining, 164–165.
32. John Miller, 239.
33. Griffith, *Battle for Guadalcanal*, 265–266, 316fn17; Kunevicius, 130; Merillat, *Island*, 260–261; Hixon, 189.
34. Muehrcke, 110–115; Griffith, *Battle for Guadalcanal*, 265–266; Wolf, 95; Hixon, 189–191.
35. Owens, 228–229.
36. Shoptaugh, 199; Muehrcke, 125–126.
37. Cronin, 75–78; George, 125; John Miller, 240–252; Griffith, *Battle for Guadalcanal*, 266–267; Muehrcke, 136, 154; Merillat, *Island*, 261–262; Hixon, 196–197.
38. Feuer, 88.
39. Wolf, 94.
40. John Miller, 220–221; DeChant, 93–94; Wolf, 12–18; Fox, 32.
41. Hoyt, *Guadalcanal*, 259; Sherrod, 118; Merillat, *Island*, 263; Wolf, 83–84; Hixon, 175–176.
42. Alexander White, 25–106; Fox, 29–32.

CHAPTER 7
JANUARY-FEBRUARY: OPERATION KE AND US VICTORY

1. Griffith, *Battle for Guadalcanal*, 284.
2. Morison, 371.
3. Charleston *Evening Post*, February 11, 1943, GenealogyBank.com.
4. US Army, *Operations of the 25th Division*, 1; Collins, 135; Bergerud, *Land War*, 180.
5. Collins, 1–67.
6. Hixon, 200–204; Cronin, 72, 75; Collins, 145, 150.
7. US Army, *Operations of the 25th Division*, 5; Collins, 149.
8. Epperson; Bergerud, *Land War*, 62–63, 199.
9. George, 118.
10. John Miller, 286–289; Collins, 156.
11. John Miller, 262–264, 271–276; Bergerud, *Land War*, 192–193; James Jones, *Thin Red Line*, 270–279; Collins, 152–155; US Army, *Operations of the 25th Division*, 46, 128.
12. Richard Johnston, 75; John Miller, 279.
13. Zimmerman, 159–161; Dower, *War Without Mercy*, 90; Merillat, *Island*, 266–268; Cronin, 72; Wyant, 64; US Army, *Translated Captured Japanese Documents*.
14. John Miller, 310.
15. Ibid., 314.
16. Ibid., 260, 285.
17. Murayama, 97–105.
18. Frank, 527.
19. Toland, 477–478, 484–486.
20. John Miller, 337–338.
21. Ugaki, 265; Hayashi and Coox, 61–65.
22. Ugaki, 319.
23. Prados, *Combined Fleet Decoded*, 345; Frank, 534–540; Hixon, 200.
24. Dull, 327–328; LeTourneau and LeTourneau, 75, 101; Merillat, *Island*, 264; Orita, 143–144.
25. Prados, *Combined Fleet Decoded*, 400–401.
26. Tillman, 124; Farrington, 150; John Miller, 230–231; Morison, 321–323, 329; LeTourneau and LeTourneau, 2–3, 16, 77–79, 287–289.
27. Morison, 323–324; Dull, 267.
28. Frank, 541.
29. D'Albas, 234; Griffith, *Papers*, Box 2, Folder 18, 3–6; John Miller, 338, 338fn13; Merillat, *Island*, 269–270.
30. Griffith, *Battle for Guadalcanal*, 279–280; Griffith, *Papers*, Box 2, Folder 18, 3–6; Toland, 487–489; Hixon, 200.
31. Muehrcke, 159–160; John Miller, 292–296.
32. Larsen, *Papers*, Debriefing-Gifu.
33. US Army, *Operations of the 25th Division*, 85–86; Collins, 158; John Miller, 301–304; Muehrcke, 160.
34. Larsen, *Papers*, Debriefing-Gifu.
35. US Army, "XIV Corps Intelligence Memorandum," 6.
36. Bergerud, *Land War*, 199.
37. Cronin, 87; Collins, 159–161.
38. Wyant, 67; Cronin, 90–92; John Miller, 332–335.
39. Wyant, 68; Hixon, 207; US Army, *Operations of the 25th Division*, iv; John Miller, 336.
40. Cronin, 86; Merillat, *Island*, 268; George, 148; John Miller, 342–346.
41. Hixon, 207; Cronin, 91–92.
42. Bergerud, *Land War*, 418; George, 153.

43. Richard Johnston, 78.
44. Toland, 489–490; John Miller, 338; Cronin, 98; Griffith, *Battle for Guadalcanal*, 284.
45. Yahachi, 132.
46. Frank, 573–574.
47. DeBlanc, 85–108; Tillman, 126–127.
48. Griffith, *Battle for Guadalcanal*, 285–286; Christ, 295; Hornfischer, 407; Prados, *Islands of Destiny*, 395; Hixon, 289–290.
49. Domagalski, 169–170, 176. The Navy report on Savo Island, completed in April 1943, criticized Bode's actions. When the report was released, Bode committed suicide.
50. Morison, 352–254.
51. Domagalski, 180; Morison, 354–355.
52. Fahey, 16–17.
53. Sherrod, 125–126; Domagalski, 181–190; Morison, 359–360.
54. Morison, 360–361; Domagalski, 193–195; Hixon, 208; Hornfischer, 406.
55. Fahey, 21.
56. Toland, 490; Griffith, *Battle for Guadalcanal*, 285–286; Hixon, 201–202.
57. Associated Press, February 5, 1943, GenealogyBank.com; Boston *Traveler*, February 9, 1943, GenealogyBank.com; Cronin, 90–92.
58. Toland, 490–491; D'Albas, 238.
59. Associated Press, Dallas *Morning News*, February 9, 1943, GenealogyBank.com; Shoptaugh, 223.
60. George, 156–158.
61. John Miller, 349; Cronin, 91–92; Collins, 164; Halsey, 140; James Jones, *WWII*, 50. On June 6, 1944, Collins commanded VII Corps when it landed at Utah Beach. It captured Cherburg and fought at the Falaise Pocket, Huertgen Forest, and the Bulge. In 1949, as a full general, Collins became Army chief of staff.
62. Toll, 443–444.
63. Morison, 371; Merillat, *Island*, 270; INS, Charleston *Evening Post*, February 11, 1943, GenealogyBank.com; Associated Press, Macon, GA, *Telegraph*, February 14, 1943, GenealogyBank.com; John Miller, 350.
64. Associated Press, Baton Rouge *State-Times*, February 10, 1943, GenealogyBank.com.
65. Associated Press, Macon, GA, *Telegraph*, February 14, 1943, GenealogyBank.com.
66. Hayes, 139, 264.

EPILOGUE

1. Griffith, *Papers*, "Kawaguchi Interview."
2. Griffith, *Battle for Guadalcanal*, 287.
3. Agawa, 374–376, 358; Ugaki, 351–359.
4. Kiyoshi, 29; Agawa, 390–392.
5. Griffith, *Battle for Guadalcanal*, 287.
6. Orita, 144.
7. Griffith, *Battle for Guadalcanal*, 285–286; Tillman, 131.
8. Griffith, *Papers*, "Miyazaki Manuscript"; John Miller, 350, 350fn69; Griffith, *Battle for Guadalcanal*, 285–286.
9. John Miller, 350.
10. Frank, 611; Ito, 83; Wolf, 111; Clemens, 292; Dull, 182; Twining, 193; Hornfischer, 437; Blum, 91–93.
11. *Mission Accomplished*, 3.
12. Sherrod, 425; Thomas Miller, 211.
13. Orita, 133; Dull, 269.

14. Cameron, 104, 112, 125; Nevins, 13.
15. Orita, 133; Griffith, *Papers*, "Miyazaki Manuscript"; USAFISPA, "Enemy Morale."
16. *1st Marine Division Commander's Final Report*, 323; Carlson, *Second Marine Raider Battalion Report*, 17.
17. Toland, 487.
18. *1st Marine Division Commander's Final Report*, 286, 314.
19. Griffith, *Papers*, Box 3, Folder 1, 1–6, 8.
20. *1st Marine Division Commander's Final Report*, 318–319.
21. Shoptaugh, 210.
22. Griffith, *Papers*, Box 2, Folder 4, 1.
23. Toland, 296, 580.
24. Griffith, "Memories and Impressions"; Merillat, *Island*, 294–298. More than one hundred thousand people today live on Guadalcanal, several times the island's 1942 population. Jacob Vouza died in March 1984 at the age of ninety-three—remarkable longevity for a man who had endured what he did. Vouza was given a state funeral in Honiara. Richter, 421.

BIBLIOGRAPHY

Agawa, Hiroyuki. *The Reluctant Admiral: Yamamoto and the Imperial Navy.* Translated by John Bester. Tokyo, New York, San Francisco: Kodansha International, 1979.

Alexander, Joseph H. *Edson's Raiders: The 1st Marine Raider Battalion in World War II.* Annapolis, MD: US Naval Institute Press, 2001.

Ambrose, Hugh. *The Pacific.* New York: NAL Caliber, 2010.

Americal Division Papers. Boxes 4A–4B, 1942–1943. US Army Heritage and Education Center, Carlisle, PA.

Asprey, Robert A. *General Alexander A. Vandegrift, USMC, Oral History Transcript.* US Marine Corps History Division Archives, Quantico, VA, 1962.

Backus, Commander Paul H. *Oral History.* Annapolis, MD: US Naval Institute Series, 1995.

Baldwin, Hanson. *Oral History.* In *Finding Aid—Solomon Islands, Guadalcanal.* US Marine Corps History Division, Quantico, VA, 1975.

Bartlett, Tom. "Japanese Warriors' Final Journey." *Leatherneck,* August 1985, 38–45.

Bartsch, William H. *Victory Fever on Guadalcanal: Japan's First Land Defeat of World War II.* College State: Texas A&M University Press, 2014.

Becton, Julian, with Joseph Morschauser III. *The Ship That Would Not Die.* Englewood Cliffs, NJ: Prentice-Hall, 1980.

Bennett, Edward S., Jr. *Papers.* Boxes 1, 2. Army Heritage and Education Center, Carlisle, PA.

Bergerud, Eric M. *Fire in the Sky: The Air War in the South Pacific.* Boulder, CO: Westview Press, 2000.

———. *Touched with Fire: The Land War in the South Pacific.* New York: Viking, 1996.

Berry, Henry. *Semper Fi, Mac: Living Memories of the U.S. Marines in World War II.* New York: Arbor House, 1982.

Blair, Clay, Jr. *Silent Victory: The U.S. Submarine War Against Japan.* Philadelphia and New York: J. B. Lippincott Company, 1975.

Blankfort, Michael. *The Big Yankee: The Life of Carlson of the Raiders.* Boston: Little, Brown and Company, 1947.

Blum, John Morton. *V Was for Victory: Politics and American Culture During World War II.* New York, London: Harcourt Brace Johanovich, 1976.

Borneman, Walter R. *The Admirals: Nimitz, Halsey, Leahy, and King—The Five-Star Admirals Who Won the War at Sea.* New York: Little, Brown and Company, 2012.

Brady, James. *Hero of the Pacific: The Life of Marine Legend John Basilone.* Hoboken, NJ: John Wiley and Sons, 2010.

Brand, Max. *Fighter Squadron at Guadalcanal.* Annapolis, MD: US Naval Institute Press, 1996.

Buell, Harold L. *Dauntless Helldivers: A Dive-Bombing Pilot's Epic Story of the Carrier Battles.* New York: Orion Books, 1991.

Calhoun, C. Raymond. *Tin Can Sailor: Life Aboard the USS* Sterett, *1939–1945.* Annapolis, MD: US Naval Institute Press, 1993.

Cameron, Craig M. *American Samurai: Myth, Imagination, and the Conduct of Battle in the First Marine Division, 1941–1951*. Cambridge: Cambridge University Press, 1994.

Campbell, John. *Naval Weapons of World War II*. Annapolis, MD: US Naval Institute Press, 1985.

Captured Documents and Material, 1943–1946. In *Finding Aid-Solomon Islands, Guadalcanal*, Box 21, Folder 19, Intelligence Reports, 1942–1946. US Marine Corps History Division Archives, Quantico, VA.

Carlson, Evans. *Second Marine Raider Battalion Report of Operations, 4 November–4 December 1942*. Box 20, Folder 34, December 1943. US Marine Corps History Division Archives, Quantico, VA.

———. *Twin Stars of China*. New York: Dodd, Mead and Company, 1940.

Carmichael, Thomas N. *The Ninety Days*. New York: Bernard Geis Associates, 1971.

Carroll, Andrew, ed. *War Letters: Extraordinary Correspondence from American Wars*. New York: Scribner, 2001.

Cates, Clifton B. "Battle of the Tenaru." *Marine Corps Gazette*, October 1943, 5–7.

Chew, John L. *Reminiscences of Vice Admiral John L. (Jack) Chew, U.S. Navy (Ret.)*. Annapolis, MD: US Naval Institute Press, 1979.

Christ, James F. *Battalion of the Damned: The 1st Marine Paratroopers at Gavutu and Bloody Ridge, 1942*. Annapolis, MD: US Naval Institute Press, 2007.

Cleary, Thomas. *Samurai Wisdom: Lessons from Japan's Warrior Culture: Five Classic Texts on Bushido*. Tokyo, Rutland, VT, Singapore: Tuttle Publishing, 2009.

Clemens, Martin. *Alone on Guadalcanal: A Coastwatcher's Story*. Annapolis, MD: US Naval Institute Press, 1998.

Collins, General J. Lawton. *Lightning Joe: An Autobiography*. Baton Rouge: Louisiana State University Press, 1979.

Combat Narratives: Solomon Islands Campaign: The Battle of Cape Esperance, 26 October 1942, and the Battle of Santa Cruz Islands, 26 October 1942. Washington, DC: Office of Naval Intelligence, 1943.

Combat Narratives: Solomon Islands Campaign: Battle of Guadalcanal, 11–15 November 1942. Washington, DC: Office of Naval Intelligence, 1944.

Combat Narratives: Solomon Islands Campaign: The Battle of Savo Island, 9 August 1942; The Battle of the Eastern Solomons, 23–25 August 1942. Washington, DC: Office of Naval Intelligence, 1943.

Combat Narratives: The Battle of Tassafaronga and the Japanese Evacuation of Guadalcanal. Washington, DC: Office of Naval Intelligence, 1944.

Conley, Sergeant Major William, USMC (Ret.). *Oral History*. Quantico, VA: US Marine Corps History Division Archives, 2007.

Cook, Haruko Taya, and Theodore F. Cook. *Japan at War: An Oral History*. New York: New Press, 1992.

Coombe, Jack D. *Derailing the Tokyo Express: The Naval Battles for the Solomon Islands That Sealed Japan's Fate*. Harrisburg, PA: Stackpole Books, 1991.

Crenshaw, Captain Russell S., Jr., USN (Ret.). *The Battle of Tassafaronga*. Baltimore, MD: Nautical Aviation Publishing Company of America, 1995.

———. *South Pacific Destroyer: The Battle for the Solomons from Savo Island to Vella Gulf*. Annapolis, MD: US Naval Institute Press, 1998.

Cronin, Captain Francis D., USA. *Under the Southern Cross: The Saga of the Americal Division*. Washington, DC: Combat Forces Press, 1951.

D'Albas, Andrieu. *Death of a Navy: Japanese Naval Action in World War II*. New York: The Devin-Adair Company, 1957.

Davis, Burke. *Marine! The Life of Lt. Gen. Lewis B. (Chesty) Puller, USMC (Ret.)*. Boston, Toronto: Little, Brown and Company, 1962.

DeBlanc, Jefferson. *The Guadalcanal Air War: Col. Jefferson DeBlanc's Story*. Gretna, LA: Pelican Publishing Company, 2008.

DeChant, John A. *Devilbirds: The Story of United States Marine Corps Aviation in World War II*. New York, London: Harper and Brothers Publishing, 1947.

Del Valle, Pedro A. "Marine Artillery on Guadalcanal." *Marine Corps Gazette*, November 1943, 9; February 1944, 39.

Domagalski, John J. *Lost at Guadalcanal: The Final Battles of the Astoria and Chicago as Described by Survivors and in Official Reports*. Jefferson, NC: McFarland and Company, 2010.

Dorris, Donald Hugh. *A Log of the Vincennes*. Louisville, KY: Standard Printing Company, 1947.

Dower, John W. "Race, Language, and War in Two Cultures: World War II in Asia." In Erinberg and Hirsch, *The War in American Culture*, 169–201.

———. *War Without Mercy: Race and Power in the Pacific War*. New York: Pantheon Books, 1986.

Drea, Edward J. *In the Service of the Emperor: Essays on the Imperial Japanese Army*. Lincoln: University of Nebraska Press, 1998.

———. *Japan's Imperial Army: Its Rise and Fall, 1853–1945*. Lawrence: University of Kansas Press, 2009.

———. *MacArthur's ULTRA: Codebreaking and the War Against Japan, 1942–1945*. Lawrence: University of Kansas Press, 1992.

———. *Nomonhan: Japanese-Soviet Tactical Combat, 1939*. Fort Leavenworth, KS: Combat Studies Institute, 1981.

Dull, Paul S. *A Battle History of the Imperial Japanese Navy (1941–1945)*. Annapolis, MD: US Naval Institute Press, 1978.

Dupuy, Trevor N., Curt Johnson, and David L. Bongard, eds. *The Harper Encyclopedia of Military Biography*. Edison, NJ: Castle Books, 1995.

Ellwood, Robert, and Richard Pilgrim. *Japanese Religion: A Cultural Perspective*. Englewood Cliffs, NJ: Prentice Hall, 1985.

Epperson, James. "Life in Guadalcanal." In *Americal Division Papers*. Army Heritage and Education Center, Carlisle, PA.

Erinberg, Lewis A., and Susan E. Hirsch. *The War in American Culture: Society and Consciousness During World War II*. Chicago: University of Chicago Press, 1996.

Ewing, Steve. *American Cruisers of World War II*. Missoula, MT: Pictorial Histories Publishing Company, 1984.

———. *Reaper Leader: The Life of Jimmy Flatley*. Annapolis, MD: US Naval Institute Press, 2002.

Fahey, James J. *Pacific War Diary, 1942–1945*. Boston: Houghton Mifflin Company, 1963.

Farrington, Arthur C. *The Leatherneck Boys: A PFC at the Battle of Guadalcanal*. Manhattan, KS: Sunflower University Press, 1995.

Felber, Abraham. *The Old Breed of Marine: A World War II Diary*. Jefferson, NC: McFarland and Company, 2003.

Feldt, Commander Eric, RAN. *The Coastwatchers*. New York, Melbourne: Oxford University Press, 1946.

Felt, Harry D. *The Reminiscences of Admiral Harry Felt, U.S. Navy (Ret.)*. Annapolis, MD: US Naval Institute Press, 1974.

Feuer, A. B., ed. *Coast Watching in World War II: Operations Against the Japanese in the Solomon Islands, 1941–1943*. Mechanicsburg, PA: Stackpole Books, 1992.

Finding Aid—Solomon Islands: Guadalcanal, Bougainville. US Marine Corps History Division Archives, Quantico, VA.

First Marine Division Commander's Final Report on Guadalcanal Operation. Phases I–IV, with appendices. In *Finding Aid—Solomon Islands, Guadalcanal*, Box 11, Folders 1–2. US Marine Corps History Division Archives, Quantico, VA.

First Marine Parachute Battalion Report on Operations: Defense of Lunga Ridge, 13–14 September 1942. In *Finding Aid—Solomon Islands, Guadalcanal*, Box 20, Folder 26. US Marine Corps History Division Archives, Quantico, VA.

First Marine Parachute Battalion Report on Operations 7–9 August 1942. In *Finding Aid—Solomon Islands, Guadalcanal*, Box 20, Folder 25. US Marine Corps History Division Archives, Quantico, VA.

First Marine Parachute Battalion Report on Operations: Tanambogo Raid, 7–8 September 1942. In *Finding Aid—Solomon Islands, Guadalcanal*, Box 20, Folder 27. US Marine Corps History Division Archives, Quantico, VA.

Forgy, Chaplain Howell M. *"And Pass the Ammunition."* Jack S. McDowell, ed. New York: D. Appleton-Century Company, 1944.

Foss, Joe, with Walter Simmons. *Joe Foss, Flying Marine, the Story of His Flying Circus as Told to Walter Simmons.* New York: Books, Inc., distributed by E. P. Dutton and Col., 1943.

Foss, Joe. "Interview of Captain J. J. Foss, Executive Officer, VMF-121." In *Finding Aid—Solomon Islands, Guadalcanal*, Box 2, Folder 20, 1943. US Marine Corps History Division Archives, Quantico, VA.

———. *Oral History Presentation.* In *Finding Aid—Solomon Islands, Guadalcanal*, Box 2, Folder 20, 1982 recording. US Marine Corps History Division Archives, Quantico, VA.

Fourteenth Corps. *Intelligence Memo No. 5: Enemy Operations on Guadalcanal, 7 August 1942—9 February 1943.* In *Finding Aid—Solomon Islands, Guadalcanal*, Box 6, Folder 8. US Marine Corps History Division Archives, Quantico, VA.

Fox, William J. "Building the Guadalcanal Air Base." In *Marine Corps Gazette.* March 1944, 27–28.

Frank, Richard B. *Guadalcanal: The Definitive Account of the Landmark Battle.* New York: Penguin Books, 1992. First published by Random House, 1990.

Freeman, Robert H. *Requiem for a Fleet: The U.S. Navy at Guadalcanal, August 1942–February 1943.* Ventnor, NJ: Shellback Press, 1985.

Friedman, Norman. *U.S. Destroyers: An Illustrated Design History.* Annapolis, MD: US Naval Institute Press, 2004.

Gailey, Harry A. *The War in the Pacific from Pearl Harbor to Tokyo Bay.* Novato, CA: Presidio Press, 1995.

Galer, Brig. Gen. Robert. *Interview.* US Marine Corps History Division Archives, Quantico, VA, conducted 1999, published 2007.

Gallant, T. Grady. *On Valor's Side.* New York: Kensington Publishing Group, 1963.

GenealogyBank.com. US newspapers, 1942–1943.

George, Lt. Col. John B. *Shots Fired in Anger: A Rifleman's View of the Activities on the Island of Guadalcanal.* Plantersville, SC: Small Arms Technical Publishing Company, 1947.

Gibney, Frank, ed. *Senso: The Japanese Remember the Pacific War.* London, Armonk, New York: M. E. Sharpe, 1995.

Gilbert, Ed. *U.S. Marine Corps Raider, 1942-3.* Oxford, UK: Osprey Publishing, 2006.

Goodman, Jack, ed. *While You Were Gone: A Report on Wartime Life in the United States.* New York: Simon and Schuster, 1946.

Griffith, Brig. Gen. Samuel B., II. "General Hap Arnold Interview." In Griffith *Papers*, Box 2, Folder 16.

———. *The Battle for Guadalcanal.* New York: Bantam Books, 1980. First published by J. S. Lippincott, 1963.

——. "Japanese Commentary on Guadalcanal." Annapolis, MD: US Naval Institute Proceedings, January 1951.

——. "Major General Kiyotake Kawaguchi Interview." In Griffith, *Papers*, Box 2, Folder 6.

——. "Commander M. Kawakami's Translation of General Sumiyoshi's Response to Griffith's Request." In *Papers*, Box 2, Folder 8e. US Marine Corps History Division Archives, Quantico, VA.

——. "Memories and Impressions: Guadalcanal and Tulagi, 1978." In *Marine Corps Gazette*, November 1978, 49.

——. "Lt. Gen. Shuichi Miyazaki Manuscript and Answers to Griffith's Questions." In *Papers*, Box 2, Folder 9.

——. *Oral History Transcript*. Interviewed by Benis M. Frank. Washington, DC: History and Museums Division, Headquarters, US Marine Corps, 1976.

——. *Papers*. US Marine Corps History Division Archives, Quantico, VA.

Groft, Marlin "Whitey." *Bloody Ridge and Beyond: A World War II Marine's Memoir of Edson's Raiders in the Pacific*. New York: Barkley Caliber, 2014.

Guadalcanal Echoes. Portland, Oregon, quarterly newsletter featuring Guadalcanal campaign veterans, 1984–2014.

"Guadalcanal: The Island of Death." Eugene, OR: Marathon Music and Video, 2000. 2 hours, 52 minutes.

Gunston, Bill. *Fighting Aircraft of World War II*. London: Salamander Books Limited, 2001.

Hailey, Foster. *Pacific Battle Line*. New York: Macmillan Company, 1944.

Halsey, William Frederick, and Lt. Cmdr. J. Bryan III. *Admiral Halsey's Story*. New York: Whittlesey House, 1947.

Hammel, Eric. *Aces at War: The American Aces Speak*. Vol. IV. Pacifica, CA: Pacifica Press, 1997.

——. *Guadalcanal: Decision at Sea: The Naval Battle of Guadalcanal, November 13–15, 1942*. New York: Crown Publishers, 1988.

——. *Guadalcanal: Starvation Island*. New York: Crown Publishers, 1987.

Hara, Captain Tameichi. *Japanese Destroyer Captain: Pearl Harbor, Guadalcanal, Midway—The Great Naval Battles as Seen Through Japanese Eyes*. Annapolis, MD: US Naval Institute Press, 2007. First published in 1967.

Harding, Stephen. *Dawn of Victory: A Sunken Ship, a Vanished Crew, and the Final Mystery of Pearl Harbor*. Boston: Da Capo Press, 2016.

Harris, Brayton. *Admiral Nimitz: The Commander of the Pacific Ocean Theater*. New York: Palgrave Macmillan, 2011.

Hart, Basil Henry Liddell. *The Defence of Britain*. New York: Random House, 1939.

Hashiba, Toyoji. *Alas, Guadalcanal: A Record of the Pacific War*. Photocopy of typewritten manuscript. US Army Heritage and Education Center, Carlisle, PA, 1980.

Hayashi, Saburo, and Alvin D. Coox. *Kogun: The Japanese Army in the Pacific War*. Quantico, VA: Marine Corps Association, 1959. First published in 1951 in Tokyo as *Taiheiyo Senso Rikusen Gaishi*.

Hayes, Grace Person. *The History of the Joint Chiefs of Staff in World War II: The War Against Japan*. Annapolis, MD: US Naval Institute Press, 1982.

Hersey, John. *Into the Valley: A Skirmish of the Marines*. New York: Alfred A. Knopf, 1943.

Hillenbrand, Laura. *Unbroken: A World War II Story of Survival, Resilience, and Redemption*. New York: Random House, 2010.

Hixon, Carl K. *Guadalcanal: An American Story*. Annapolis, MD: US Naval Institute Press, 1999.

Hoffman, Lt. Col. Jon T., USMCR. *Chesty: The Story of Lieutenant General Lewis B. Puller, USMC*. New York: Random House, 2001.

——. *Once a Legend: "Red Mike" Edson of the Marine Raiders*. Novato, CA: Presidio, 1994.

Holmes, W. J. *Double-Edged Secrets: U.S. Naval Intelligence Operations in the Pacific During World War II.* Annapolis, MD: US Naval Institute Press, 1979.

Hooper, Vice Admiral Edwin B. *Oral History.* In *U.S. Naval Institute Oral Histories.* Annapolis, MD: US Naval Institute Series, 1978.

Horne, Gerald. *Race War: White Supremacy and the Japanese Attack on the British Empire.* New York, London: New York University Press, 2004.

Hornfischer, James D. *Neptune's Inferno: The U.S. Navy at Guadalcanal.* New York: Bantam Books, 2011.

Hough, Lt. Col. Frank O., USMCR; Maj. Verle E. Ludwig Jr.; and Henry J. Shaw Jr. *Pearl Harbor to Guadalcanal: History of U.S. Marine Corps Operations in World War II.* Vol. I. Nashville, TN: Battery Press, 1993.

Hoyt, Edwin P. *Guadalcanal.* Lanham, MD: Scarborough House, 1981.

——. *How They Won the War in the Pacific: Nimitz and His Admirals.* New York: Weybright and Talley, 1970.

——. *Japan's War: The Great Pacific Conflict, 1853 to 1952.* New York, St. Louis, San Francisco: McGraw-Hill Book Company, 1986.

——. *The Kamikazes.* New York: Arbor House, 1983.

——. *Yamamoto: The Man Who Planned Pearl Harbor.* New York, San Francisco: McGraw-Hill Publishing Company, 1990.

Ienaga, Saburo. *The Pacific War: World War II and the Japanese, 1931–1945.* New York: Pantheon Books, 1978.

Inui, Lt. Genjirou. *My Guadalcanal.* Parts I, II. Nettally.com/jrube/Genjirou/genjirou.htm.

Ito, Masanori. *The End of the Imperial Japanese Navy.* New York: Jove, 1984. First published in 1962.

James, D. Clayton. *The Years of MacArthur.* Vol. II, *1941–1945.* Boston: Houghton Mifflin Company, 1975.

"Japanese Prisoner of War Reports." In *Finding Aids—Solomon Islands, Guadalcanal,* Box 21, Folder 8. US Marine Corps History Division Archives, Quantico, VA.

Jentschura, Hansgeorg, Dieter Jung, and Peter Mickel. *Warships of the Imperial Japanese Navy, 1869–1945.* Annapolis, MD: US Naval Institute Press, 1977.

Johns, J. Murray, and Bill Compton. *Guadalcanal Twice-Told.* New York, Washington, DC: Vantage Press, 1978.

Johnston, Richard W. *Follow Me: The Story of the Second Marine Division in World War II.* New York: Random House, 1948.

Johnston, Stanley. *The Grim Reapers.* New York: E. P. Dutton and Company, 1943.

Jones, F. C. *Japan's New Order in East Asia: Its Rise and Fall, 1937–45.* London, New York, Toronto: Oxford University Press, 1954.

Jones, James. *The Thin Red Line.* New York: Avon Books, 1975. First published in 1962 by Charles Scribner's Sons.

——. *WWII.* New York: Grosset and Dunlap, 1975.

Jurika, Stephen. *The Reminiscences of Captain Stephen Jurika Jr., U.S. Navy (Ret).* Annapolis, MD: US Naval Institute Press, 1979.

Keene, R. R. "Gung Ho: The Long Patrol." *Leatherneck,* November 1992, 68–75.

Kiyoshi, Kiyosawa. *A Diary of Darkness: The Wartime Diary of Kiyosawa Kiyoshi.* Edited by Eugene Soviak. Princeton, NJ: Princeton University Press, 1999.

Koburger, Charles W., Jr. *Pacific Turning Point: The Solomons Campaign, 1942–1943.* Westport, CT, London: Praeger, 1995.

Kunevicius, Alex. *585 Raids and Counting: Memoir of an American Soldier in the Solomon Islands, 1942–1945.* Jefferson, NC, London: McFarland and Company, 2011.

Kurzman, Dan. *Left to Die: The Tragedy of the USS Juneau.* New York: Pocket Books, 1994.

Laing, William H. *The Unspoken Bond: Stories About the Naval Hospital Corpsmen and the Marines They Served With.* London, Canada: Third Eye, 1998.

Lane, Lt. Col. Kerry L., USMC (Ret.). *Guadalcanal Marine.* Jackson: University of Mississippi Press, 2004.

Larsen, Lt. Gen. Stanley. *Papers.* US Army Heritage and Education Center, Carlisle, PA.

"The Lost Fleet of Guadalcanal." National Geographic documentary, 2003. 113 minutes.

Layton, Rear Adm. Edwin T., USN (Ret.). *"And I Was There": Pearl Harbor and Midway—Breaking the Secrets.* New York: William Morrow and Company, 1985.

Leatherneck, Magazine of the Marines. Quantico, VA: Marine Corps Association and Foundation, Serial, 1917–.

Leckie, Robert. *Challenge for the Pacific: Guadalcanal: The Turning Point of the War.* New York: Bantam Books Trade Paperbacks, 2010. First published in 1965 by Doubleday.

——. *Helmet for My Pillow: From Parris Island to the Pacific.* New York: Bantam Books Trade Paperbacks, 2001. First published in 1957.

——. *Strong Men Armed: The United States Marines Against Japan.* New York: Bonanza Books, 1962.

Letourneau, Roger, and Dennis Letourneau. *Operation KE: The Cactus Air Force and the Japanese Withdrawal from Guadalcanal.* Annapolis, MD: US Naval Institute Press, 2012.

Lince, George. *Too Young the Heroes: A World War II Marine's Account of Facing a Veteran Enemy at Guadalcanal, the Solomons, and Okinawa.* Jefferson, NC, and London: McFarland and Company, 1997.

London, Jack. *The Cruise of the Snark.* www.gutenberg.org/files/2512/2512-h/2512-h.htm.

Lord, Walter. *Lonely Vigil: Coastwatchers of the Solomons.* New York: Viking Press, 1977.

Loxton, Bruce. *The Shame of Savo: Anatomy of a Naval Disaster.* Annapolis, MD: US Naval Institute Press, 1994.

Lundstrom, John B. *Black Shoe Carrier Admiral: Frank Jack Fletcher at Coral Sea, Midway, and Guadalcanal.* Annapolis, MD: US Naval Institute Press, 2006.

——. *The First Team and the Guadalcanal Campaign: Naval Fighter Combat from August to November 1942.* Annapolis, MD: US Naval Institute Press, 1994.

——. "Frank Jack Fletcher Got a Bum Rap, Part Two." In *Naval History* 6, no. 3 (Fall 1992). www.usni.org/magazines/navalhistory/1992-09/frank-jack-fletcher-got-bum-rap-part-two.

Maki, John M. *Japanese Militarism: Its Cause and Cure.* New York: Alfred A. Knopf, 1945.

Marion, Ore J. *On the Canal: The Marines of L-3–5 on Guadalcanal, 1942.* Mechanicsburg, PA: Stackpole Books, 2004.

Mason, John T., Jr., ed. *The Pacific War Remembered: An Oral History Collection.* Annapolis, MD: US Naval Institute Press, 1986.

McCandless, Bruce. "The *San Francisco* Story." In *U.S. Naval Institute Proceedings* 84 (November 1958): 35–53.

McEnery, Jim, with Bill Sloan. *Hell in the Pacific: A Marine Rifleman's Journey from Guadalcanal to Peleliu.* New York: Simon and Schuster, 2012.

McEniry, Col. John Howard, Jr. *A Marine Dive-Bomber Pilot at Guadalcanal.* Tuscaloosa: University of Alabama Press, 1987.

McMillan, George. *The Old Breed: A History of the First Marine Division in World War II.* Washington, DC: Infantry Journal Press, 1949.

Mears, Lt. Frederick. *Carrier Combat.* Garden City, NY: Doubleday, Doran and Company, 1944.

Merillat, Herbert Christian. *Guadalcanal Remembered.* New York: Dodd, Mead and Company, 1982.

——. *The Island: A History of the First Marine Division on Guadalcanal, August 7–December 9, 1942.* Boston: Houghton Mifflin, 1944.

Miller, John, Jr. *Guadalcanal: The First Offensive*. Old Saybrook, CT: Konecky and Konecky, 1948.

Miller, Nathan. *War at Sea: A Naval History of World War II*. New York: Scribner, 1995.

Miller, Thomas G., Jr. *The Cactus Air Force*. New York: Bantam Books, 1987. Originally published in 1969.

Millett, Allan R. "Guadalcanal and Martin Clemens." In Clemens, *Alone on Guadalcanal*, 1–30.

———. *Semper Fidelis: The History of the United States Marine Corps*. New York: Macmillan Publishing, 1980.

Mission Accomplished: Interrogations of Japanese Industrial, Military, and Civil Leaders of World War II. Edited by US Army Air Force staff. Washington, DC: US Government Printing Office, 1946.

Moore, Right Rev. Paul, Jr. "The Making of a Marine on Guadalcanal." In Mason, *The Pacific War Remembered*, 123–131.

Morison, Samuel Eliot. *The Struggle for Guadalcanal, August 1942–February 1943*. Annapolis, MD: US Naval Institute Press, 2010. First published in 1949.

Morris, C. G. and Hugh B. Cave. *The Fightin'est Ship: The Story of the Cruiser* Helena. New York: Dodd, Mead, 1944.

Moskin, J. Robert. *The U.S. Marine Corps Story*. New York, San Francisco: McGraw-Hill, 1982.

Mrazek, Robert J. *A Dawn Like Thunder: The True Story of Torpedo Squadron Eight*. New York, Boston, London: Little, Brown and Company, 2008.

Muehrcke, Robert C. *Orchids in the Mud: Personal Accounts by Veterans of the 132nd Regiment, 1941–1945*. Chicago: J. S. Printing, 1985.

Murayama, Sgt. "A Japanese War Diary." Translated by Robert D. Thornton. In *Western Humanities Review* IV, no. 2 (Spring 1950): 95–106.

Musicant, Ivan. *Battleship at War: The Epic Story of the USS Washington*. San Diego, New York, London: Harcourt Brace Jovanovich, 1986.

Naval History magazine. Annapolis, MD: US Naval Institute Press, bimonthly, 1987–.

Naval Institute Proceedings magazine. Annapolis, MD: US Naval Institute Press. Series, 1874.

Navy History and Heritage Command. www. History.navy.mil/research.html.

Nelson, Sergeant O. W. Jr. "Cowboy Pilot." *Leatherneck*, September 1945, 67.

Nevins, Allan. "How We Felt About the War." In Goodman, *While You Were Gone: A Report on Wartime Life in the United States*, 3–27.

Newcomb, Richard F. *Savo: The Incredible Naval Debacle Off Guadalcanal*. New York: Holt, Rinehart and Winston, 1961.

New York Times archives. nytimes.com.

O'Donnell, Patrick K. *Into the Rising Sun: In their Own Words, World War II's Pacific Veterans Reveal the Heart of Combat*. New York: Free Press, 2002.

Ohmae, Captain Toshikazu. "The Battle of Savo Island." In *United States Naval Institute Proceedings* 83, no. 12 (December 1957): 1263–1278.

Okumiya, Masatake, and Jiro Horikoshi, with Martin Caidin. *Zero!* New York: Dutton, 1956.

Orita, Zenji, with Joseph D. Harrington. *I-Boat Captain*. Canoga Park, CA: Major Books, 1976.

Ortega, Pharmacist's Mate First Class Louis. *Oral History*. Washington, DC: Naval History and Heritage Command, Navy Library, 2000.

Owens, William J. *Green Hell: The Battle for Guadalcanal*. Central Point, OR: Hellgate Press, 1999.

Paige, Mitchell. *A Marine Named Mitch: An Autobiography of Mitchell Paige, Colonel, U.S. Marine Corps Retired*. New York, Washington, DC: Vantage Press, 1975.

Pacific War Online Encyclopedia. www.pwencycl.com.

Peatross, Maj. Gen. Oscar. *Bless 'Em All*. Huntsville, AL: Raider Publishing, 1995.

Perrett, Bryan. *Why the Japanese Lost: The Red Sun's Setting*. Barnsley, South Yorkshire, UK: Pen and Sword Military, 2014.

Petty, Bruce M. *At War in the Pacific: Personal Accounts of World War II Navy and Marine Corps Officers*. Jefferson, NC: McFarland and Company, 2006.

———. *Voices from the Pacific War: Bluejackets Remember*. Annapolis, MD: US Naval Institute Press, 2004.

Phillips, Sid. *You'll Be Sor-Ree! A Guadalcanal Marine Remembers the Pacific War*. New York: Berkley Caliber, 2010.

Pintwala, Ken. "Albert A. Schmid, Guadalcanal Hero." *Leatherneck*, August 1986, 30–35.

Prados, John. *Combined Fleet Decoded: The Secret History of American Intelligence and the Japanese Navy in World War II*. New York, Random House, 1995.

———. *Islands of Destiny: The Solomons Campaign and the Eclipse of the Rising Sun*. New York: NalCaliber, 2012.

Quirk, Brian J. "Reflections on Carlson's Raiders." In *Marine Corps Gazette*, August 2001, 58–61. First published in March 1944.

Raider Patch newsletter. Huntsville, AL: US Marine Raider Association. Series, quarterly.

Rasor, Eugene L. *The Solomon Islands Campaign: Guadalcanal to Rabaul: Historiography and Annotated Bibliography*. Westport, CT: Greenwood Press, 1997.

Reeder, Lt. Col. Russell, Jr. *Fighting on Guadalcanal*. Quantico, VA: Marine Corps Combat Division Command, 1991. Interviews conducted in 1942 and 1943.

Rhoades, Lt. Cmdr. F. A. "Snowy," RAN. *Diary of a Coastwatcher in the Solomons*. Fredericksburg, TX: Admiral Nimitz Foundation, 1982.

Richter, Don. *Where the Sun Stood Still: Guadalcanal, August 7, 1942—February 8, 1943*. Calabasas, CA: Toucan Publishing, 1992.

Rogal, William W. *Guadalcanal, Tarawa, and Beyond: A Mud Marine's Memoir of the Pacific Island War*. Jefferson, NC: McFarland and Company, 2010.

Roosevelt, Franklin. Digital Collections. www.fdrlibrary.marist.edu/archives/collections.html.

Sakai, Saburo, with Fred Saito and Martin Caidin. *Samurai!* New York: Dutton, 1957.

Satterfield, John. *We Band of Brothers: The Sullivans and World War II*. Parkersburg, IA: Mid-Prairie Books, 1995.

Sbrega, John J. *The War Against Japan, 1941–1945: An Annotated Bibliography*. New York: Garland Publishing, 1989.

Schom, Alan. *The Eagle and the Rising Sun: The Japanese-American War, 1941–1943, Pearl Harbor Through Guadalcanal*. New York: W. W. Norton, 2004.

Shaw, Henry I., Jr. *First Offensive: The Marine Campaign for Guadalcanal*. Washington, DC: History and Museums Division, Headquarters, US Marine Corps, 1992.

Sherrod, Robert. *History of Marine Corps Aviation in World War II*. San Rafael, CA: Presidio Press, 1980. First published in 1952.

Shillony, Ben-Ami. *Politics and Culture in Wartime Japan*. Oxford, New York: Clarendon Press, 1991. First published in 1981.

Shoptaugh, Terry L. *They Were Ready: The 164th Infantry in the Pacific War, 1942–1945*. Valley City, ND: 164th Infantry Association of the United States, 2012.

Sledge, E. B. *With the Old Breed at Peleliu and Okinawa*. New York: Ballantine Books, 2010. First published in 1981.

Smith, George W. *The Do-or-Die Men: The 1st Marine Raider Battalion at Guadalcanal*. New York: Pocket Books, 2003.

———. *Carlson's Raid: The Daring Marine Assault on Makin*. Novato, CA: Presidio Press, 2001.

Smith, Maj. John, USMC. "Interview of Major John Smith, VMF-223." In *Finding Aid—Solomon Islands, Guadalcanal*, Box 2, Folder 7, 1942. US Marine Historical Division Archives, Quantico, VA.

Smith, Michael. *Bloody Ridge: The Battle That Saved Guadalcanal*. Novato, CA: Presidio Press, 2000.

Smith, Michael W. *The Emperor's Codes: The Breaking of Japan's Secret Ciphers*. New York: Arcade Publishing, 2001.

Smoot, Roland N. *The Reminiscences of Vice Admiral Roland N. Smoot, U.S. Navy (Ret.)*. Annapolis, MD: US Naval Institute Press, 1972.

Stafford, Cmdr. Edward P., USN. *The Big E: The Story of the USS* Enterprise. Annapolis, MD: US Naval Institute Press, 2002.

Stille, Mark E. *The Imperial Japanese Navy in the Pacific War*. Oxford, UK, and New York: Osprey Publishing, 2013.

Tanaka, Vice Admiral Raizo. "Japan's Long Struggle for Guadalcanal." *United States Naval Institute Proceedings* 82, no. 7 (July 1956): 687–699.

Thach, Adm. John S., USN (Ret.). *Reminiscences*, Vol. I. Annapolis, MD: US Naval Institute Press, 1977.

Thobaben, Robert G., ed. *For Comrade and Country: Oral Histories of World War II Veterans*. Jefferson, NC: McFarland and Company, 2003.

Thomas, Gen. Gerald C, USMC (Ret.). *Oral History*. Interviewed by Bemis M. Frank. Washington, DC: History and Museums Division, Headquarters, US Marine Corps, 1966.

Thomason, Col. John W., Jr. *And a Few Marines*. New York: Charles Scribner's Sons, 1943.

Tillman, Barrett. *Wildcat: The F4F in World War II*. Annapolis, MD: US Naval Institute Press, 1983.

Toland, John. *The Rising Sun: The Decline and Fall of the Japanese Empire, 1936–1945*. New York: Bantam Books, 1981. First published by Random House in 1970.

Toll, Ian W. *The Conquering Tide: War in the Pacific Islands, 1942–1944*. New York: W. W. Norton, 2015.

Torgerson, Capt. Harry. *Oral History*. In *Finding Aid—Solomon Islands, Guadalcanal*, Box 20, Folder 27. US Marine Corps History Division, Quantico, VA.

Tregaskis, Richard. "The Best Soldier I Ever Knew." *Saga* magazine. In Tregaskis, *Papers*.

———. *Guadalcanal Diary*. New York: Random House, 1943.

———. *Papers*. Laramie, WY: American Heritage Center, University of Wyoming.

Twining, Merrill B. *No Bended Knee: The Battle for Guadalcanal: The Memoir of Gen. Merrill B. Twining, USMC (Ret.)*. Edited by Neil Carey. Novato, CA: Presidio Press, 1996.

Ugaki, Matome. *Fading Victory: The Diary of Admiral Matome Ugaki, 1941–1945*. Translated by Masataka Chihaya. Pittsburgh, PA: University of Pittsburgh Press, 1991.

Updegraph, Charles L., Jr. *U.S. Marine Corps Special Units of World War II*. Washington, DC: History and Museums Division, Headquarters, US Marine Corps, 1972.

US Army. "XIV Corps Intelligence Memorandum No. 5. Enemy Operations on Guadalcanal, August 7, 1942 to February 9, 1943." In *Finding Aid—Solomon Islands, Guadalcanal*, Box 6, Folder 8. US Marine Corps History Division Archives, Quantico, VA.

———. *Operations of the 25th Infantry Division on Guadalcanal*. Army Heritage and Educational Center, Carlisle, PA, 1994.

———. "Translated Captured Japanese Documents." In *Finding Aid—Solomon Islands, Guadalcanal*, Box 21, Folder 19.

———. "XIV Corps Intelligence Memorandum." In *Finding Aid—Solomon Islands, Guadalcanal*. US Marine Corps History Division Archives, Quantico, VA.

United States Army Forces in the South Pacific Area (USAFISPA). In *Finding Aid—Solomon Islands, Guadalcanal*, Box 6. US Marine Corps History Division Archives, Quantico, VA.

———. "Enemy Morale and Supply." In *Finding Aid—Solomon Islands, Guadalcanal*, Box 6, Folder 37. US Marine Corps History Division Archives, Quantico, VA.

———. "Report on Captured Letter and Extracts from Diary of a Japanese Aviator, 17 Dec. '42." In *Finding Aid—Solomon Islands, Guadalcanal*, Box 6, Folder 36. US Marine Corps History Division Archives, Quantico, VA.

United States Naval Institute Oral Histories. Annapolis, MD: US Naval Institute Series.

United States Naval Institute Proceedings. Annapolis, MD. Serial.

USS Enterprise *Action Report, 13–15 November 1942*. Washington, DC: US Department of the Navy, Serial 0019, 1942.

USS New Orleans *Torpedo Damage Lunga Point 30 November 1942: War Damage Report No. 38*. Washington, DC: US Hydrographic Office, 1943.

USS San Francisco *Gunfire Damage: Battle of Guadalcanal 13 November 1942: War Damage Report No. 26*. Washington, DC: US Hydrographic Office, 1943.

USS South Dakota *Gunfire Damage: Battle of Guadalcanal 14–15 November 1942: War Damage Report No. 57*. Washington, DC: US Hydrographic Office, 1947.

USS Washington *Damage Report, Battle of Guadalcanal 14–15 November 1942*. Washington, DC: US Hydrographic Office.

Vandegrift, Gen. A. A. *Once a Marine: The Memoirs of General A. A. Vandegrift, United States Marine Corps, as Told to Robert B. Asprey*. New York: Ballantine Books, 1966.

Walker, Brett L. *A Concise History of Japan*. Cambridge, UK: Cambridge University Press, 2015.

Walt, Gen. Lew, USMC (Ret.). *Oral History*. US Marine Corps History Division Archives, Quantico, VA, 1967.

Warner, Denis, and Peggy Warner. *Disaster in the Pacific: New Light on the Battle of Savo Island*. Annapolis, MD: US Naval Institute Press, 1992.

Weschler, Thomas R. *Reminiscences of Vice Admiral Thomas R. Weschler, U.S. Navy (Ret.)*. Annapolis, MD: US Naval Institute Press, 1995.

Western Humanities Review. Salt Lake City: University of Utah. Series, 1947–.

White, Alexander S. *Dauntless Marine: Joseph Sailer Jr., Dive-Bombing Ace of Guadalcanal*. Fairfax Station, VA: White Knight Press, 1996.

White, William Richard, and Ben Wofford. *The Marine: A Guadalcanal Survivor's Final Battle*. Annapolis, MD: US Naval Institute Press, 2002.

Whyte, William H. "Hyakutake Meets the Marines, Part II." In *Marine Corps Gazette*, August 1945, 32–37.

———. *A Time of War: Remembering Guadalcanal, a Battle Without Maps*. New York: Fordham University Press, 2000.

Williams, Gary. *Guardian of Guadalcanal: The World War II Story of Douglas A. Munro, United States Coast Guard*. West Chester, OH: Lakota Press, 2014.

Willmott, H. P. *The Barrier and the Javelin: Japanese and Allied Pacific Strategies, February to June 1942*. Annapolis, MD: US Naval Institute Press, 1983.

Winton, John. *ULTRA in the Pacific: How Breaking Japanese Codes and Cyphers Affected Naval Operations Against Japan, 1941–45*. Annapolis, MD: US Naval Institute Press, 1993.

Wolf, William. *13th Fighter Command in World War II: Air Combat over Guadalcanal and the Solomons*. Atglen, PA: Schiffer Military History, 2006.

Wolfert, Ira. *Battle for the Solomons*. Boston: Houghton Mifflin Company, 1943.

Woods. Lt. Gen. Louis, USMC (Ret.). *Oral History*. Interviewed by Benis M. Frank. US Marine Corps History Division Archives, Quantico, VA, conducted 1968.

Wukovits, John. *American Commando: Evans Carlson, His World War II Marine Raiders, and America's First Special Forces Mission*. New York: NAL Caliber, 2009.

———. *Hell from the Heavens: The Epic Story of the USS* Laffey *and World War II's Greatest Kamikaze Attack.* Cambridge, MA: Da Capo Press, 2015.

Wyant, William K. *Sandy Patch: A Biography of Lt. Gen. Alexander M. Patch.* New York, Westport, CT, London: Praeger, 1991.

Wylie, Joseph C., Jr. *The Reminiscences of Rear Admiral Joseph C. Wylie, Jr., U.S. Navy (Ret.).* Annapolis, MD: US Naval Institute Press, 2003.

Yahachi, Ishida. "Ghosts of Soldiers Lost on Guadalcanal." In Gibney, *Senso*, 131–132.

Young, Edward M. *F4F Wildcat vs. A6M Zero-Sen: Pacific Theater 1942.* Oxford, UK: Osprey Publishing, 2013.

Youngdeer, Robert. *Oral History.* Quantico, VA: US Marine Corps History Division, 2008.

Zimmerman, John L. *The Guadalcanal Campaign.* Washington, DC: Historical Division, Headquarters, US Marine Corps, 1949.

INDEX